D1559677

WITHDRAWN

HEMINGWAY'S THEATERS
OF MASCULINITY

HEMINGWAY'S THEATERS OF MASCULINITY

Thomas Strychacz

LOUISIANA STATE UNIVERSITY PRESS

BATON ROUGE

Designer: Andrew Shurtz
Typeface: Minion
Typesetter: Coghill Composition Co., Inc.
Printer and binder: Thomson-Shore, Inc.

LIBRARY OF CONGRESS
CATALOGING-IN-PUBLICATION DATA:
Strychacz, Thomas F.
Hemingway's theaters of masculinity / Thomas Strychacz.
p. cm.
Includes bibliographical references and index.
ISBN 0-8071-2906-2 (alk. paper) — ISBN 0-8071-2925-9 (pbk. : alk. paper)
1. Hemingway, Ernest, 1899–1961—Characters—Men.
2. Hemingway, Ernest, 1899–1961—Knowledge—Psychology.
3. Masculinity in literature. 4. Men in literature. I. Title.
PS3515.E37Z8826 2003
813'.52—dc21
2003012837

Portions of this work appeared previously in the following publications and are reprinted
here with permission, possibly in slightly altered form: "Dramatizations of Manhood in
Hemingway's *In Our Time* and *The Sun Also Rises*," *American Literature* 61, no. 2 (1989):
245–60. "'The Sort of Thing You Should Not Admit': Hemingway's Aesthetic of Emotional
Restraint," in *Boys Don't Cry? Rethinking Narratives of Masculinity and Emotion in the U.S.*,
ed. Milette Shamir and Jennifer Travis (New York: Columbia University Press, 1996),
141–66. "Trophy Hunting as a Trope of Manhood in Hemingway's *Green Hills of Africa*,"
Hemingway Review 13, no. 1 (1993): 36–47. Copyright © 1993 by the Ernest Hemingway
Foundation. All rights reserved. "*In Our Time*, Out of Season," *The Cambridge Companion
to Hemingway*, ed. Scott Donaldson (Cambridge: Cambridge University Press, 1996), 55–86.
Reprinted with the permission of Cambridge University Press. "'Like Plums in a Pudding':
Food and Rhetorical Performance in Hemingway's *Green Hills of Africa*." *Hemingway
Review* 19, no. 1 (2000), 23–46. Copyright © 2000 by the Ernest Hemingway Foundation.
All rights reserved.

CONTENTS

ACKNOWLEDGMENTS

No man is an island, as Hemingway recognized, and in writing this book over several years I have incurred more debts than I can say or possibly remember. I would like to thank my students at Mills College, who have always proven a wonderful resource for testing out new ideas on Hemingway; and especially Hannah Love, who helped edit and polish the manuscript with tremendous care. Readers have offered invaluable advice and influenced my thinking over the years, notably Scott Donaldson, Debra Moddelmog, and Edmund Reiss. The anonymous reader at Louisiana State University Press made very helpful suggestions. Friends in Mere, Wiltshire, made it all worthwhile as I worked on writing the bulk of the manuscript. A Meg Quigley fellowship and several grants from Mills College allowed me to dedicate summers to working on this project. And, last but not least, my family deserves a vote of thanks for putting up with Hemingway for so long. Much love to Kathryn, Nicholas, Daniel, and Isabel. This book's for you.

HEMINGWAY'S THEATERS
OF MASCULINITY

Performing Hemingway

MICHAEL PALIN'S recent *Hemingway's Chair* (1998) features a character named Martin Sproale, a mousy English post office clerk, whose one claim to adventure in his unspectacular life lies in his admiration for Papa Hemingway. Drinking grappa in his bedroom, surrounded by Hemingway memorabilia, Martin at one point early in the book salutes a gigantic photograph of a vulnerable-looking Hemingway adorning his wall—the only one, according to Martin, in which the "Great Man seemed not to be performing or posing."[1] Under Hemingway's gaze, Martin, to girlfriend Elaine, appears to become a "different man from the one she knew" (30). Enter Ruth Kohler, American scholar, writing a biography of Hemingway and his women, who discovers that a man who "hero-worshipped the old bastard" (80) can help her with the dense aura of verisimilitude she needs, not by providing information but by actually *playing* Papa Hemingway to her Pauline Pfeiffer (and later Jane Mason). Ruth's book—and Ruth and Martin's ensuing love affair—thus take shape around role playing and a series of role transformations in which Martin not only acts like Hemingway but begins to look like him too. Their relationship is consummated amid Hemingwayesque dialogue (" 'You ever made love in a church, Papa?' 'Hell no,' he grunted. 'Too cold' " [214–15]) and character changes that transform the standoffish Ruth into Jane Mason and the clumsy Martin into a self-assured lover. By the novel's end, Martin—having sabotaged, Robert Jordan–like, attempts to move Britain's communications systems into the twenty-first century—has fled to America, where we find him winning the Papa Look-Alike Competition in Key West and telling Ruth "Legends never die!" (280).

1. Michael Palin, *Hemingway's Chair* (New York: St. Martin's Press, 1998), 14. This work will hereinafter be cited parenthetically by page number in the text.

Palin's conceit of characters who disrupt their claustrophobic lives by emulating Hemingway's larger-than-life example turns out, on nearer inspection, to be much more complex than it seems and certainly germane to the thesis of this study of Hemingway's fiction. For though we are set up in the early stages of the novel to discover a true Papa (the vulnerable Papa of the photograph) beneath the glitzy surface of his posing, the notion that performances construct identity recurs with more seriousness as the novel progresses. If a photograph of Hemingway can be said to describe truly the Great Man (the one pose in which he seems not to be posing), does not the photograph of Martin that lands on Ruth's desk at the end—displaying the "best ever" (279) look-alike, whose "uncanny" resemblance to Papa "could have fooled the family"—possess the same ontological status (for it is still a pose that is somehow not a pose)? If the post office clerk embodies his role with enough verisimilitude both to terrify Ruth (210) and to excite her (213), how can we distinguish between him playing an eccentric role and him becoming his role? Should we say that his actions mask the original Martin or express one of the potential selves an "original" mask concealed? And if Martin becomes a "real man" by resurrecting the legendary Hemingway, can we really separate a "real" Hemingway (the vulnerable man) from his legend? Martin's psychic odyssey suggests otherwise. If Martin is still himself, or more of a self, or more of a man, while looking and acting like Ernest Hemingway, it would appear that the process of attaining a real (manly) self is commensurate with the performances that express it. Since Hemingway seems psychically and physically "there" in the person of Papa Martin, the two, we might as well argue, are one, and a novel that begins with the solid, predictable, though slightly eccentric figure of Martin Sproale ends by countenancing the radical notion that posing as someone else can fashion a new, ontologically secure identity. Performing Hemingway, puzzlingly enough, is the same as being Hemingway.

Not surprisingly, critical interpretations of Hemingway's work are frequently caught in the double bind intimated by the subtitle of this introduction and enacted in Martin's escapades. Scholars, like Michael Palin's characters and Palin himself, have long been fascinated by the pose of Hemingway's tough, charismatically overbearing personality—and the potential vulnerabilities underlying it—and nothing has been more characteristic of Hemingway scholarship than its reliance on biographical material in order to mediate aesthetic and philosophical problems in his work. That focus has often proved illuminating. Hemingway scholarship in the 1980s and 1990s was led forward by a number of biographies inspired by the opening of the Hemingway collection at the John F. Kennedy Library.[2] And even the best interpretive work to come out of that reevaluation, which in recent years has begun to propel Hemingway into the forefront of gender studies, relies heavily on psychoanalytic insights into his life.[3] As often, particularly in recent years, the biographical focus of Hemingway studies has had a deleterious effect on his old reputation as culture hero. When I was a graduate student at Princeton, I attended a lecture where Nina Baym gave an impromptu demonstration of how Hemingway might have opened and closed a car door like a matador gracefully and professionally pulling a cape before the muzzle of a raging bull. Like "bad Hemingway" writing contests, the demonstration was very funny and quite unfair and also telling: it was as if Hemingway's inimitable style had been so long under the gaze that there was little left of it beyond its imitability.

Equally unsurprising, evaluations of Hemingway's work—perhaps more so than in the case of any other writer—seem unable to ignore the he-man roles Hemingway performed in life and often wrote about. Most readers acquainted with Hemingway's biography assume that he truly inhabited his performances of manly actions. For these readers he is an exemplar of ideal masculine roles or, more usually, an author invested to his detriment in the "glorification of machismo, blood sports, physical violence and war."[4] This is particularly true in the wake of feminist studies now that his pursuit of stereotypically masculine experience—war, hunting, fishing, boxing—has come to seem extremist or (what is worse) lugubrious. But even pre-feminist critics found it necessary to bracket off his more outrageous chest-thumping as exterior to his best fiction and endemic to his worst. Edmund Wilson, to cite an early instance, argued that Hemingway prostituted his talent to his celebrity status, for he is "beginning to be imposed on by the American publicity legend which has been created about him."[5] That judgment echoes down the annals of Hemingway criticism. Lionel Trilling, perhaps most famously,

2. See the biographies by Peter Griffin (1985), Kenneth Lynn (1987), Jeffrey Meyers (1985), and Michael Reynolds (1986, 1989).

3. I am thinking of interpretive work like Mark Spilka's *Hemingway's Quarrel with Androgyny* (1990), Debra Moddelmog's *Reading Desire: In Pursuit of Hemingway* (1999), and Carl Eby's *Hemingway's Fetishism* (1999).

4. Jeffrey Meyers, *Hemingway: A Biography* (New York: Harper/Perennial, 1985), 3.

5. Edmund Wilson, "Letter to the Russians about Hemingway," in *Hemingway: The Critical Heritage,* ed. Jeffrey Meyers (Boston and London: Routledge and Kegan Paul, 1982), 218.

argued that one can and must distinguish between Hemingway the man and Hemingway the artist: "Hemingway the 'artist' is conscious, Hemingway the 'man' is self-conscious; the 'artist' has a kind of innocence, the 'man' a kind of naivety; the 'artist' is disinterested, the 'man' has a dull personal ax to grind; the 'artist' has a perfect medium and tells the truth even if it be only his truth, but the 'man' fumbles at communication and falsifies."[6] Still others found little to admire in Hemingway grinding his personal axes, particularly of the self-consciously masculine variety, but endeavored to delineate more complex narratives of the roles Hemingway traversed in his life. Philip Young's extremely influential interpretation of Hemingway's work in terms of the physical and psychic wounds overcome by the man is a fine example.

In many ways, Hemingway must be held responsible for the strong biographical focus to interpretations of his work. Few writers have played to the public more effectively. In early Paris days, Robert McAlmon presciently called him the "original Limelight Kid."[7] An "incorrigible attention-getter and impresario of his need to be situated always centre-stage," the writer who is "always center stage, overpowering the nominal subject,"[8] Hemingway arguably made his entire life a calculated attempt to keep himself and his works in the public eye. And if not always calculated, so many events of his life seemed shaped and governed by an overriding desire to display himself in a tough masculine role. Leicester Hemingway commented that Hemingway always "needed someone he could show off to,"[9] a trait that his biographers consider intensified in the early 1930s, when, as Jeffrey Meyers writes, he began to "indulge in heroics, to boast, to swagger, to suppress the sensitive side of his nature and to cultivate the public image." One famous encounter in Max Perkins's office between Hemingway and Max Eastman, the writer who had recently accused him of shaping a "literary style . . . of wearing false hair on the chest," has Hemingway ripping open his and Eastman's shirts in order to demonstrate his superior hirsuteness. At another moment during World

6. Lionel Trilling, "Hemingway and His Critics," in *Hemingway and His Critics: An International Anthology,* ed. Carlos Baker (New York: Hill and Wang, 1961), 61.

7. Quoted in Malcolm Cowley, *A Second Flowering: Works and Days of the Lost Generation* (New York: Penguin, 1980), 61.

8. A. Robert Lee, introduction to *Ernest Hemingway: New Critical Essays,* ed. A. Robert Lee (London: Vision Press, 1983), 8; John Raeburn, *Fame Became of Him: Hemingway as Public Writer* (Bloomington: Indiana University Press, 1984), 15.

9. Leicester Hemingway, *My Brother, Ernest Hemingway* (Cleveland: World, 1962), 117.

War II a shell hit the headquarters where Hemingway, General Buck Lanham, and artist John Groth were eating, causing everyone to duck under the table or into the cellar. "Hemingway alone," notes Meyers, "continued to eat and drink as if nothing had happened," a mixture of "bravery and bravado" that Meyers considers "impressive if adolescent."[10] Hemingway biographies are packed with similar instances of his commitment to evidencing some sign of authentic manhood—and with similarly irritable accusations of adolescent posturing.

In all scenes like these, critics tend to anatomize Hemingway's he-man heroics in terms of a maze of subconscious yearnings toward a bravura masculine role: the scenes evidence what Hemingway would have *liked* to be secure about, but clearly was not. And the reason we know he was not secure about his manhood is because he chose to evidence it. This formulation allows us to explain a distinction between bravery and bravado that might seem a little perplexing as soon as we think to inquire how showing a hairy chest or a calm indifference to death is a reliable index to the way Hemingway really felt. In Meyers's anecdote from World War II, for example, what prohibits us from interpreting Hemingway's actions as those of a perfectly brave man? It would seem that we are prohibited, rather surprisingly, simply because of the presence of an audience. With an audience (Groth, Lanham) watching, actions that might otherwise be understood as evidence for manhood can only be interpreted as Hemingway's need for *evidencing* manhood. Such actions actually tell us nothing about Hemingway's real state of mind; but they tell us much about cultural proclivities toward understanding true manhood as self-contained, self-possessed, and antagonistic to self-display. Ripping open Max Eastman's shirt, in other words, is a direct violation of the protocols "real men" share and thus an obvious sign that Hemingway's claim on authenticity ("I really am a man") is fake and interpretable as swaggering and bluster. Indeed, Hemingway is doubly damned, for it would seem that he (of all men!) ignores protocols that are to others so obvious that Meyers does not even bother to inform us how he knows that Hemingway's actions mix bravado in with their bravery.

Scenes like this, however, are susceptible to a different analysis that reads them as staged actions activating codes both theatrical and cultural that reads them, in short, as acts of genuine theater. This is not to say that Hem-

10. Meyers, *Hemingway*, 237, 96, 402.

ingway was always deliberately acting for an audience, though many episodes of his life (like the shirt-ripping) do seem self-consciously witty. Nor is it to say that Hemingway's life composed an intentional and critical reflection on cultural codes of manhood. But to think of Hemingway's performances as being motivated by the presence of and by his awareness of an audience makes a profound difference in the way we might interpret them. The scholars' and biographers' emphasis on Hemingway's poses pays some attention to the fact of an audience. To Meyers, as we have seen, the fact that others witness Hemingway's calm indifference to the shelling is crucial; his playing to them marks his divergence from self-possessed manhood. But this emphasis on *Hemingway's* posturing obscures the effect of his *audience.* Groth and Lanham (and also Meyers and any other reader of this episode) must be present culturally more than physically. The audience must be prepared to read the situation and activate cultural codes about manly behavior, one of which is that men commonly watch other men perform as men; another of which is that men performing as men are frequently seen as faking their manhood; another of which is that men can decide differently about whether other men are faking (as do, presumably, Groth, Lanham, and Meyers); and another of which is that men performing must be aware at some level of the ability of audiences to activate these codes.

In this sense, one's temptation to criticize Hemingway for swaggering like an adolescent might yield to a more deliberate assessment of the entire structure of the dramatic scene, which now speaks to a powerful collusion between actor and audience and an intense dependence on preexisting codes about how men should perform for other men. The shirt-ripping episode does not in any simple way reveal a man who swaggers; it reveals a male's need to fashion signs for an audience in hopes of being interpreted as a man. Likewise, the falling-shell episode does not in any simple way reveal Hemingway's adolescent bravado; it reveals a theater of manhood-on-display in which the audience's interpretive and evaluatory responses crucially affect its dramatic significance. Read this way, the meaning of scenes of Hemingway posturing cannot be confined to an assessment of his character. They mark the moments at which manhood-fashioning must be read as complex social practices configured within a theatrical structure, and at which claims on manhood must be seen to be overtly rhetorical. To anticipate a later discussion: such scenes can be read as "gests" in the Brechtian sense of drama that grasps and exposes the socially constructed performances of everyday life.

6

Accounts of Hemingway's fiction have always played a major part in framing the discussion on Hemingway's life-performances. *Hemingway* has often been held to have succumbed to various anxieties about lacking virility and thus given a studied performance of manhood; and some of his characters (like Harry Morgan and Richard Cantwell), unworthy of being dubbed men, are sometimes thought to have been infected by their author's posturing. But few doubt that Hemingway considered the pursuit of an idealized, full manhood to be a worthy and to-be-longed-for goal that motivated his fiction, even when, or perhaps especially when, no character achieved that ideal. As Hugh Kenner explains succinctly, "Hemingway's [characters] are divided by their knowledge or ignorance of what the self-sufficient man ought to know."[11] And the values the self-sufficient man ought to know have never been associated with self-staging. The "old Hemingway" values were of "isolation, inarticulateness, self-sufficiency"[12] sneered Philip Rahv in 1935; others, more kindly disposed, have read those values as autonomy, silent endurance, and self-possession. But the true man, the man that Hemingway tried assiduously and perhaps anxiously to delineate in his fiction, was surely not to be confused with the pompously overbearing figure Hemingway cut in life. It seems more obvious that what Hemingway lacked as a man must have motivated the pursuit of authentic masculinity in his fiction. Conversely, the ideal of authentic masculinity broached in his work is what convinces us that Hemingway's life-performances do in fact imply a profound lack. Accusations that Hemingway in life was "only" performing thus go hand in hand with a powerful recuperation of "full manhood" in the best of his fiction, where ideal traits like self-control, quiet endurance, living by a code, and a desire for independence and autonomy can be understood as motivating the most potent of his characters or as representing that which his characters have unfortunately lost or struggle to reclaim. This dynamic interrelationship between Hemingway's fiction and his life has always ruled out the kind of argument I made for Palin's *Hemingway's Chair,* where, it seemed, "just performing" might actually constitute identity.

It is therefore not surprising that no one has considered the possibility that the extravagant performances of Hemingway's life urge and support an ac-

---

11. Hugh Kenner, *A Homemade World* (New York: Morrow, 1975), 135.

12. Philip Rahv, "The Social Muse and the Great Kudu," in *Ernest Hemingway: The Critical Reception,* ed. Robert O. Stephens (New York: Burt Franklin, 1977), 186.

count of theatricalized masculinity in his fictional narratives of manhood-fashioning. This study does so, and in the process disagrees in diverse ways with the kind of long-established notions about Hemingway's work noted above. It argues that Hemingway's constant urge toward self-dramatization can be taken as an appropriate and powerful trope for the way his male protagonists emerge into manhood before an evaluating audience. Hemingway's male characters are constituted as men through their public relationship with an audience rather than through achieving autonomy; and by performance rather than by a process of internal transformation. Hemingway emphasizes the *theatrical representation* of masculinity. As a corollary, I argue that Hemingway's narrative art constantly represents masculinity as temporary and subject to abrupt change rather than stable and permanent; as relational and contingent rather than self-determined; as the function of insubstantial codes and evaluating audiences rather than the sole possession of code heroes; as negotiated and constructed rather than constitutive of an essential identity. The codes of manhood to which Hemingway's male characters look for psychological sustenance are themselves staged, and conducive to role-playing rather than to settled identities. Masculinity in Hemingway can be seen more profitably as a trope that must be negotiated into meaning by means of a changing structural relationship between character, masculine code, and legitimating audience.

The claim for a theatrical representation of manhood has several profound consequences for reading Hemingway. First, it focuses new attention on one of the most time honored assessments of Hemingway's style, which is that its tough, emotionally restrained, laconic concision is deeply masculine, and that Hemingway's "fall" into rhetoric in the early 1930s denotes a failure or crisis of style and masculinity together, after which Hemingway's work could only parody its former glory. This study contends not only that reading Hemingway's fictions under the rubric of a stylized narrative concision is at variance with their rich rhetorical performances but that rhetoricity itself—the self-conscious display of language for the purpose of invoking and commanding an audience—creates a mode of theatrical representation that Hemingway exploits in varied and subtle ways to trouble conventional interpretations of masculine style. The metaphoric density, emotional excess, linguistic oddities, and rhetorical games of Hemingway's work should be read as a serious attempt to articulate, and to involve readers in articulating, processes of manhood-fashioning.

8

The second consequence of a theatrical representation of manhood, as the preceding point implies, is that Hemingway's audiences must play a major role in the construction of his meanings about manhood. This is true in the sense that Hemingway carefully delineates specific roles for his readers, as scholars such as Walter J. Ong and James Phelan have argued; and it is true in the larger sense I shall argue here, which is that readers, along with fictive audiences in the text, are positioned to watch and evaluate Hemingway's characters.[13] Indeed, this study traces a series of roles for Hemingway's readers, both past and present. It argues in Chapter 1 that Hemingway scholars have codified essentialist concepts of manhood, uncompromised by any hint of theatricality or pose, from narrative evidence that, as this study (and several other recent studies) demonstrate, is by no means overwhelmingly in its favor. And it shows throughout that Hemingway fosters a variety of interpretive stances for readers (not one, as I think both Ong and Phelan imply), particularly when it comes to questions of masculinity. Indeed, this study maintains that paying attention to the way readers respond, or might respond, to issues of masculinity in Hemingway's work greatly complicates what has usually seemed a firmly settled issue; and, conversely, approaching masculinity in Hemingway as an unsettled and unsettling issue draws our attention to the remarkable negotiations readers undergo in responding to Hemingway's narrative strategies.

These points dispute from the outset some of the most common judgments of Hemingway's work, namely, that in its focus on isolated men enduring their existential woes it disregards the historical, social, and economic conditions of the twentieth century; that, as a corollary, it attempts to set up transhistorical ideals of heroic masculinity in the midst of radical changes in the sociohistoric status of men; and that Hemingway's "masculine" style in and of itself builds a kind of aesthetic monad—a linguistic erasure of history. So powerful are these concepts that even when the troubles plaguing men are found to have local causes in the First World War or in the Parisian "lost

---

13. See, for instance, Walter J. Ong's reading of the opening lines of *A Farewell to Arms* in his "The Writer's Audience Is Always a Fiction," *PMLA* 90 (1975): 12–15; and two works by James Phelan: "The Concept of Voice, the Voices of Frederic Henry, and the Structure of *A Farewell to Arms*," in *Hemingway: Essays of Reassessment,* ed. Frank Scafella (New York: Oxford University Press, 1991), 214–232, and "Distance, Voice, and Temporal Perspective in Frederic Henry's Narration: Powers, Problems and Paradox," in *New Essays on "A Farewell to Arms,"* ed. Scott Donaldson (Cambridge: Cambridge University Press, 1990), 53–74.

generation," scholars have usually found Hemingway's sense of manhood to rest stably on the transhistorical ground of the real nature of men: these characters are men plunged into and tested by war, not characters for whom war defines the possibilities of their manliness. Against the grain of these interpretations, this study argues that manhood-fashioning for Hemingway is irredeemably social in the sense that theatrical gestures staged before an audience comprise manhood and compromise its ontological purity. As our attention shifts from an imaginary plenitude to the *process* of manhood-fashioning, we regain the option of focusing on the historical and cultural conditions within which human beings obtain, in the words of Bertolt Brecht, their "social individuality." So strikingly does Hemingway render problems of masculine identity that I will argue that his body of work equals and in some ways predicts the formidable critique of masculinity raised by feminist studies over the past four decades.

Each chapter in this book advances different perspectives on the theatrical representation of masculinity in Hemingway's work. Chapter 1 performs a reading of "The Short Happy Life of Francis Macomber" with the double goal of, first, demonstrating how a concept of theatricalized manhood opens up new readings of one of Hemingway's best-known and most-discussed stories and, second, situating Hemingway's analysis of masculine self-dramatization within current accounts of gender-as-performance in order to elaborate a more theoretically grounded approach. In addition, Chapter 1 begins an investigation into how critical interpretations of Hemingway's work have evaded or reconstrued the evidence for masculine self-dramatization in order to preserve idealized concepts of masculinity. Thereafter, chapters are organized in roughly chronological fashion. Chapter 2 extends these issues by exploring the dramatization of manhood and the role of an evaluating audience in the early *In Our Time* (1925) and *The Sun Also Rises* (1926). It traces some of the implications an account of role-playing in Hemingway's work might have for the twinned concepts of code and code hero, and concludes with a revisionary reading of how Jake Barnes's failures to dramatize himself authoritatively enough shape and constrain his narration of Pedro Romero's actions.

Taking their cue from Hemingway's next major novel, *A Farewell to Arms* (1929), Chapters 3 and 4 explore issues of violence in Hemingway—the topic that has probably done most to open his work to a wide-ranging feminist critique—and its relationship to his rhetorical and narrative representation of theaters of masculinity. There are indeed connections to be made between writing and fighting in Hemingway's work, but in a very different way than most of his critics have assumed. Chapter 3 examines Hemingway's two major war novels, *A Farewell to Arms* and *For Whom the Bell Tolls* (1940), in terms of a metaphor, "theater of war," that each work makes apt and problematic in different ways. In *Farewell,* the "Show" has often been read as a testing ground for the true nature of men; yet Frederic Henry's many masquerades put into question precisely the truth, naturalness, and permanence of masculine identity. Against a still more somber backdrop of the formidable disciplining of the male gaze under totalitarianism, *Bell* poses the travails of Robert Jordan, whose fascination with the power of a panoptic master-eye is countered by the demands of dramatizing his authority to Pablo, Pilar, and the other partisans—only to find Pablo demonstrating a mastery of self-dramatization from which Jordan could learn much. In many ways, I shall argue, "cave theater" in *For Whom the Bell Tolls* anticipates the contemporary attack on the totalitarian male gaze formulated by poststructuralism, feminism, and postcolonial theory.

Chapter 4 is pivotal in this study. It focuses on a work—*Death in the Afternoon* (1932)—that has proved central to Hemingway studies in at least three ways. The novel elaborates the significance of the bullring, long held to be the exemplary Hemingway arena where men violently attain manhood. It states the author's important aesthetic criteria of "real things" and emotion-into-action. And it has frequently been read as a work whose complete lack of emotional restraint marks it as the beginning of the long downward slide of Hemingway's career. This chapter contends that *Afternoon* is less a handbook of bullfighting than a guide to the multiple modes of performance undertaken by men. But it is also a work whose rhetorical performances—at odds with its announced modernist principles of aesthetic restraint—must be taken as a serious attempt to confuse straightforward articulations of masculinity. Representations of manhood built around rhetorical performance are scandalously contradictory or equivocal, and emerge as a critique of the many ways readers have used Hemingway's aesthetic criteria to consolidate a philosophy of masculinist modernism.

Chapters 5 and 6 continue this theme of rhetorical performance. They are grouped together under their concern for the ways Hemingway employs trophies as tropes of, and as a critique of, manhood, focusing particularly on the manner in which fictive audiences and Hemingway's readers are led to grapple with the signs that are supposed to represent manliness. Chapter 5 begins with a revisionary reading of the little-admired *Green Hills of Africa* (1935), showing how Hemingway's self-dramatizations and hunt for trophies can be read as a deconstruction of masculinity, now understood as a trope subject to the freeplay of language. Far from being an aberration in Hemingway's canon, the book provides a crucial articulation of the way in which the meanings of masculine codes must be negotiated into significance. Chapter 5 continues its exploration of metaphors of manhood by examining the significance of trophies and tropes—in particular the bull's head and Manuel's coleta—in "The Undefeated."

A brief analysis of Hemingway's posthumous novel *The Garden of Eden* (1986) concludes Chapter 5. In this study I have opted to focus on works Hemingway published in his lifetime to avoid the problem of dealing with someone else's editorial decisions and to afford readers full accessibility to the fiction with which I deal. But Catherine's and David's experiments with the fluid dynamics of masculinity—focused on the trope of boyish hair—are such a striking corroboration of my argument about earlier Hemingway works that it seemed worth living with the necessary provisionality of any thesis about this work. I have chosen to use the heavily edited published text because *any* interpretation of this sprawling manuscript posits, or assumes, a set of intentions on Hemingway's part that one simply has no way of proving—it is not as if the manuscript represents Hemingway's final thoughts. And this strategy has the obvious advantage of allowing any reader to follow my argument.

I consider next in Chapter 6 "Big Two-Hearted River" and *The Old Man and the Sea* (1952), Hemingway's most remarkable (and quite different) attempts to shape a nontheatrical construction of masculine identity. "Big Two-Hearted River" shows how the depiction of a man off alone leads to ironic conclusions: a man under these circumstances may not be a man at all. My reading of the marlin-trophy in *Old Man,* however, demonstrates that audiences are absolutely crucial to the meanings about masculinity generated by Santiago. Although the claim seems puzzling at best, I shall argue that the work is deeply imbued with a theatrical construction of masculine identity. This section of the chapter, moreover, investigates the spectatorial roles that might be undertaken by the readers of Hemingway's work. That theme, implicit everywhere in this study, is broached more particularly in my analysis of "The Undefeated" and becomes central to my reading of *The Old Man and the Sea.*

Recent scholarly works by Spilka, Messent, Comley and Scholes, Moddelmog, and Eby have made Hemingway's representation of gender and sexuality come to seem a much more complex and multifaceted concept. The numerous and varied scholarly exegeses of his work over the last two decades are in part, no doubt, a response to the protocols devised by post-feminist movements like gender studies and the New Men's Studies, for whom the construction and interpretation of masculinities has taken a newly complex turn. But those exegeses also suggest that his work continues to pose the right kind of provocative questions. At this point in time, it would seem very much to Hemingway's advantage to have inspired the kind of fierce debates about male characters and masculine style that have distinguished his fiction from the beginning; indeed, his work and its reception has come to compose an archive of changing articulations of manhood over the course of the twentieth century. But too few of the appraisals of and attacks on Hemingway have given his work credit for the *way* he instigates these debates. It is certainly time to present not so much a "*nuevo* Hemingway,"[14] as Comley and Scholes put it in their recent book, but a defamiliarized Hemingway whose narrative and rhetorical strategies will seem disconcertingly different from those that have been thought to typify his work.

14. Nancy R. Comley and Robert Scholes, *Hemingway's Genders: Rereading the Hemingway Text* (New Haven: Yale University Press, 1994), 146.

CHAPTER 1

Unraveling the Masculine Ethos in
"The Short Happy Life of Francis Macomber"

ACCORDING TO THE APPRAISAL of cold-eyed hunting guide Robert Wilson, the key event in "The Short Happy Life of Francis Macomber" is the wild car chase across the African plains that leaves two buffaloes dead and one seriously wounded, Margot Macomber white-faced and terrified, and Francis Macomber a man. Precipitated without forethought into violent action, Macomber enters into his manhood in his thirty-fifth year and, if the story's title is any indication, begins a short happy life that ends a few minutes later with Margot's bullet in his brain. Wilson considers that Macomber has been reborn into manhood, for the latter's transformation is "More of a change than any loss of virginity. Fear gone like an operation. Something else grew in its place. Main thing a man had. Made him into a man."[1] Wilson, documenting the emergence of that phallic "Something," configures Macomber's mawkish attempts to express his new-found courage around codes of heroic deportment: the quotation from Shakespeare that Wilson embarrassedly recites, the knowledge that it "Doesn't do to talk too much about all this," the sudden camaraderie that allows Macomber to instruct his wife "If you don't know what we're talking about why not keep out of it?" The scene is consummate Hemingway. Male bonding, the initiation into manhood, the discovery of codes of graceful and appropriate behavior, a privileging of action over mere words translated out of an aesthetics of emotional restraint—all of these seem archetypal, even stock, gestures from what has always seemed Hemingway's infatuation with hard-boiled masculine identity, behavior, and style. And they set up what is for many critics the interpretive crux of the story: the moment when Margot

1. Ernest Hemingway, *The Snows of Kilimanjaro and Other Stories* (New York: Scribner's/ Collier, 1986), 150. This work will hereinafter be cited parenthetically by page number in the text.

Macomber, perhaps jealously resenting her husband's new-found power over her, perhaps shooting at the charging buffalo in token of a new-found respect for him, sends her bullet into his head.

Its ending has made "The Short Happy Life of Francis Macomber" the most anthologized, the most representative and, perhaps oddly, the most controversial short story in the Hemingway canon. On the one hand, the ending seems a definitive expression of Hemingway's iceberg theory of writing whereby an economy of narrative information allows the reader to infer an untold tale of offstage occurrences, hidden motives, and psychological and emotional complexities. As Hemingway phrased it in *Death in the Afternoon* (1932), writing truly was a matter of putting down "what really happened in action" and stating purely "the real thing, the sequence of motion and fact which made the emotion."[2] The conclusion of "The Short Happy Life" exploits such strategies with characteristic compression. On the other hand, scholars have debated back and forth for decades about how to read a number of narrative cruxes: Does Margot intend to kill Macomber? Is Wilson a real or fake code hero? Does Macomber become a man in the last moments before his death? The only truly consistent trend amid the controversies is that scholars, probably seduced by straightforward pronouncements like "the real thing" and "what really happened," have always thought that there should be answers to these questions.

Widely variant readings of "The Short Happy Life" should give us pause before making categorical statements about what really happens in this sequence of actions. Negotiating what Hemingway omits from his narratives, in fact, is a deeply problematic activity, for modernist strategies of narrative gaps, omissions, abrupt juxtaposition, and lack of authorial closure impose strictures on the acquisition of absolute knowledge. In "The Short Happy Life," the logic of narrative omissions forever defers the moment when we might determine the meaning of, say, Margot's shot. The evidence for any final reading of Margot's actions and motives is simply inadequate. The narrative eschews interior monologue; presents consequences rather than initial actions; and palms off what appears to be an omniscient statement that Margot Macomber "shot at the buffalo" without assuring us that a vestige of subconscious hostility did not affect her aim. If Hemingway typically allows us to intuit a narrative whole from carefully selected parts, in this case Macomber's

---

2. Ernest Hemingway, *Death in the Afternoon* (New York: Scribner's 1932), 2.

death makes us aware that the parts cannot be understood without prior knowledge of the whole—for the individual actions that might lead us to understand Margot's motivation are themselves comprehensible only once we have understood her motivation. A bullet strikes Macomber's head; but we cannot know whether the bullet was delivered accidentally or with malice aforethought until we know Margot's intention; and we cannot know what Margot's intention was from the described action of the bullet striking her husband's head.

We seem on firmer interpretive ground with the assertion that in the final scenes Macomber becomes a fully self-controlled and self-determined man. At one point during the buffalo charge, the narrative portrays Macomber "aiming carefully," a phrase that echoes Wilson's actions during the earlier scene when he "aimed carefully" at the charging lion. Not only does that phrase enhance arguments for a growing likeness between Wilson and Macomber; it seems to present a new Macomber, now carefully self-controlled in the face of enormous danger and independent of Wilson's help. Macomber's independence is crucial, for it is on that ground that so many scholars have anchored the manliness of Hemingway's characters. For Mark Spilka, Hemingway's heroes must establish "private and imaginative frontiers," which reminds us that for Earl Rovit Hemingway's stories documented the travails of the "isolate self," for Philip Young the code hero "builds what he lives by" out of the compromises of his life, and for Carlos Baker the Hemingway hero must "learn his own way to a great extent independently of every other man."[3] Guided by critical opinion and by telling phrases like "aiming carefully" and, later, "stood solid," we might piece together a whole man from the fragmented perceptions of the charge.

Such a reading conforms to traditional perspectives of Hemingway's ethics and aesthetics and is certainly a viable interpretation of the story. But this reading is not self-evident. Phrases like "aiming carefully" and "stood solid" do not in and of themselves bespeak a new, manly Macomber; aiming carefully and standing solidly are simply what one does to stay alive. Nowhere, in fact, do the concluding scenes of Macomber's lone conflict with the buffalo

---

3. Mark Spilka, "The Necessary Stylist: A New Critical Revision," *Modern Fiction Studies* 6 (1960): 292; Earl Rovit and Gerry Brenner, *Ernest Hemingway* (Boston: Twayne, 1986), 37; Philip Young, *Ernest Hemingway: A Reconsideration* (New York and Toronto: Rinehart, 1952), 74; Carlos Baker, *Hemingway: The Writer as Artist* (Princeton: Princeton University Press, 1952), 156.

guarantee conventional interpretations of Hemingway's masculine ethos. We learn about Macomber's transformation in incomplete ways: from Margot's and Wilson's perspectives; from partial judgments omnisciently narrated (Macomber, for instance, was "still exploring his new wealth"); from Macomber's statements; and from actions undertaken. These fragments of what we do know about Macomber are constellated around an absent center: the lack of any interior monologue or omniscient narrative that might have given us direct access to Macomber's sense of his own transformation. Indeed, one problem with interpreting Macomber's fortitude before the buffalo as a sign of his new manliness is that its depiction of pure action portrays Macomber acting without conscious reflection. The buffalo scene presents a rush of unmediated physical action: "Macomber, as he fired, unhearing his shot in the roaring of Wilson's gun, saw fragments like slate burst from the huge boss of the horns, and the head jerked, he shot again at the wide nostrils and saw the horns jolt again and fragments fly, and he did not see Wilson now." Composed out of a jumble of simple perceptions and complex linguistic constructions (such as the wonderful phrase "unhearing his shot"), the passage balances intensely realized details against syntactic distortions and narrative elisions. The passage brilliantly evokes the psychological experience of the instantaneity of action with its run-on phrases ("the head jerked, he shot again") and odd time compressions: Macomber sees "fragments like slate" erupt "as he fired" rather than after he fires. A series of dissociations characterize Macomber's experience. He fires twice and both times sees fragments fly, yet these impressions are juxtaposed rather than rationally conjoined (that is, fragments fly because a bullet strikes). Similarly, the buffalo's head jerks presumably because of the bullet striking, but we are left with an isolated perception: "and the head jerked."

Though Macomber this time stands his ground rather than fleeing, the scene is rendered with a syntactically scrambled yet precisely observed detachment that puts in doubt the distinction between bravery consciously founded on a new code of behavior and mere action bereft of thought and conscious control. Such questions are always implicit in Hemingway's strategic displacement of emotion into action, but they are particularly pressing here because Macomber's transformation into manhood is usually categorically associated with reflective, purposive action: one naturally expects Macomber as a new man to determine his own fate before the charging buffalo with the self-consciousness of Robert Wilson, who is articulate about his hunting principles and possesses a credo drawn from Shakespeare. But we cannot tell whether Macomber's conduct in front of the buffalo suggests purposive action or the abrogation of conscious thought; he carries out a bravura performance of Wilson's manly codes without revealing the self-determining motivations that would make such actions significant. "The Short Happy Life" is thus most provocative in making the fate of Macomber's manhood undecidable. More precisely, perhaps, manhood appears and disappears before our eyes as we activate one or another competing paradigms of identity in the story: Macomber as self-determining man or Macomber as unthinking actor.

Why then—and how—have critics acquiesced to readings that are nowhere specified in the text? One reason may be the very familiarity of Hemingway's narrative conversion of emotion and interior consciousness into action, which has become such a cornerstone of understanding his aesthetic principles that critics have largely ceased to feel the interpretive pressures such principles place on them. Hemingway's most influential critics have tended to assume that one can stand in the presence of the true, real, whole narrative lacking from the text yet represented by it; they have assumed an uncomplicated passage from the signifier of the text to the signified of the implied, true (and whole) narrative. To Carlos Baker, for instance, the submerged parts of Hemingway's narrative icebergs are "mostly invisible except to the patient explorer," to whose enlightened and disciplined eyes Hemingway's stories (in Baker's enigmatic phrasing) "tell nothing but the truth in a way that always allowed for telling more than the truth." Joseph Warren Beach likewise credits Hemingway with the "esthetic principle of economy" so skillfully employed that the "discriminating reader will not long miss it."[4]

Beach's comment puts the problem of "The Short Happy Life" in a nutshell. Discriminating readers of Hemingway usually have little trouble discerning what he omits in any of his fictions; typically, they infer a pattern from other events and statements in the story, from similar moments in other stories, and from what they think they know of Hemingway's life and writing career. But discriminating readers have constantly argued about what the narrative omissions of "The Short Happy Life" mean. And that has pressured them to articulate assumptions—the "common sense" approaches and hidden theoretical underpinnings—that normally remain unspoken. That disclosure

4. Baker, *Writer as Artist*, 117; Joseph Warren Beach, *American Fiction, 1920–1940* (New York: Macmillan, 1941), 111.

affords startling opportunities for revising standard lines of inquiry. It suggests that hidden assumptions about masculine style, codes, and identity, upon which critics present an almost complete show of unanimity, have always played an active role in temporarily resolving disputes about Hemingway. It suggests that resolution has been possible *because* these assumptions have generally been "understood" and thus omitted. And, as we shall see, it suggests the more particular thesis that Hemingway studies have always contained a deeply worrying tautology: problems in Hemingway's representation of masculinity have been referred to commonsense notions about his style while problems in his style have been addressed by commonsense notions about his narrative representation of masculinity.

In the following pages I explore three related aspects of Hemingway's representation of masculinity in "The Short Happy Life." First, I examine the ways in which scholars have brought to bear on his texts a multitude of powerful ideas—a fetish of virile masculinity, his masculine style, masculine codes, and code heroes—whose effect has been to smooth away interpretive cruxes and close narrative gaps. Arguing that the story unsettles a too-simple understanding of masculine codes, I turn next to an analysis of how covert assumptions about a stable and consistent masculine identity have made these codes seem to "work" despite the evidence arrayed against them. Holding to a newly cautious sense of the fluidity of Hemingway's characters, I conclude with a study of theatrical representations of manhood in "The Short Happy Life" and the implications thereof. Theatricality provides a far-ranging critique of codes of manhood and the assumptions about male identity that underpin them, and allows new ways of thinking about Hemingway's style. To that end, this chapter elaborates a more cogent account of theatricality by way of Bertolt Brecht's concept of the *gest*, which has an important function in my work. It secures the alienating (but also relational) aspects of a theatrical representation of manhood I will claim for Hemingway's work—and perhaps helps us to see why so many scholars would want to put his work beyond the reach of theatricality. Finally, it allows me to link Hemingway to recent trends in gender studies, notably in the work of Judith Butler, which have emphasized the role of performance in constructing gendered identities.

As early as the late twenties, readers had begun to claim that Hemingway's style somehow represented or spoke for codes of masculinity. Sometimes that connection was made directly: his style is "masculine"[5] and "brutally masculine"; it demonstrates "inarticulate masculinity"; it is the production of one of the few "whole men" in American letters.[6] Sometimes that connection was posed in the form of associated metaphors like "hard," "virile," "tough." Hemingway, for instance, writes a "lean, hard, athletic narrative prose,"[7] his language has a "tough resilience," "propulsive force," "unbounded vigor," "ferocious virility"; is "hard-boiled," "clean and virile"; his "stubby verbal forms" display the "brute, rapid, joyous jab of blunt period upon period." As one writer said in a classic pun, Hemingway is a "professional Hard Guy." And sometimes that connection was made within a labyrinth of metaphoric associations, as when D. H. Lawrence places Hemingway as the descendant of the "lone trapper and cowboy" whose motto is "Don't get connected up" and whose stylistic correlative is the brevity of sketches that are "so short, like striking a match . . . and it's over."[8]

Later writers extend these assertions into important and much more self-conscious accounts of Hemingway's artistic development. Philip Young provides a classic example: "Hemingway's style is the perfect voice of his content. That style, moreover, is the end, or aim, of the man. It is the means of being the man. An old commonplace takes on new force: the style *is* the man." Young has in mind the wounded Hemingway hero whose only recourse is the "rigid restraint which the man feels he must practice if he is to survive," which is evoked by "laconic and carefully controlled" conversation, a "hard and clean prose style," and the "intense simplicity of the prose." Prose style and heroic, disciplined action are thus interchangeable for Young; style is deeply masculine because it embodies the responses to the travails suffered by Hem-

---

5. See, for instance, K. S., review of *Men Without Women*, in ed. Stephens, 62; Lawrence S. Morris, "Warfare in Man and Among Men," in ed. Stephens, 45; J. B. Priestley, review of *A Farewell to Arms*, by Ernest Hemingway, in *Hemingway: The Critical Heritage*, ed. Jeffrey Meyers (Boston and London: Routledge and Kegan Paul, 1982), 137.

6. "Writer," in ed. Stephens, 13; Lewis Garnett, "Books and Things," in ed. Stephens, 83; Allen Tate, review of *The Sun Also Rises*, in ed. Meyers, *Critical Heritage*, 14.

7. "Marital Tragedy," in ed. Stephens, 32.

8. "Preludes to a Mood," in ed. Stephens, 7; "Preludes," 8; Cleveland B. Chase, "Out of Little, Much," in Stephens, 41; Cyril Connolly, review of *Men Without Women*, in ed. Meyers, *Critical Heritage*, 111; Schuyler Ashley, review of *In Our Time*, in ed. Stephens, 11; K. S., in ed. Stephens, 62; Paul Rosenfeld, "Tough Earth," in ed. Stephens, 9; "Stiff Upper Lip," in ed. Stephens, 144; D. H. Lawrence, review of *In Our Time*, in ed. Meyers, *Critical Heritage*, 73.

ingway's sense of threatened manhood. Hugh Kenner, less favorably inclined toward Hemingway in his influential book on American modernism, *A Homemade World* (1975), also reads style in terms of masculinity: Hemingway poses as a writer for whom "style cancels 'style.'" But since his characters are satisfied only when the "things men do are . . . done accurately and well, which means done with style," his work can only foster a "rhetoric of evasion." Faith Pullin is still more hostile to the gendered implications of Hemingway's style. Committed to the "exact and detailed reporting of the experience of sensations of an extreme kind" and featuring isolated male protagonists who exist only within the "moment of action," Hemingway ignores character and in particular the humanity of his female characters, and in so doing constructs (as Pullin's title announces) a "secret language of hate." Style and language for Pullin are thus deeply male—and misogynist.[9]

Intimate relationships between style and masculinity in Hemingway's work have been made to function in numerous ways. In the decades prior to the advent of feminism, the rapidly formed consensus about Hemingway's masculine style was easily tied to a modernist aesthetic—a "whole system," as Malcolm Cowley puts it, of "practical aesthetics"—that depended on aligning narrative strategies of omission with what seemed to be typically masculine virtues of emotional restraint. His younger self was searching, Hemingway claims in *Death in the Afternoon,* to "put down what really happened in action; what the actual things were which produced the emotion that you experienced." Emotion might be thought of as being submerged, iceberg-like, beneath the surface of the text, invisible, potent, leaving on display only those actions that are, in Ezra Pound's assessment of the modernist response to Victorian poetics, "austere, direct, free from emotional slither."[10] Emotion was not exactly to be erased from narrative but omitted within a strategy of metonymic displacement, which would allow writers to avoid overtly emotional displays while granting informed readers the ability to make narrative gaps, hesitancies, and omissions signify.

As Pound's comments make clear, Hemingway's thoughts on writing accord with other modernists, who worked, in Imagist poems, manifestoes, and

9. Young, 174–80; Hugh Kenner, *A Homemade World* (New York: Morrow, 1975), 147, 151, Faith Pullin, "Hemingway and the Secret Language of Hate," in *Ernest Hemingway: New Critical Essays,* ed. A. Robert Lee (London: Vision Press, 1983), 184, 178.

10. Cowley, *Second Flowering,* 63; Hemingway, *Afternoon,* 2; Ezra Pound, "A Retrospect," *Literary Essays of Ezra Pound,* ed. T. S. Eliot (New York: New Directions, 1968), 12.

in concepts like T. S. Eliot's "objective correlative," to curtail Victorian senti-mentalism and to trim the rhetorical excess they saw as its aesthetic sign. Modernism was to be hard-boiled and tough-minded, taciturn and "mascu-line"; it was specifically designed to contravene the outmoded tendencies of an earlier time, when emotional display and rhetorical overflow were thought appropriate. Gendered concepts of emotional and rhetorical restraint thus played a major role in structuring and supporting what was supposed to be innovative about modernist aesthetics, construing manhood as a function of modernist style and legitimating modernism as a form of pure masculine ex-pression. Hemingway's style played a marked role in configuring that field of "masculinist 'Modernism.'"[11] As early reviewers suggested, long before Hem-ingway codified modernist principles of style in *Afternoon* they already seemed obvious in his lean, hard prose and in the "masculine" emotional restraint implied by his tactics of omission; and they seemed already embodied in his code heroes, those tough, taciturn exemplars of autonomous manhood whose devotion to a private code of action demonstrated and authenticated the manly "real thing."

Readers have closed narrative gaps at the end of "The Short Happy Life"—in particular the problem of whether Macomber becomes a man—by employing versions of this relatively unproblematic gendering of modernist style. The logic is elegant. If to "mouth it up" is unmanly, as Wilson seems to consider, then neither Macomber nor Wilson dare speak of Macomber's com-ing to manhood; their silence "speaks" it. Their silence is thus exemplary of, and comprehensible in terms of, a long tradition whereby Hemingway's nar-rative lacunae have been read as the quintessence of modernist style, which in turn implies a masculine psychic economy of emotional restraint. Impor-tantly, those beliefs cannot be and need not be derived simply from his written texts; they already inform the reader's largely unarticulated assumptions that restraint characterizes masculinity; that narrative silences are somehow "about masculinity" and in many ways present the solution to problems of masculinity; and that such narrative strategies, modernist in mode, carry a weighty aesthetic value. Just as importantly, those beliefs need not be tied to Macomber himself. Refusing to "mouth it up" can after all be a pose; and scholars do sometimes read Macomber, the character, as a failure. What

11. Celeste M. Schenk, "Charlotte Mew," in *The Gender of Modernism: A Critical Anthol-ogy*, ed. Bonnie Kime Scott (Bloomington: Indiana University Press, 1990), 317.

seems beyond doubt is the supposition that Hemingway's bedrock beliefs in masculine identity and authoritative codes of conduct like taciturnity and endurance do not in and of themselves pose interpretive dilemmas. In this light, it seems counter-intuitive, perhaps even nonsensical, to read Hemingway's narrative gaps as posing a series of problems: How do we know Macomber becomes, or fails to become, a man? What are the signs of manhood amid the narrative silences? Might a strategy of narrative omission provide a critique of masculine taciturnity? Why does Macomber need to be watched into manhood?

As I remarked, however, "The Short Happy Life" has prompted scholars to "mouth it up" by uttering codes normally too deeply held to need much articulation. That ironic move—uttering what really needs to stay silent—deserves careful analysis, for it draws attention to the powerful rhetorical strategies scholars have deployed to retain a sense of a self-evident masculinity-that-need-not-be-spoken, which can be resurrected at will to negotiate narrative gaps and make them signify manhood. The long-running controversy between Warren Beck and Mark Spilka provides a good example. In his efforts to criticize Robert Wilson and rehabilitate Margot Macomber, Beck, according to Spilka, derives an "absurd interpretation" by reading "The Short Happy Life" idiosyncratically and in isolation from the rest of Hemingway's work.[12] What really happens to Macomber, Spilka argues, can be constructed contextually from a larger knowledge of Hemingway's "working vision of experience" that profoundly informs every aspect of his writing.[13] Wilson, for instance, is not the limited and imperceptive hunter that Beck portrays, but a man who "does 'guide' others through . . . tests, and teaches them their inward meaning. His code is used, moreover, to expose and amend the inadequacies of wasteland life."[14] Characterizing dignity, integrity, and self-determination in his embarrassed yet firm commitment to his Shakespearean code, Wilson becomes another of those Hemingway heroes who "establish private and imaginative frontiers, or reassert them, in opposition to society." Without comprehending that, Macomber's "accession to manhood would be the smaller thing it in fact becomes in Beck's reading."[15]

12. Mark Spilka, "Warren Beck Revisited," *Modern Fiction Studies* 22 (1976): 247.

13. Mark Spilka, "The Necessary Stylist: A New Critical Revision," *Modern Fiction Studies* 6 (1960): 287.

14. Spilka, "Stylist," 292.

15. Spilka, "Warren Beck," 249.

Discussions of Robert Wilson, which began by seeing him as code hero to the cowardly Macomber[16]—a notion that visibly shaped Spilka's "working vision" of Hemingway's work—have more recently questioned the hunter's moral values and the reliability of his observations. Many scholars, for instance, have faulted him for his amoral opportunism (his tryst with Margot) and for his unethical conduct during the hunt (pursuing the buffalo in the car).[17] But critics have almost always agreed with Spilka's basic premises. John J. Seydow's attack on Francis Macomber's "spurious masculinity," for instance, argues that Macomber is inexperienced rather than a coward; that facing the charging buffalo is not manly but foolish; and that his moment of courage is anyway too short to reveal a true accession to manhood. Macomber, in fact, has been intimidated into assuming the "spurious values of the selfsame person [Wilson] who had cuckolded him." But Seydow is not claiming that, for Hemingway, masculinity is somehow spurious. Actually Seydow recognizes the spuriousness of Wilson's values by way of an authentic measure of manhood drawn from Hemingway's other work—a measure that is indistinguishable from the "standard of manhood" that Carlos Baker argued Wilson represented and from the "working vision of experience" that Spilka employed to promote the same character. Otherwise at odds, Baker would surely agree with Seydow when the latter claims that, for Hemingway, "heroism, and its generic synonym, manhood, occurs when an individual, aware that he is face to face with apparent death, conducts himself with 'grace' at 'the moment of truth.' "[18]

On the one hand, then, a wide variation of critical opinion characterizes questions about which men and which incidents manifest manhood. On the other, that variation is all but obscured by subjecting dissent about individual cases to a prior agreement that secure and inviolable forms of manhood are

16. Young, 69–70.

17. Critics have tended to criticize Wilson's behavior (see Cheatham, Hutton, Baym) or view him as a complex figure who cannot be simply identified with Hemingway's values (see Gebhardt, Lounsberry, Paul R. Jackson), or as a character in need of the codes earlier critics saw him as representing (Lounsberry). Even Baym, whose essay "Actually, I Felt Sorry for the Lion" goes furthest toward challenging conventional readings of "The Short Happy Life," is more interested in rehabilitating Margot as a strong character than reevaluating Hemingway's larger conception of masculinity.

18. John J. Seydow, "Francis Macomber's Spurious Masculinity," Hemingway Review 1, no. 1 (1981): 39; Baker, Writer as Artist, 189; Spilka, "Stylist," 287; Seydow, 40.

nonetheless to be found in Hemingway's work. That agreement exercises an intense power. The masculine codes underpinning critical approaches do not even have to be inscribed into the text in order to function in critical readings. The codes represent a cross- and intertextual organization of Hemingway's thoughts about manhood; and extratextual examples of authentically manly grace-under-pressure are always available if the buffalo charge (of all things!) does not serve to exhibit it. Indeed, it is possible that these codes function more powerfully when they are found to be omitted from the text altogether and therefore resistant to individual cases of code-breaking. By indicting Wilson and Macomber for grievous misconduct based on standards derived from other texts (say, Manuel's true heroism in "The Undefeated" or Santiago's in *The Old Man and the Sea*), critics preserve by way of contrast a working definition of manhood. The characters are not man enough—and that is how we know what it takes to be man. Wilson, then, may not live up to his own values, but masculine values of fearlessness, independence, grace in the face of death, taciturnity, and "holding tight," all loosely embodied in the quotation from Shakespeare and the warning not to "mouth it up," remain unsullied in this story and in other works by Hemingway.

These codes of manhood attempt to secure what Jacques Derrida would call a metaphysics of presence in and beyond individual works by Hemingway. They seem self-evident, as though they need no discussion, explanation, or supplement. This is not to say that self-evident truths are necessarily obvious. To Spilka, for instance, it is Beck who makes the error of assuming that meaning lies innocently in a narrative like "The Short Happy Life." A truer understanding of Hemingway's work can only come as the product of hard work and experience as we seek the horizon of our "working vision of experience." Without that hard-won knowledge, one might fall into the trap of assuming what some readers (like Beck) might consider the more obvious interpretation of the story, which is that Wilson's code *causes* his unpleasant form of manhood. In an odd sense, Spilka plays a Hemingwayesque code hero to readers, warning them that what is obvious and what is spoken must yield to hidden, enduring truths. It is a brilliant strategy for demolishing obvious readings *because* they are obvious. But Spilka's more complex interpretive framework merely defers the moment when what is self-evident to him—that is, what is made self-evident in and through that interpretive framework—can be broached. Wilson can now be seen to have been a paradigm of manliness all along: he is a true guide; he exposes the inadequacies of wasteland life; he establishes private frontiers. Aspects of Hemingway's work are thus just as transparent and beyond negotiation for Spilka as for Beck; Spilka merely shifts his epistemological grounds to a vaster cultural, historical, and biographical arena where "obvious" readings can be compared with interpretations that are more fully grounded in a deep knowledge of Hemingway's work and world.

Yet it is telling that so many scholars agree in principle about Hemingway's working vision of manliness but disagree so entirely about which exemplary characters or dramatic incidents support that vision. As any reading of "The Short Happy Life" shows (including this one), we cannot legitimately assume the sufficiency of a code of manhood apart from examples of it. Macomber's actions do not speak for themselves. The mere fact of facing down a charging buffalo is meaningless (or stupid); what makes Macomber's actions manly, according to those readers who see him suddenly a "man," is the code and the contextual meanings that invest his actions with significance. *Choosing* to face down the buffalo in full knowledge of possible death might be a legitimate display of Wilson's "something" that has made Macomber a man. Articulated codes seem to confirm as signs of manhood what might otherwise be mistaken as thoughtless action or mere physical motion. By the same token, articulated codes are meaninglessly abstract until backed by appropriate action and thus made to signify masculinity. No amount of "mouthing" from Macomber about his courage could make him into a man; and no statement that men stand their ground before charging animals could make Wilson a man had he run from the lion. Characters like Macomber and Wilson must do more than speak their manhood; they must demonstrate it in action. And they must do more than act; their actions must be reciprocally informed by a code.

Likewise, at some crucial juncture scholars who wish to preserve the purity of masculine codes that not even the Wilsons of the world can sully must read the codes in a dynamic relationship with actions designed to express them. These critics must be able to do more than extract from the story a code of manliness (such as holding to a code of taciturnity); they must speak for or against the notion that the taciturn Wilson is a man. To do otherwise is simply to defer the moment when two critics at loggerheads over a character like Robert Wilson must, to secure their principal grounds, search for agreement on a truly exemplary male character. Such agreement, when and if found, might retrospectively foster a sense that codes of masculine deportment precede particular incidents and even seem to be unaffected by the poor behavior of individual characters. Hemingway's codes in this retrospective light appear self-evident. But they appear so because the search for agreement has been premised on the need to confirm what both parties already think they know. The codes have already been evidenced. They must already have been engaged—articulated, demonstrated, or simply assumed as part of Hemingway's "working vision of experience"—prior to the moment of being subjected to the problematic antics of a Wilson or Macomber, when readers are susceptible to the "error" of deciding that characters like these make a very poor case for manhood indeed.

"The Short Happy Life" frees us to embrace the error, however, not by insisting that Wilson is a poor tutor and inconsistent role model for the codes he espouses but that the codes he espouses are internally incoherent and even contradictory. The Shakespeare quotation with which Wilson blesses Macomber's initiation into manhood, for instance, articulates a philosophy of individual power and integrity based on a near-fatalistic acceptance of death. Accepting that a "man can die but once" makes a male into a man, for the loss of fear gives a man the power to undertake any action, however terrifying; it signifies independence from consequences. Ulterior and exterior considerations vanish; past failures and humiliations disappear. Macomber simply acts, and in so doing seems to exemplify the key value of autonomy that underpins the various estimations of Hemingway's codes. For Carlos Baker, as we have seen, the Hemingway hero must "learn his own way to a great extent independently of every other man"—and in particular independently of other women. Wilson, for instance, is "the man free of woman and of fear."[19] Hemingway's men without women seek personal codes of graceful conduct in the face of a hostile, repressive, or chaotic world.

But in "The Short Happy Life" the male characters' pursuit of autonomy is thoroughly compromised by the authority they need to exercise over Margot. Macomber's coming of age, according to Wilson, signifies a loss of fear; but it also signifies the loss of fear *of* Margot. Macomber's retort to his wife ("If you don't know what we're talking about why not keep out of it?"[151]) gives credence to Wilson's statement that the three have witnessed the "end of cuckoldry" (150). But Macomber's new-found potency (his ascendancy over his wife) and the camaraderie he suddenly forges with Wilson suggest something quite different from autonomous manhood. Autonomy, in fact, is rec-

19. Baker, *Writer as Artist*, 156, 189.

ognized at this point as the independence to reconfigure a relationship on one's own terms. The influential interpretations of both Baker and Young, oddly enough, recognize that fact without consciously articulating it. Though "free of woman," Wilson, for Baker, is the "judge who presides, after the murder, over the further fortunes of Margot Macomber" and whose "dominance over the lady is apparent from the moment she sees him blast the lion." Young is still more forthright: "Francis Macomber, when under the tutelage of the hunter Wilson, learns courage and honor and to embrace the code. . . . When he attains this manhood he regains the ithyphallic authority he had lost and his wife, now panicky herself in her new role, must destroy him literally. Before he became a man she had committed adultery almost in his presence, knowing him helpless to stop her. When he becomes a man, and she can no longer rule him . . . she sends a bullet to the base of his skull."[20] Both critics identify manhood with autonomy and indeed liberation ("she can no longer rule him"), yet both covertly read Macomber's transformation in relational terms. Macomber flowers under the tutelage of Wilson; and, crucially, Macomber's newly discovered manhood enables him to dominate a relationship in which he was once dominated. Quite against the grain of their articulated arguments, Baker and Young intuit a complex, dialogic sense of manhood, which now appears to consist of standing alone against impending death but also of standing with a man and above a woman.

Wilson's relationship to Margot provides an example exactly analogous to Macomber's. His code of courage and professionalism inspires not only Francis but, presumably, Margot, who publicly kisses Wilson after witnessing her husband's humiliating flight from the lion and who later sleeps with the hunter. For his part, Wilson seems the quintessential "man free of woman." He accepts Margot into the double-sized cot brought to accommodate rich women on safari, but seems indifferent to the prospect of losing her again to the now manly Macomber. The end of Macomber's cuckoldry, in fact, would be a "damned good thing." Yet Wilson's final dealings with Margot suggest a dynamic not of indifference but of dominance. "Why didn't you poison him?" (154) inquires Wilson after Macomber's death and, whether Margot (sub)consciously killed her husband or is merely mourning his passing, his gibes and innuendoes place her, at least in his mind, squarely on the defensive. Having wrung a "please" out of Margot—like a parent to a recalcitrant child—Wilson

20. Ibid., 189–90; Young, 70.

28

finally deigns to stop. But Wilson is not motivated simply by anger at Margot for ending her husband's brief manhood. For after learning that Wilson stood to lose his license and business after chasing the buffaloes by car Margot, as Francis puts it to Wilson, "has something on you" (147). A desire for self-preservation, if not a cruel glee at turning the tables on Margot, sharpens Wilson's attack on her at the end. Wilson regains his independence from Margot like Francis Macomber's coming of age: by asserting Margot's dependence.

Critics have only been able to see Wilson and Macomber as truly autonomous men by ignoring the fact that independence seems possible only at the expense of dramatizing one's control over another's dependence. The worrying corollary—worrying to those who hold to a self-evident masculine ethos in Hemingway's work—is that the story's codes of masculinity subvert themselves *in the way that they function* to make males into men. Being a man in "The Short Happy Life," in other words, means so many contradictory things. If facing a charging buffalo represents Macomber's (and Wilson's) manly independence from fear, facing down Margot (securing her dependence) becomes an equally authoritative sign. Critics have ignored the profound discrepancy in "The Short Happy Life" between manhood-as-autonomy and manhood-as-authority and failed to realize that the exercise of one implies the exercise of the other. Both actions are supposed to signify manhood; the problem is that the two actions signify it in incompatible ways.

This interpretation, to be clear, does not mean that Macomber or Wilson are torn or split personalities or that they necessarily struggle to resolve the contradiction or that the contradiction simply bespeaks their deficiencies. My emphasis has fallen on the fact that the codes subvert each other, not that Macomber's and Wilson's characters subvert the codes. It is important, however, to think through the implications of resorting even at this late stage to a version of the common manhood-saving maneuver whereby the practices of a male character are differentiated from the code he supposedly embodies. We might argue that Wilson and Macomber, as ironic as this might sound, sacrifice their manliness to their misogyny. Their obsession with defeating Margot wrecks what is supposed to be the goal of Hemingway men: their pursuit of a true code of autonomous masculinity. In that case they simply stand in need of the correction that the codes purport to supply; Macomber's and Wilson's problems lie not in manhood but in the fact that they are not yet truly autonomous, not yet truly men.

But to argue so is to depend on several covert, and simple, but very powerful assumptions: that manhood exists prior to and separate from the actual actions undertaken by males; that males can therefore be "not-men" but that manhood always exists to be learnt or won; that manhood is the remedy for "not-men"; and that therefore, crucially, manhood signifies wholeness, completeness, and consistency. This last assumption in particular governs any critical strategy that seeks to understand Hemingway's work by way of the "full man" code hero or by way of codes of manhood to which his broken men could and should aspire. And it governs the interpretive strategies of readers in the concluding scenes of the story. Because we are not privy to Macomber's thoughts while the buffalo charges, his response can only be read as signifying autonomy by supposing that he has substituted self-possessed wholeness for his earlier dependence on Margot and Wilson; and can only be read as heroic and manly by assuming a continuity between his final actions and what immediately precedes them (his excited confidence and Wilson's assessment of Macomber's new manliness). The proposition that to be a man is to be whole allows a reader thus critically fortified to have little trouble in moving from a sequence of events to an understanding of Macomber's true (and new) self. Narrative intervals are not read as intervals at all because a paradigm of continuous, linear identity underpinning the final scene of Macomber's life contextualizes and stabilizes his actions and scholarly interpretations alike, filling the gaps with the certainty that Macomber, having been transformed into a man, will not only stay a man but will not be transformed again.

Given the enormity of Macomber's putative change into manhood, however, it would seem more pressing to place the logic of consistent identities under scrutiny. In fact "The Short Happy Life" gives ambiguous support for a paradigm of consistent and stable identity. On the one hand, the narrative emerges from the consequences of long-lasting, calcified relationships: Macomber knowing that Margot "would not leave him ever now" (139); Margot knowing "too much about him to worry about him either"; Margot having, to no avail, "done the best she could for many years back" (151). Wilson, too, finally quotes "this thing he had lived by"—the code, a touchstone of personality, that has constantly defined and given meaning to his life over many years. Memory plays a crucial role. It encodes the essence of determining influences over a number of years, providing a stable, guiding narrative that allows actions like Wilson's prowess at killing or Margot's infidelity to be comprehended as characteristic and predictable. What has been known, indeed, often stifles healthy change. Wilson tries to comfort Macomber by saying "Any one could be upset by his first lion. That's all over" (129). But Macomber knows that "it was not all over." Similarly, Macomber's idea that "I can fix it [his shame] up on buffalo" (126) confuses Wilson: "Perhaps he had been wrong . . . You most certainly could not tell a damned thing about an American. He was all for Macomber again. If you could forget the morning. But, of course, you couldn't."

That these quiet assumptions about stable constructions of selfhood have fundamentally shaped interpretations of the story, competing theories of Margot's motivations for firing the rifle clearly suggest. For Young and Baker, Margot is a murderer; for Beck, she is not; Arnold E. Davidson argues that Margot is simultaneously a "would-be rescuer and a successful murderer." Taking one important step further, Roger Whitlow realizes that many critics, hastily assembling a coherent narrative out of multiple and often contradictory details, have constrained the complexity of her actions. Margot can only be reviled as a "bitch-murderess," for instance, through an "unfathomable extrapolation" from the story. But Whitlow also proceeds to orchestrate complex narrative events within a paradigm of consistently motivated identity when attempting to prove the "murder thesis" wrong. Having determined that Macomber's three shots should take fewer than four seconds, Whitlow continues: "This means that Margot Macomber, being farther away, would probably not have seen the buffalo charge out of the brush until a moment after Francis sees him (thereby losing at least part of a second). She has slightly more than three seconds, then, to see the buffalo, note that Francis is standing directly between the buffalo and herself, realize that such a position could make the murder of her husband appear to be an accident . . . and fire. . . . Simply impossible."[21] Not impossible, however, if one imagines that Margot from her different angle had spotted the buffalo *before* Macomber and Wilson had, or if one imagines that Margot had already decided to shoot and put it down to firing at some imaginary vulture—notions that are no more or less suspect than trying to elaborate a coherent sequence from a passage whose very syntax enacts the confusion it portrays. Whitlow himself, in other words, extrapolates from the text, assuming first that Margot is a certain kind of char-

---

21. Arnold E. Davidson, "The Ambivalent End of Francis Macomber's Short, Happy Life." *Hemingway Notes* 2, no. 1 (spring 1972): 15; Roger Whitlow, *Cassandra's Daughters: The Women in Hemingway* (Westport, Conn., and London, England: Greenwood Press, 1984), 66–68.

acter (one who would need to make a snap judgment rather than having decided to shoot first and account for it later) and then inferring a sequence of events from what such a character makes possible. None of these critics assumes—except in one limited sense I shall consider shortly—that Margot's motivations are undecidable because she, like Macomber, is subject to abrupt and unexpected transformations.

In fact, the narrative just as easily supports an interpretation of characters who are indeterminate because fundamentally changeable. Despite Wilson's claim that one could not "forget the morning," the narrative demonstrates that the events of the morning, and even those of the night, can be forgotten. Everywhere, in fact, the narrative is marked by flux and bewildering discontinuities. Margot might be, as Wilson would have it, simply cruel, but she walks away from the table crying; she walks away crying, but reappears twenty minutes later "looking refreshed and cheerful and quite lovely" (126) and claiming to have "forgotten the lion." Moreover, Margot transfers her affections to the killer Wilson because her husband has proven himself to be a coward; but when Macomber's sudden enthusiasm for the kill proves that he is not a coward she (so the murder hypothesis goes) shoots him. That hypothesis propounds the greatest transformation of all, from sullen wife to murderer. Margot's changeability thus presents a dilemma to those attracted by a notion of stable identity, though, in her case, Hemingway criticism has always offered a simple answer: women, particularly the "rich bitch" variety, are illogical, flighty, and changeable, and their unpredictability represents not complex characterization but "everything that is confusing, ambivalent and threatening" to the male.[22] Women's motivations are undecidable because they are women.

This may be true of Margot; but we can only establish flightiness as an attribute pertaining to rich *women* if the men of the story appear stalwart, consistent, and predictable. The logic of the story suggests otherwise. In fact Macomber nowhere behaves more like Margot than when he makes his quantum leap into manhood. Manhood-fashioning does not extend characteristic behavior but is defined by sudden new beginnings, summarized best by Margot's contemptuous remark that "You've gotten awfully brave, awfully suddenly" (151). Forgetting the adultery that had obsessed him on the morning of the buffalo hunt, Macomber feels "absolutely different" (149) after pursuing

22. Pullin, 182.

the buffalo, and Wilson ponders "Yesterday he's scared sick and today he's a ruddy fire eater." We are told that "For the first time in [Macomber's] life he really felt wholly without fear" (148), but fear itself seems to be a new manifestation in Macomber's life: "more than shame he felt cold, hollow fear in him. The fear was still there like a cold, slimy hollow in all the emptiness where once his confidence had been" (129). His confidence emptied into a void, Macomber next indicates that he would "like to clear away that lion business" (128) and thus void the fear—an eventuality that Wilson suggests does occur: "Fear gone like an operation. Something else grew in its place." Against the grain of stabilizing codes and faulty relationships too long remembered, Macomber proceeds to his new manhood by way of abrupt change, forgetfulness, and a peculiar dynamic of hollowing out and clearing away.

Men and women together in "Short Happy Life" participate in a logic of sudden transformation of identity whereby Macomber's apotheosis matches Margot's abrupt "enamelled . . . female cruelty" (127). What may prove true for all gender roles, however, is emphasized in the case of Macomber's transformation. Whether or not manhood resembles womanhood, the male characters in the story certainly accord manhood the prestige reserved for impressive and singular events. Their emphasis calls attention to the collective critical amnesia that counts on a stable construction of identity in the face of an event that everyone involved views not as a continuation but as an origin. That amnesia tells us much about the critics' own assumptions about manhood. Manhood, it seems, must already be known to be nonlinear and discontinuous in one powerful sense: it emerges during a single, crucial transition that males undergo on their way to becoming men. The moment of becoming a man signifies not a random disruption of male identity but an expected, necessary, and predictable transformation; it is the one moment when male identity becomes completely restructured, allowing new perspectives on remembered experiences and ensuring new patterns of appropriate conduct. The acquisition of manhood seems not to disturb paradigms of stable identity partly because it is held to be a unique event rather than a function of random change, and partly because its uniqueness is predicted and indeed made necessary by the conventional pattern of development that boys (should) undergo. It occupies the structural center of the individual male personality.

Once that center has been articulated, the very meaning of a stable and consistent identity changes. Until the moment of transformation, critical readings imply, Macomber (and all boys and not-men) suffer from a debilitating centerlessness: the ingrained patterns of his life can only be defined in terms of lacking manhood. Lack is precisely the reason why the destructive patterns of Macomber's life have become ingrained. The acquisition of manhood therefore becomes the one permissible disruption within a paradigm of stable identity because it is the change that alone makes male identity significant. It authenticates identity by transforming boys, or not-men, into true men, at which point masculine identity can be simply hypostasized. One can thus suppose Macomber's conversion to manhood to be stable because it replaces what Macomber so unproductively was with an identity that is for the first time self-aware and self-determining. By its very definition, manhood is autonomous and not subject to the vagaries of personality characterizing the childish Macomber or the flighty Margot. What this suggests is not so much that scholars have grounded their faith that Macomber remains a man in a paradigm of stable identity, but that a faith that males can transform themselves into authentic men underpins their faith in stable identity.

There is something deeply tautological about this appraisal of manhood: the acquisition of manhood seems problematic, but only because those who have not achieved it are not yet men. Manhood once acquired seems beyond question; actually it is accounted the solution to the problem. Masculinity becomes something that Wilson exemplifies and Macomber attains, or that Wilson makes spurious, or that Wilson and Macomber both lack, but which is in every case the structural center of the various interpretive codes—a center that is, as Derrida writes, thought to be outside structurality itself because it is that which structures the codes rather than itself being constructed.[23] Critics making this assumption of the inviolable, unproblematic, and continuous nature of masculinity in Hemingway's work have been freed to shape a "working vision of experience" uncovering universally identifiable "Hemingwayesque" features like code hero and "rich bitch," and thus to illuminate what would otherwise seem prohibited by a strategy of narrative omission. It has enabled critics to make the story work in marvellously authoritative ways as a representative Hemingway fiction. And it has allowed critics to sketch the lineaments of a classic modernist text and simultaneously construe a paradigmatic account of manhood-acquisition.

23. See Jacques Derrida, "Structure, Sign, and Play in the Discourse of the Human Sciences," in *Writing and Difference,* trans. Alan Bass (Chicago: University of Chicago Press, 1978).

Concepts of inviolate manhood and stable character-formation continue to shape contemporary studies of Hemingway and indeed of modernism in powerful ways. They mark, for instance, Sandra Gilbert and Susan Gubar's reading of "The Short Happy Life" in their influential *No Man's Land* (1988), which argues for a "link between male discontent and masculinist backlash" in male modernist texts, noting that "modernist men of letters sought to define appropriately virile reactions" in response to the perceived infringements of female writers. Arguing that Hemingway like other male modernists reacted to a nightmarish landscape of "no-manhood" by depicting impotent males and attacking potent females, Gilbert and Gubar focus on the conclusion to "The Short Happy Life," where Margot responds to Macomber's "courageous confrontation with a buffalo by accidentally-on-purpose shooting him." They continue: " 'Why didn't you poison him? That's what they do in England,' Wilson scathingly remarks, for, though Wilson may be in some ways a problematic character, Hemingway's tale implies that Macomber is trapped in a dire double bind: whether he is cowardly or courageous, unmanned or manly, his wife is determined to betray him."[24] My own interpretation of "The Short Happy Life" puts in question almost every aspect of Gilbert and Gubar's reading. We cannot tell, I have claimed, whether Macomber is courageous or whether Margot shoots "accidentally-on-purpose"; we certainly cannot tell whether Margot is "determined to betray him"; and Wilson's problematic character casts doubt precisely on categories of judgment like "cowardly or courageous, unmanned or manly." Gilbert and Gubar assume the lucidity of what is actually indeterminate (like Margot's betrayal of her husband) and subordinate the significance of what is problematic (like Wilson's character).

Above all, despite the superficial attention to Wilson's problematic character and the question of whether Macomber is "unmanned or manly," Gilbert and Gubar's reading depends on putting into play the same circular logic I have already addressed in Hemingway scholarship whereby manhood as a structural but absent center can always be activated. A concept of manhood beyond any problematic of the story governs the binary opposition "unmanned or manly." If it did not—if the construction of manhood itself were al-

24. Sandra Gilbert and Susan Gubar, *No Man's Land: The Place of the Woman Writer in the Twentieth Century,* vol. 1, *The War of the Words* (New Haven: Yale University Press, 1988), 36–37, 41.

lowed to be the problem—Gilbert and Gubar would have to subject the oppo-sition itself to scrutiny. But they cannot, for they put this interpretation of "The Short Happy Life" to the larger service of configuring the battle lines of an "ongoing battle of the sexes."[25] The erasures and key assumptions I outline above suggest that their reading has been made to conform to, rather than truly evidencing, binary gender relationships and male misogyny in the early twentieth century. Their thesis necessitates a series of interlocked perceptions: Margot must be determined to betray her husband; the problem of Wilson's character might puzzle but must not intrinsically affect our interpretation of the story; above all, Macomber must face a binary "double bind" of manhood or "no-manhood." Though Gilbert and Gubar seek to envision a "vexed ter-rain"[26] of modernist writing, what is truly vexing to their hypotheses is the possibility that Margot does not seek to betray her husband, or the possibility that the story critiques Wilson's domineering performances—or, as we shall see, the possibility that manhood is nothing more *than* its performances.

Most contemporary studies of Hemingway depict a much more complex attitude toward gender issues in his work; indeed, it might be said that the attempt to debunk what Nancy R. Comley and Robert Scholes call the myth of Hemingway's "monolithic masculinity" is *the* characteristic of contemporary Hemingway scholarship. Peter Messent, for instance, reads Hemingway's work with an eye to a "new fluidity as far as categories of masculinity and femininity go," and Comley and Scholes concur, tracing the complexity of Hemingway's attitudes toward such issues as fathering, homoeroticism, trans-vestism, impotence, and divorce. But affiliations with concepts of stable mas-culinity still exist in their work. Messent argues that Hemingway's persistent "cult of virility" prevents a truly explosive upsetting of gender roles because "any ambiguity of response is covered over in the containments that finally take place; in the reimpositions of new (though limited) forms of 'masculine' authority." And Comley and Scholes's provocative account of homoerotic de-sire in Hemingway's work focuses on covert implications that are nowhere directly expressed by Hemingway. They admit that the "usual view of Hem-ingway's interest in sexuality," which is the "locker-room sort, kidding-with-the-guys but fiercely heterosexual in its focus, treating homosexuality as either a joke or a horror," is "not . . . entirely wrong." The "locker-room joker,"

25. Ibid., xii.
26. Ibid., xiii.

however, sometimes makes way for "someone else, someone denied," who does not "speak of this pure vision of masculinity or in a single macho voice."[27]

Comley and Scholes thus accent a repressed ("someone denied") and dialogic (not "single") voice, which, in the case of a book like *Death in the Afternoon*, exists in opposition to, but is necessarily conjoined with, its "phallic (or, perhaps better, cojonic) text." The phallic/cojonic text of the virile Hemingway is thus not disavowed but placed out of bounds, partly because it is the "usual view," and hence seemingly something that can be assumed anyway, and partly because, as Peter Messent says, it is "difficult to provide a strong defence of Hemingway's sexual politics" when he enters the mode of the locker-room joker. Comley and Scholes thus appear to discover in Hemingway's narrative omissions the antidote to the popular view (and often the scholars' view) of an author who has "eaten too many criadillas [bull's testicles]." Yet a "pure vision of masculinity" is just as legible and undeniable in this cojonic text as it ever was. The only difference is that now that "pure vision," being but one among the range of Hemingway's voices, can be largely omitted from consideration on the grounds that it is too obvious or too unattractive. Despite the fact that in the case of Hemingway Comley and Scholes could hardly agree with Gilbert and Gubar's reductive reading of male modernist writers, it is telling that their brief comments about "The Short Happy Life" as a story about the "loss and recovery of honor" and about Margot as a "rich bitch" sound remarkably like the commonplace readings that emerge from *No Man's Land*.[28]

This reading of "The Short Happy Life" contends that a principle of stable masculinity has consistently appeared as the (sometimes displaced) center of appraisals of Hemingway's work, and that the frequency and congruity of these acts of evaluation have done much to convince readers that narrative gaps can be bridged, significations restored, and cogent principles of masculinity adduced. I have argued, furthermore, that "The Short Happy Life" unsettles the masculine ethos of autonomy and self-determination so assiduously maintained by generations of scholars on at least two counts: it confuses manhood-as-autonomy and manhood-as-authority; second, it puts

27. Comley and Scholes, ix; Peter Messent, *Modern Novelists: Ernest Hemingway* (New York: St. Martin's Press, 1992), 87, 98; Comley and Scholes, 110, 111.

28. Comley and Scholes, 111; Messent, 83; Comley and Scholes, 109, 8, 40.

in doubt paradigms of consistent, stable identity. But both interpretations—the one implying that masculinity is derived relationally and the other implying that it can never be whole, self-identical, and consistent—can be theorized differently within what I call a theatrical representation of manhood. Indeed, my account of "The Short Happy Life" has already begun to suggest that codes of tough, autonomous manhood are particularly fragile at the points where being in charge of oneself depends on the necessity for *being seen* to be in charge. Wilson and Macomber have to display their power over Margot; many watchers evaluate Macomber's early humiliation; Macomber comes to manhood under the eye of Wilson and Margot. Moreover, the omissions of the story's concluding scenes exert a pressure on readers to play an active role in evaluating the actions of Hemingway's male characters; to a remarkable extent, as we have seen throughout this chapter, scholars have felt called upon to reenact Wilson's appraising glances in their work. In "The Short Happy Life," audiences of all kinds demand attention. It is to the theatricalization of masculinity we must now turn in order to extend and sharpen this new sense of the richly contradictory representation of manhood in Hemingway's work.

In the midst of Macomber's stumbling excuses for not going into the tall grass after the wounded lion, a telling action occurs. Offended by Macomber's vaguely murderous suggestion that they send in beaters before the hunters themselves, Robert Wilson "looked at him [Macomber] appraisingly" (134). Without quite realizing the extent of Macomber's terror, Wilson nevertheless performs the role we would expect of the tutor, appraising the nature of Macomber's problem and clarifying the conduct expected of him. That Wilson completely mistakes the extent of Macomber's cowardice and only later "felt as though he had opened the wrong door in a hotel and seen something shameful" (135) is interesting but less important than the fact of his appraising gaze. His glance marks him out as the authority figure (even if he initially observes wrongly) and, not incidentally, reminds us that from the beginning of the story Macomber's humiliation has been witnessed by a series of audiences. As the story begins, Macomber's return from lion hunting has just been celebrated—a "demonstration" (121) from which the gunbearers who were on the scene refrain, for Macomber has "just shown himself, very publicly, to be a coward" (122). That scene specifically recalls a staged drama, for Macomber becomes conscious of his behavior when "standing by himself in the clearing where he had run, holding a loaded rifle, while two black men and a white man looked back at him in contempt" (137–38). On returning to the car Macomber finds his wife unable to look at him, precisely because, he realizes, she has witnessed the whole performance: "Looking across the stream to where the gunbearers were skinning out the lion he could see that she had been able to see the whole thing." Triangulated by contemptuous gazes, Macomber must later suffer his "personal boy" (124), newly apprised of the actual circumstances of the hunt, "looking curiously at his master" at dinner.

The importance of these appraising glances becomes clearer when we recognize the extent to which they actually create the meaning of Macomber's actions. Macomber's flight from the lion, which concludes with knowledge of his cowardice derived from those gazes, begins with an unsettling response to the lion's "swishing rush in the grass." The "next thing he knew," the narrative tells us, "he was running." It is as if *Macomber* does not run but is merely there to register his running as an involuntary action separate from himself. That peculiar sense of disconnection continues in the swirl of the long, brilliantly conceived sentence that follows:

> He heard the *ca-ra-wong!* of Wilson's big rifle, and again in a second crashing *carawong!* and turning saw the lion, horrible-looking now, with half his head seeming to be gone, crawling toward Wilson in the edge of the tall grass while the red-faced man worked the bolt on the short ugly rifle and aimed carefully as another blasting *carawong!* came from the muzzle, and the crawling, heavy, yellow bulk of the lion stiffened and the huge, mutilated head slid forward and Macomber, standing by himself in the clearing where he had run, holding a loaded rifle, while two black men and a white man looked back at him in contempt, knew the lion was dead. (137–38)

Intense and impressionistic flashes of observation (the "horrible-looking" lion, the "red-faced" Wilson, the "short ugly rifle") appear out of the syntactic swerves of a sentence that seems to have no obvious coherence. "He heard the *ca-ra-wong!* of Wilson's big rifle, and again in a second crashing *carawong!* and turning saw the lion," the sentence begins. "[A]nd again in a second crashing *carawong!*" is mystifying until we realize that it does not begin a new clause but requires us to reinsert the first: "and again [he heard Wilson's big rifle] in a second crashing *carawong!*" "[I]n a second," moreover, sounds momentarily like a reference to duration rather than frequency, so that again we struggle to locate our syntactic place in Macomber's panicked flight.

Thereafter, perspective in the sentence lunges from the lion to Wilson to the lion and then, in an odd finale, back to Macomber: "the huge, mutilated head slid forward and Macomber, standing by himself in the clearing where he had run, holding a loaded rifle, while two black men and a white man looked back at him in contempt, knew the lion was dead." The end of the sentence returns Macomber to reflective rather than impressionistic consciousness of external things (he "knew the lion was dead"). That knowing is syntactically deferred, however, until we recognize that, before the eyes of Wilson and the gunbearers, Macomber's experience of disconnected, chaotic actions has taken on the pattern and meaning we associate with drama. They read his involuntary actions as though they constitute a script. On Macomber's part, his realization that his panicked actions have been read as a performance precedes and governs his return to reflective consciousness and self-awareness of his humiliation. Out of his loss of self-control emerges a "self" (i.e., that of a coward) configured primarily around the surprisingly powerful act of being watched.

Though Macomber promises Margot that "We'll put on another show for you tomorrow" (127) shooting buffalo, his statement only partially clarifies the significance of the lion-show. In fact, Macomber does not perform in any sense of the word. He does not perform (carry out) his duty as a man or as a white man (according to Wilson, at least, "no white man ever bolts" [125]). Nor does he perform in the sense of acting out an appropriate role before an audience; he has not even been aware of the presence of an audience. But Macomber correctly interprets the lion hunt as a "show" insofar as his relationship with everyone on the safari and his very consciousness of himself emerges out of his non-performance (not-doing) being witnessed as a performance (a poor show). Not surprisingly, Macomber's coming of age during the buffalo hunt hinges on his sudden command over his stage-presence. "Look at the beggar now" (150), thinks Wilson of the transformed Macomber. Instead of the appraising, contemptuous, or evasive glances that characterized Wilson earlier in the story, the two men now look at each other on an equal footing. Wilson advises Macomber not to talk about his newfound heroism, for instance, while "looking in the other's face" (151). As he moves toward the wounded buffalo in the brush, Macomber this time invites Margot's attention to his new confidence: "Macomber, looking back, saw his wife, with the rifle by her side, looking at him. He waved to her" (152).

We have seen that many critics at this point attribute to Macomber a wholesale personality change that governs his newly minted independence from Margot, from Wilson's aid, and from the humiliating self-display during the scene with the lion. But the narrative obtrudes the issue of self-display, inviting us to read Macomber's transformation in terms of the kinds of performances he manages. His early lack of self-control turning into a later desire to act courageously and not "mouth it up too much," Macomber more than adequately demonstrates his mastery of the code by way of a drama of legitimating glances he now seems to control. Yet mastery of self-staging cannot be conflated with self-mastery. The emphasis on masculinity as performance in both the lion and buffalo scenes—Macomber as coward and Macomber as hero—radically challenges the conventional sense that males acquire manhood in Hemingway's work by themselves, for themselves, and off by themselves. The problem in "The Short Happy Life" is not that Macomber fails Wilson's early appraisal of him (that is, Macomber fails to be a man) but that throughout the story Macomber's lack of or coming to manhood must be appraised (that is, social codes fashion the possibilities of manhood). Subject to and therefore contingent upon the scrutiny of an audience, Macomber in his thoroughly staged final moments (waving at Margot, for instance, to attract her attention) demands a radical rethinking of his "independence," which must at the very least be considered along with his audience's decision to validate or reject his gestures toward manhood.

We can begin to move toward a more firmly theorized sense of this theatrical representation of manhood in Hemingway's work by considering the odd case of those few writers who have dealt at length with the importance of audiences, performers, and arenas in Hemingway's fiction, who argue for a special intensity or insistence about the way he stage-manages scene and character and turns his narrators into spectators or spectator-participants—yet who nonetheless manage by an interpretive sleight of hand to circumvent the implications of their insights. Jackson J. Benson's analysis of Hemingway's game metaphors, for instance, leads him to a very perceptive account of typical structures in Hemingway's work, where a "whole scheme of self-dramatization" arises from the game player taking a "role in front of spectators, often with accompanying costume, prescribed actions and lines, and characteristic apparatus and setting." The bullfight is a prime example: "Of tremendous importance to Hemingway is the presence of an audience . . . which observes and judges the behavior of the bullfighter in relation to the game context. As a metaphor, this actor-audience relationship is rather strange in its application to the fictionalization of aspects of life other than the bullfight, for the protagonist of courage becomes tied to the existence of an observer."[29] It is in fact "necessary in Hemingway's fiction that [the central character] be observed, that his condition and achievement be witnessed and recognized." That function is carried out by "another 'self,' standing between the audience and the footlights" and by the reader, who is "usually offered the opportunity to be observant and appreciative."[30] But Benson makes this "strange" actor-audience relationship even stranger by denying the more unsettling aspects of his account of masculine self-dramatization. Despite Benson's remark about Hemingway's protagonists being "tied to the existence of an observer," for instance, he theorizes their role in terms like the "self-reliant hero," a "continuing struggle to achieve a masculine independence," and a situation in which the "unit of ultimate moral responsibility is the individual." The possibility of a synergistic relationship between protagonist and audience, which Benson often entertains, fades into a conventional treatment of characters striving for independence in scenes where self-dramatization yields to "self-imposed integrity."[31]

Christian Messenger reaches the same point by way of a wholly different approach. His analysis of the bullfight works by distinguishing the "popular sports spectacle," which is commercial and secular, from ritual drama, in which the audience participates with the matador in seeking a transcendent and religious experience of their "primitive cultural roots." Hemingway must "frame the spectacle in ritual meaning." The act of "heroic witnessing" is valuable not in itself but as an "extension of the ritual moment."[32] In an important sense the spectacle is not to be considered as spectacle at all. It signifies only as a conduit to the ritual moment that transcends both time and space—at which point, as in Benson's reading, the enabling roles of hero/matador and audience become unimportant and the dangerously commercial elements of the spectacle can be ignored. Benson and Messenger, in fact, both promote readings that bracket off self-dramatization as lacking in substance: it is what certain men display en route to their self-sufficient masculine selves but what

29. Jackson J. Benson, *Hemingway: The Writer's Art of Self-Defense* (Minneapolis: University of Minnesota Press, 1969), 73, 140–41.

30. Ibid., 71, 141.

31. Ibid., 30, 6, 43, 76.

32. Christian Messenger, *Sport and the Spirit of Play in American Fiction: Hawthorne to Faulkner* (New York: Columbia University Press, 1981), 241–43, 253.

hardly counts toward a definition of masculinity itself. The effect is to place beyond the reach of criticism—because it is held to be a given, a working vision of experience that constitutes what readers are able to say about Hemingway—a concept of self-sufficient masculinity, even as performance obtrudes with an almost puzzling insistence as *the* principle that must be repeatedly restrained, structured, and "frame[d] . . . in ritual meaning" in order to bring about the transcendent purity of the ultimate masculine state.

Why then should men performing under conditions of theatricality prove so threatening in accounts of Hemingway's work? We can begin to move toward an answer by considering the nature of the theatrical medium itself, and then more particularly by engaging the theories of Bertolt Brecht. The "only thing that all forms of theatre have in common," Peter Brook argues, is the "need for an audience." Alan Read agrees, though with a slightly different emphasis: "theatre is a public act" and as such is a "process of building between performers and their constituencies." The presence of an audience shapes human beings into actors and builds space into a theater where dramatic acts are publicly consummated. "I can take any empty space and call it a bare stage," states Brook, and continues: a "man walks across this empty space whilst someone else is watching him, and this is all that is needed for an act of theatre to be engaged."[33] Acts of theater must therefore be invoked (one calls a space a stage), and they demand a certain kind of attention (an action becomes *acting* while someone is watching). The stage thus appears to be a peculiarly uncertain and transient terrain. It exists, according to Brook and to Read, at the moment when a willed act of calling-to-attention temporarily engages actor and audience in the transformation of space. A theatrical plenitude depends, oddly, on acts of emptying-out. It is that which, by definition, cannot be sustained.

Stagecraft also insists on the presence of the body on stage and in the audience: theater is an "expressive practice that involves an audience through the medium of images at the centre of which is the human body."[34] Yet though bodies are actually present, actors participate in a complex transformation of their everyday selves wherein their bodily presence becomes the medium for

33. Peter Brook, *The Empty Space* (New York: Atheneum, 1980), 127; Alan Read, *Theatre and Everyday Life: An Ethics of Performance* (London and New York: Routledge, 1993), 5; Brook, 9.

34. Read, 10.

acts of representation. Actors both present and represent; they are, as human individuals, both present and absent. The actor is the "paradigm of one who stands in for another," a statement that nicely captures the ambiguity of an act that can be imagined as an alienation, hollowing out, or loss of the "one" who represents, or even as an augmenting or doubling of identity, so that the one becomes one and another.[35] Drama entertains the possibility that both space and identity must be emptied for them to become dramatically full. That augmented (or alienated) identity cannot be sustained, for it is subject to the duration of the performance, though it may be repeated as subsequent performances take place. By the same token, that act of transformation whereby a human individual becomes a stage character is not wholly within the control of the actor. It cannot merely be willed into existence, for it depends on the structure of the drama (typically a script) and on a productive engagement between actor and audience. Actors rehearsing their lines in private may carry out the very same verbal and bodily gestures as on stage without bringing a theatrical experience into being, for inherent in the concept of dramatic acting is the sense of acting for another and before the gaze of another.

Yet theater is not only a public but a social act, and in that sense we cannot afford an abrupt distinction between theater and everyday social life. The public does not merely gaze in a neutral, anonymous, and universal recognition of the actor's role but is itself constituted within a matrix of historical and cultural variables, which can be spoken of in terms of a sociology of theater (how, for instance, different stage technologies affect the possibilities of drama) or in terms of the broader concerns of cultural studies (how questions of gender, class, race, or economic structure shape the very notion of what an audience is and does). Constructions of stage and character reveal social structures. Moreover, they reveal the very constructedness of social life. These ideas can be elaborated by introducing a concept drawn from Bertolt Brecht's repertoire of dramatic innovations: the social *gest*. Brecht's neologism suggests both *gesture* and *gist*. Gestic theater is the dramatic moment that captures the gist of patterns of social behavior: to "view things gestically," as Terry Eagleton states in his gloss on Brecht's theory, is to "catch the gist in terms of the gesture." However, Brecht argued, "Not all gests are social gests": "The attitude

---

35. Bruce Wilshire, *Role Playing and Identity: The Limits of Theatre as Metaphor* (Bloomington: Indiana University Press, 1982), xiii.

of chasing away a fly is not yet a social gest, though the attitude of chasing away a dog may be one, for instance if it comes to represent a badly dressed man's continual battle against watchdogs. One's efforts to keep one's balance on a slippery surface result in a social gest as soon as falling down would mean 'losing face'; in other words, losing one's market value." At the same time, Brecht inveighs against the tendency in drama to abstract human character from its social context: the "artist is not happy," Brecht claims sarcastically, until the "man becomes just Man; his gest is stripped of any social individuality; it is an empty one, not representing any undertaking or operation among men by this particular man." If human beings are constructed within particular social realities, the tendency to universalize empties human life of the richness and plenitude of its social being. We must not misread the attempt to keep one's balance on a slippery slope as a metaphor for the human condition, but grasp it as an act shaped by and betokening particular market forces that in turn constrain a host of other human attributes: body and facial gestures; the experience of gazing at someone falling; being gazed at. Yet, it must be said, the social gest captures the gist of human behavior within an ensemble of social relations by refusing to claim anything more than a temporary and provisional representativeness. The social gest truly accounts for patterns of social behavior while recognizing the materiality of human life as nothing other than constructed; it hollows out, as Eagleton puts it, the "imaginary plenitude of everyday actions."[36] It represents a space of negotiation—a moment when truth-claims are revealed as rhetorical performances and performances as the only (social) truth. The crucial strategy of gestic theater, famously, is the *Verfremdungseffekt:* the act of staging the routine and natural-seeming and ostensibly universal practices of everyday life in such a way as to alienate them from the conditions of their making and, by making them strange, to admit new (and revolutionary) perspectives.

It is because of this productive engagement between the ambiguous presence of the human/actor on stage and the social construction of identity that the metaphor of performance has recently become so important to emerging discussions about the concept of gender. Gender studies, which explore the relationship of gender to formations of power, have long emphasized the con-

36. Terry Eagleton, *Against the Grain* (London: Verso, 1986), 168; Bertolt Brecht, *Brecht on Theatre: The Development of an Aesthetic,* ed. John Willett (New York: Hill and Wang, 1964), 104; Eagleton, 167.

struction of gendered identities within a sociohistorical matrix. Indeed, it is the constructedness of gender that is usually held to define its difference from the category of sex, which marks natural and permanent divisions between male and female. More recently, theorists have begun to question even the naturalness of sexual difference, arguing that we cannot know even sexual identity in any ontologically pure sense. Categories of sex are themselves the product of discursive systems and formations of power. Discussions of sexual differentiation, in fact, are always already embraced by the rubric of gender— though, to be sure, as Judith Butler argues, the assumption that sexual differentiation into male and female is natural and absolute can be held responsible for the binary oppositions that mark cultural constructions of gender. What constrains the formation of gendered identities is not permanent biological or psychological characteristics but the effect of repeated discursive acts and practices in the cultural field, and it is this reflection that has led scholars to begin to formulate theories of gender as performance. Butler asks: "In what senses, then, is gender an act? As in other ritual social dramas, the action of gender requires a performance that is *repeated*. This repetition is at once a reenactment and reexperiencing of a set of meanings already socially established; and it is the mundane and ritualized form of their legitimation."[37] Gender, in short, must be theorized in terms of performance, though it is important to recognize that the consequences of such performances often concern what seems interior and private and that Butler does not construe gender identities solely in terms of being enacted before a legitimating audience. Gender is a performance that does not depend on the moment of theater, as I have begun to argue is the case in "The Short Happy Life." Theatricalizations of gender (such as drag) nonetheless render visible the constructedness of gender in powerful ways, and there is a more general sense in which gender relationships are the function of iterations in the social field that must at some point be displayed, watched, imitated, and re-performed.

The gendered subject, for Butler, might be said in Brechtian terms to be gestic; a man can never be just Man. Repetitive legitimating acts of gender script the acts of individual humans, creating roles as part of a "public action" whose aim "cannot be attributed to a subject, but, rather, must be understood to found and consolidate the subject."[38] To "be" a man or woman is thus to

37. Judith Butler, *Gender Trouble: Feminism and the Subversion of Identity* (New York: Routledge, 1990), 140.

38. Ibid., 140.

act out socially sanctioned roles, and indeed to iterate them endlessly in social gests of all descriptions, even though in the process those roles may well come to seem self-evident and permanent. Like Brecht, then, Butler refutes the "imaginary plenitude of everyday actions," particularly insofar as they undergird feminist interpretations of gender; her "genealogical critique," unlike many other feminist paradigms analyzed in *Gender Trouble* (1990), "refuses to search for the origins of gender, the inner truth of female desire, a genuine or authentic sexual identity."[39] Building on this gestic foundation, Butler's understanding of the possibilities for changing gendered relationships of power is also strikingly similar to Brecht's. Because gender is gestic and thus emphatically not self-identical, the social production of gendered modes of behavior cannot articulate perfect iterations or construct a seamless whole. Far from being monologic, power is complex and unable wholly to constrain or compel the gendered subject. Subjects, locked into formations of power working through the discursive realms that constitute them, experience multiple and contradictory processes of gender-fashioning. A *Verfremdungseffekt*—the alienating or making strange of what has hitherto appeared timeless and natural—must be possible at seams where the constructedness of the often shaky edifice of gender-fashioning becomes apparent. At such points the "abiding gendered self will then be shown to be structured by repeated acts that seek to approximate the ideal of a substantial ground of identity, but which, in their occasional discontinuity, reveal the temporal and contingent groundlessness of this 'ground.' The possibilities of gender transformation are to be found precisely in the arbitrary relation between such acts, in the possibility of a failure to repeat, a de-formity, or a parodic repetition that exposes the phantasmatic effect of abiding identity as a politically tenuous construction." Gender, as Butler states lucidly, can be "rendered thoroughly and radically *incredible*."[40] It is worth emphasizing the fact that this process of rendering something incredible is created, like Brecht's gestic theater, by way of a reciprocal relationship between socially contingent and thus mutable acts on the one hand and the alienating efforts of the analyst on the other. Discontinuities in the cultural field allow and perhaps invite a de-forming analysis; but the analyst must bring to the cultural field an ability to look beyond essentialist explanations of human phenomena. Like Brecht's man on the slippery slope,

39. Ibid., viii.
40. Ibid., 141.

the gendered subject requires the scrutiny of observers attuned to the thoroughly performed and processual nature of social life.

It is important to note that Brecht's and Butler's concepts of identities caught within relationships of performance do not suggest the enactment of hollow, fake versions of real human beings, as though the gest were little more than a trivial jest. Far from it. The strategies with which Brechtian drama draws attention to its constructedness indicate the brute materiality of strategies of representation rather than the fragility of dramatic representation. As Butler argues, moreover, reading gender as performative does not mean that gender roles are thereby empty or less distressing to real people constructed by and through them. A hermeneutic of performance implies that one cannot read cultural phenomena as if there were some solid and unchanging ground, embodying eternal meanings, against which the transience of theatrical representation could be identified. That being the case, the quest for essence is futile or deeply nostalgic. By the same token a hermeneutic of performance undertakes to enter the sliding ground of signification, which renders meaning contextual and constative utterances rhetorical, by way of an interpretive mode that is itself temporary and aware of its own staging but is for all that no less "real."

These characteristics of drama begin to explain why elements of theatricality in Hemingway's work—modes of self-dramatization, role-playing, the way in which space transforms into theater-space, the activities of various audiences—have always proved so problematic to scholars attentive to their presence. His fiction creates a gestic theater of masculine representation. And the implications of that theatrical mode are immense. As Brecht and Butler recognize in various ways, the staging of mundane obvious- and natural-seeming social practices within a defamiliarizing context has the effect of unraveling them, showing that their obviousness is a result of repetitive performances rather than of some universal essence. Hemingway's staging calls a masculine self into being and calls it into question with the same gesture. Macomber and Wilson (and many more of Hemingway's male characters) do indeed act out and speak for masculine codes of conduct, and in this sense their actions conform to and represent a cultural faith in an absolute and universal masculinity. Macomber's final wave to Margot, for instance, demonstrates the kind of confidence that grounds typical readings of him becoming a man, and counterbalances the scene of the lion charge in which watchers defined his character. In certain senses, we would indeed be justified in calling him a "man." The concluding scenes show Wilson believing that Macomber has become a

man; they imply that Macomber feels the same; they hint, more circum-
spectly, that Margot recognizes the fact; readers, too, have always felt the pressure to make (or question) that determination. But Hemingway's insistently
theatrical strategies of stage-managing displace and hollow out the naturalness
of those moments. They invite us to ask: Why does what Macomber is about
to perform (do) as a "man" depend on performing (dramatizing himself) for
Margot? Why would a visible sign of an internal transfiguration even be necessary? Why Margot? How does Margot's watching reconfigure Macomber's
relationship to Wilson and the gunbearers? How does being watched suddenly
become authoritative, when during the lion charge it signified humiliation?
What are the other implications of class and race that structure the possibilities of who waves and who gets to watch? Questions like these call attention
to the provisional contexts within which Man becomes "man."

Macomber's wave creates a form of *Verfremdungseffekt*. It shows the distance he has traveled from his earlier humiliation while refusing to guarantee
that he is established on an independent footing; it shows him acquiring typical gestures of masculinity while simultaneously revealing those gestures as
posed. Macomber is the quintessential actor who "stands in for another," representing a "man" by displaying the signs that carry cultural connotations of
manhood. Crucially, that pose is not hollow. As Brecht and Butler make clear,
drawing attention to the constructedness of social roles does not empty
human life of meaning; it simply re-locates the meaning of human life within
the rich, but provisional, plenitude of social codes. To argue that Macomber
poses as a man does not necessarily diminish him—as soon as we accept that
Hemingway's male characters pose their way into manhood by enacting appropriate gests. If one becomes a "man" theatrically, and cannot become a
man any other way, the theatrical pose ceases to carry the imputation of failure, as it must to those who see Macomber (and other Hemingway characters)
aspiring toward an ideal of "full," self-identical manhood. Indeed, one could
conceivably re-cast masculine authority in terms of mastery of the stage and
thus preserve the essential outlines of Hemingway scholarship: his code heroes
would still be code heroes, his misogyny still misogyny. As many feminists
have noted, showing the constructedness of gender is not the same as disman-
tling the relationships of power the system allows.

But Hemingway's theatrical representation of manhood preserves a more
critical edge than that, and one sign is precisely the intensity and ingenuity
with which scholars have tried to avoid its presence. Like Benson and Messen-

ger, who substitute formalized, controlled gestures for provisional acts of theater, timeless ritual for the constructedness of social reality, and "celebrants"
for an audience, scholars have tried to defuse the moment of masculine display (whenever acknowledged) and its implications of provisionality and constructedness. In part this is because the gest of masculinity assumes a
correlation with social relationships of power, masked though they be. Brecht
asks in his drama: who gains power, over whom, by what means, and in which
historical circumstances? To read gestically is thus to represent an "undertaking or operation among men by [a] particular man" within a specific social
setting and to reveal manhood within the conditions of its making. It is not
simply *that* the theatrical maneuvers and rhetorical poses through which
Hemingway's male characters come (or fail to come) to manhood question
essentialist, transhistorical concepts of manhood. It is *the way* that the maneuver, the pose, the rhetoric obtrude, so that one cannot simply accept mastery
of the theatrical moment as an unquestionable, logical, and worthy prerogative of men.

The presence of audiences plays a crucial role in constructing the nature
of this theatrical mode in Hemingway's fiction. As we have seen, audiences
call acts of theater into being; the need for an audience prevents an individual
from willing theater into being; and audiences are what mark theater as an
irrevocably communal form of artistic expression. For Brecht, the engagement
between actor and audience metaphorizes the social ground of art and puts
into effect the disturbing possibilities of the *Verfremdungseffekt*. Watching un-
covers the mode of doing something, demonstrating that the meaning of actions is derived from socially constructed and agreed-upon codes. In "The
Short Happy Life," Macomber's wave to Margot before he goes into action
against the buffalo is again instructive. It invokes an audience and stage, and
sets up an expectation that subsequent actions carried out will create, and be
meaningful within, a shared context: they will signify *to Margot* (and perhaps
to Wilson and the gunbearers) something about Macomber's newfound courage. Once the buffalo charges, it is certainly true that Macomber seems un-
aware of Margot watching; he sees Wilson briefly and then, as the buffalo
looms and his attention narrows, "he did not see Wilson now" (153). But Margot has been watching. One aspect of the final scenes that no one has thought
to remark in the desire to figure out whether Margot means to kill Macomber
is that in order to make the shot she must have been enacting the role he
intends her to play as he walks away. Margot's shot restores as a quiet but

insistent element the theatrical impulse that initiates the scene—and must motivate Macomber's sudden desire to stand solid—but which Macomber and most readers appear to have forgotten.

As the fact that no one has really noted Margot's role implies, the dramatic context of the final scenes is compelling but by no means self-evident. It too must be adduced from what has been omitted. But the significance of the dramatic context is not thereby limited to the readers who wish to, or happen to, see its presence. Its presence instead underscores the fact that the final scenes co-opt readers into watching and evaluating Macomber's actions and thus repeating willy-nilly the mini-dramas already staged within the text. Dozens of accounts of the buffalo charge suggest that readers have indeed taken to heart that profound narrative pressure to evaluate a sequence of actions, which in themselves possess no inevitable meaning, and make them signify (or question) manhood. One can opt out of this responsibility only in the limited sense that one can deny its existence, for the point is that the narrative omissions of the concluding scenes mean that one must construe the meaning of actions (they are not self-evident) and that as soon as one construes meaning one is acting like Margot or Wilson or the gunbearers, to whom actions are performances. Whatever we decide—Macomber as self-sufficient hero or posturing actor—Hemingway's gests unmask the relationships of power that allow practices of reading to construe the meaning of narratives, calling attention even to the acts of interpretation that try to deny the contextual and theatrical production of meaning. Thinking through and "feeling through" the significance of narrative gaps, readers must perform like Brechtian audiences who negotiate the communal value and meaning of social practices. Therefore, though we may not know it, decisions about codes of masculinity can only be temporarily resolved and comprehended through the act of critical performance. Their value is inherently rhetorical, the product of a particular argumentative strategy developed for a particular kind of audience.

This is not to say that readers have completely free rein. Indeed, the most subtle aspect of the story is that theaters of manhood seem so commonplace as to incite little or no attention. Macomber understands intuitively the humiliating stage on which he first appears—he recognizes instantly what meaning Wilson and the gunbearers will bestow on his flight—and at the end plays to the crowd (inviting Wilson's and his wife's gaze) without forethought or comment. Generations of scholars have negotiated the ending of the story similarly without forethought or comment, disagreeing indeed over whether

Macomber really becomes a man, but agreeing to overlook the much more obvious fact that the ending, evincing that "process of building between performers and their constituencies" Read sees as fundamental to theatrical experience, demands our participation and evaluation. An admission like that would certainly be fatal to any interpretation of uncompromised, autonomous manhood, and perhaps for that reason the process has been obliterated. But this is not at all the same as saying that the process is invisible. I began this chapter by arguing that readers were too familiar with Hemingway's strategies of narrative omission and too ready to impute to them the significance of masculine restraint. It now appears that this familiarity derives from a deep-seated knowledge about the invisible but integral role observers play in theaters of manhood and that the codes of manhood Hemingway articulates in "The Short Happy Life" are defined not by taciturn heroes but by *taciturn watchers* who stand quietly, invisibly off-stage, unconcerned with their participatory and evaluatory role precisely because that role is so fundamentally constitutive of the process of manhood-fashioning.

"The Short Happy Life of Francis Macomber" can indeed be seen as representative of Hemingway's fiction. But its depictions of manhood as a performance within the purview of an audience's empowering acts of watching suggest that the story will never articulate an ideal of full manhood. Staging alienates the story's ostensibly confident assertions about the inalienable duties and prerogatives of men. Masculine display implies a loss of autonomy and authority to the audience and challenges customary formulations about the myth of the autonomous, virile male, associated with the emergence of a whole, coherent, hypostasized masculine self, which persist even in the revisionary works of the last fifteen years. And interpretations of the story demonstrate the importance of readers, interpreters, and audiences who have over the decades through repeated acts of inquiry disseminated concepts that seem to possess the weightiness of everyday fact and created that which seems unexceptionable, natural, and "understood." In contrast, a thematics of performance opens the way for interpreting Hemingway's characters in terms of role playing within a theatrical construction of narrative. It allows the possibility of theorizing his sense of masculinity in terms of performance, self-dramatization, and rhetoricity. It resurrects the possibility of creative freeplay in the construction of masculine roles. And it argues for a quite different set of reading strategies than the ones that have typically governed the interpretation of Hemingway's work. That these ideas can be extended to Hemingway's other works in still more complex ways, ensuing chapters attest.

CHAPTER 2

Dramatizations of Manhood in *In Our Time* and *The Sun Also Rises*

IN THE BULLRING, men are made or unmanned. The "kid" in the first bull-fight vignette of *In Our Time* submits to the code of the ring and, by killing five times, reaches his majority. Then, remarks the narrator, he "sat down in the sand and puked and they held a cape over him."[1] Such modest conceal-ment does not satisfy the delighted crowd, which "hollered and threw things down into the bullring," recognizing that this kid has "finally made it" to manhood. Villalta, the matador at the height of his powers, plays to the crowd more deliberately. His killing becomes a test of intense watching as he "sighted" the bull along the sword blade with the bull "looking at him straight in front, hating." With Villalta's life and manhood on the line, the crowd watches and roars with every pass of the muleta. The vignette refers repeatedly to the spectacle of the bullfight. "If it happened right down close in front of you, you could see Villalta snarl at the bull and curse him," begins the narra-tor: the observer becomes "you" the reader, and Villalta the cynosure of all eyes. At the end, Villalta's "hand up at the crowd" announces the successful completion of this ritual of manhood—and acknowledges its essentially theat-rical nature.

Hemingway, as Leo Gurko neatly puts it, "made himself master of the small arena," an observation that applies not only to the bullring but to many other symbolic spaces—houses and hotels, bedrooms, camps and clearings—

1. Ernest Hemingway, *In Our Time* (New York: Scribner's, 1925), 83. This work will here-inafter be cited parenthetically by page number in the text. Parts of this chapter were first published in "Dramatizations of Manhood in Hemingway's *In Our Time* and *The Sun Also Rises*," *American Literature* 61, no. 2 (1989). 245–60, and in *"In Our Time*, Out of Season," in *Companion to Hemingway*, ed. Scott Donaldson (Cambridge: Cambridge University Press, 1996), 55–86.

that take on the characteristics of a ceremonial arena.[2] These arenas are rich in significance. The bullring's physical characteristics sanction—and configure—the rituals enacted there. Empty space becomes ordered space, providing necessary boundaries within which potentially chaotic action might reveal a comprehensible structure. In turn, as critics argue and Hemingway seems to suggest, the small arena permits men to display their mastery over other creatures and, perhaps more importantly, over themselves. Ritualized actions serve as index to the masculine codes practiced by the bullfighter. Villalta's "hand up at the crowd"—like Macomber's wave to Margot—is a vitally gestic part of that ritual. The gesture demands the crowd's attention and respect while reminding it of the stylized (phallic) thrust that dispatched the bull. Conversely, breaking those masculine codes disrupts the space of the ring. The bad bullfighter of Chapter XI, for instance, suffers the humiliation not only of symbolic castration ("some one cut off his pigtail") but of the crowd invading his territory as it "came over the barrera and around the torero."

Yet by themselves a bullfighter's actions are insufficient to affirm (or to make a travesty of) the ritual act. Space becomes arena only within the presence of an audience, which, acting as an agent of legitimation for ritual gestures made in the ring, assimilates all action to performance and invests performance with value. Part of the audience's function is to appraise rituals of manhood and bestow praise or condemnation on the protagonist—a particularly important role if we take the matador's actions as somehow representative of masculine codes of behavior. And such moments of evaluatory watching are not confined to bullrings: many different individuals or groups of characters function as audience in Hemingway's work. By the same token, the kid and Villalta are just two of many characters whose potency as men depends on their ability to transform space into spectacle; and the bad bullfighter of Chapter XI is one of many who fail to master an audience. In a paradox whose resolution is crucial to my argument, the characters who succeed and those who fail to master the arena are often one and the same, though caught in different circumstances. Continuing to elaborate my argument about "The Short Happy Life," this chapter contends that Hemingway's logic of performance precludes consistency and stability of character in these works and that manhood-fashioning must be analyzed in terms of theatrical-

2. Leo Gurko, *Ernest Hemingway and the Pursuit of Heroism* (New York: Thomas Crowell, 1968), 230.

ized arenas, audiences, shared social codes of watching and evaluation, and role-playing. Manhood for Hemingway, in short, is thoroughly gestic.

Of the five Nick Adams stories that begin *In Our Time*, "Indian Camp" is the most remarkable, treating with extraordinary delicacy the cultural, familial, and gender conflicts so central to the collection. Appropriately, the story concerns origins: not only birth, and not only Nick's untimely initiation into an adult world of blood and death, but the origins of a bitter racial conflict between Native and white American. The first scene of the story opens on what we soon know to be a doctor's humanitarian mission: "At the lake shore there was another rowboat drawn up. The two Indians stood waiting" (16). Yet immediately it presents an archetypal moment of a different sort. Boats beached, Indians waiting, whites debarking: the scene of whites arriving in the New World or encountering tribes within the New World is strong in cultural memories, pictured over the centuries in scores of illustrations and books. The similarities continue, for the narrative reenacts a subsequent history of dispossession, annexation, betrayal, and death. To the doctor and Uncle George, the mercy mission affords the opportunity for revisiting a form of Manifest Destiny upon the Indian camp. They play the role of the Great White Father, bringing to birth a child/nation supposedly deficient in civilized attributes. Uncle George even "gave both the Indians cigars," thus usurping the role traditionally accorded the father in Anglo-American culture as well as iterating a long history of territories purchased by means of trinkets and other cheap gifts. Still more effectively, as the doctor deploys his medical expertise in the cabin he implies by contrast the Native Americans' ignorance of hygiene and medical procedure. His actions and words suggest their general cultural incompetence—a reading supported by the feeling of distanced superiority he shows (or at least affects) when the woman screams: "her screams are not important. I don't hear them because they are not important." What is important, apparently, is to preserve the history of this cultural and racial domination, for the doctor proceeds to sketch out the narrative he wishes to write: "That's one for the medical journal, George. . . . Doing a Caesarian with a jack-knife and sewing it up with nine-foot, tapered gut leaders."

Though recurring images of doorways link the cabin metaphorically to the womb, the entrance of Nick's father quickly transforms womb-space into a masculine arena and associates the baby's struggles to be born with other barely repressed racial and social conflicts. In particular, "Indian Camp" concerns a struggle for masculine authority, which Nick's father tries to master by directing the visual dynamics of a space transformed from shanty/womb to operating theater. That shift in the metaphoric meaning of the cabin-space keys a series of cultural and sexual overthrows in which male midwives (three whites and three Indians) supplant the traditional roles of the "old women" (16) of the camp and in which the white doctor supplants the cultural and parental authority of the Indian father. According to the narrative, the three white characters transgress what has traditionally been an intimate female space. The doctor has been called only after customary procedures of birth, which tacitly preclude the presence of men, fail: "She had been trying to have her baby for two days. All the old women in the camp had been helping her."

While this situation allows the doctor to demonstrate his skill, it seems to have degraded the Indian father, who has had to share his wife's experience of giving birth. After all, the "men" (not the "*other* men") of the camp have "moved off up the road to sit in the dark and smoke out of range of the noise she made." In a futile attempt to follow the appropriate masculine role, the Indian father is also smoking and will soon bury his head in blankets to summon his own darkness. Indeed, the Indian father's cultural role has been jeopardized in several ways. He cannot "father" the child in the sense of bringing it to life and consciousness, and he has lost control of his own space (the cabin). In each case, the white doctor—the "great man," as Uncle George somewhat sarcastically labels Nick's father—symbolically usurps the Indian father's role. Even the father's posture (he lies in the other bunk with a cut that prefigures his wife's) physically aligns him with his wife. The father's presence is thus doubly problematic: helpless to escape, he symbolically occupies a female role while prevented by his sex from trying to help. The doctor, on his part, not only transgresses an age-old custom (and possesses a knowledge of the woman's sexuality previously appropriate only to the husband and the "old women"), but gives rise to the suspicion that the old customs are no longer valid and powerful anyway.

Already displaced from the authority of the other men's positions "off up the road," the Indian father bears unwilling witness while the white doctor dramatizes his superior medical skills. Critics have defended Nick's father on the basis of his pragmatic handling of the operation, but the real point is that he constantly dramatizes his pragmatism, especially before the eyes of his son, whom he insistently invites to watch: "You see, Nick, babies are supposed to be born head first," "See, it's a boy," "You can watch this or not, Nick." The doctor plays out a fantasy of being both director and star actor in his own operating theater. His expert perception and appraisal of the medical situation calls for an audience to appraise him, and his several attempts to explain and show the mysteries of birth to his son suggest less a detached interest in Nick's education than a desire to educate Nick's perception of him. Indeed, as the operation progresses the doctor's sense of his potential audiences becomes more expansive, including not only George to whom he boasts about his accomplishments, and not only the Indian father whose attention he tries to attract, but an imagined audience of his peers in some future medical journal.

Attending to the complex play of gazes in the story tells us much about relationships of power. It reveals, for instance, interesting (but oddly skewed) analogies between the paired set of fathers and sons—for the newborn child is also a boy. The Indian father who, according to Nick's father, "couldn't stand things" (19), hides his face by rolling over against the wall. And it is Nick whose actions correspond: "He was looking away so as not to see what his father was doing"; "Nick did not watch" (17). Deprived of fatherhood and manhood, the Indian father plays the inappropriate role of son to the usurping white father. The relationship between Nick and his father thus represents and articulates the unvoiced relationship between the doctor and the Indian father. The doctor revels in emphasizing the inequality of that relationship by pressuring Nick to accept his authority. When Nick answers "I know" to the revelation that "This lady is going to have a baby, Nick," for instance, his father replies: "You don't know. . . . Listen to me." Later, the doctor refers to the details of the operation ("You can watch this or not, Nick, just as you like"; "There. That gets it") in direct proportion to Nick's unwillingness to watch. The doctor insists on his son's failure to watch rather than his putative freedom ("just as you like"). He is not inviting him to undergo a bloody initiation into a frightening adult world so much as reminding Nick (and, as a corollary, the Indian father) of the toughness and ability to "face" the adult world that the boy clearly lacks.

At other times, however, the doctor loses his grasp on the play of glances that hitherto he commanded with ease. Though the Indian father actively shuns the audience that could witness his degradation—his vision is blocked by the wall he rolls over against and the blanket that covers his head—his self-willed blindness has complex consequences. The refusal to be seen signifies his humiliation, but it also frees him from watching the doctor's performance. The doctor's subsequent move, as he "mounted on the edge of the lower bunk with the lamp in one hand and looked in" at the dead man, demonstrates the paradoxical efficacy of the suicide. The doctor's action, which suggests an attempt to force the "proud father" to acknowledge the doctor's pride in his own skill (and perhaps in the enlightened, civilizing influence he seems to feel he represents) suddenly forces him into the role of observer. Even more telling, his action switches Nick's attention from one proud father to the other: Nick "had a good view of the upper bunk when his father, the lamp in one hand, tipped the Indian's head back." From Nick's point of view, his father has become lamp-bearer to illuminate the Indian father's final self-dramatization. (We might note that on the doctor's arrival, the role of watcher and lamp-bearer was played by an "old woman"). Though the tableau is nothing more than a symbolic victory for the Indian father, the doctor does quickly lose his "post-operative exhilaration."

The characters in "Indian Camp," in other words, play several roles in succession or even simultaneously as the nature of their performance and the function of the audience changes. The rapid transformation of roles in the cabin (the doctor becoming the "great man" and surrogate father to the Indian child, the Indian father becoming, as it were, both son and wife) suggests the friable, temporary, and constructed nature of masculine (and feminine) roles. Doubled characters merely emphasize this malleability of role. Though the two fathers might suggest an identity of authority and role, the fact that they possess very different standings in the play of glances that construct meaning and authority in the cabin demonstrates that paternal authority, at least, is not contingent merely on being a father. Nor can we distinguish forms of paternal authority on the basis of racial difference, for even in "Indian Camp" the doctor's authority is not absolute. It grows—and diminishes—with his precarious ability to play to an audience. Authority, it seems, is not vested in the man but in the man's role; and the role depends on how easily external factors (such as race, culture, class, medical expertise, and so on) can be brought to bear on a particular situation.

The next story in *In Our Time*, "The Doctor and the Doctor's Wife," underscores this point by replaying the drama of power and humiliation contained in "Indian Camp" while reversing the earlier story's dramatic structure: three Native Americans are invited into the doctor's garden, and this time it is the doctor's authority that suffers. The doctor's garden, cleared from the surrounding forest and fenced in (as the presence of gates attests), becomes a highly charged symbolic space in which the doctor and the three Indians enact a drama of great significance for their authority as men. Like "Indian Camp," this story describes the wielding of personal power against a backdrop of cultural conflict. The quarrel over the stolen logs, to begin with, disguises the fact that the garden (like the logs) has been expropriated from the Native Americans in the first place. The mark of the scaler's hammer in the log shows that it belongs to "White" and McNally, which gives rise to a double irony: the mark exposes the historic truth of Boulton's remark that "You know they're stolen as well as I do," in the sense that White has stolen from the Indian, but the immorality of the act comes home to the doctor only in the idea of a white stealing from White. In "Indian Camp," the doctor relied on superior technology to support a symbolic appropriation of the cabin-space. In "Doctor's Wife," with the fact of appropriation suddenly evident, the moral superiority of white culture is shown to be a mere covering for an aggressive exploitation of natural resources. Tellingly, Boulton's first action with the log is to have the obscuring dirt cleaned off: "Wash it off. Clean off the sand. . . . I want to see who it belongs to" (24).

These moral conflicts key the cultural and racial power plays with which this story is concerned. Playing star surgeon in "Indian Camp," the doctor transformed the Indian's camp into a metaphoric arena; Boulton, conversely, threatens to turn the doctor's garden into a real arena (a boxing ring) that will display physical strength rather than scientific know-how. Appropriately, Hemingway emphasizes the play of glances between audience and the (potential) protagonists: "Dick Boulton looked at the doctor," Eddy and Billy Tabeshaw "looked at the doctor," they "could see from his back how angry he was," they "all watched him walk up the hill and go inside the cottage." Although the doctor tries to reciprocate in kind (he "looked at Dick Boulton"), he sees only Boulton's conviction of superiority: "He knew how big a man he was." The paradoxical nature of evaluatory watching is evident here, for whereas an audience empowered the doctor in the Indian's cabin, here it lays bare his inadequacy. Shamed by his ignominious retreat, the doctor withdraws (like the Indian father in "Indian Camp") from the gaze of spectators, leaving the garden/ring in their possession. Doubles once more abound, this time across the boundaries of individual stories. The doctor now reprises the role of the humiliated Indian father while Boulton, playing the doctor's part, appropriates the garden for a drama of his own devising, in which he has convincingly upstaged the doctor and dispossessed him of his manhood.

Back in the cottage, the doctor pumps shells in and out of his shotgun in a masturbatory attempt to regain his lost confidence in his manhood—first to prove that he is a "man" and, second, to demonstrate his access to the cultural and technological prowess that "won the West" for white settlers. Having put away the gun, however, the doctor's humiliations continue. Sent on an errand by his wife to find Nick, he must first apologize for slamming the screen door, unlike Dick Boulton, who deliberately leaves open the gate into the woods. But the errand does give him the opportunity to reprise the father-son relationship played so powerfully at the end of "Indian Camp." Nick's "I want to go with you" (27) allows his father to reassert an authoritative role ("His father looked down at him") in a way that is reminiscent of "Indian Camp": the son sitting in the stern of the boat, his father authoritatively rowing. But the likeness is only superficial. The doctor's escape into the woods merely points up his inability to confront his wife directly. Moreover, the impetus for their retreat comes from Nick, who "know[s] where there's black squirrels." Having lost the authority he possessed while rowing and steering the boat, and having forfeited the privileged knowledge he tried to impart to Nick in the cabin and boat, the doctor follows the leader into the woods his child knows better than he.

At the end of the first section of the Nick Adams stories, "The Battler," which features an avatar of Nick's father in Ad Francis, links together many of the functions of the symbolic arena registered so far and suggests new perspectives on the role of men within it. Bugs and Ad Francis's camp directly recalls "Indian Camp" (and "The End of Something") and the transgressions enacted there. Once again, "The Battler" evokes disputed territories, threats of humiliation, and symbolic evictions. "Who the hell asked you to butt in here?" (59) asks Ad Francis, a question the brakeman who knocks Nick off the train might also have asked. Like Dick Boulton, both Francis and the brakeman wish to transform enclosed spaces into symbolic arenas—in this case boxing rings—in which men compete to demonstrate their manhood. Nick's poor performance on the train (the "lousy kid thing to have done") inspires only a new devotion to self-dramatization and to that correlation between evaluatory watching and male identity. Touching his black eye, Nick, rather mysteriously, "wished he could see it," and then apparently tries to see his reflection: "Could not see it looking into the water, though" (53). While berating himself for his immaturity, he nonetheless prizes the black eye as one sign of his initiation into manhood: "That was all he had gotten out of it. Cheap at the price." In lieu of the hollering crowd at the bullfight in Chapter IX, Nick, another "kid," tries to become the audience to the spectacle of his own maturation. Self-display puts him in mind of what he must remember not to do again.

The ensuing scene bears out that correspondence between manhood and performance. Nick enters the firelit clearing to find Francis using him as audience to Francis's exhibition of toughness. Francis constantly refers to the importance of visible wounds as an index of toughness, acknowledging, for instance, Nick's black eye with his first words ("Where did you get the shiner?") before going on to dramatize his own battered face: "Look here!" and "Ever see one like that?" The echoes of the doctor's comments to Nick in "Indian Camp" are telling, for both insistently draw attention to the iconography of their professions. The doctor's surgical skill warranted the attention of the other "midwives"; and Francis's "pan," manifesting his performances in the ring, signifies his indomitable courage to a fellow battler: "I could take it," "They couldn't hurt me." That delight in displaying his battered face provides a key to his behavior during the rest of the story. For his failure to get Nick's knife destroys his self-image, carefully maintained before the younger man, of the heroic prizefighter. Consequently, like the doctor who is transformed from medical marvel to lamp-bearer in "Indian Camp," Francis becomes the frustrated but passive observer: "The little white man looked at Nick," "He was looking at Nick" (repeated twice), "Ad kept on looking at Nick," "He glared at Nick." Such manic staring suggests Francis's humiliation; it also suggests the root of his humiliation. For Francis, more than anyone else in the Nick Adams stories, has been battered in the public eye: first in the ring, where he "took too many beatings," and then in the papers, because his wife "Looked enough like him to be twins." Like the matador who admits "I am not really a good bull fighter" (95), Francis's shame has grown because of the crowds that witness it. His compensatory solution in the clearing is to recall the scene of his most successful dramatizations of physical prowess: the boxing ring. Thus he does not swing wildly at Nick but adopts the stance of the trained boxer, stepping "flat-footed forward." But the battler's attempt at self-dramatization merely parodies his earlier ability to dominate arenas as he falls unconscious in the most dishonorable way possible—being hit from behind.

It is tempting to read Ad Francis in terms of the archetypally beaten but undaunted Hemingway hero, avatar of Nick Adams himself. Nick, as Bugs says, has "got a lot coming to him," and the ensuing vignette describing Nick's wounding connects him to the beatings suffered by Ad Francis. Each acts, indeed, as if the presence of marks somehow constituted proud manliness.

Francis's mutilated face signifies "I could take it," while Nick's black eye connotes for him a transition from the acts of a "lousy kid" to a new maturity: "They would never suck him in that way again." But Hemingway confronts quite different dilemmas about masculine identity in "The Battler." Nick knows Francis "by name as a former champion fighter," and the narrator, at the moment when Nick refuses him the knife, calls him the "prizefighter"; Francis, it seems, has become commensurate with his role, named and remembered by and through performances enacted for others and identifying himself with a set of remembered movements. Yet identity suffers when performance no longer serves. Clubbed by Bugs in an ugly parody of a boxing match, he fails to perform the expected role and falls unconscious— indicative, perhaps, of his profound absence of self. Moreover, the story reveals the inadequacy or even inappropriateness of masculine codes of conduct that issue in Francis's confused, self-destructive courage and Nick's wavering command over his conduct. In his first conversation with Francis, for instance, Nick first admits his lack of inner resilience, denying that he is "a tough one," then attempts to fall back on the aggressive role that Francis expects of him and that Nick deems appropriate to the situation: "You got to be tough." In fact neither Francis nor Nick carries off the role of tough fighter: Nick is identified as a "kid," while Francis ends with his face looking "childish" in repose. Though both Nick and Francis carry the signs of beatings, each errs in interpreting the visible marks as signifying toughness. As the next chapter shows, Nick will again be "sucked in" and still more severely wounded, while for Bugs Francis's mutilated face merely suggests the unheroic possibility that he "took too many beatings."

Interestingly, critics persuaded by the wounded hero hypothesis read a character's marks in the heroic spirit of Nick and Francis, who are convinced that they "could take it," rather than as a sign of foolishness. Philip Young, most obviously, constructs his compelling and influential account of Hemingway's work by universalizing the wound that Nick receives in the war. The "culminating blow in the spine," Young writes, is "symbol and climax for a process that has been going on since we first met Nick." It represents the psychic and physical wounds Nick has experienced and will undergo, as well as the wounds suffered by other characters, such as Jake Barnes and Colonel Cantwell. Though the wound is an "outward and visible sign of an inward and spiritual dis-grace," it is nonetheless responsible for the masculine codes of discipline and restraint that for Young characterize Hemingway's adult male.[3] Nick in "Big Two-Hearted River," as Young is careful to point out, is a man rather than a boy, damaged, to be sure, but still a "man who knows his way around."[4] Experiences like the caesarean in "Indian Camp" and his "shiner" in "The Battler" do not imply Nick's boyhood so much as an emerging manhood; receiving *the* wound from which all other wounds derive meaning constellates diverse experiences into a pattern that now seems to have been present all along. The overarching trajectory of a journey to manhood now appears as the hidden meaning and value of each one of those early encounters. Put differently, we understand the hollowness of boyhood experiences by figuring back from whatever value—discipline, courage, holding tight, suffering wounds, enduring pain—is held to characterize a man. The outcome is threefold. First, boyish actions are not understood as problematic in their own right but only insofar as they fail to measure up to actions performed by a man; masculine codes themselves are not recognized as the problem boys must face. Second, a man's problems are inflicted upon him from outside sources (epitomized by the bullet that hits Nick's spine) rather than from the codes that seem to sustain him. Third, manhood emerges as a stable and solid quality, capable of being encoded and employed in many different situations.

A story like "The Battler" and other stories of the young Nick Adams, however, give little cause for certainty on any of these points. "The Three-Day Blow," in which we find Nick pondering the wisdom of breaking up with Marjorie, demonstrates Hemingway's acute insights into the early travails of manhood-fashioning. The story portrays with a kind of relish the spartan but comfortable appurtenances of a world without women, where Nick and Bill drink, talk about sport, hunting, fishing, writing, and women, and shape a masculine paradise familiar from dozens of boys' stories of adventure. According to Leslie Fiedler's classic *Love and Death in the American Novel* (1959), such scenes are also familiar as the primal material of American literature in books where the male protagonist must leave behind society and the women who embody it in order to achieve freedom and self-determination. As a consequence, male characters in American literature remain boys, forever seeking a pristine boyhood paradise free of the responsibility of adult, heterosexual relationships. "Once a man's married he's absolutely bitched," Bill states in succinct praise of Nick's breaking off "that Marge business", with Marge

3. Young, 13.
4. Ibid., 27.

around, in fact, "we wouldn't even be going fishing tomorrow" (46–47). Despite Nick's ambivalent feelings about renewing a relationship with Marjorie, the story provides evidence of the adolescent, tough posturing of which his detractors accuse Hemingway, and which, not surprisingly, has been interpreted by many feminist writers as signifying a deep-rooted hostility toward women.

There is much to recommend Fiedler's account and other critiques of Hemingway's stories insofar as they accurately describe the codes that govern Nick and Bill's behavior and conversation. But the story explores the socially constructed nature of those codes and exposes their contradictions rather than representing them as the standards to which Nick and Bill should aspire. Both Nick and Bill, for instance, resist a world of consequences, though for crucially different reasons. For Bill, the consequences of marriage are destructive and should thus be avoided, an act that leaves a man free while symbolically asserting the power of masculine agency and volition. For Nick, picking up Bill's hint that he "might get back into it again," the consequences of the breakup appear suddenly reversible. "There was not anything," according to Nick, "that was irrevocable." But Nick himself has just given an example of something that is: "All of a sudden everything was over. . . . I couldn't help it. Just like when the three-day blows come now and rip all the leaves off the trees" (47–48). Nick here might simply be in the maudlin stages of incipient drunkenness, but his image conforms more closely than the boys' fantasies of volitional action to the world of inescapable contingencies that Hemingway depicts. The three-day blows occur in fall for a predictable length of time; they are irrevocable and consequential. They mean that it is "getting too late to go around without socks" (40) and that the "birds will lie right down in the grass with this" (49). And they inevitably limit action, for, as Bill proclaims at the end, "You can't shoot in this wind."

Unable to shoot, the two nevertheless carry their guns when setting off to find Bill's father, determined, in spite of the storm, to conform to a masculine code of potent action. Like the shotgun in "The Doctor and the Doctor's Wife," the guns are useless, but are powerful reminders of the (phallic) masculine authority Nick and Bill hope to inherit. The guns signify not an intention to kill but a desired form of conduct. In what has come to seem the archetypal Hemingwayesque gesture of grace under pressure, Nick and Bill value their ostensible goal less than the process of trying to achieve it. Indeed, the entire story concerns processes of behavior: how to drink, how to use practical symbols in a narrative, how to love women, and even, as the intoxicated Nick struggles in with a beech log, how to pick up spilled apricots: "He laid the log down and picked up the pan. It had contained dried apricots, soaking in water. He carefully picked up all the apricots off the floor, some of them had gone under the stove, and put them back in the pan. He dipped some more water onto them from the pail by the table. He felt quite proud of himself. He had been thoroughly practical" (44–45). Nick sets the spilled apricots to rights using the kind of ritual thoroughnesss and care that seems more pertinent to the Villalta bullfighting vignette and to "Big Two-Hearted River." But his drunken lucidity (which even includes a wonderfully slurred run-on sentence in "picked up all the apricots off the floor, some of them had gone under the stove") imparts an unsettlingly comic feel to these scenes of heroic action. Similarly, Nick and Bill attempt to abide by paternal codes and prohibitions even when they are blatantly ludicrous. Bill, for instance, says with regard to whisky that there is "plenty more but dad only likes me to drink what's open," because he "says opening bottles is what makes drunkards." If opening bottles really made drunkards, of course, Bill should never open another bottle. Nick, on the other hand, had thought that it was "solitary drinking that made drunkards," a difference of opinion that is quietly suppressed in their quest for cohesive standards of conduct. For Nick and Bill, the point is not to question the appropriateness of the injunction but to internalize the appropriateness of making codes. The story persuades us that Hemingway's intent might be parodic rather than celebratory. Nick and Bill naively and unsuccessfully try to imitate the codes of true manhood; but because those codes appear to govern even the most inappropriate and trivial situation, they testify to their own limitations.

The problematic nature of those codes becomes particularly evident in stories like "The End of Something" and "Cat in the Rain," in which masculine roles are subtly inhabited by women. In "The End of Something," for instance, we might read Nick's taciturn treatment of Marjorie as setting the scene for the ensuing display of precise professionalism and careful mastery of emotion that, to many, characterize the manly conduct of Hemingway's heroes. As fishing expert, moreover, Nick holds the upper hand in the play of glances that, once more, transforms this camp into an arena. At one point Nick appraises her work ("Nick looked at her fish") and advises: "You don't want to take the ventral fin out." So proficient is he that we may miss Hemingway's provocative critique of Nick's fumbling attempts to perform an adult masculine role. For Nick's treatment of her arises out of the threat of being out-performed. Marjorie proves every bit as adept as Nick, rowing while "holding the line in her teeth" at one point, smartly "row[ing] up the point a little way so she would not disturb the line," then driving the boat powerfully "way up the beach." As Nick finally admits, Marjorie is less an apprentice than an equal: "You know everything. That's the trouble. You know you do. . . . I've taught you everything. You know you do. What don't you know, anyway?" (32–34).

The fact that Marjorie can match Nick's expertise, experience, and toughness threatens him precisely because the acquisition of such attributes has traditionally been the prerogative of a male. As a consequence, "The End of Something" subverts the "heroic" qualities usually identified in Hemingway's male characters. In particular, the story reveals Nick's heroic pose of cool detachment to be contingent not on his authority but on a double fear of humiliation. First, Marjorie vies with Nick to possess the role he attempts to make his own. Though Philip Young makes some intriguing connections between Nick Adams and Huckleberry Finn (both are "masculine and solitary and out-of-doors . . . and fond of . . . hunting and fishing"), it is Marjorie who in this story exhibits the panache and strength of a Huck Finn.[5] Second, and perhaps more worrying, Marjorie demonstrates that these manly characteristics do not automatically accrue to any male. To be *male* is not the same as being a *man*, but what is a man if Marjorie can possess all the requisite attributes? One might argue that Nick in adolescent fashion is only aping the characteristics that will define the true Hemingway hero. The example of Marjorie, however, suggests the opposite: that there is something deeply problematic about the way masculine codes of behavior initiate boys into manhood.

If the model of Huck Finn reconfigures our easy expectations about roles appropriate to Nick and Marjorie, the woman in "Cat in the Rain" brings to our attention the potentially malleable nature of role-playing itself. The two Americans stopping at the unnamed hotel of an unnamed Italian seaside resort "did not know any of the people" (91) at the hotel and are themselves not known. Tourists without tourism, the Americans are stripped of everything but the most rudimentary roles. George spends the story reading, his wife wishing for whatever she does not have. The narrator, moreover, constantly identifies them in the simplest and most generic way, labeling the woman "the

5. Ibid., 202.

American wife," "the wife," and then "the American girl," while designating to George the position of "her husband" and then, even more indifferently, "The husband" (91–92). Tellingly, when going downstairs the American wife thinks of the padrone first as the "hotel owner" and then "hotel-keeper"; the maid, whose umbrage at the American wife's speaking English hints at depths of character never revealed in the story, remains "the maid."

These epithets hint at a cultural baggage of stereotypical roles that circumscribe the characters' lives yet are not adequate to the task of expressing their deepest desires and fears. This is particularly true of the "American wife," whose barely conscious feelings of entrapment and yearnings for powerful models of behavior make her one of Hemingway's most sensitive portraits of a female character. That portrait is nowhere more profound than in the rich metaphoric relationship the narrative draws between the woman and the cat. Initially the cat, which is "crouched under one of the dripping green tables . . . trying to make herself so compact that she would not be dripped on," represents the woman's own claustrophobia in the hotel room, where she stands at the window looking out. While the cat wishes only to escape the rain, however, the woman wants to break through the protective shelters that confine her. Her mission to rescue the cat reveals a fantasy of escape *into* the rain. Yet, ambivalently, she wishes to rescue the cat by securing it more completely within her hotel room. After her abortive venture into the rain, in fact, the fantasy she weaves around the cat suggests a longing for a traditionally feminine and maternal role: "I want to pull my hair back tight and smooth and make a big knot at the back that I can feel. . . . I want to have a kitty to sit on my lap and purr when I stroke her." The "kitty" substitutes for what she lacks: perhaps the lack of a child and certainly the complete lack of emotional and physical contact from George. The maternal woman/"kitty" relationship thus doubles for the (conventionally) romantic one between the male lover and female object of affection. The latter roles both depend on George's ability or willingness to restore a conventional paternalism.

The point, however, is not that Hemingway maneuvers the woman back into the position of "American wife," but that none of her fantasies affords her a stable and sustaining role. Her predicament is evident in her relationship to the padrone of the hotel, which recalls and extends the tense cultural engagements of the early stories. To begin with, the wife liked the hotel keeper. She "liked the deadly serious way he received any complaints. She liked his dignity. She liked the way he wanted to serve her." After her mission to find the cat, however, the woman's reaction is more complex: "As the American girl passed the office, the padrone bowed from his desk. Something felt very small and tight inside the girl. The padrone made her feel very small and at the same time really important. She had a momentary feeling of being of supreme importance" (93). The servant-to-queen relationship augments the woman's sense of superiority as a wealthy American tourist. Even more ironically, the padrone assumes the conventionally romantic gestures of the lover, bowing to the woman, catering to her every whim, and finally offering her the gift (the cat) she wanted most of all. George instructs her "Don't get wet" (92) and halfheartedly offers to retrieve the cat, but it is the padrone who actually causes the woman to be sheltered and the cat to be found. By quietly anticipating and performing every action for her, however, the padrone also ensures that her experience will remain vicarious. As surrogate lover/father, he merely confirms the uselessness of her existence. Feeling "very small," the American girl thus becomes child to the protective father and realizes her "supreme importance" only within his strict limits. The conclusion to the story, in which the woman receives her heart's desire, is thus a brilliantly parodic fairy-tale ending. "I want a cat. I want a cat now. If I can't have long hair or any fun, I can have a cat," complains the woman, only to have a cat miraculously delivered. But with her articulated wants so comprehensively assuaged and her fantasies made real, the ill-defined and chaotic yearnings that the cat symbolizes remain unfulfilled. And worse: by getting exactly what she said she wanted, the woman loses the means for expressing metaphorically the true extent of her predicament. The problem the story poses, then, is not that George fails to measure up to the woman's romantic fantasy of being treated like a princess but that such culturally sanctioned roles are themselves not generative or appropriate to her desires. We see this most clearly when, by playing dutiful hero to the woman's fantasy of being rescued, the padrone causes her fantasy of heroic rescue to *succeed.*

The mock fairy-tale ending brings to ironic closure the story's dynamic of displacement and substitution most clearly figured in the relationship between woman and cat. Expatriated from their own country, prevented by the rain from being tourists, and, it appears, alienated from each other, the American tourists seem lost in a freeplay of substitutive elements. Linguistically, this dynamic is signaled by the sliding of "cat" into "kitty" and the frequent displacement of one language for another: "brutto tempo. It's very bad weather," and the conversational sequence that goes "A cat?" "Si, il gatto." "A cat?" But other forms of substitution pervade the story. The woman's longing for the cat, as many interpretations have pointed out, may represent a baby or perhaps, as Carlos Baker has it, "comfortable bourgeois domesticity."[6] Her desire for long hair substitutes for an emotional attachment to her husband; the padrone substitutes for her husband; the maid, sent by the hotel-keeper to protect her from the rain, symbolically enacts his role, while replacing the woman's yearning for escape with an umbrella-protected charade; and the woman's gazing into the rain represents a stifled desire for action.

Enmeshed in a play of substitutions, the woman struggles to express authentic and original desires as if to bring to an end the bewildering freeplay of sliding roles. In one of the key substitutions of the story, the woman wishes to discard the sense of boyishness and immaturity associated with short hair and grow the long hair that signifies womanhood. The fantasy that long hair grants access to true womanhood seems to reveal to her the truth about her frustration, which can now be explained away as having short hair, "looking like a boy," and thus acting out an inappropriate role. The authenticity of long hair suggests that she is only metaphorically female—a substitute for a true, long-haired, and womanly self. This substitution has the power to end the play of substitutions as the woman imaginatively dons the authentic sign of womanhood, hitherto obscured by her illusions of grandeur and her perverse misinterpretation of appropriate gender roles. At this point one is tempted to read the story as a parable of expatriation in which traditional gender roles, imbued with meaningful, authentic, and regenerative codes of conduct, have yielded to inappropriate and inadequate replacements. Thus, we might argue, George, passively reading, reneges on a potent, masculine role while the "American girl" substitutes boyish fashion for her womanly prerogatives. Such unnatural pursuits condemn them, like many other characters in *In Our Time* (such as Krebs in "Soldier's Home" and the couple in "Out of Season"), to near-paralysis.

But "Cat in the Rain" does not imply that expatriation has divorced George and his wife from sustaining patterns of behavior. In fact, it is the traditional roles themselves that seem to force the American woman into a logic of displacement by inviting her to speak her frustration in a false language of authenticity. Though her fantasy of long hair posits a movement from metaphor (looking like a boy) to the real (being a long-haired woman), her ac-

6. Baker, *Writer as Artist*, 135.

tions imply the opposite. During her thorough survey of her face in the mirror, for instance, the woman merely engages culturally constructed types of femininity that place her squarely within the purview of objectifying gazes: "She studied her profile, first one side and then the other. Then she studied the back of her head and her neck." Her conclusion, after asking George to observe her too, is that "I get so tired of looking like a boy." But this traditionally narcissistic perusal of her own beauty, culminating in a claim on the "feminine" prerogative of long hair, places her as a center of attention emptied of true authority. Her attempt to command center stage merely entangles her in culturally sanctioned images; a potential power over the gaze becomes submission to the way women and men are supposed to look. Tellingly, her next action is to direct her gaze outwards—a gaze that, though empty in terms of specific motivation, suggests her yearnings for potent observation: "She laid the mirror down on the dresser and went over to the window and looked out."

The woman, then, can only study her reflection and invite George's gaze within a theater of culturally approved appearances that is by definition out of her control; her only mode of expressing authenticity is to draw attention to a cult of beautiful womanhood whose limitations are evident in her ambivalent response to the padrone and in George's waning interest in her looks. The woman is most displaced from her amorphous desires for liberation when most assiduously performing the role expected of a woman. (Tellingly, she wants to make of that long hair a "big knot.") Indeed, the mock fairy-tale ending wholly deflates the victory of the authentic over the metaphoric, for the arrival of the authentic and actual in the shape of the cat effectively brings to an end the frustrating but revealing course of the woman's metaphoric expression of her predicament. Though the substitutive rhetoric of longing for the "kitty" obscures the true sources of her frustration, it at least allows a series of metaphoric reflections that keep alive her sense of frustration. Her dilemma, at least in part, is how to keep the freeplay of metaphor alive.

While the woman in "Cat in the Rain" and Marjorie play relatively minor parts in *In Our Time,* the import of their actions is crucial to an understanding of Hemingway's work. Their actions and longings combine traditionally male and female perspectives. Marjorie, expert on the water and more resilient than Nick, makes her own proud exit from the camp. The woman in "Cat in the Rain" wants to be rescued, but also to be the rescuer; she refuses to let her husband get the cat for her, preferring to experience the traditionally masculine role of self-liberation. The fact that the padrone circumvents the woman's fragile rebellion is perhaps less important than the fact of the rebellion, which reveals that women, like men, harbor urges toward heroic action. If so, this story, like "The End of Something," urges the possibility that identity is culturally constructed rather than biologically ordained. The American wife's paralysis might be seen more fruitfully within a matrix of social repression rather than as her biological destiny. The characters of Marjorie and the American woman, moreover, inveigh against the tendency of many critics to construct a limited classification of female types. Roger Whitlow in *Cassandra's Daughters* (1984) rightly condemns the propensity to categorize Hemingway's female characters and argues that they are more complex than his most influential critics (of which Whitlow provides a long list) credit. Comley and Scholes's recent *Hemingway's Genders* suggest that Whitlow's argument has not been entirely persuasive. They argue that Hemingway "worked all his life with a relatively simple repertory of male and female figures, modifying and individuating them with minimalist economy," a repertory that the title of Chapter 2 defines as "Mothers, Nurses, Bitches, Girls, and Devils." For Comley and Scholes, whatever complexity Hemingway manages in his female characters arises from a kind of elaborate cutting and pasting: what makes Brett in *The Sun Also Rises* "interesting as a character," for instance, is the way that "Hemingway has assigned her qualities from both sides of his gendered repertory of typical figures."[7]

This neo-structuralist reading of Hemingway, which sees his narrative method as selecting and combining from a paradigm class of feminine elements, underestimates the full range and depth of Hemingway's female characters. Like all typologies of Hemingway's characters, each putative category assimilates and erases all idiosyncrasies and potential points of difference. And like all typologies, it assumes the presence of qualities (such as bitchiness or devilishness) with the force of ideal essences. On the other hand, Whitlow, who tends to read those characters simply as fully dimensional human beings (he wonders, for instance, how Marjorie felt about the breakup with Nick), misses the crucial importance of role-playing in Hemingway's narrative.[8] To read the woman in "Cat in the Rain" as simply a woman misses the specific ways in which womanhood is constructed (and found wanting), in which the

7. Comley and Scholes, 23, 45.
8. Whitlow, 88.

woman herself assigns others to certain roles, and in which the woman tenta-tively inhabits roles that American and Italian cultures place out of bounds. What makes her interesting as a character, to rephrase Comley and Scholes, is her *experience* of the simple repertory of female roles she is expected to play, yet cannot.

These rereadings of Marjorie and the American woman parlay into a much more thoroughgoing critique of roles and role-definitions in Hemingway's work. As we have seen, until recently the most influential thrust of Heming-way criticism construed his male characters in terms of their adherence to specific categories of male experience and behavior—the code hero and tutor being the most famous, though by no means the only ones. Delbert E. Wylder, for instance, though rightly disagreeing with the easy code hero/Hemingway hero thesis, simply goes on to construct a more elaborate classification in his *Hemingway's Heroes* (1969): we now have the sentimental hero of *The Torrents of Spring* and the tyrant hero of *Across the River and into the Trees*, among others. Whatever the many virtues of his analysis, Wylder must still ignore or assimilate potentially disruptive aspects of a character's behavior in the pro-cess of defining what typifies it. The example of Ad Francis in "The Battler" suggests how problematic such attempts are. It is not just that Francis's tough pose masks a deep fragility, but that the story questions whether one can dis-tinguish his pose from his authentic self. Having knocked Francis uncon-scious, Bugs argues that "I have to do it to change him when he gets that way." But does Francis change from "crazy" belligerence to the "normal" man whom Nick overhears saying "I got an awful headache, Bugs"? Or does he change from a normal state of craziness, attributable to his having sustained too many beatings, to a temporary state that is merely manageable? Since Francis "won't remember nothing of it" (60), there is a sense in which his personality is fundamentally incoherent; what defines him is not so much his craziness as the changes he undergoes, which, once forgotten, cannot be as-similated into a coherent sense of identity. Nick Adams, as the analogies be-tween him and Ad Francis suggest, experiences similar changes as he shifts from "kid" to adult ("They would never suck him in that way again") and from victim to "tough one." We might even argue that Nick's famous state-ment in Chapter VI that he and Rinaldi are "Not patriots" has something of the force of "not patriots *anymore*," and that his comment thus suggests that he has been sucked into patriotism by more pernicious lies. In that case he has indeed forgotten the lessons of "The Battler."

What used to be one of the most problematic aspects of "The Battler"—its homoerotic underpinnings—is pertinent to this question of role-playing. The story, as Philip Young coyly states, "can have only one very probable interpretation," which is that the "tender, motherly, male-nursing Bugs is too comfortable in the relationship with the little, demented ex-fighter" and that it is "not only Ad who is 'queer.'" This all-male colloquy in the wilderness, replete with phallic imagery of knives and a cosh that had a "flexible handle and was limber in [Nick's] hand," certainly supports Young's point. But his contention that the theme of homoeroticism is "normally used by Hemingway as it is used here—a kind of ultimate in evil" does the story, and indeed his own reading, a disservice.[9] For if Bugs is gay, he is also, as Young points out, motherly; and lest this association between homoeroticism and mothering be construed as portraying Bugs as one more Bad Mother in *In Our Time*, we should also note that Bugs addresses Nick with the respectful "Mister Adams." (It is Francis who addresses Nick as "kid" and "Nick.") If anything, Bugs provides an important counter to the brakeman, who exemplifies lies and brutal "masculine" aggression. And if Francis is gay, his struggles to survive the many beatings he has endured potentially mark him as heroically masculine—if, for instance, we read back from Hemingway's aphorism in *Death in the Afternoon* that "you will find no man who is a man who will not bear some marks of past misfortune."[10] Moreover, Nick's interest in Bugs's cosh and the proliferating analogies between Francis and Nick would suggest that Nick himself is at least symbolically implicated in the story's rich homoerotic overtones. The story presents no necessary or logical contradiction between homoeroticism and masculinity—between, that is, a "transgressive" male sexuality and "normal" manly behavior.

The story does, however, suggest that "normal" behavior contains a carnivalesque diversity of potential, and ever-changing, roles; it permits Bugs to be motherly and an avatar of the brakeman (for Bugs not only coshes Francis but has been in jail for "cuttin' a man"). But it is not only that Young's "probable interpretation" can be stood on its head so that aspects of masculinity and motherhood can be read as entangled within the purview of homoeroticism. What is truly transgressive about the story is that it refuses to specify a fundamental social and sexual role for Bugs and Francis. Because "The Battler"

9. Young, 11.
10. Hemingway, *Afternoon*, 99–100.

omits any authoritative indication of the couple's homoeroticism, it permits a constant permutation of interpretive judgments. The story can be interpreted as justifying Young's point that Nick can or should learn to construct a more complete masculine identity out of his awareness of Francis's failures, so that, for instance, Nick carries away a sense that "You got to be tough"— though tempered with a sane contempt for empty violence and abnormal relationships. Equally, the story could be interpreted as suggesting Nick's fascination with the wide range of behavioral patterns liberated by the "abnormal." Equally, we might argue that the story simply exhibits a wide range of behaviors, none of which should be judged either normal or abnormal. The point is that each of these potential interpretations (among many others) depends upon stabilizing one foundational element out of a play of possibilities. Once a foundation has been adduced, it rigorously governs subsequent readings. In Young's reading, for instance, the assumption that Nick encounters a brutally abnormal relationship between Francis and Bugs assimilates the concept of motherliness, which is similarly made suspect by virtue of its transgressive relationship to "normal" manliness. A man, that is, should not be a mother, though a queer male might be motherly. The possibility that Bugs could be a motherly man (whether queer or not) puts in doubt the very grounds of Young's assumption—though, by the same token, the story also puts in doubt the extent to which one could construe the presence of a motherly man into an affirmative view of homoeroticism.

My point is not to castigate Young for covert homophobia but to criticize the all too overt tendency in Young and most other scholars toward assuming the stability of Hemingway's concept of manhood. Actually, the constant displacements of role in narratives like "The Battler" and "Cat in the Rain" problematize the very idea of masculinity, and not simply because Nick is fascinated by limber blackjacks, Bugs shows propensities for mothering, and the woman in "Cat in the Rain" exhibits fantasies of heroic conduct. More profoundly, these stories consistently put in question available categories of judgment. Hemingway's genius is to place constant interpretive pressure on us to make decisions about actions and values appropriate to men or women—as when Dick Boulton thinks about "how big a man he was" or when the American tourist gets "tired of looking like a boy"—while asking us to recognize how hazardous is the task of negotiating definitions that are rarely specified in the text. Categorical definitions within these stories are finalized only at the risk of ignoring the logic of narrative decentering contained within their gestic structure. What seem to be fairly straightforward representations of masculine and feminine types—Francis enduring the beatings, the woman in "Cat in the Rain" wanting long hair and a kitty—turn out to be much more complex negotiations of roles and values. Some roles that scholars have considered to represent the heart of Hemingway's concept of manhood, such as the taciturn man dealing expertly with intransigent experience, are treated ironically. Other roles possessing cultural sanction, such as the woman wishing for long hair, are exposed as inadequate shams.

The signs that construct masculine and feminine roles, in fact, are constantly shown to be transient and subject to negotiation: the Doctor who dominates the operating theater of the cabin thus suffers humiliation in the arena of his own garden, just as Ad Francis's attempt to dominate the camp suddenly changes to the image of his body in "childish" repose. Masculinity and femininity are fundamentally metaphorical in the sense that they possess no categorical or absolute value. They demand negotiation, not only in the sense that audiences within narratives need to observe, judge, and interpret the value of a man's actions, but in the sense that readers, as I argued in the case of "The Short Happy Life," must construe the significance of actions that simply do not speak for themselves. In judging whether Bugs is a motherly man, or a motherly gay (and therefore to Hemingway not a "man" at all?), or androgynous, or a sensitive (and thus "real"?) man, we become aware of our predilection for strong definitions of masculinity and femininity that the story, just as surely, puts in question.

Conventional assessments of Hemingway's work conclude that attaining manhood—as in the numinous moments when the "kid" becomes a man and when Villalta kills—promises to deliver the true meaning of a man's life. My reading of these stories suggests instead that meaning in Hemingway's work is always negotiable. His fiction concerns both the ways in which masculine and feminine roles are performed; and it foregrounds the ways in which readers perform definitions of masculinity and femininity. Reading "Cat in the Rain" in terms of the woman's attempts to dramatize herself amid the gazes of husband, padrone, maid, and mirror suggests something of the potential malleability of performed roles. At the same time, we should recognize that to argue that the woman in "Cat in the Rain" pursues "masculine" fantasies of rescue and self-liberation is as much a construction of the evidence as to argue that Bugs demonstrates "feminine" delicacies of tenderness and nurturing. It may be that Bugs's particular quality of tenderness should not be confused with mothering or that the American wife's "masculine" longing to break out of her room should not be equated with Nick's desire to separate from Marjorie. In each of these readings a conventional interpretation of "masculine" and "feminine" has been brought to bear from outside the story itself. The result would be the same, however, if we chose to define these terms more unconventionally—through, say, Hélène Cixous's notion of linear masculinity and oceanic femininity.[11] My point is that Hemingway's fiction forces us to try out various constructions of masculinity and femininity while recognizing that we are merely staging significations that have no eternal or absolute validity.

JAKE BARNES AND THE "HARD-EYED PEOPLE":
MANHOOD-FASHIONING IN *THE SUN ALSO RISES*

In *In Our Time*, Hemingway turns repeatedly to the arenas where, he suggests, men act out their dramas of power and shame. Some of these characters (such as Boulton and Villalta) demonstrate the authority accruing to the successful self-dramatist. More often, exposure to the watching crowd brings humiliation: in crucial scenes, characters like Ad Francis and Nick's father reach center stage only to display their inadequacy. Audiences may be disappointing, as Nick realizes in Chapter VI, but they do play a crucial part in the fashioning of manhood. They function as legitimating agents for men's images of themselves while problematizing the articulation of a secure and stable masculine identity. These narratives displace self, as it were, into seeing, and thus disrupt a monologic representation of masculinity by way of a theatrical experience that emphasizes the stage/arena, staged actions, watching audiences, and gestic role playing. Though Hemingway is primarily concerned with masculine identity, we have also seen that female characters like Marjorie and the American wife contribute to a more general sense that human identity rests precariously on the possibilities of role playing.

Jake Barnes, in *The Sun Also Rises*, shares with Nick Adams the displacement of self into seeing amid a landscape of theatricalized and carnivalized actions that are, if anything, more insistently woven into the narrative fabric than in *In Our Time*. Jake himself is primarily responsible, as many critics

---

11. See, for instance, Hélène Cixous, "The Laugh of the Medusa," trans. Keith and Paul Cohen, *Signs* 1 (1976): 865–80.

DRAMATIZATIONS OF MANHOOD

have pointed out, since his role as observer-participant dominates the novel's narrative trajectory, constantly drawing attention to the multiple acts of watching that shape his identity and that lead, ultimately, to his psychological travail in the arenas where men demonstrate their potency. This sense that Jake's watching embroils him with other characters in theatricalized arenas has, however, received little attention. Critics usually construe Jake's watching as a mode of detachment, though opinions vary as to whether detachment signifies a pure and objective disinterest or an unfortunate passivity. James T. Farrell noted that Jake's occupation as journalist "tends to develop the point of view of the spectator," and others concur. Edwin Burgum claims that Jake is a "disinterested observer," Carlos Baker that Jake is a "detached observer looking on at aimless revels which at once amused him and left him sick at heart." As a variation on this theme, Benson argues that Jake is a "developing character whose awareness and commitment is shaky until the end of the novel" when he finds the "bitter detachment" that other critics posit as his defining characteristic. At this point, Jake "finally becomes his own man." The main disagreement with this sense of Jake as the fatally or successfully detached observer has come from those who, like H. R. Stoneback, argue that Hemingway is "one of the great cartographers of the *deus loci*" and that Jake's role as an observer-figure at sacred places adds a mythic and transcendent resonance to his spectatorial abilities.[12]

Yet the most immediate impression of Jake's watching in *The Sun Also Rises* suggests neither detachment nor spirituality; his watching reads as a compensatory mechanism operating within an economy of lack. Early in the novel, Jake reports, "I looked at myself in the mirror of the big armoire beside the bed," thinking "Of all the ways to be wounded" (30).[13] The term "myself," interestingly, signifies in contradictory ways. On the one hand, it represents a productive combination of body and the conscious gaze. Seeing is responsible

12. James T. Farrell, "The Sun Also Rises," in *Ernest Hemingway: Critiques of Four Major Novels,* ed. Carlos Baker (New York: Scribner's, 1962), 5; Edwin Berry Burgum, "Ernest Hemingway and the Psychology of the Lost Generation," in *Ernest Hemingway: The Man and His Work,* ed. John K. M. McCaffery (Cleveland: World Publishing, 1950), 315; Baker, *Writer as Artist,* 77; Benson, 40; H. R. Stoneback, "From the rue Saint-Jacques to the Pass of Roland to the 'Unfinished Church on the Edge of the Cliff,'" *Hemingway Review* 6, no. 1 (fall 1986): 27.

13. Ernest Hemingway, *The Sun Also Rises* (New York: Scribner's, 1926). This work will hereinafter be cited parenthetically by page number in the text.

for awareness of being, though there also seems to be an "I" that precedes the act of watching ("I looked") that is reducible neither to the imaged body nor to the act of watching. On the other hand, because "myself" also refers metonymically to the genitals—the male equipment that (supposedly) establishes a masculine self—the term also represents an absence (either of penis, testicles, or both). In this sense, Jake sees nothing at all or not enough: an absence or a lack. He faces the conundrum of watching a self into being that is simultaneously revealed to be missing or lacking. He is simultaneously "myself" and "not-myself."

What remains to his advantage, it seems, is the act of watching and being watched, which at once represents his loss/lack of physical completeness and sexual potency and compensates for it. The theatricality of watching "myself" at least allows him to represent a lost plenitude to himself, though it is by the same token a precarious and possibly inauthentic substitute for the whole self that equivocally appears when he looks into the mirror. Watching and being watched establishes selfhood; yet it establishes selfhood in terms of loss/lack. Not surprisingly, then, Jake demonstrates a vexed relationship to the acts of seeing that sustain and, it might be said, create him. Jake remarks early on that "I have a rotten habit of picturing the bedroom scenes of my friends" (13). His impotence has transformed his friends' acts into theater and himself into director, a habit of voyeurism that appears to be at once a product of and compensation for his inability to participate in his own bedroom scenes. Similarly, his self-disgusted comment that "I liked to see [Mike] hurt Cohn" (148) suggests a burden of desire, anger, and guilt cathected onto the act of seeing.

The scene at the Irati River—which critics persist in reading as an edenic interlude between the hellish scenes at Paris and Pamplona—indicates further some of the complicated roots of Jake's voyeurism. Bill, producing his haul of four trout, lays them out on the grass and asks:

"How are yours?"
"Smaller."
"Let's see them."
"They're packed."
"How big are they really?"
"They're all about the size of your smallest." (120)

In this conspicuously phallic show-and-tell, Jake refuses the competitive display that would mark his as "smaller." His act of looking (at Bill's trout) doubles for the display he will not make; his assessment of the size of Bill's trout relative to his own covers for the assessment he will not allow Bill. A refusal to put his (Jake's) on display thus reconfigures the play of glances around an absence (the absent trout/phallus)—with the unforeseen consequence that this absence generates both the rich rhetorical play of the passage and its fascination with a dynamic interplay of probing, competing, and revealing glances. At the same time, Jake rather slyly reserves to himself the role of evaluation. Like the earlier scene where Jake watches himself in the mirror, this moment at the Irati River suggests the equivocal dynamic of watching and being watched: watching and evaluating grants Jake a measure of authority in scenes where men compete against and test each other, yet he forfeits the self-display that seemed so problematic when "I looked at myself" in the mirror, but which characterizes the confidence of Bill and Pedro Romero.

In still another sense, Jake's "rotten habit" corresponds to that passionate witnessing which is his afición. They "saw that I had afición" (132), claims Jake of Montoya's friends, as if afición is a matter of seeing true rather than of interrogation. Several other characters comment on Jake's perceptiveness. Romero remarks: "I like it very much that you like my work. . . . But you haven't seen it yet. To-morrow, if I get a good bull, I will try and show it to you" (174). And when Jake advises Montoya (to the hotel keeper's pleasure) not to give Romero the invitation from the American ambassador, Montoya asks Jake three times to "look" (171–72) for him. Cast as the archetypal observer by other men who accept his evaluations of their endeavors, Jake has managed to transform observation itself into a kind of powerful witnessing—though the closing scenes at Pamplona will show how flimsy his authority truly is. Not surprisingly, after Jake assists Brett to seduce Romero Montoya responds to what he perceives as the American's betrayal of afición by refusing the gaze that signifies a commonality and community of interest: Montoya "bowed" (209) upon meeting Jake and Brett on the stairs; on departure, the hotel keeper "did not come near us" (228).

Jake Barnes is thus much more than a recording eye or a detached observer occasionally implicated in the immoral conduct of his expatriate friends. My point, though, is not simply to characterize Jake's habit of watching as less disinterested and more of an activity than critics usually grant, but to show that he employs some of the functions of gazing within a theatrical representation of manhood. His status as spectator-participant underpins Hemingway's sense of manhood-fashioning as a performance carried out before an evaluating audience. Jake's acts of gazing—as opposed to Benson's account of Jake becoming "his own man" in "bitter detachment"—can never be separated from the structure of authority and humiliation that inform his (and others') gestures toward manhood. But it would be a mistake to construe Jake's dependence on watching as signifying his lack of manhood, as though his status of observer, perpetually cut off from the activities of real men, were the consequence of his genital injury. On the contrary: Jake, as odd as it sounds, exemplifies the condition of manhood. As the above example of Bill's flaunting of his trout suggests, and as Romero's bullfighting will demonstrate still more effectively, Jake is not alone in working within a visual economy of display and spectatorship. If his habit of observing places him in the important but apparently subsidiary role of passionate witness (aficionado), the novel also draws our attention to the general economy of lack, facing all men, within which observing and being observed become functional, and within which both imply lack. Jake watches others to compensate for his sexual impotency; but the need to be observed on the part of those in the novel who are not generally recognized to be in need of support (like Romero) testifies to a situation in which the male self is never felt to be complete, authentic, and independent.

Approved by the adoring crowd as well as by Jake's expert appraisal, Romero's victories in the bullring after the beating by Cohn are not only the narrative conclusion of Book II but the focus of Jake's own attempts to redeem his impotence. Jake perceives Romero's painful trial in the ring as a testing and affirmation of the matador's spirit—and perhaps, since Jake is another survivor of Cohn's assaults, as a vicarious affirmation of his own: "The fight with Cohn had not touched his spirit but his face had been smashed and his body hurt. He was wiping all that out now. Each thing that he did with this bull wiped that out a little cleaner" (219). Romero's process of recuperation, to Jake, depends upon a complex relationship between being watched and disavowing the watching audience (Brett in particular). For *Sun,* and for Hemingway's early work in general, interpretation of this passage is crucial: "Everything of which he [Romero] could control the locality he did in front of her all that afternoon. Never once did he look up. He made it stronger that way, and did it for himself, too, as well as for her. Because he did not look up to ask if it pleased he did it all for himself inside, and it strengthened him, and yet he did it for her, too. But he did not do it for her at any loss to himself. He gained by it all through the afternoon" (216). Jake's conundrum of profit and loss (if Romero did it "all" for himself, what could be left for Brett?) involves, once again, the matador's intimate relationship with his audience. Unlike Villalta in Chapter XII of *In Our Time*, who played self-consciously to the crowd, Romero "did not look up" and thus, according to Jake, "did it all for himself inside." Even at the end of the fight, when the crowd raises him in triumph, this most reticent of actors tries to resist: "He did not want to be carried on people's shoulders" (221). Yet by defying the rules of performance in Hemingway's quintessential arena, Romero appears to Jake to increase the potency of his actions—a formulation that seems to justify scholarly accounts of his detached heroism and to contradict those many scenes in *In Our Time* and *Sun* where a man's prestige is seen to depend on the legitimating approval of an audience.

Most critics have concurred with Jake. Few characters in Hemingway seem to fit more exactly the profile of the tutor or code hero, whose governing feature, according to Earl Rovit, is his "self-containment" (39). Lawrence R. Broer speaks of the "self-contained Romero," Mark Spilka agrees that Romero's "manhood is a thing independent of women," and Allen Josephs has recently written in a similar vein that Romero is "an innocent."[14] Yet Romero's mode of asserting his manhood is far more self-consciously part of a "system of authority" (185) than Jake (like the critics) perceives: he performs as close to Brett as possible; he follows the wishes of the audience when, with the second bull, "the crowd made him go on" (219), and proceeds to give a complete exhibition of bullfighting. He also holds his posture as consciously as any actor: he "finished with a half-veronica that turned his back on the bull and came away toward the applause, his hand on his hip, his cape on his arm, and the bull watching his back going away" (217). In the bullfight, Romero dispenses with the audience only because the audience is there. He never once looks up, because the arena supplies an audience that looks down, celebrating his actions for him. At the dramatic climax of the fight, the presentation of the bull's ear to Brett takes on significance precisely because it happens before an audience. As Jake describes it, Romero "leaned up against the barrera and gave the ear to Brett. The crowd were all about him. Brett held down the

14. Lawrence R. Broer, *Hemingway's Spanish Tragedy* (University, Ala.: University of Alabama Press, 1973), 49; Mark Spilka, "The Death of Love in *The Sun Also Rises*," in *Twelve Original Essays on Great American Novels*, ed. Charles Shapiro (Detroit: Wayne State University Press, 1958), 250; Allen Josephs, "Toreo: The Moral Axis of *The Sun Also Rises*," *Hemingway Review* 6, no. 1 (1986), 92.

cape." The crowd here is not merely an element of the scene: it is "all about," the element that creates a scene, converting the act of giving into a ceremony and transforming these actors into celebrities.

Romero, as the scene in the café with Brett and Jake shows, is an accomplished actor. During the conversation he "tipped his hat down over his eyes and changed the angle of his cigar and the expression of his face. . . . He had mimicked exactly the expression of Nacional" (186). The cigar itself is a kind of stage prop marking him as one of the "bull-fighters and bull-fight critics," who are all smoking cigars, and that continues to invest him with authority when he joins Brett and Jake. Jake intimates that Romero continues smoking despite his "very nice manners," for the cigar, as Jake observes, "went well with his face." Though Brett at one point tells Jake "I can't look at him" (184), Romero (in a foreshadowing of his later performance in the bullring) is eager to display himself, quickly inviting Brett to "look" and "see [the] bulls in my hand." In the next chapter, Mike's account of Cohn's beating of Romero (learnt secondhand from Brett) attests once more to Romero's prowess at self-display. Mike casts Cohn as the villain in a melodrama of humiliation—it is Cohn who wishes to create a "Damned touching scene" (201) in making Brett an honest woman, who cries, and who wants to shake hands with Romero in a lugubrious gesture of respect and reconciliation. But Romero—whose willingness to continue the battle with Cohn despite its one-sided nature has usually been taken to signify a code of indomitable courage—plays a crucial role in this "touching scene." The struggle, after all, is enacted before the eyes of Brett (who later recounts it to Mike for yet another dramatization). Defeated by Cohn's superior technique, Romero can only gain face by prolonging his heroic resistance to the point where an outclassed boxing performance can be seen as a gesture of pride in the face of physical defeat, and where physical loss can be transformed into a theater of evaluatory watching. Romero's sole statement during his punishment ("So you won't hit me?"), which is intended to incite a resumption of the conflict, can therefore be read as an act of profound courage—in which, as Melvin Backman writes, the "hard male core of the young bullfighter could not be touched by Cohn's punches"—or a melodramatically conceived throwing down of the gauntlet to an equally theatrical rival.[15] In this latter sense, Romero's work in the bullring should be seen not

15. Melvin Backman, "Hemingway: The Matador and the Crucified," in ed. Baker, *Hemingway and His Critics*, 247.

so much as a "wiping . . . out" (219) of the beating by Cohn than as a resumption of the code of display that the scene with Cohn and Brett exemplifies.

Considering the subtle but insistent theatricality of Romero's performances, the motives behind Jake's assertions that the matador does it "all for himself inside" become more complex than critics have generally recognized. Christian Messenger is not unusual in claiming that Romero "provides Jake Barnes with a hero whom Jake can learn from and appreciate by spectatorial comprehension of the sporting rite."[16] Yet Jake's role at the ringside is actually far more than that of spectator and student of Romero's expert work with the bull. Jake represses the element of theatricality in Romero's actions because of his own failure in crucial scenes to control the way he displays himself; a more complete characterization of Jake must include the dramas of humiliation in which he plays the leading role. The key scene in which he tacitly pimps for Brett in the café, which as we have already noted features Romero's successful self-dramatization, becomes even more of a theatrical event when we figure in Jake's role. His ambiguous brief from Brett is to "see me through this" (184), and Jake literally watches the relationship between Romero and Brett into being. If Brett, through embarrassment or nerves, cannot at first look at Romero ("I can't look at him"), Jake has no such compunction: observing that Romero is "nice to look at," Jake proceeds to give a detailed description and then notes that "I saw he [Romero] was watching Brett." Romero twice more "looked at her across the table" (186, 187)—glances that bracket Brett's study of his hand—before Jake leaves after Romero's "final look to ask if it were understood." "It was," Jake comments wryly, "understood all right."

Many things are potentially understood in this exchange of glances between Romero and Jake. Though Jake acts as consultant to an incipient love affair, his actual role and authority is ambiguous. It is unclear, for instance, whether "it" refers to a contract fashioned between men—a kind of transfer of Brett from impotent watcher to potent matador—or to Jake's understanding of Brett's desires. In either case, the inquiring glance that Romero directs at Jake only bestows on him titular authority. Acting as mediator, translator, and consultant to the desires of others, Jake takes center stage only to discover his own humiliation. For his account of the evaluatory glances at the table have thus far obscured the presence of yet another audience to his actions. On leaving the café, Jake notes that the "hard-eyed people at the bull-fighter

16. Messenger, 251.

table watched me go" and comments dryly that it "was not pleasant." Several things are not pleasant for Jake here: the sense that Romero has usurped him sexually, and the sense that he has betrayed his tough masculine role by pimping for Brett. Above all, it is not pleasant that his failures are played out before a crowd of aficionados who watch and judge him. The whole scene thus comprises a series of actions framed by diverse glances: Romero watches Brett for signs of attraction; Jake watches Romero's victorious campaign for Brett; and the aficionados watch the entire show. In this theater of seduction, the role of watcher constantly switches function. The hard-eyed aficionados' stares come as an unpleasant shock to Jake; his watching, in contrast, appears only as a function of Romero's need for an audience. Though in some ways Jake has powerfully shaped the scene in this theater-café by directing the liaison of Brett and Romero, he does not control the play of glances. By the end of the scene, he is effectively "looked down," and looked down upon, by Romero and the aficionados.

Jake's appreciation of Romero's disdain for the crowd in the bullring takes on a richer significance in the context of his humiliating failure to dramatize himself sucessfully before the "hard-eyed people." In the café, for the first time in the novel, Jake inadvertently steps into the part hitherto enacted by characters like Romero and Dick Boulton: a man dramatizing his manhood before other men (and, in this case, Brett). Every potent action of Romero's in the bullring thus recalls a double failure on Jake's part: he fails to perform a tough masculine role in the café and then betrays, before his co-aficionados, his compensatory ability to watch and evaluate the masculine behavior of another. Such betrayals inform Jake's fascination with Romero's performance in the bullring. Romero "did it all for himself inside," but Jake does it for Brett; Romero scripts the killing of the bull, but Jake directs in accordance with Brett's script of seduction; Romero does not look up, disdaining the audience yet inviting applause, while Jake suffers the stares of the "hard-eyed people." Jake's fascination with Romero's display and his corresponding desire to play down the importance of self-display both arise from his humiliating lack of mastery over his own performances.

This interpretation of Jake as an interested (and failed) participant in scenes of masculine display illuminates two more aspects of the final bullfight. First, it helps to account for the long passage on Belmonte. Another man who has a "crowd . . . actively against him" (214) and who proves to be a secret observer of Romero ("Belmonte watched Romero too, watched him always without seeming to"), Belmonte has similar motives to Jake: both men have suffered the contempt of the crowd, and both jealously watch Romero enact what they may never again possess. And Belmonte sketches a possible role for Jake. For Belmonte, at least according to Jake, is "utterly contemptuous and indifferent" to the crowd that scorns him and, in our last glimpse of him, able to ignore the evaluatory stares altogether: he "leaned on the barrera below us, his head on his arms, not seeing, not hearing anything, only going through his pain." But Jake's answer is to attempt to return to the aficionado role he has forfeited, telling Brett to "Watch how" and comparing his knowledge of Romero's perfect handling of the visually impaired bull with that of the "Biarritz crowd," who misread Romero's actions as cowardice and who prefer "Belmonte's imitation of himself or Marcial's imitation of Belmonte." In contrast to Belmonte's indifference to the crowd, Jake searches for a way to resurrect the privilege of watching, and it is telling that as this lengthy scene unfolds the crowd plays an increasingly effective and even intrusive role. It showers Belmonte with "cushions and pieces of bread and vegetables," "made a great row" when it "wanted the bull changed," "made [Romero] go on" fighting his last bull, and is finally "all about him" and "all around him" during the concluding celebrations. If Romero's performances represent and recall all that Jake lacks, Jake's insistence on the role played by the crowd at the final bullfight at least serves to remind us of the crowd dynamics that structure Romero's own "system of authority."

Watching Romero typifies Jake's role in *The Sun Also Rises*. But the key scenes where Pedro Romero performs before the eyes of Brett and Jake—exemplified by Romero's command over the bullring—force a complete reconsideration of the usual claims about the masculine, moral, mythic, or spiritual significance of the ritual encounter, and about the psychic renewal Jake gains from it. Neither Jake's refusal to take center-stage nor his ability to transmit heroic and mythic values to his various audiences are compelling reasons for accepting at face value his role of detached, heroic witness. Instead, his expert analysis of the various arenas where men perform reveals the problematic nature of manhood-fashioning. As the mirror scene suggests, Jake struggles to construe a workable identity out of a precarious dynamic of presence/absence. Watching others substitutes for the lack of visible signs of maleness that keep him, it seems, from competing with other men in displays of masculine prowess. Lacking confidence in a masculine presence that exists prior to the play of evaluating glances, he constructs Romero as the type of man who "did it all for himself inside" while obsessively recording the details of Romero's performance. Watching, ironically, projects his unfulfilled desire for a masculine plenitude beyond the purview of watching.

But in *The Sun Also Rises* no man escapes from theatricality and self-dramatization into the full presence of autonomous selfhood. The point is worth emphasizing lest it seem that Jake's humiliation and the power of Romero's performance, arising from the kind of masculine show-and-tell staged on the Irati River, simply suggest the bullfighter's phallic power and the watcher's obvious lack. That Romero stages himself authoritatively while Jake (apart from his poor display before the "hard-eyed people") manages to avoid center-stage does not in the end suggest that each character finds a different way to manhood or that the novel argues for a dialectic of man/not-man or that the novel constructs its theaters only for those who lack the full male equipment. Indeed, because Jake, lacking his "manhood," must overtly struggle to construct a sense of masculine selfhood, it is Jake rather than Romero who exemplifies the novel's metaphorics of manhood-fashioning. Romero's and Jake's distinct roles bespeak the same structure of performance, and in that sense both confront the same peril of lacking or losing manhood.

My account of manhood-fashioning in *The Sun Also Rises* and *In Our Time*, building on my earlier analysis of "The Short Happy Life of Francis Macomber," suggests that Hemingway's fictions affirm a concept of masculinity that is multiply transformed and subject to rupture, inconsistency, and lack. This sliding of masculine identities and the inevitable deferral of a complete and autonomous masculine self, which is constantly being filled, voided, and refashioned before an audience, must, I argue, be read as a theatrical imperative experienced by men (if not women as well). Hemingway's work thus sustains a provocative interpretation of his characters' travails. Jake Barnes's obsession with Romero's performances springs from a vexed relationship with the very modes of masculine display that structure his identity. And the dynamic of man/not-man that characterizes Jake's mirror-gaze is consistent with the structural relationship between protagonist and audience experienced elsewhere in Hemingway's work. Nick's father switches from master of the operating theater to the humiliated husband of his own house and garden; Macomber voids his hollow fear to become a man, determined to display his new understanding of the code; and Wilson, giving up the "thing he had lived by" in several different misdemeanors against the logic of his own code, is thereby unmanned. It is in an effort to explore further the implications of theatricalized masculine behavior that the next chapter turns to Hemingway's theaters of war.

CHAPTER 3

Hemingway's Theaters of War:
A Farewell to Arms and For Whom the Bell Tolls

A COMMON IDIOM speaks of a "theater of war."[1] The phrase refers to the scene of action; the place where martial operations are undertaken. Building on that original image, the twentieth century has added other terms: the "show," staging operations, a "circus," acts of war, the European Theater, and so on. But in what ways could war be said to be theatrical? Because movements of soldiers and armaments and the battles in which they will be employed are scripted, or directed, by generals who remain behind the scenes, taking no hand in the stage-action itself? Because war operations are obsessively watched, depending for their successful outcome on the quality of visual information obtained? Because such obsessive watching transforms terrain into a kind of arena? Because, as in all theater, actions undertaken under the eyes of others somehow liberate a superabundance of meaning, so that these are not simply men fighting but men fighting *for* (their country, freedom, each other, their pride)? The issue is worth pondering because in many respects Hemingway's war stories appear to have little to do with theatricality. A dramatic scene like the broken-legged mules in the water at Smyrna, which fascinated Hemingway enough for him to publish three versions of it, is dramatic only in the loose sense of shocking or sensational; the fact that the event was witnessed at all has nothing to do with the exigencies that drove the baggage handlers to it.[2] Hemingway's war characters, moreover, tend to be men "in the trenches" far removed from the supposedly all-seeing generals who

1. According to the *Oxford English Dictionary*, the term "theater" was used to designate the scene of a non-dramatic action as far back as the sixteenth century, though usage in something like its modern form seems to date from the nineteenth century. Mendel in his *Art of War* (1879), for instance, speaks of the "theater of operations of an army."

2. Hemingway published versions of this event in *In Our Time* and *Death in the Afternoon*, and then excerpted the section from *Afternoon* as "A Natural History of the Dead."

direct the show. Frederic Henry's wounding, which many Hemingway critics and biographers interpret as a re-telling of *the* seminal experience of Hemingway's life, comes apropos of nothing: "I ate the end of my piece of cheese and took a swallow of wine. Through the other noise I heard a cough, then came the chuh-chuh-chuh-chuh—then there was a flash, as when a blast-furnace door is swung open."[3] The action that takes place is unscripted, meaningless; the shell is flung blindly; beyond the mere fact of the Austrian artillery having observed the enemy lines, there is no sense that an audience makes a difference to unfolding events. And, certainly, no one witnesses whatever there is to be seen when Frederic Henry "felt myself rush bodily out of myself."

Subsequent pages, however, return Henry to life amid a series of oddly drawn poses. The following exchange, for instance, takes place with the British ambulance driver who helps him:

> "They tell me you're an American."
> "Yes."
> "I'm English."
> "No!"
> "Yes, English. Did you think I was Italian?" (61–62)

Henry, having already referred to the man as the "Britisher" (61), does not think of him as Italian, and his "No!" is a piece of comic sarcasm that we understand but the Britisher misses. (The Britisher also pats Gordini's shoulder, missing the fact that it is smashed.) Within a few sentences, however, the Britisher, trying to get Henry early treatment, puts his faculty of misinterpretation to different use:

> "Here is the American Tenente," he said in Italian.
> "I'd rather wait," I said. "There are much worse wounded than me. I'm all right."
> "Come, come," he said. "Don't be a bloody hero."

Henry's deadpan presentation of this exchange encourages multiple interpretations. The Britisher reads his protestations as an excessive self-dramatization—though it is unclear whether the Britisher thinks of Henry as being

---

3. Ernest Hemingway, *A Farewell to Arms* (New York: Scribner's, 1929), 58. This work will hereinafter be cited parenthetically by page number in the text.

truly heroic at an inappropriate moment (he is being unnecessarily stoic), or simply falsely heroic at an appropriate moment (the moment calls for stoicism, but the man does not believe him).

Henry's actual words could be taken either way. "I'd rather wait" sounds genuine enough, but it is followed by "There are much worse wounded than me," which is certainly true, but smacks enough of the realm of comic-book heroes for the Britisher to perceive it as a merely rhetorical exercise. "I'm all right" is patently untrue. But that last response does allow Henry to claim kinship with the man who has quietly provided a role model for him throughout this whole scene: Gordini. Gordini, "white and sick" after his shoulder was smashed, brings the Britisher for Henry so that the Tenente can have his injuries treated first; "wince[s] and smile[s]" when the Britisher pats his shoulder; and, in response to Henry's question, says "I am all right" (which Henry repeats in his very next speech). Smiling through his pain and caring for Henry first, Gordini cuts a more heroic figure than Henry, who quite unstoically berates his (also wounded) bearers when falling shells cause them to drop him ("If you drop me again"; "You sons of bitches"). We might then read Henry in this passage as neither heroically trying to defer his treatment nor quite posing as a hero but as someone who, by imitating Gordini, tries to reproduce an appropriately heroic role. The Britisher's admonishment to not "be a bloody hero" suggests that Henry's masquerade is still evident. The narrative frame for this moment provides additional evidence: it is preceded by Henry pretending not to know that the Britisher is British, and followed by the Britisher introducing him to the surgeons under aliases: "He is the legitimate son of President Wilson"; "The only son of the American Ambassador."

The scene of Henry's wounding, which begins with a completely unscripted event and ends with Henry posing or at least learning how to pose properly, adds a crucial dimension to the idea of a theater of war in Hemingway's work. Theaters of war set up exemplary situations in which soldiers, under extreme duress, demonstrate (or fail to demonstrate) that they are men. In one sense, generations of Hemingway scholars have not only recognized this fact, they have often made it a cornerstone of their interpretations. Using *The Sun Also Rises* as a representative text for his chapter on "The War and the Postwar Temper," for instance, Frederick J. Hoffman in his much-reprinted *The Twenties: American Writing in the Postwar Decade* (1949) argues that one of the main themes emerging from World War I was "testing the true nature of men."[4] Arguments like these are flawed, for if males do in fact have a true (that is, essential, transhistorical) nature, it would seem incommensurable with any specific and transient set of circumstances like a war. Hoffman actually conflates two approaches to understanding male experience—the first implying a true nature of man that all males presumably possess, or must work toward, whether or not they participate in a war, the second interpreting the kind of actions males undertake in wartime as *representing* a universal ideal of manliness.

But Hoffman's sleight of hand allows him to finesse the troubling conclusion that males might need war in order to dramatize themselves. Hoffman's account of men at war depends on the kind of strategy we have already seen operating in the work of Benson and Messenger whereby self-dramatization appears only as the agent of its own undoing. On the one hand, the "Show" shows what males are made of; it makes males into men by allowing them to represent themselves appropriately; and acts of representation are necessary because the true nature of men cannot be known until put to the test. Manhood, it seems, must be shown to be known. On the other, imputations of theatricalized warfare can be discarded on the grounds that the true nature of men, being interior and somehow always and already present, cannot be conflated with or be contingent on the external display that brings it into being. The scholarly understanding of Hemingway's theater of war has typically been a beautifully wrought paradox: the true nature of men calls into being the acts of representation that are necessary for revealing the true nature of men.

But Hemingway's two great war novels, *A Farewell to Arms* and *For Whom the Bell Tolls,* insist on exploring the full metaphoric weight of "theater of war" and in so doing problematize in a rather different way from his critics the relationship between manhood and war. In the earlier novel, Frederic Henry's various masquerades, of which the scene with the Britisher is only one, suggest that war does indeed allow males to represent manhood. But *Farewell* never loses sight of the theatricality of such representations. And its theaters of war compose an ambiguous analysis of the dramatizations war enforces and of the self-dramatizations war reveals, urging us to explore the possibility that war metaphorizes the acts of self-representation males undertake when not at war. *For Whom the Bell Tolls,* however, demands a very different analysis. The later

4. Frederick J. Hoffman, *The Twenties: American Writing in the Postwar Decade* (New York: Free Press, 1966), 77.

novel depicts a situation all too familiar to the later twentieth century: a crisis of encroaching totalitarianism figured in unidentifiable systems of power and ruled by an invisible master-eye signifying fantasies of absolute domination. The novel is as magisterial an inquiry into the Western fascination with the dominating (male) gaze and with military intelligence as Luce Irigaray's *Speculum of the Other Woman* (1985) and Michel Foucault's *Discipline and Punish* (1977). Theater—and in particular the many instances of "cave theater" that characterize Robert Jordan's attempts to gain control of the guerrilla band— allows a trenchant critique of the fascist gaze, not so much because it offers a potent strategy of resistance but because it subjects the exercise of male power to a human audience.

FREDERIC HENRY: HIS MASQUERADES

As Frederic Henry nears the site of his wounding, he finds that the "road was crowded and there were screens of corn-stalk and straw matting on both sides and matting over the top so that it was like the entrance at a circus" (49). A major soon informs him that it is going to be a "one-road show" for the ambulances seeking to remove injured men. The metaphors are quite in keeping with the insistently theatrical atmosphere of the war as Henry establishes it in the first chapters of the novel. "We were supposed to wear steel helmets even in Gorizia," says Henry, "but they were uncomfortable and too bloody theatrical in a town where the civilian inhabitants had not been evacuated" (29). As suspect are the other paraphernalia of war: the "real" English gas masks that are beginning to replace presumably unreliable ones, and the pistols. Henry notes that: "You were liable to arrest if you did not have one worn in plain sight. Rinaldi carried a holster stuffed with toilet paper. I wore a real one and felt like a gunman until I practised firing it. . . . then the ridiculousness of carrying a pistol at all came over me and I soon forgot it and carried it flopping against the small of my back with no feeling at all except a vague sort of shame when I met English-speaking people" (30). Humiliation, in fact, seems to come readily to Henry in the Italian army. After saluting Catherine Barkley, he ponders that it was "impossible to salute foreigners as an Italian, without embarrassment. The Italian salute never seemed made for export" (23). In all of these instances, Henry's self-consciousness transforms the quite deadly functions of war into theater. Real helmets, pistols, and salutes become stage-props, Henry's pistol as useless as Rinaldi's toilet-paper-stuffed holster. The gesture of salute, for Henry, becomes a gest, transforming the war into a series of signifying practices.

Henry's cross-cultural role as an American Tenente in the Italian army contributes to his sensitivity toward the responses of "foreigners" and thus fosters his early sense of the war as a rather ridiculous piece of theater. His role certainly draws the attention of other characters in the novel. Earl Rovit and Gerry Brenner note that "Henry is, in a sense, playing a double masquerade. He is to Ferguson a sneaking American hiding in an Italian uniform; to Rinaldi, he is an Italian pretending to be an American."[5] We have seen also that Henry pretends momentarily not to know that the Britisher is British. And an exactly analogous scene occurs in the dressing station to which the Britisher's intervention causes him to be brought when one medical captain (who knows that this is the "American Tenente" [63]) signs off with "Vive La France." "He's an American," corrects one of the other captains, misinterpreting (like the Britisher) the joke; to which the first captain replies (like Henry posing to the Britisher): "I thought you said he was a Frenchman. He talks French" (64). Yet another early scene at which Henry translates for Rinaldi has the Italian claiming "But Scotland is England" (21) and the Scot Ferguson claiming "We do not like the English" before explaining to Rinaldi why she does like Catherine Barkley despite the fact that she is English. Ferguson's admonitory "You mustn't take everything so literally" could stand as epigraph to the many early comic scenes of cultural clash and misinterpretation— particularly because it seems evident that *Ferguson* takes Rinaldi's joke too literally, unable, like the Britisher and the other captain, to see through the masquerade.

As the twinned themes of love and war in the novel promise, Ferguson's words also apply to Henry's relationship to Catherine Barkley, which, early in the novel, seems composed almost entirely of masquerades: Henry seeing his conquest of Barkley "all ahead like the moves in a chess game" (26), or thinking that she might pretend that he is "her boy that was killed" (40), or playing the "rotten game" (32) of saying he loves her, which she requires and he supplies. The narrative marks the "little show" of his protestations of love in overtly dramatic terms: Barkley scripts Henry's responses ("Say, 'I've come back to Catherine in the night'" [31]; "You did say you loved me, didn't you?") and later reveals she has been aware of the "show" all along. For his

5. Earl Rovit and Gerry Brenner, *Ernest Hemingway* (Boston: Twayne, 1986), 84.

part, Henry is conscious that "This was a game" (32). In one sense, one might expect nothing else of Barkley and Henry. Having lost her first love to the war and realized the folly of propriety (he "could have had anything he wanted if I would have known" [19]), Barkley is disposed to enter precipitately into a relationship with Henry; and, for his part, he cynically thinks, Catherine is better than "going every evening to the house for officers where the girls climbed all over you" (31). The "show" does not exactly assert the fakery of their relationship; it illuminates the early stages of a relationship that, under the impress of war, must develop too rapidly to be anything but self-conscious role-playing.[6]

Nonetheless, the early scenes of *A Farewell to Arms* demonstrate that Henry's pose as a "bloody hero" after his wounding is no isolated incident; it is part of a near epidemic of posings, self-conscious self-dramatizations, and counterfeit identities. The environment of war alienates the normally invisible and imperturbable conventionality of things.[7] It gives rise to all manner of linguistic and cultural confusions and makes those confusions susceptible to theatricalization ("Viva la France!"). And, as Gerry Brenner writes neatly, the "military landscape abounds in irrationality."[8] Its rigidly literal rules (salute, wear helmets, carry a pistol) collide with brute reality, appearing humiliatingly to be little more than a useless show. Nothing, as Ferguson warns, can be taken literally, least of all the guidelines devised by the war machine to further its course. In all cases, supposedly stable categories of definition—identity, nationality, men and women in love, manly heroism—are revealed to be gestic. In this sense, war itself is not theatrical; but its disruptions make theater of human relationships by removing the security of conventional social arrangements. It is the *Verfremdungseffekt* par excellence.

One could of course argue that Henry's early masquerades say less about

6. As Ernest Lockridge argues in a slightly different way: "Motivated by the agonizing grief and loss that she still feels after a year of mourning, Catherine Barkley is acting out . . . a one-sided, therapeutic game of 'pretend.'" "Faithful in Her Fashion: Catherine Barkley, the Invisible Hemingway Heroine," *Journal of Narrative Technique* 18, no. 2 (spring 1988): 173.

7. Robert E. Gajdusek agrees, arguing that: "In war, the inability to maintain identity, thus losing integrity, is studied as the cost of disguise, desertion . . . the casting off of significant duties, roles, and established definitions." "*A Farewell to Arms:* The Psychodynamics of Integrity," *The Hemingway Review* 9, no. 1 (fall 1989): 28.

8. Gerry Brenner, *Concealments in Hemingway's Works* (Columbus: Ohio State University Press, 1983), 29.

the theatrical effects of war than about his immature perceptions of warfare and human relationships. After all, the novel opens on what Henry calls a "picturesque front" (20) where there is "no work" (20) for the nurses and where the Austrians barely shell the town. Its picturesqueness does not last long. The steel helmet, "bloody theatrical" in Gorizia, presumably saves his life during the shell burst (his skull is nearly fractured as it is); and during the retreat from Caporetto he does indeed become a "gunman" with a pistol, shooting down a deserter. Moreover, the comic masquerades surrounding issues of nationality and language turn deadly serious when he is apprehended at the bridge over the Tagliamento and an officer notes that he "speaks Italian with an accent" (238). To the battle police, Henry thinks, "I was obviously a German in Italian uniform" (240). Having escaped and thought "clearly and coldly" (247) about his plight, Henry reaches what seems a major turning point in the novel: the moment when he realizes that "it was not my show any more" (248). The metaphor indicates his determination not to attend the "Show" again as well as his rejection of the "outward forms" (248) of the war, like the stars of rank he removes from his uniform. And it indicates his determination to put an end to the masquerades that characterize his initial response to the war and to Catherine. His relationship to Catherine Barkley, indeed, would seem the main beneficiary of this straightforwardness, unless we date a new honesty in their relationship to Barkley's earlier arrival at Henry's hospital room: "When I saw her I was in love with her. Everything turned over inside of me" (98). As Frederic J. Svoboda remarks, the moment potentially marks the emergence of a "new seriousness" in the novel.[9]

This interpretation of Henry's diminishing penchant for masquerade corresponds to a time-honored way of reading the novel, which holds that the narrative traces his development from callow youth to a man mature in the ways of love and war. The "initiation of Frederic Henry comes gradually," Ray B. West argues. Benson agrees, writing that Hemingway's male characters are usually "developing characters" and that by the end of the novel Henry has "learned to love," though he will also have to learn how to lose that love. In a similar vein, J. Bakker argues in speaking of Henry that a "Man gains wisdom in defeat." And James F. Light writes of an early "naivete that Lt. Henry

9. Frederic J. Svoboda, "The Great Themes in Hemingway: Love, War, Wilderness, and Loss," *A Historical Guide to Ernest Hemingway,* ed. Linda Wagner-Martin (Oxford: Oxford University Press, 2000), 161.

must—and does—lose."[10] In terms of these readings, we could not argue that the war's disruptions *force* humans into masquerade. Rather, it seems as though Henry either initially misinterprets the true nature of war (its bloody theatricality turning out to be merely bloody) or must learn to pursue an authentically nontheatrical life of his own despite the propensity of war to transform the human condition into a cruel jest/gest.

Even the most sanguine interpretations of Frederic Henry have had to observe at least some of the marks of war upon him: his multiple defeats, the atmosphere of loneliness and loss, his shell-shock, his occasional callousness. But critical accounts that emphasize his education and gradually emerging determination to forge an authentic way of life have given rise to a particularly powerful construction of American masculinity. For though Henry is physically and psychically damaged, and therefore potentially a seriously disabled spokesman for masculine values, it has always been possible to recuperate them on the basis of his representativeness. As Philip Young has argued, Henry is a "man who stands for many men. Thus it is that when historians of various kinds epitomize the temper of the American twenties and a reason for it the adventures of that lieutenant come also invariably to mind." In fact Henry's story, according to Ray B. West, is a "parable of twentieth-century man's disgust and disillusionment at the failure of civilization."[11] Whatever

10. Ray B. West, "*A Farewell to Arms,*" *The Art of Modern Fiction,* ed. Ray B. West and Robert W. Stallman (New York: Holt, Rinehart, and Winston, 1949), 632; Benson, 82, 112; J. Bakker, *Ernest Hemingway: The Artist as Man of Action* (Assen, Netherlands: Van Gorcum, 1972), 96; James F. Light, "The Religion of Death in *A Farewell to Arms,*" *Modern Fiction Studies* 7 (summer 1961): 170. Robert W. Lewis also writes that Henry has "undergone an initiatory and learning experience that he is now ready to interpret." For Edgar Johnson, the war forces Henry to shuck off his rejection of society and responsibility and accept a "vision of cosmic cruelty." John Killinger, though accepting the existential bleakness of the novel, feels that by the end of the novel "death means rebirth for the existentialist hero." James Phelan, too, argues that though the "world has destroyed [Henry's] life by destroying Catherine," Henry's final mature voice and action, developing over the course of the novel, are "controlled and dignified." Robert W. Lewis, *Hemingway on Love* (Austin: University of Texas Press, 1965), 39; Edgar Johnson, "Farewell the Separate Peace," in ed. McCaffery, 142; John Killinger, *Hemingway and the Dead Gods* (Lexington: University of Kentucky Press, 1960), 47; James Phelan, "The Concept of Voice, the Voices of Frederic Henry, and the Structure of *A Farewell to Arms,*" in *Hemingway: Essays of Reassessment,* ed. Frank Scafella (New York: Oxford University Press, 1991), 229.

11. Young, 62; West, 622.

Henry's failings as a man, then, they could always be masked by his metaphoric struggles on behalf of Man.

The power of such a strategy depends in part on the early proclivity of literary historians to characterize the historical and cultural temper of "lost generation" modernism in terms of the First World War and its aftermath—and thus to read constructions of gender in the context of a sociopolitical event that by definition seemed to belong to a male order of experience. In *The Twenties,* Hoffman does begin his chapter on *Sun* by citing the war novels of Willa Cather, Edith Wharton, and Dorothy Canfield. But they are included to demonstrate the oversimplicity of a female response, for "non-participants, women for the most part . . . saw the issues of the war much more simply (and therefore more 'clearly') than did the writers of the so-called war generation." Compared to the young men who were "very close to, or right in, the thick of the fighting," these novelists' experience could only be "secondhand"—though at this point, to be accurate, it is male *experience* rather than *maleness* as such that dictates literary value.[12] Hoffman goes on to argue, however, that the "postwar American" is "abnormally sensitive to a form of experience that may best be described by the term 'violation'" and that "war literature" was defined by themes like "the war as a monstrous hoax" and "the war as a means of testing the true nature of men and of reclassifying them morally." At a stroke, Hoffman erases putative distinctions between typical male and female experiences of the war in favor of a "postwar American" whose "war literature" must exclude that of the female novelists.[13] Hemingway's fascination with "testing the true nature of men" thus becomes universalized. The idea is not simply the obsession of a wounded man; it places him among those who—unlike Hoffman's "Miss Cather"—truly "faced the present."[14]

For scholars who wrote history in terms of the front-line (and thus male) experience of death and disillusionment, an entire aesthetic code could be seen to derive from those principles. As Malcolm Cowley remarks, war—or at least the "revolt against big words and noble sentiments" in the war—helped to "shape the prose style of a generation."[15] What Cowley put so simply in his powerfully hagiographic style, dozens of other canon-makers ex-

12. Hoffman, 68, 72, 70.
13. Ibid., 77
14. Ibid., 71.
15. Cowley, *Second Flowering,* 16, 17.

pounded in more complex formulations. The war forced (male) writers to value simple, plain language over the inflated rhetoric of propaganda machines;[16] to value tight-lipped endurance amid a landscape of mechanized slaughter;[17] and to find an aesthetic suited to expressing a profound sense of exhaustion, brutality, and disillusionment.[18] The principles Hemingway expressed in *Death in the Afternoon* were thus easily associated with a tight-lipped response to the war and to the "exhaustion" of a postwar "lost generation." The discipline of an aestheticized emotional restraint—displacement of emotion into action, putting down only what really happened, questing for a near-unattainable "real thing"—seemed most appropriate to a situation where the conditions of modernity were brutalizing language, emotion, and identity.

This reading of history and of modernist aesthetics was clearly a deeply gendered response. Its gendered nature could also be at once assumed and dismissed: the front-line experience of war was distinctively male but representative of the conditions of modernity. This sleight-of-hand maneuver had profound consequences. Male experience mattered not in and of itself but because history, if it was to speak to all people, seemed to require the mediation of men who had witnessed its terrors. A potentially gendered response (particular, that is, to certain men) had to be raised into the generally human, and the historical experience of men placed on an ahistorical footing. Men were indeed constructed by their historical circumstances as they searched for solutions to an overwhelmingly brutal world, literary historians held, and it is on that basis that modernist aesthetics could be read as speaking to and for the modern world. But of necessity the homology between a modernist aesthetic and male experience erased the particularity of the represented experience of men. On this basis, Frederic Henry's failings—his various masquerades, for instance—could be both admitted and comfortably overlooked. It was men's *representativeness* and not the representation of *men* that seemed crucial to discovering the essence of the early twentieth century.

16. See, for instance, Cowley and Stanley Cooperman, *World War 1 and the American Novel* (Baltimore: Johns Hopkins, 1967).

17. See, for instance, Alfred Kazin, *On Native Grounds* (Garden City, N.Y.: Doubleday, 1956), 253.

18. See, for instance, Mark Schorer, "The Background of a Style," *Kenyon Review* 3 (winter 1941): 103; Kazin, 253; Marcus Cunliffe, *The Literature of the United States* (London: Penguin, 1954), 239–93.

In the later twentieth century, however, readers have been increasingly skeptical of claims that Frederic Henry attains (or is meant to be shown as attaining) a newly mature code of conduct or enlightened perspective on a shattered world, putting in question, as they have done so, his status as representative Man. The narrative, as Michael Reynolds writes dryly, "does not reflect well on the displaced American." Brian Way argues that he remains "self-indulgent or self-pitying," Svoboda that he is "immature, indeed babyish," Broer that he is as "emotionally disabled" as all early Hemingway heroes. Moreover, as Broer also points out, the "notion of role-playing and false identity is one consistently associated with Frederic." Peter Messent has argued a similar point much more stringently, noting that the "masquerade motif" continues, and in fact intensifies, through the later stages of the novel.[19] The donning of civilian clothes marks a particularly strong reversion to earlier scenes of masquerade: "In civilian clothes I felt a masquerader. I had been in uniform a long time and I missed the feeling of being held by your clothes" (260). Messent comments: "If his uniform gives him a provisional but thoroughly unconvincing identity, once it is removed his self apparently loses rather than gains shape. . . . Instead of the revelation of this self's 'essence,' just another false front appears. The stripping-off of uniform reveals a masquerade self not a 'real' one."[20] And subsequent scenes keep revealing further masquerade selves: the "comic opera" (304) of the arrest in Switzerland; Henry and Barkley pretending to be cousins and then man and wife; Henry's beard making him look like a woodcutter (323) and a "fake doctor" (340).

Interpretations like these, refuting any sense that Henry becomes a more authentic man and lover, or simply a sadder and more enlightened person, insist that Henry must be construed as a masquerader to the bitter end. But to what purpose? Messent's conclusion that these shifting articulations of identity indicate the "vulnerability of the self" is certainly a valid one, and it aligns him with the many critics who have looked to the First World War as one of the primary causes of a decentered and destabilized masculine self.[21] And it is possible to read Henry's final masquerades as mere confirmation

19. Michael Reynolds, "*A Farewell to Arms*: Doctors in the House of Love," in *The Cambridge Companion to Hemingway,* ed. Scott Donaldson (Cambridge: Cambridge University Press, 1996), 124; Brian Way, "Hemingway the Intellectual: A Version of Modernism," in ed. Lee, 165; Svoboda, 162; Broer, 42, 58; Messent, 60.

20. Messent, 60.

21. Ibid., 61.

that these isolated individuals, Catherine and Frederic, are still very much trapped within the logic of a "theater of war." The death of Catherine's first love at the Somme leads to their initial love-charades and ultimately to the unmarried haste with which she sleeps with the wounded Henry and thus to the various enforced poses (as skiers, tourists, cousins, man and wife) he and Barkley must enact in Switzerland. And there is a powerful sense that Henry's confession "In civilian clothes I felt a masquerader" haunts the end of the novel, for he is still liable to be shot as a deserting soldier. To the Italian authorities, in other words, he *remains* a soldier masquerading as a civilian, not a civilian who has shucked off the masquerade of being a soldier. In this reading, masquerade simply describes the proliferating disruptions occasioned by war, even when its victims operate under the auspices of the "separate peace" they think they have found in Switzerland.

But there are problems with holding the war causally responsible for the novel's masquerades. For one thing, as many commentators have pointed out, Catherine Barkley's and the baby's deaths speak to biological imperatives (narrow hips and a choking umbilical cord) rather than the war. Though the timing of their deaths depends on the haste with which Barkley and Henry enter into a relationship, and though the operating theater in the novel's final scenes bears a metaphoric relationship to earlier war scenes, the deaths seem to stand outside the purview of the war-world itself. The hospital world of the novel that Michael Reynolds describes in a recent essay seems to stand for the human condition, not the sickness of war, even though the "drive to propagate in the close proximity of death [is] played out against the backdrop of ritual violence."[22] Indeed, the "bright small amphitheatre of the operating room" (346) where three nurses watch the caesarean from the gallery (and try to get Henry to watch), where a life-and-death struggle is played out against the audience's levity ("We're just in time. Aren't we lucky?"), could be taken instead as the novel's fundamental metaphoric staging ground. In this case, the drama of the operating theater bespeaks the human condition, and its meanings underpin the various theaters of war and human masquerades narratively preceding it. This kind of theater is not gestic; it dramatizes the way masks come off as death takes center stage.

If so, it is a mode of drama that Henry neither wants to watch nor performs in his own life. As we saw earlier, Henry's first stint in the operating

22. Reynolds, "Doctors in the House of Love," 124.

room transformed it into gest as he learned appropriate manly roles and became the center of swirling confusions about identity and nationality. The final death scenes, moreover, show a character increasingly committed, in his tough taciturnity, to a narrow but very potent cultural code of emotional restraint. Apart from some cool reflections on death ("You died. You did not know what it was about" [350]) and one passionate outburst ("Oh, God, please don't let her die" [353]), Henry retains a scrupulous hold on his emotions. The ending of the novel has him saying, famously, "I do not want to talk about it." One can of course read between the lines to the turmoil he feels he must control. But the point is that our very need to read between the lines compels us to recognize his desperate urge to complete the mask he now inhabits. His detailed descriptions of his meals (the "waiter brought a dish of sauerkraut with a slice of ham over the top and a sausage buried in the hot wine-soaked cabbage" [340]); his stoic acceptance of his son's death ("'So he's dead'" [349]); and even momentary glimpses of fear ("I was afraid of the numbers above two" [345])—all remind us of the effort that is going into generating his masquerade. But how far does the masquerade extend? Henry's tight hold on his emotional responses is powerful enough that some critics have argued that he is actually glad that Catherine Barkley dies. Should we then read "Oh, God, please don't let her die" as the authentic Frederic Henry behind the culturally appropriate mask—a last glimpse, perhaps, as the mask closes around him—or as the role that the more callous Henry simply feels he should try out?

Unlike Barkley, Frederic Henry demonstrates throughout a psychological and cultural rather than a biological determination of self. The wounds to his body demand appropriate role-playing, not the desperate applications of gas that Catherine demands and he administers in order to try to mask her real, perfectly nontheatricalized suffering. Indeed, the biological determinism she displays motivates him, I have argued, into shaping the mask of tough taciturnity that defines his identity at the end. Henry's sense of theater operates quite differently from Barkley's; and she therefore cannot be held to speak for the human condition in some "all the world's an operating theater" motif. (Nor does Barkley necessarily speak for all women, as if she represents some conventional sense of women being trapped by their own female bodies.) We can never be sure, in other words, when Henry's masks are off. His masks define him. And perhaps the best evidence is the aspect of his career that has done most to convince critics that he is the victim of the war or only finds himself after the war: the separate peace that transforms his masquerade as soldier to his role as civilian. There is a sense (the Italian authorities' sense), as I suggested above, in which Henry remains a soldier masquerading as a civilian after his famous plunge into the Tagliamento. But there is a more important sense in which the novel places in question the very categories of soldier and civilian as essential, enduring descriptions of male identity. Henry, for instance, acquires the characteristics of soldiering and being a civilian with equal awkwardness: early on he finds the salutes and military gear theatrical; and after his escape from the army, his first attempt to change into a civilian fails, as the proprietor of a wine shop tells him: "Do not go about with that coat. . . . On the sleeves it shows very plainly where the stars have been cut away" (255). Having entered into another masquerade on the train to Stresa (by wearing his friend Simmons's clothes), Henry states how much he feels the "masquerader" (260). But the aviators on the train "were very scornful of a civilian my age."

The point is not so much that clothes define the man or even that the removal of each "uniform" reveals yet another facade (as Messent suggests), but that the novel shows all categorical definitions of Henry's identity to be thoroughly contextual. Markers of identity such as the pistol, salutes, military uniforms, and Simmons's clothes signify who Henry is with certainty—during the moment of performance. On the train to Stresa, as far as the Italian authorities are concerned, Henry really is a deserter; to the aviators, Henry really is a civilian; to the questioners on the banks of the Tagliamento, he really is a traitor; to Barkley's hairdresser, she and Henry really are married. It is because performances of identity are always being taken as real that some masquerades are never uncovered (as when the Britisher or the medical captain fail to "get the joke") and some masquerades seem indistinguishable from the real (can we really tell when Henry first loves, or if he ever does love, Catherine Barkley?). And it is for the same reason that masquerades are consequential (Henry could be shot if discovered as a deserter in Italy and can really be safe as a tourist in Switzerland). But their very consequentiality—their having real effects in the real world—only demonstrates the power of social codes functioning through the scenes of their performance. The question, then, of whether Henry is a deserter or a civilian at the end is undecidable because all categories of identity are performative and locked into their dramatic context; and to decide that Henry is, say, still "really" a soldier/deserter is merely to step into the logic of the novel whereby performances are taken as real.

By the same token, we cannot say that the war causes Henry's masquerades: since his civilian and his military identities are constructed in the same way, we have no grounds for distinguishing between a theater of war provoking civilian masquerades on the one hand, and war-identities simply taking on a masquerade-function already deeply embedded in civilian society on the other. It is not surprising, then, that Henry's attempt to display a heroic toughness after his wounding ("I'm all right") puts us in mind of the taciturn role he perfects after Catherine Barkley's death ("I do not want to talk about it") while confounding any attempt to read one as the cause of the other. Because Henry's is a retrospective narration—its opening scenes written after Barkley's death—we can only speculate how we are meant to interpret his tough taciturnity. Does his response to her death dominate the narrative that chronologically follows this event, and thus frame the scene of his wounding? Or does narrative causality take precedence, so that the appropriately heroic role and tone he tries to attain after his wounding frames his response to her death? Does the physical wounding frame the psychic wounding, or vice versa? These questions have to be unanswerable. But the questions also imply misleadingly that one or more actual events in his life motivate Henry's masquerades; his masquerades, that is, are unique to him and his situation. In fact, as the scenes following his wounding suggest, Henry's main concern is the performance of appropriate social roles dominated by a cultural ethos of masculine emotional restraint. In this sense, all scenes, military and civilian, are consistent with the theaters of manhood Hemingway depicts in other works.

In the final scenes of the novel, Catherine Barkley calls for a (gas) mask: to keep up the illusion that she is a "good wife and [will] have this child without any foolishness" (336); and to prevent herself from "going all to pieces" (344), thereby maintaining a sense of a coherent self in the face of overwhelming pain. The mask, as she says on numerous occasions, "doesn't work at all." In one of the ironic confusions *A Farewell to Arms* constantly generates, this scene of an English woman dying is anticipated early in the novel by Henry's new gas mask, his "real mask" (specified as English), and which does seem to work, at least metaphorically, through the endless masquerades that distinguish his career. But the notion of a "real mask" captures the unsettling implications of this novel's theater of war. Do Henry's masks mask the real horror (of war, of life) but suggest some authentic man beneath—one, say, with the insight to write this narrative? Or do his masks define the real Henry, so that we should simply recognize the power of performances to constitute a sense of solid, immutable identities? Perhaps we cannot decide the issue. But we cannot decide the issue because Henry's narrative offers too many competing possibilities—the man who never learns to leave his masks behind, the man who learns to use his masks successfully, the man who learns to throw off his masks—for us to identify the essential Frederic Henry. The narrative— Henry's narrative—is the "real mask," promising a revelation of masculine identity that, when it comes, seems to be composed of a formidable array of still more masks.

WRITING THE "GLORIOUS DISCIPLINE OF INDISCIPLINE": PANOPTIC GAZE AND CAVE THEATER IN *FOR WHOM THE BELL TOLLS*

Few of the carefully detailed instruments of war in *For Whom the Bell Tolls* play a more intricate role in the novel than Robert Jordan's watch; and few allow us to tap more readily into the novel's profound concern with "watching" and masculinity. "What a watch," exclaims Rafael upon receiving it from Jordan: "Look at what complications. Such a watch should be able to read and write. Look at what complications of numbers. It's a watch to end watches."[23] The watch's ubiquitous presence serves to remind Jordan (and us) of the urgent passing of time in a novel obsessed with temporality, whose protagonist counts the hours remaining until the "show" ("Twenty-four hours in a day would be threescore and twelve for the three full days" [166]) and spends time trying to slow the luminous hands on the watch dial (378). But the watch's complications ramify through the novel. Like some gypsy Walter Benjamin entranced by a store-display of the latest consumer items, Rafael draws attention to the watch's fetishistic attributes. Its "complications of numbers" attest to a world outside Rafael's ken, though his wry awe and bemusement (and perhaps amusement) suggest equally an education of the gaze. Rafael pays no attention to market value. He marvels instead at what the watch represents to the man who owns it: complicated systems for seeing time, waging war, and even, since such a watch "should be able to read and write," for a new construction of identity. The watch can simply be enjoyed

23. Ernest Hemingway, *For Whom the Bell Tolls* (New York: Scribner's, 1940), 79. This work will hereinafter be cited parenthetically by page number in the text.

for its aesthetic qualities, but it also implies a new and unfamiliar scopic regime based on "watching."

When Jordan asks Rafael to "tell time" (79), the gypsy responds facetiously with a little narrative organized around essential bodily functions: "Twelve o'clock mid-day. Hunger. Twelve o'clock midnight. Sleep. Six o'clock in the morning, hunger. Six o'clock at night, drunk." But Jordan has in mind a much more complicated extension of the human sensorium in asking Rafael to "See at what intervals the guard is relieved at that bridge." The loan of the watch expedites a strange crossing of spatial and temporal coordinates, for Rafael should now be able to spatialize time (watch time passing) and make space temporal (measure the duration of what he sees). He should be able to "See . . . intervals," a usage that confuses Rafael ("Intervals?"), in part because the term refers equivocally to an operation that one can time as "space-between" or measure as "time-between." Jordan manages this feat: when fifteen planes fly over, he "pushed the knob that set the second hand to clicking" and begins to collate time elapsed with distance traveled (he "looked at his watch. By now they should be over the lines" [76]). Jordan even accompanies the ticking of his watch with an unfolding plane's-eye panorama of Spain: "Five minutes would carry them there [to the lines]. By now they're well beyond the pass with Castile all yellow and tawny beneath them now in the morning, the yellow crossed by white roads and spotted with the small villages and the shadows of the Heinkels moving over the land as the shadows of sharks pass over a sandy floor of the ocean."

A response to Pilar's question "What do you do with the watch?" could then take many forms. Jordan simultaneously looks at his watch and watches from the cockpit of the Heinkel bombers; he enters the aesthetic domain of colorful images and comprehends the predatory power of the machines. His enhanced chrono-vision even allows him to inhabit land, air, and sea. Though Rafael does not match Jordan's capabilities, his brief possession of the watch has intriguing effects. In testimony to a new organization of space-time, Rafael returns the watch amidst a telling transformation of metaphors. He refers to Jordan's watch as a "chronometer" (190), while Jordan's "intervals" have become, in more usual parlance, a "watch." "I stayed until they changed the watch," Rafael says, defining a period of watching that, with the aid of Jordan's watch, can now be articulated in precise temporal terms: "It was changed at noon and at six." By intensifying his powers of vision, Rafael's "watching" grants him a new ability to articulate and record the passage of time; to intervene in the ceaseless flow of seconds by marking intervals; and to penetrate the visual and temporal logic of the enemy. In the hands of his mentor, Jordan, such information allows a crucial dovetailing of guerrilla-time and fascist-time; his plan must account for and step inside the logic of the fascists' watch-maneuvers if it is to succeed.

In point of fact, Jordan does not need his watch to organize the attack on the bridge, which is synchronized with the sound of the Republic's bombardment. But Jordan's fascination with the illuminated dial marks a profound shift in the experience and manipulation of space-time. The partisans know night time by sunset, dawn, and the passage of moon or stars (or, as Rafael says, by sleep and hunger and drunkenness); time is subject to vision, but one is aware of time passing rather than *the* time. One can only know one's general location within an amorphous interval between the ambiguous markers of light and dark. Watch-time imposes a logic of near-endless subdivision and coordination within a continuum of discrete moments that are themselves invisible. Time as structure becomes visible to an internal eye; the watch is only an outward manifestation of an internal shift in logic. Even without a watch one could conceivably know that it was 2:50 A.M. from "how low the stars had swung." But one could only do so, or even wish to do so, by understanding the logic of time as a system divorced from the watching of cosmic motions (so that time can measure anything). The corollary is that watch-time reconstructs the act of watching. Watching time makes it possible to carry out precisely coordinated military maneuvers overnight. Golz surveys the forthcoming battlefield (429) at the same moment that Jordan observes the sentry through his field-glasses (433); and Golz, like Jordan, is aware of the panoply of forces at his command both within and without his actual field of vision. It is their misfortune that the fascists comprehend and indeed master the same internal logic.

Rafael might well joke that Robert Jordan's watch should be able to read and write, for it denotes a mastery of the visual field that philosophers and historians identify most clearly with yearnings toward a literate and rational comprehension of social, geographical, and scientific spaces during the Enlightenment. The Enlightenment thus serves as a kind of master trope for what Martin Jay has called the "Empire of the Gaze": the fascination with the ability of the gaze to survey, organize, discipline, and master the entire terrain of modernity. Jay, like many other writers on the hegemony of vision, is strongly critical of the Western ideal of the detached, disinterested observer whose all-seeing eye dominates the visual and epistemological field. One of its severest critics is Michel Foucault, whose account of Jeremy Bentham's Panopticon, which "provided a formula applicable to many domains, the formula of 'power through transparency,' subjection by 'illumination,'" creates what Foucault calls a "space of exact legibility" within which culture and the human subject is reconstructed according to the disciplinary gaze.[24]

These critiques of the privileged but potentially despotic gaze are firmly anchored to a larger critique of masculine vision and authority. David Michael Levin argues that the "vision which dominates our ocular culture is haunted by the specters of patriarchal rule: the rule of the masculine is both cause and effect of an ocularcentrism which privileges the autonomy-drive of vision and rewards its aggressiveness, its hunger for control." Luce Irigaray in *Speculum of the Other Woman* agrees, tracing back the various forms of masculine scopic power to Plato's allegory of the cave in the *Republic*. That master-parable of humans emerging into the Father-Sun of Reason grounds, in Andrea Nye's words, the "speculative constructions of metaphysics as well as the spectacular skills of technical science." For Nye, the hidden (and terrifying) burden of Plato's *Republic* is the alliance it forges, at the genesis of Western metaphysics, between vision and military science. Plato's soldier-philosopher weds a fantasy of privileged cognition (the all-seeing consciousness) to the gaze of the male military master. The "metaphysician's eye," in fact, "is a refinement of the general's eye: abstract, all-encompassing, unemotional, pitiless."[25] Henceforth, according to Nye, a (masculine) metaphysics of presence is mediated by military and imperial power, just as Western military might is rooted in the urge of political, psychic, and aesthetic economies to subject everything to the disciplinary and imperial eye. Late-twentieth-century military technologies have indeed multiply enhanced the visionary capabilities of the human eye. Satellite surveillance and computer-and-laser-guided bombs are just two of the mechanisms whereby the human eye exfoliates

24. Martin Jay, "In the Empire of the Gaze," in *Foucault: A Critical Reader*, ed. David Couzens Hoy (Oxford: Basil Blackwell, 1986), 175; Michel Foucault, "The Eye of Power," in *Power/Knowledge: Selected Interviews and Other Writings 1972–1977*, trans. Colin Gordon et al. (New York: Pantheon Books, 1980), 153–54.

25. David Michael Levin, "Decline and Fall: Ocularcentrism in Heidegger's Reading of the History of Metaphysics," in *Modernity and the Hegemony of Vision*, ed. David Michael Levin (Berkeley: University of California Press, 1993), 205; Andrea Nye, "Assisting at the Birth and Death of Philosophic Vision," in ed. Levin, 364, 373.

through virtual electronic circuits, monitoring multiple forces, trajectories, and images with the kind of thoroughness and sophistication Plato's philosopher-king could only intuit. The military dream of absolute surveillance thus brings to a focus in modernity the prophetic gaze of antiquity: Plato's detached observer emerges in the military eye invisible behind its electronic outriders, while the republic subject to the philosopher's eye transforms into a global Panopticon overseen by disciplinary formations. The male philosopher's eye embeds itself within a formidable will to power.

Of all Hemingway's books, *For Whom the Bell Tolls* shows the most concern with the exercise of scopic regimes of power. The novel portrays in the figure of Robert Jordan a prototypical master of the disciplinary gaze, whose watch evidences the kind of expert supervision men need in order to kill well. It might be argued, of course, that the partisans (and the Republicans) are in desperate need of the kind of ordering and controlling gaze Robert Jordan offers. The Republicans suffer, in Jordan's neat phrase, from the "glorious discipline of indiscipline" (370). Others agree. Trying to strengthen his resolve to stand watch in the freezing cold, Anselmo tells himself that "All through this war we have suffered from a lack of discipline and from the disobeying of orders" (192). Early in the war at Segovia, Anselmo says, the Republicans "did not truly understand what we were doing, nor how it should be done" (42). Jordan supplies the necessary corrective instruction. After shooting the cavalryman, Jordan gives Agustín an important lesson in positioning the machine gun to create an appropriate killing field, commenting "You see? From there it was useless. . . . See? Look now. All that is dominated" (272). Later, he orders the construction of a "good blind" for the gun and "showed them [Primitivo and Agustín] where to place a man high in the rocks to the right where he could see all the country below" (276). It would seem that Jordan's task is necessarily to educate the gaze of these cave-dwelling partisans if the bridge is to be blown and the country "dominated." In a war where even "conscientious objectors weren't exempted. . . . No one was exempted. It came to one and all alike" (276), and where atrocities are a regular part of military campaigns, such knowledge can be crucial to the survival not only of the partisans and the Republic but even, if we are to believe Jordan's hyperbole, the "future of the human race" (43).

Yet one could also take Hemingway to task for indulging fantasies of male power and surveillance that only masquerade as historical necessity. One trend of Hemingway criticism has always condemned what Richard B. Hovey terms Hemingway's fascination with the death-urge (Thanatos). Hovey, Broer, and Bakker are among many who gauge the value of Hemingway's work in terms of the success of his struggle against his obsession with killing and with his "mystique of death."[26] Though Robert Jordan is usually exempted because of the (putatively) moral essence of his work, it might be argued that he is also, as Michael Reynolds puts it in an article on Hemingway's debt to the popular western, one of the "warriors, gunmen, enforcers, men with the abilities to kill dispassionately" who people his later works. Jordan's defense of killing as a means to an end, his cool competence, his fascination with efficient watching and killing at a distance, his acknowledgment that he enjoys killing (287), his ability to separate emotional attachments from the demands of his task, all depict a figure who is, in Pilar's words, a "very cold boy" (91). And perhaps more than that: Bruce Henricksen, noting that the "values implied in the subtext [of *In Our Time*'s bullfighting vignettes] have disturbing affinities with fascist fantasies," argues that in general "Hemingway's texts . . . wed killing (not always unconsciously) to aesthetics and creativity." Henricksen's article, which suggests that Hemingway's modernist aesthetic actually "functions as an alibi for the violence that is being celebrated" is pertinent to *Bell* insofar as its plot depends on a logic of surveillance and killing that its moral register seems to justify.[27] The novel, a critical reading might hold, normalizes the exchange of vision for supervision by making the latter seem a necessary part of everyday life behind enemy lines. It carefully disguises its fetish of militarism under the logic of moral necessity and, still more cleverly, inscribes it into a plot that results in noble failure. It performs the double task of exploring the guilty pleasures of militarism while ostensibly mourning the passing of brave fighters who not only suffer the exigencies of history (by giving and receiving death) but find glory thereby. Indeed, it might be argued that Jordan's death and the probable failure of Golz's offensive point up precisely what the Republic lacks: a truly efficient use of various technologies of dealing death. The novel's affinities with a fascist mas-

26. Richard B. Hovey, *Hemingway: The Inward Terrain* (Seattle: University of Washington Press, 1968), 105; see also Broer, 20–21, 84–87; Bakker, 154–69.

27. Michael Reynolds, "Hemingway's West: Another Country of the Heart," in *Blowing the Bridge: Essays on Hemingway and "For Whom the Bell Tolls,"* ed. Rena Sanderson (New York: Greenwood Press, 1992), 28; Bruce Henricksen, "The Bullfight Story and Critical Theory," in *Hemingway's Neglected Short Fiction: New Perspectives,* ed. Susan F. Beegel (Ann Arbor: UMI Research Press, 1989), 115, 116, 114.

culinity, in short, are mandated and justified by the supreme moral imperative of fighting fascism.

Another way of saying this is that *For Whom the Bell Tolls'* fascination with the will to power expressed in the supervisory gaze could be said to crush the gestic possibilities contained within the metaphor of a "theater of war." Whereas Frederic Henry's masquerades unsettled our sense of war as a test of true manhood, Robert Jordan's drive to watch, supervise, and dominate the country suggests a new and ominous panoptic space in which the directors control everything through their gunsights and other technologies of supervision, in which the "actors" are never aware of the watched space within which they move, and in which, under the scrutiny of anonymous eyes, there exists no mechanism for defamiliarizing or alienating actions from themselves. These forms of watching bestow a potentially God-like power on those who master the appropriate disciplines and technologies. And, to reverse Brecht, they transform men back into Man, though a Man now possessed of enormous scopic and military power within a fascist fantasy of total domination.

Yet *For Whom the Bell Tolls* also composes a powerful return to Hemingway's theaters of masculine representation. The many competitions between Jordan and Pablo to take center-stage among the partisans make for rich cave-theater; and the capable dramatic presence of Pilar within that theater extends the significance of "masculine" self-dramatization in ways that were only implied in *In Our Time*. Robert Jordan plays a significant role here insofar as he carries with him into the cave new techniques of disciplined supervision, only to find them useless on the stage of cave theater. These scenes are crucial to an understanding of Hemingway's work because they adumbrate a concept of masculinity that cannot simply be explained in terms of despotic gazing. In this sense, *For Whom the Bell Tolls* resists any straightforward connection between masculinity and fascism. If the most fervent criticisms of Hemingway's work—his defense of aggressive virility, his obsession with killing, his misogyny—can all be understood as criticisms of a displaced and fetishized militarism, cave theater tackles head-on the implications of the will to power expressed in the general's gaze, which, as Nye holds, becomes a master-trope of masculine, metaphysical, and perhaps even narrative supervision. This is not to say that cave theater succeeds. The novel is unabashedly pessimistic about the growing power of fascistic military supervision and struggles to negotiate the question of its relevance to the nascent republic. Cave theater might even be said to be a classic example of the "glorious discipline of indiscipline" that haunts the Republican cause. Nonetheless, the carnivalesque dramatizations of masculinity in the partisans' cave and the complex, ever-shifting questioning of gender roles to which they lead ultimately restore faith in the possibilities of gestic transformation—in the very possibilities of change for which the new republic ideally stands. The abstract and potentially supreme power of fascist supervision, however deeply imbued with male longings for an unending and immutable gaze, is a terror from which this novel recoils.

From the beginning of the novel, Robert Jordan demonstrates a penchant for theatricality. Knowing that Anselmo fears running from battles, Jordan assures the old man that he will receive the support of firm commands: "We will be together. . . . I will tell you what there is to do at all times" (43). "For us will be the bridge and the battle, should there be one," Jordan then announces, thinking that "saying it in the dark, he felt a little theatrical but it sounded well in Spanish." These statements, which follow immediately upon the neo-biblical rhetoric of "It will be written," and which are followed by profundities like "that bridge can be the point on which the future of the human race can turn," suggests the fragility of his attempts to bolster Anselmo's confidence. According to Jordan, Anselmo speaks "honestly and clearly and with no pose, neither the English pose of understatement nor any Latin bravado"; Jordan, clearly attuned to the subtleties of heroic posing, labels himself by contrast a "windy bastard." While it would not do to judge Jordan's character by a few sentences of the convoluted and often contradictory passage of his thoughts, his attitude toward Anselmo is quite in keeping with his attempts to test, evaluate, and master the partisans in the first hours of his arrival by transforming the cave and its environs into arenas of self-dramatization.

Even before the important confrontations between Jordan and Pablo in the cave, the novel suggestively probes that relationship between a theatrical representation of masculine prowess and the scopic regime inhabited by men under the conditions of modern warfare. Meeting for the first time, Jordan and Pablo begin to assess each other in a climate of mutual distrust, each determined to penetrate false appearances: Jordan does "not like the look of this man" (9) who is leader, while Pablo asks Jordan to "justify your identity." Both men then engage in a series of evaluatory tests that are importantly different in their methodology and consequences. Jordan, handing over his identification, observes the fact that Pablo "opened it, looked at it doubtfully and turned it in his hands," and notes "So he cannot read." Next inviting Pablo to look at the seal, Jordan again insists "Have you never seen it?" Fresh from his mapping and surveying of the territory, the American unsurprisingly extends to Pablo the same test of literate scrutiny and, finding the guerrilla leader wanting, adds that one seal is "S. I. M., the service of the military intelligence. The other is the General Staff." "Have you never seen it?" situates both men in a power game that is endlessly replayed in this novel, whereby men attempt to manipulate and dominate scenes of masculine representation. Pablo, Jordan implies, is not enough of a leader to interpret the signs that constitute "military intelligence," whose logic disseminates through the order of writing and through the written and signed order. Emphasizing that Pablo proves his "loyalty through . . . acts," Jordan forges his own alliance with the "intelligence" characteristic of military surveillance, discipline, and logocentrism. Jordan implies that his eye sees through and beyond Pablo's; and, since Anselmo watches this exchange, Jordan ensures that Pablo's seeing-deficit is seen to exist.

If Jordan stakes his authority on "military intelligence," Pablo tests Jordan's vision against what we might call "horse-sense" when he asks the American whether he "see[s] a defect" (13) in one of the horses. Jordan, who has already been "Sorting them out carefully with his eyes after he had seen them first together," realizes now that "his papers were being examined by the man who could not read." Subjecting the horses to a further scrutiny (he "watched the horses circle the corral, stood watching them a minute more, as they stood still"), Jordan shows himself capable of a sorting, marking, and ordering that does not arise out of or lead to a systematic and clinical knowledge. Jordan's interpretation here is emotive rather than detached (the "best horse . . . has a swelling on the upper part of the cannon bone that I do not like"), and communal rather than hierarchical (the horse's swelling "is nothing," Pablo adds to Jordan's diagnosis, "He knocked it three days ago"). Horse-sense, moreover, depends not on abstract diagnoses but on narratives remembered or imagined: the "hoof was like that when we took her," recalls Pablo, the horse could "break down if she travels over much hard ground," suggests Jordan. If Jordan typically favors the supervision required by "military intelligence," then, he also demonstrates his expertise in other forms of knowledge more traditionally and less systematically ordered. As important, he demonstrates his expertise in front of an audience composed of Pablo and Anselmo, the latter being sufficiently impressed, "seeing that Robert Jordan knew horses" (15), to speak his mind fully.

In these early scenes Jordan convincingly displays his mastery of military intelligence and horse-sense. But it is not surprising that Jordan, imbued with his faith in the disciplined gaze and inhabiting a military landscape of written orders, surveillance, and killing fields dominated through gunsights, should interpret Pablo's illiteracy as a profound deficit. Pablo, to Jordan, cannot properly "read" military situations; though Pablo has survived all his engage-ments and recognizes the dangers of the bridge-blowing, he has no compre-hension of the larger military picture visible to more inclusive and detached observers like Jordan or Golz. Yet the novel is equivocal about the respective merits of Pablo's and Jordan's performances. Pablo survives to dramatize himself once more as the leader of the partisans; and, as Jordan himself notes on several occasions, Pablo has a firmer understanding of the danger of this operation than any other partisan. (During the first confrontation in the cave, Pablo asks, "Am I the only one who sees the seriousness of this?" to which Jordan adds silently, "I believe so . . . Except me. You can see it and I can see it" [54]). In the matter of foresight Pablo, who at least contemplates the man-ner of the band's escape from the vicinity of the bridge, shows himself to be Jordan's equal and probably his superior. It is perhaps not so much Pablo's weakness (as Jordan claims) but the perception that the onetime scourge of the fascists is a "very strong man" (9) (as Anselmo notes) that informs Jor-dan's many attempts to out-perform Pablo in the cave.

Jordan enters the cave for the first time having provisionally scripted the scene to come and bearing stage props: cigarettes and, on second thought, the two packs of dynamite that metonymically attest to the power of the dyna-miter. The heavy packs replace the erstwhile leader's lost equipment—the "two stones" (194) of the castrated boar in Anselmo's image, the "lost eggs" (199) in Jordan's—and prepare us to read the performances in the cave spe-cifically as dramas of manhood-fashioning and masculine humiliation. From the moment Jordan enters the cave, he comprehends it as an arena within which he must assert his mastery over various glances. Reaching his hand am-biguously toward his hip pocket, and keeping his audience guessing as to whether he will produce his pistol, Jordan is aware of a complex interplay of looks: "Pablo watched him. He knew they were all watching him, too, but he watched only Pablo" (50). That need for a clear perception of his strategic position is established the moment Jordan enters the cave. He files away the various positions of the partisans in the cave, offering cigarettes to the three unknown members though he "was not looking at them yet" (49); concentrating on Pablo, however, he does not neglect to note that "one man took cigarettes and two did not." A little later, he decides that he "had better look at the other three and try to see where he stood," though he defers that action until he has mocked and provoked Pablo with his suggestive talk of bitter medicine (51). As that provocation implies, Jordan is acutely aware not only of the necessity for clear perception but of the power of being watched. Having asked for wine and received only Pablo's sullen "There is little left," Jordan at once attempts to sharpen his image of masculine authority by ordering "the girl" (Maria) to bring him water. Back in command, Jordan crafts the charged moment when he reaches for his flask (or pistol). Even the drawn-out ceremony of drinking absinthe, which Jordan informs Maria is "too strong" for her, and which Pablo and the rest of the partisans shun, is designed to leave the group with the impression that Jordan alone can face the "real absinthe."

Subsequent events, however, begin to demonstrate the flaws in Jordan's makeshift staging of his authority. When Jordan confesses to Rafael his idea to kill Pablo, Rafael replies, "Surely all could see that. Every one noted your preparations" (61). But what Rafael sees is subject to important differences of interpretation. For him, events were staged for the (failed) purpose of killing Pablo ("What do you think that all waited for? What do you think the woman sent the girl away for?"). For Pilar, in contrast, killing Pablo was "not necessary. I was watching thee. But thy judgment was good" (68). In different ways, both Pilar and Rafael are wrong. Pilar does not wait for Pablo's death, and she almost certainly sends Maria away not to incite violence but to protect Maria. Yet Jordan refrains from shooting Pablo not so much because of good judgment but, as he explains to Rafael, because he has insufficient information to gauge the effect of his actions: "I thought it might molest you others or the woman" (61). Assassinating Pablo secretly, Jordan tells Rafael, is not the way to "act for the cause"; but the preferred alternative, which is to kill Pablo by deliberately provoking him in public, fails because of Jordan's lack of knowledge of the dramatic context within which his actions are displayed and perceived. Both Pilar and Rafael during their respective conversations with Jordan call him "young" (61, 68), and it is thus not surprising that in between those conversations Jordan follows Pablo to the horses in the dark but cannot decide what to do. In contrast to Jordan's seemingly complete unmasking of Pablo's pretensions to manhood in the cave, Jordan's surveillance is now unable to penetrate the ethical and psychological complexities of the situation: he "sat watching him, trying to think his problem out clearly" (63). Though Jordan leaves the cave having replaced Pablo with trustworthy Pilar as titular head of the band, it cannot be said that Jordan succeeds in his ambition to script and direct the proceedings in the cave-arena. Indeed, at the crucial moment when Pablo passes command to Pilar, it is Pablo who brings to a crisis and seems to master the drama of glances: "Pablo looked at her and you could tell nothing of what he was thinking by his face. He looked at her quite deliberately and then he looked across the table at Robert Jordan. He looked at him a long time contemplatively and then he looked back at the woman. . . . [He was] looking the woman straight in the face and he was neither dominated by her nor seemed to be much affected by her" (57). For all Jordan's joke about "lost eggs," Pablo seems adept at watching from cover ("you could tell nothing of what he was thinking") and at comprehending the dramatic context within which various glances take on significance. Pablo, in fact, is more given than Jordan to a profound theatricalization of war. The killing of the fascists in the plaza, as recounted by Pilar, is a masterpiece of participatory theater within which Pablo plays the parts of actor and director interchangeably.[28] Blocking the streets "as though to organize the plaza for a *capea* [amateur bullfight]" (103), Pablo arranges the two lines of men with flails so that each must participate and each must watch others participating. Pilar's metaphors appropriately evoke the theatrical dimension of the scene: "[Pablo] placed them in two lines . . . as they stand in a city to watch the ending of a bicycle road race with just room for the cyclists to pass between, or as men stood to allow the passage of a holy image in a procession." In the spirit of carnivalesque overthrow that marks every moment of Pilar's narrative of the killings, she adds the perspective of the protagonists of Pablo's drama: "from the doorway of the *Ayuntamiento* [town hall], looking across the plaza, one coming out would see two solid lines of people waiting."

Though this "shameful . . . spectacle" (110) comes to a rowdy end with the killing of Don Anastasio, the massacre that follows demonstrates again the theatricality of what Pilar calls Pablo's "conception" (118). The scene in the

---

28. Lionel Trilling makes a similar argument in a critical register when he remarks of "good moments" like the massacre in the square that "one has the uneasy sense that they are rather too obviously 'performances.'" Lionel Trilling, "An American in Spain," in ed. Baker, *Ernest Hemingway,* 78.

town hall reveals at least a double drama. Inside, Pablo dramatizes his power over the fascists' lives by displaying first to the priest and then to Don Pepe the key that will unlock the door and allow the mob to enter. Like some devilish incarnation in a medieval mystery play perverting the scripts of sacred ritual, Pablo parodies the role of Saint Peter (holding the keys to life and death). Outside the hall, Pilar and the drunkard provide an audience both to the massacre and to Pablo's self-satisfied acting and stage-managing. Less saint than ruthless Hollywood director, Pablo, watched by Pilar, "sat in the big chair with his shotgun on his knees, watching." Pablo's sole disappointment is that the denouement of the killing of the fascists did not go according to his personal script: "All day I had waited for the death of the priest. I had thought he would be the last to enter the lines. I awaited it with great anticipation. I expected something of a culmination." Pablo's confession reveals an almost Aristotelian conception of tragedy. He requires a rising action, a dramatic conclusion, eloquent "lines," and a doomed protagonist—the priest—who is supposed to die with dignity.

Pablo's own acting in the cave is far from that of a great tragedian, but his affinity for theatrical modes of expression is constantly and subtly on display. Prior to the second major confrontation between Pablo and Jordan in the cave, for instance, Pablo masterfully redefines Jordan's carefully constructed image of masculine authority. The scene begins with Jordan ordering Maria to "Hunt me a pair of socks" (202) and earning from Pilar the epithets "Lord and Master," a comment that Jordan jokingly parries and intensifies by asking Maria, "Thou canst not dry them [his feet] with thy hair?" This humorous play of sexual cave-politics quickly turns serious with Pablo's insults about Jordan's masculinity ("it seems to me that with enough *cojones* you would not wear skirts" [206], "Don Roberto has no beard" [210]). Pablo gives the lie to the supposition that this early talk of Jordan's mastery is mere humor. Among other things, this banter foregrounds Pablo's humiliation in the arena he once dominated and underscores Jordan's claims to leadership. But Pablo cleverly disguises his intentions by alternating between aggressive provocation and maudlin regret for the killing of the fascists. He constantly dramatizes his drunkenness ("I am drunk, seest thou" [215]), and on three separate occasions Primitivo and Agustín tell Jordan to "Pay no attention to Pablo" (209, and 206, 211). From behind the mask of drunkenness, Pablo provokingly claims "I do not provoke" (212).

Jordan, who eventually realizes that Pablo is "not so drunk" and that "I had better watch myself" (211), has no more success in transforming play-acting into action than Agustín, who repeatedly strikes Pablo. Because Jordan has not in Pablo's words the *"cojones"* to "assassinate" (213) him, the scene remains merely theatrical in the sense that one meaning of performance (doing something) is always displaced into another (watching people act). Brilliantly, Pablo both acknowledges and disguises his thorough comprehension of drama by charging *Pilar* with stage-managing the provocation: "I am not to be provoked," he tells Jordan, "signal to the woman it was not successful" (212). His tactic is effective not only because he implies that Jordan is being directed rather than acting as a free agent but because Jordan—Lord and Master of the cave—takes direction from a woman ("Ask the woman. She commands" [211]). Jordan's lame response "I provoke thee for myself" cannot erase his feeling that "this had all been gone through before . . . [and that] he was playing a part from memory of something that he had read or had dreamed." His attempt to supervise the arena of the cave ended for a second time, Jordan admits to Pablo "I am learning much from thee." And Pablo, even after pushing past the blanket that covers the mouth of the cave, cannot resist a final curtain call: the snow is "still falling, *Inglés*."

Pablo's inclinations toward theatricality are worth emphasizing because they help us to address two crucial questions about manhood-fashioning: first, the question of how Pablo despite his multiple humiliations survives to redeem his manhood among the partisans and, second, the question of how the novel negotiates the relationship between theatrical representations of manhood and the masculine impulse toward the supervisory gaze. In the first case, Pablo survives a threefold overthrow of his erstwhile authority: the arrival of the young foreigner; the band's allegiance shifting to Pilar; and, according to the other partisans, the cowardice that has already reduced his effectiveness. His cave-theatrics might then be seen as an emptying-out of his earlier command over the killing of the fascists, where his capacity to be seen and acknowledged as supreme arbiter of his enemies' fate went hand in hand with his ability to stage-manage their demise: potent self-dramatization has come to mere play-acting. As his return to the cave after disposing of the detonators suggests, however, Pablo's manliness seems not at odds with but intimately bound up with its theatrical construction. Pablo's odyssean return may well be his finest hour on stage. At one point Pilar remarks "So much theatre tires me" (390) and, though she intends only to hide her emotion, her point is well taken insofar as it accurately assesses the profusion of roles Pablo's return allows. It allows him to demonstrate his superior percipience ("Nine of you could never have done it. . . . I knew that last night when the *Inglés* explained it") and his courage ("I am not a coward"), while his dramatic reappearance underscores the metaphoric significance of his oft-repeated statement "I am back." Back as leader and as man, his return also restores his command over the unstable dynamic between looking and being looked at: though he enters the cave "looking toward no one in particular," the scene ends with him looking "Pilar in the eyes again and this time he did not look away. He kept on looking at her squarely." The passage emphasizes the reciprocity of this theater of manhood-fashioning: his power to gaze at Pilar dovetails with the new respect her look grants him, and her respect is won by his newfound power to gaze "squarely" at her.

His confession that the new guerrillas he has brought "think I am the leader," moreover, is a brilliant artifice that resonates with significance in many different ways. In one sense, his heroic humility convinces Pilar to restore to him the mantle of leadership: "Thou art [leader]. . . . If thee wishes." In another, Pablo's pretence underscores the fact that to the members of the other bands there is no perceptible difference between performance (theater) and formal authority: to them, Pablo being the leader and acting the leader comes to the same thing. At least on this occasion, performance (theatricality) constitutes leadership. The point is a crucial one, for it would seem that the partisans' account of Pablo's downfall and resurgence as leader and as man suggests precisely the opposite: that his status depends on the quality and number of warlike activities rather than his acting, and on his failure to perform his duty rather than his failure to dominate the cave-arena. It might even be argued that staging himself to the band after Jordan's arrival simply represents his struggle to recover what Pilar calls the last "remnants of manhood" (209) in him. His eventual ability to speak "simply" and to look "squarely" at Pilar thus suggests a new blunt honesty beyond the prevarications and pretence of earlier scenes. In this reading, the other partisans' assumption that Pablo is the leader might be seen as justified by his night of riding, by his newly mature reflection on his role, and by his courageous return to his band. Despite Pilar's remark that "So much theatre tires me," and despite her unbelieving "Thy mother!" to Pablo's seemingly lugubrious comment that "after I had thrown away thy material I found myself too lonely," we cannot dismiss the possibility that Pablo's return is a genuine volte-face signaling a new devotion to the Loyalist cause and to his resurrected manly courage.

Nevertheless, in still another sense Pablo's remark "They think I am the leader" must be read ironically, for this pretend-leader is only pretending to lead: he has actually plotted their murders. Pablo looks "squarely" at Pilar for the first time when he refers to the new partisans as "*buenos,*" and Pilar is unintentionally accurate when she adds "*Buenos y bobos.* Good ones and stupids." If Pablo might be accounted a true leader of his band for providing enough horses for the escape, we cannot ignore the fact that Pablo squarely misrepresents his intentions to the new partisans and to Pilar. But the men from the other bands are not wholly mistaken in trusting the authenticity of Pablo's command, for the theater of the cave has constantly demonstrated that leadership must be dramatized in order to be recognized as authentic. Pablo is supremely skilled at self-representation; and the question of how Pablo is restored so unexpectedly to manhood would be meaningful only if there were a principle of manhood beyond representation that Pablo has irretrievably sacrificed. Pilar's accusation that Pablo has lost the last "remnants of manhood," Anselmo's image of the castrated boar, and Jordan's parable of the "lost eggs" all fundamentally miss the point, which is that Pablo has all along retained control of the theatrical apparatus with which to dramatize his return to manhood. There is no distinction between the way he provokes and directs the second confrontation with Jordan and the way he stages his dramatic return, though the outcome seems very different. The narrative does not guarantee a difference between manhood and the pose of manhood. In its reticence about stating how deeply Pablo's theatricality informs his return, the narrative dramatizes the possibility that manhood and its performance are simply interchangeable.

Indeed, during the first showdown with Pablo the person who most successfully governs the theater of masculine representation is a woman. Though the epithets most often used to describe Pilar in this scene suggest a subservient role ("wife of Pablo," "woman of Pablo"), it is Pilar who surprisingly ousts Pablo from his position as leader. Her interpretation of the unfolding drama is percipient: she sends Maria out of the cave at the moment when Jordan believes "it is going to come now" (52) and insists on the correctness and propriety of her statement that "I command." And though for much of this scene Jordan barely registers her presence, it is Pilar who quickly establishes her credentials as consummate actress, "mimicking a visit to a bedside" (55) of a gored matador, and, in a parody of Pablo's decaying courage, "imitating the weak voice of the wounded bull fighter." Pilar's booming voice supplants the "almost effeminate" voice of the failed self-dramatist (Finito, the matador) in her little allegory of theatrical misconduct, while providing a suitably dramatic focus for the exchange of roles taking place in the cave. Pilar not only evaluates Pablo (as she evaluates Finito), but, through Jordan's eyes, assumes the man's phallic power in dominating the arena: Pilar stands "proudly and confidently holding the big spoon as authoritatively as though it were a baton." It might be argued, with some justice, that Pilar's wielding of the baton is only temporary and that, in contrast to her proud stance in this early scene, she restores the role of leader to Pablo with fuzzy sentimentality: "'Thou,' she said and her husky voice was fond again. 'Thou. I suppose if a man has something once, always something of it remains'" (391). The transience of her authority however, demonstrates exactly the opposite of her supposition. Pablo, out-performed by a woman, awaits not the resurgence of that ineffable "something" but a superior performance. By the same token, Pilar's assured performance in the first confrontation with Pablo cannot be dismissed as mere theater. Her appropriation of the phallic signifier of manhood suggests the friable nature of gender roles, but to argue that gender roles are performance-based does not empty them of significance to those whose sense of reality is informed by and through such performances. Pilar's claim on the (putatively masculine) leader's role by virtue of performance is no less authentic than Pablo's assertion of his prerogative by virtue of sex.

Robert Jordan's attempts to extend the regime of the general's eye into the cave-theater thus underestimate the variety and subtlety of dramatic performances possible there. Jordan enters the cave for the first time consciously resolved to master its ambiguous visual spaces by playing the simultaneous roles of performer and magisterial spectator. Presenting himself to the spectators as the dynamiter with *cojones* (two heavy packs), Jordan is equally confident that his knowledge and awareness illuminate the complexities of cave-politics; before the first showdown with Pablo, he is sure that he can distinguish between protagonist (Pablo) and spectators (Pilar, the "wife of Pablo," and the three men in the shadows). But the cumulative pattern of plot events—including the intrusion of random and unforeseen events like the snowfall or the theft of his detonators—increasingly belies Jordan's early confidence that he might see through to a comprehensive knowledge and mastery of people, events, and situations. Above all, cave-theater constantly thwarts Jordan's desire to master and discipline the visual terrain. His watch, with its "complications of numbers," does not equip him to command the complex and unexpected events of the cave, where his attempt to finesse the problem of Pablo is followed by Rafael's arguably correct criticism of his actions, where Pilar confidently usurps her husband's role, and where Pablo's stagy return arguably empties of meaning Pilar's fond aphorism that "if a man has something once, always something of it remains." Cave-theater partakes of the carnivalesque. It baffles Jordan's attempts to master terrain and people in an ordered and disciplined way, instituting instead what Jordan (scornfully) calls the "glorious discipline of indiscipline." Pablo, tracing his trajectory from humiliated coward to returning hero, upsets the very notion of the gaze as a function of a masculine will to power. Performance, which implies the importance of being watched and thus being subject to a glance that is intransigently other, negates the principle of abstract and invisible surveillance and the possibility of an eye that masters all within the visual and epistemological field.

As long as the many performances undertaken by the characters of this novel keep alive an irrevocable element of freeplay, no one character attains a complete and controlling perspective. After Pablo's enigmatic return, Jordan is simply at a loss to understand this "strange man" (404). Shaking Pablo's hand in the dark, Jordan expects the hand to feel "reptilian"; in fact, Pablo has a "good hand in the dark." And though Jordan guesses what Pablo will do to the new men, his outrage is limited to "that is his, not mine. Thank God I do not know these new men." Pablo's comment that the "*Inglés* and I understand one another" implies Jordan's tacit acquiescence in a strategy he has already dismissed while trying to deal with Pablo: assassination. Pablo's "good hand in the dark" thus leads us to one of many interpretive cruxes. Should we read Pablo's good hand as signifying the essential worthiness of the man beneath the rough exterior? Or as being good at "dark" and nefarious activities? By the same token, should we admire this manly handshake for what it implies about enterprises undertaken with resolve and purpose, or deride the illicit bargain struck between two opportunists who are willing to sacrifice allies for the sake of their individual goals? We could as easily read this scene as the unmanning of Jordan as the restoration of manly camaraderie. We cannot even be sure that Pablo's "strange, firm, purposeful hand" is not simply one more staging of his suddenly restored heroism, in which case it signifies not Pablo's true nature but his success as an actor. The scene forecloses the difference between the authentic and the performed self. Jordan has no independent and detached perspective from which to gauge the authenticity or theatricality of Pablo's handshake; indeed, he himself participates in the reconstruction of Pablo by choosing to place confidence in the "good hand in the dark" as if, despite the monstrous acts Pablo has planned, it represents after all the true man.

Performance, then, always compromises Jordan's moves toward establishing a panoptically complete supervision of terrain and character. Performance upsets absolute knowledge and the clear-sighted gaze, leaving Jordan and us to guess at the meaning of handshakes in the dark. Yet the fact that Jordan never sees and knows enough paradoxically only confirms the hegemony of super-vision, which operates beyond any source of knowledge to which Jordan has access, including Gaylord's. (Golz, a Gaylord's regular, does not know his attack is doomed until the arrival of Jordan's brief.) What dooms the larger offensive is the presence of systems and the existence of knowledge beyond the grasp of any individual Republican. In foreseeing the attack, fascist military intelligence has already proved superior to the S. I. M. that (in Pablo's words) justifies Jordan's identity. Minor successes such as Jordan's blowing the bridge and Pablo's escaping with his much-reduced band of partisans count for little against the presentiment that all such attacks will fail under the scrutiny of the fascist gaze. Tellingly, the nature of that gaze is never specified; we never see the network of spies or the modes of transmitting information that must be in place to monitor the Republican offensive. Such power is anonymous and invisible, and the genius of *For Whom the Bell Tolls* is to dramatize the potency of fascist super-vision by making it disappear from the novel's microscopic depiction of action and psychological complexity while holding it responsible for the novel's macroscopic depiction of a military cause going inescapably awry. And unlike Jordan in the cave, fascist super-vision is indifferent to the power of individual performances: the fact that Jordan blows the bridge does not materially affect the counter-attack to which Golz's offensive will shortly fall prey. If fascist power is not truly all-seeing and all-knowing, then, it stakes its claim to a regime of supervision by virtue of having settled this military encounter before the novel even opens.

The masculine will to power in *For Whom the Bell Tolls* is thus in one sense undermined only to be superimposed in another register. On the one hand, cave-theater exposes the hollowness of men's pretensions to leadership: not because Jordan and Pablo lack that "something" Pilar fondly recalls as her husband's strength but because that masculine "something" must always be acted out as part of a competitive display, and as such must be negotiated into significance by the gaze of others. Backed by military intelligence and by complicated systems for mapping, watching, and representing, Jordan still cannot fully maintain his authority amid an array of glances that seems to argue against the existence of a single master gaze. On the other hand, cave-theater itself seems insignificant in light of abstract and almost wholly unseen technologies of mechanized doom. No act of self-dramatization undertaken by Jordan or Pablo matches the forces that launch the planes and the tank that leads to Jordan's death. Indeed, the logic of the general's eye, inscribed within the goggled pilots, their planes, and covert spying rings, implies the end of theatricality. The pilots are impervious to the gaze of the other; and the spies are so efficient that they barely warrant a mention in the novel despite being responsible for the collapse of the Loyalist hopes. Fascist supervision operates by way of invisible efficiency and abstract surveillance that erases any productive exchange between (male) character and audience.

The relationship between scopic regime and theatricality is thus a vexed and complicated one in *For Whom the Bell Tolls*. At the very least, the novel must be said to play off against each other quite disparate senses of masculinity. The novel records the deployment of a panoptic gaze whose identity could be read (as Nye and Irigaray argue) as essentially masculine; yet, despite Jordan's attempts to inculcate new technologies of perception, the theatrical construction of masculine identity in the cave upsets the very premises of panopticism. The men who participate in cave-theater cannot be described or judged by the putatively masculine order of supervision—though they do suffer its consequences. By this logic, any attempt to comprehend masculinity solely by way of masculine supervision must fail, for masculinity is in at least some of its manifestations that which reintroduces theatricality and a carnivalesque overthrow of monocularcentrism. Acknowledging the appeal of panopticism to men at war, Hemingway's work resists the argument that the masculine gaze can be reduced to the horizon of the general's eye. There is even an odd sense in which the theater of masculine representation recuperates the very principle of freeplay and indeterminacy from the totalizing effects of fascist supervision and thus actually represents what would be for Nye and Irigaray a counter-masculinity. This claim might appear to reintroduce via the backdoor the figure of a traditional male hero, rebel and upholder of anarchic freedoms. Yet it need not do so, for cave-theater takes the construction of masculinity, as it were, beyond masculinity. Though males in Hemingway's work are typically the ones who seek authority and suffer humiliation in moments of self-dramatization, cave-theater countenances Pilar's intervention and construes it as a logical implication of "masculine" dramatization. It countenances a conception of human identity that is still fluid and replete with multiple possibilities for self-fashioning. It is not even, it seems, the sole prerogative of men.

CHAPTER 4

Real Things and Rhetorical Performances in *Death in the Afternoon*

THE MAIN BODY of the text of *Death in the Afternoon* concludes with a famous piece of advice to aspiring writers: "Let those who want to save the world if you can get to see it clear and as a whole. Then any part you make will represent the whole if it's made truly."[1] To be sure, these syntactic nightmares of sentences are often quoted only in part. In the first sentence, clarity depends on distinguishing its constituent parts in order to see that Hemingway is referring to those who *want to* and not those who want *to save*, though, confusingly, those who *want to* do in fact want to save the world. And clarity in the second depends on negotiating the enigmatic pronoun reference in the second sentence, where for a moment "it" seems to refer to "world" rather than "part" (and actually does make a strange kind of sense). But Hemingway's advice is particularly appropriate to the rhetoric of his own book, which so often invokes synecdochic principles of discourse whereby parts are made to stand for wholes. Madrid, for instance, though it has "none of the look that you expect of Spain" (51), in fact captures the "essence" (51) of the country. Likewise, the nobility of the bulls is said to be "the most extraordinary part of the whole business" (113) of bullfighting, in fact the "primal root of the whole Spanish bullfight" (113). In some sense a bull's nobility must not only allow an artistic performance to take place; it must contain within it the ideal form of the bullfight. To grasp the bull's innate quality is to grasp the principle of the entire conflict. In the same way, Hemingway seems to be suggesting, some

---

1. Ernest Hemingway, *Death in the Afternoon* (New York: Scribner's, 1932), 278. This work will hereinafter be cited parenthetically by page number in the text. Part of this chapter was first published in "The Sort of Thing You Should Not Admit: Hemingway's Aesthetic of Emotional Restraint," in *Boy's Don't Cry? Rethinking Narratives of Masculinity and Emotion in the U.S.*, ed. Milette Shamir and Jennifer Travis (New York: Columbia University Press, 2002), 141–66.

principle of construction intrinsic to the making of *Death in the Afternoon* allows any part of it to signify the whole.

Critics have noted that *Death in the Afternoon* doubles as Hemingway's "Baedeker of the bullfight" and as his most important aesthetic manifesto, and it is usual, as I have just done, to read Hemingway's descriptions of bullfighting as displaced accounts of writing, and vice versa.[2] The discussion is worth pursuing again at greater length, however, because it begins to bear on the larger preoccupation of this chapter, which is the relationship of Hemingway's style to the concept of manhood. As we saw in Chapter 1, few ideas about Hemingway have proved as enduring in the popular and scholarly imaginations as the supposition that his style is masculine or represents his predilection for virile masculinity in a variety of metonymic displacements: lean, hard, muscular, tough, hard-boiled, and so on. It is as if Sandra Gilbert and Susan Gubar's punning connection of pen/penis, which represents the phallic fount of male creativity, were more obvious in Hemingway's work than in most male writers—indeed, more than obvious if style, as Philip Young wrote, "*is* the man."[3] Young's formulation, if accurate, would seem to allow Hemingway's readers no room even for punning connections, for the man would *be* straightforwardly and unequivocally there in textual form. It would bring Hemingway's principle of synecdoche newly to life, the part (style) now standing for the whole (man).

This relatively firm consensus about Hemingway's style is remarkable in the sense that his fiction does not refer self-consciously to its own virile masculine virtues; critics must draw out an interpretation that Hemingway's work omits but presumably everywhere implies. And it is remarkable in the sense that many Hemingway works, including, as we shall see, *Afternoon* itself, have been read as an utter travesty of a true masculine style. Nonetheless, at face value *Death in the Afternoon* presents compelling support for this nexus of key critical notions about Hemingway's work. The book relates the bullfighter's performance to the writer's work in ways that seem to afford the writer a particularly courageous and manly role. When he writes of spectators learning to "appreciate values through experience," seeking "honesty and true, not tricked, emotion," and desiring "purity of execution of all the suertes" (12), Hemingway directs our attention to his own crafting of the "real thing," with

2. Baker, *Writer as Artist,* 143.
3. Young, 180.

its emphasis on truth, purity, and actual experience; when he writes of it taking "more cojones to be a sportsman when death is a closer party to the game" (22), he reminds us of his determination to tackle head-on the idea of violent death in his fiction. We can therefore understand Lawrence Broer's argument that the "image of the matador" in Hemingway's work is a "symbol of the best a man can be in a violent and irrational world—a model of manhood and integrity after which he would pattern his major fictional heroes" and which inspires the "ideas and artistic methods he employs."[4]

The problem with arguments like Young's and Broer's is not so much that they pose a connection between masculinity and style as that their categories of judgment mutually reinforce each other in a comfortable submission to what, in Chapter 1, I critiqued under the rubric of Spilka's "working vision of experience." Just as narrative gaps in "The Short Happy Life," I argued, were easily closed by what critics thought they knew about Hemingway's sense of manhood, so, here, Hemingway's sense of manhood subtends and is in turn guaranteed by style. That laconic, hard and clean style, for Young, assures us that the wounded Hemingway hero will not self-destruct; and the model of manly integrity posed by the matador, for Broer, convinces us that Hemingway's artistic methods will conform to the "best a man can be." But in what sense does the mazy tangle of Hemingway's advice to writers ("Let those who want to save the world . . .") conform to an aesthetic and ideal of hard, clean prose? If those concluding statements of principle really do represent the whole—the whole man as well as the whole text—should we not rather impute to this text an aesthetic and a representation of manhood that is chaotic, muddled, downright contradictory, or determinedly rhetorical?

This chapter argues that Hemingway's principles of clarity, trueness, wholeness, and the "real thing"—in short, everything that is usually taken as a straightforward description of his aesthetic and as a heartfelt guide to full manhood—must be read as profoundly rhetorical. Meanings in *Afternoon* are a series of possibilities staged in full recognition of *their effect as arguments on an audience.* They lead to the conclusion that Hemingway is a master rhetorician, not to conclusive propositions about some masculine "real thing" understood as a property of style and modeled on the conduct and art of the matador. There are several corollaries to this thesis. It will become apparent that scholars have been right to read the art of the matador as an apt meta-

4. Broer, vii, vi.

phor for Hemingway's style but wrong to thereby traduce his style as a failed attempt to mimic in prose the matador's beautifully restrained and disciplined suertes. My emphasis will be on the one aspect of the matador's performance that usually receives short shrift: its dramatic staging before, and for the sake of, an audience. In this respect, the matador's dramatic command of the arena/stage stands in for the writerly games of the rhetorician. As an audience is crucial to the significance and appraisal of a matador's performance, moreover, so Hemingway's text constantly keeps our role as an audience of readers alive and invested in a purposeful negotiation of the relationship between style and masculinity. The implications of Hemingway's rhetorical performances are profound for an understanding of his representation of masculinity. For if style *is* the man, as Philip Young propounded, it would seem that the man—writer and fighter both—is hopelessly indebted to a mode of self-fashioning that is theatrical, rhetorical, stylized, and audience-bound. And it would seem the stagy and often playful discourse of hesitancy and indeterminacy in *Afternoon* challenges the most salient features of a putative masculine style: that simple, direct, straightforward, unemotional, unsentimental pursuit of the "real thing."

Hemingway's aesthetic of synecdoche implies a powerful sense of epistemological security. His desire "to try to present the bullfight integrally" (7) supposes the possibility of apprehending the bullfight as an integral and integrated whole, where the emphasis lies first on the complete experience and second on the relationship between the parts that form the complete experience. These different emphases in fact distinguish the responses of amateur spectator and aficionado. Women who might be discomforted by the bullfight Hemingway advises to sit in the gallery, for "You might enjoy the fight from there where you will see it as a spectacle and not care for it at all if you sat closer so that the details destroyed the effect of the whole" (33). Experts, however, may sit in the gallery because they "can see details even though a long way from them and want to be high enough up so they can see everything that happens in any part of the ring in order to be able to judge it as a whole" (32). The expert judge, that is, views the bullfight as an integrated whole that emerges out of the harmonious relationship between various parts; amateurs, lest they miss the whole in the confusion of parts, are invited to view the bullfight as an integral whole. In each case—whether one intuits the principle of the bullfight or whether one constructs the whole from its constituent parts (each containing the essence of the whole)—it would seem that the bullfight is made as "truly" as Hemingway hopes his own work will prove. Writing and bullfighting alike must possess qualities that are permanent, communicable, determinate, and even transcendent for "any part you make" to "represent the whole if it's made truly." Only thus could spectators "sense the meaning and end of the whole thing even when they know nothing about it" (8).

The ostensible security of synecdochic construction permeates *Afternoon.* It illuminates, for instance, Hemingway's iceberg theory of writing: "If a writer of prose knows enough about what he is writing about he may omit things that he knows and the reader, if the writer is writing truly enough, will have a feeling of those things as strongly as though the writer had stated them. The dignity of movement of an ice-berg is due to only one-eighth of it being above water. A writer who omits things because he does not know them only makes hollow places in his writing" (192). Hemingway clearly employs the metaphor of the iceberg for its synecdochic properties. As the visible iceberg implies at least some properties of the whole iceberg, so does Hemingway's writing imply that which is unsaid but which must somehow inhabit the interstices of the text. The reader's task, if not easy, is at least determinate. Like the spectators who "sense the meaning and end of the whole [bullfight] even when they know nothing about it," readers of fine prose find their experience structured by the writer's process of truly and completely knowing. The reader stands in the presence, as it were, of a plenitude of meaning that is never quite written but always comprehensible, and is certainly not to be confused with the vacancies or "hollow places" of the poor writer. That plenitude arises out of a set of specific techniques. His younger self was searching, Hemingway claims in *Afternoon,* to "put down what really happened in action; what the actual things were which produced the emotion that you experienced"; he was working to get the "real thing, the sequence of motion and fact which made the emotion and which would be as valid in a year or in ten years or, with luck and if you stated it purely enough, always" (2). These last much-quoted statements provide a rationale for the synecdochic principles the book so often invokes. What shapes and stabilizes the movement from part to whole, so that writer and reader might ultimately know what is true and pure writing, is the relationship between writing and the "actual things" that give rise to it—a relationship that must itself be seen as synecdochic if writing is to be considered of a piece with the sequence of motion and fact (the "real thing") rather than merely a recording or transcription.

Such statements, more obviously than anywhere else in Hemingway's work, unfold into a metaphysics of presence. The fine writer articulates the true and the pure; invokes a potentially comprehensible whole; integrates parts into a complete whole; crafts narrative gaps that contain rich plenitudes of meaning; and realizes a formidable bond between writer and reader that allows (for the right reader at least) a perfect transmission of feeling. Most startlingly, writing in these statements seems to go beyond representation and instead becomes the "real thing." It is as though the "real thing" actually banishes writing in favor of those "actual things" one might consider outside the purview of textuality, or as though (in a quite contemporary way) Hemingway sees no necessary difference between the life of the text and the textuality of real life. In the same way, Hemingway later insists that the writer's task is to create "people not characters" (191) and that it is only when the writer "can make people live" that the book remains as "a whole; as an entity; as a novel" (191). Oddly, the book achieves its greatest stature at the moment when its capacity to create "people not characters" seems to erase its very being as a book.

An aesthetic that constantly blurs the distinction between the aesthetic and the real, however, also puts in question the principle of synecdoche. A mode of writing in which "any part you make will represent the whole" would seem to make it a deeply figurative practice that constantly draws attention to the nature of representation. Writing that gives up its ontological status as writing to become the "real thing," in contrast, eschews representation in favor of presentation. Parts, in this reading, only present the "actual things" themselves; signifiers lose their identity to the signified; the book surrenders all possibilities of figurative play. Hemingway's ideal of pure writing would seem to be Roland Barthes's "degree zero" of style, a style losing all trace of its identity in its capitulation to the real. One could not test out pure writing against the "actual things" that gave rise to it, moreover, because the external standard of measurement (the real things whose sequence the writing attempts to capture) would have collapsed with the closing of the gap between writing and the "real thing." Hemingway's aesthetic principles thus place the reader in something of a quandary, for they make claims for the profound power of figurative writing to represent while simultaneously seeming to displace writing altogether. One can always argue that Hemingway is speaking figuratively and that by the "real thing" he means something like a perfect *simulacrum* of the real. But now our dilemma deepens. For if at the moment Hemingway seems most explicitly to be denying the figurative power of language our only option is to claim that he is being figurative, how shall we ever know if and when the writer achieves the real thing, or even what it is?

Hemingway's ostensibly forthright comments about writing early in Chapter 1, moreover, are much more consistently qualified than rapid summaries of his positions allow: he considers that putting down what really happened in action is not so much his achievement as his "greatest difficulty," while the supplemental statement "aside from knowing truly what you really felt" gives rise to some doubt about which problem is the writer's most pressing. A triple emphasis on *trying* to learn to write, moreover, modifies each articulation of his philosophy. That hesitancy might be put down to disingenuous modesty (that is, the real thing was beyond me; but no longer) if not for the ensuing discussion of the tendency "when you really begin to learn something about a thing not to want to write about it but rather to keep on learning about it always." That process must always elude the inquirer for "every year I know there is more to learn" (4). This philosophy seems at odds with earlier statements. On the one hand, Hemingway countenances a form of making whereby the "real thing" is apprehended and made valid "always"; on the other, puzzlingly, the writer's subject evades complete comprehension so that it is always to be learnt. Mere difficulties can be surmounted; but the possibility of perpetually incomplete learning baffles the promise of a lasting and transcendent aesthetic experience.

Critics, by and large, have smoothed away Hemingway's confusion—or the confusion he intends to capture—usually managing to construe a cogent philosophy out of aesthetic statements that individually present severe problems of interpretation and that can be made to add up to a collective whole only with great difficulty. Carlos Baker, for instance, remarks that the "primary intent of [Hemingway's] writing . . . has been to seize and project for the reader what he has often called 'the way it was,'" but goes on to assume and emphasize that Hemingway means "reproducing . . . 'the way it was.'" And Baker, like many other critics looking to support various aesthetic theories, quotes the writer's ideas piecemeal. He, for instance, conjoins fragments of Hemingway's statements into an aesthetic principle entitled "the discipline of double perception," by which he means seeing objects from slightly different angles to produce a "unified picture." In a more recent example, Paul Civello's "Hemingway's 'Primitivism': Archetypal Patterns in 'Big Two-Hearted River,'" which concerns the mythic and ritualistic aspects of that story, concludes with the statement that Hemingway "succeeds in creating his own artistic ideal, the 'real thing': the work of art that would not spoil with time, but would remain valid 'always.' "[5] In one sense, Civello's and Baker's mining of the manifesto-like properties of *Afternoon* seems perfectly appropriate, for Hemingway's aesthetics of the "real thing" does suggest the transhistorical, "unified," and archetypal experience we associate with myth. In another, the irony is obvious: Hemingway's synecdochic principles can only be made to work by utilizing them in fragments.

In light of this more cautious approach to Hemingway's aesthetics, we might return to the statement that begins this chapter: "Let those who want to save the world if you can get to see it clear and as a whole. Then any part you make will represent the whole if it's made truly" (278). Asserting the value of seeing the world "clear and as a whole," Hemingway seems to construct an aesthetic favoring truth, simplicity, clarity, and determinacy. But the cogency of such principles comes apart in the muddy syntax of these two sentences. As I have suggested, the construction "want to/save the world" and the float-ing "it" seem designed to baffle an aesthetic of clarity; so too does the caveat "*if* it's made truly." The use of "you," moreover, confuses the issue further, for though the use of second-person implies advice to an aspiring writer (as I assumed at the beginning of this chapter), Hemingway persistently employs "you" to signify a quasi-first-person, sometimes with the force of "one." One hesitates, therefore, between reading these sentences as advice to someone else or as the author's formulation of his personal aesthetic code. Reading the sen-tences in context scarcely helps, for the final paragraph of the book runs the gamut of pronouns, beginning with "a country you love very much" (which seems obviously to refer to Hemingway himself), moving to "he" (Rafael), then "I," then, more mysteriously, "we" ("We've seen it all go") before the "you" currently under discussion, before concluding still more puzzlingly in the passive voice ("there were a few things to be said"). Why then transpose "you" for "I" in a paragraph that already features Hemingway speaking as "I"? Are we to assume that I, you, and we (and the passive) compose together the Hemingway persona? Or that you and we signify Hemingway in conjunction with all like-minded readers, so that the Hemingway persona composes us? Or that Hemingway is dramatizing the difficulty of seeing the world (or a sentence) "clear and as a whole"? Or that Hemingway is deliberately confusing

5. Baker, *Writer as Artist*, 48, 57, 55; Paul Civello, "Hemingway's 'Primitivism': Archetypal Patterns in 'Big Two-Hearted River,' " *Hemingway Review* 13, no. 1 (fall 1993): 14.

issues of agency and communities of readers by obsessively changing pronouns? My point here is not that we should choose, but that there is nothing transparent or self-evident about Hemingway's aesthetic principles—and thus, ultimately, about the idea and ideal of manhood they have always been held to imply or embody.

Death in the Afternoon, as this brief discussion of Hemingway's aesthetic principles suggests, composes a labyrinthine rhetorical display. This is true from the very beginning of Chapter 1, even though it opens with Hemingway making statements that seem to support an aesthetic of rigorous truth-telling: "I found the greatest difficulty, aside from knowing truly what you really felt, rather than what you were supposed to feel, and had been taught to feel, was to put down what really happened in action." So Chapter 1 begins with Hemingway faulting his expectations ("I expected to be horrified"), his reading ("most people who wrote of it condemned bullfighting outright"), and the "modern moral point of view" (1) that considered the killing of the horses indefensible. Moreover, the book is written as a corrective to journalism (2), "various guides to Spain" (29), and the "mysticism of such a book as [Waldo Frank's] *Virgin Spain*" (53). Such conventional and learnt perspectives are to be rejected in favor of telling "honestly the things I have found true about it," and *Afternoon* constantly invokes, as we have seen, a mode of "writing truly" (192) that reaches its apotheosis in the idea of the "real thing." But the first paragraph concludes on a very different note. Hemingway admits that his readers' fineness of feeling may be greater than his, adding: "But whoever reads this can truly make such a judgment when he, or she, has seen the things that are spoken of." If the very point of Hemingway's aesthetic is to deliver the "real thing" to the reader in contrast to false perceptions, however, and if writing truly enough allows "any part you make [to] represent the whole," it would seem that the reader should not need to be present at an actual bullfight. If a true appreciation of the bullfight must wait for an actual visit, no amount of "writing truly" could ever be enough. That desire to "present the bullfight integrally" must always founder on the fact that a real bullfight is absent from the pages of the book.

The point is important enough that Hemingway returns to the subject at the end of the first chapter, where he attempts to portray the work of the bullfighter Cagancho, who

> sometimes standing absolutely straight with his feet still, planted as though he were a tree, with the arrogance and grace that gypsies have and of which

all other arrogance and grace seems an imitation, moves the cape spread
full as the pulling jib of a yacht before the bull's muzzle so slowly that the
art of bullfighting, which is only kept from being one of the major arts
because it is impermanent, in the arrogant slowness of his veronicas becomes, for the seeming minutes they endure, permanent. That is the worst
of flowery writing, but it is necessary to try to give the feeling, and to
someone who has never seen it a simple statement of the method does not
convey the feeling. Anyone who has seen bullfights can skip such flowerishness and read the facts which are much more difficult to isolate and
state. (13–14)

The passage turns, in part, on the issue of imitations. Cagancho, possessing the kind of authentic arrogance and grace that gypsies have, would therefore seem to be the real thing against which any other bullfighter's grace must
appear an "imitation." Flowery writing, similarly, is held to be only imitative
of "the facts" and the experience of watching a bullfight. Actually, the passage
is a good deal more complex. If Cagancho only "sometimes" performs truly,
it could hardly be said that he absolutely embodies qualities that are contingent on the moment of performance; moreover, if all arrogance and grace
only "seems" an imitation of that possessed by gypsies, how can we be sure
that gypsies actually possess the original and authentic expression of these
qualities? Can we be sure that the truth about arrogance and grace has not
succumbed to rhetoric (in the sense of overblown, hyperbolic language)—or
what Hemingway terms "flowerishness"? It is as if Hemingway, far from
knowing truly and writing purely about arrogance and grace, is merely defer-
ring the moment when absolute knowledge of them could be gained.

But we also have to ask what is wrong with "the worst of flowery writing"
if it does "try to give the feeling" of watching a bullfight and if technical explanations, which have no room for flowerishness, are "like the simple directions
which accompany any mechanical toy and which are incomprehensible"
(179). Hemingway's self-conscious criticism is puzzling, for beautifully sculp-
ted phrases like "the cape spread full as the pulling jib of a yacht," placed
delicately in a sentence that strives to mimic, in its rising crescendo of dove-
tailed clauses, Cagancho's slow and statuesque suertes, appears to fulfill Hemingway's own criterion for writing that endures always: capturing the
"sequence of motion and fact which made the emotion." One might argue
that metaphors like "planted as though he were a tree" and "cape spread full

as the pulling jib of a yacht" are contrived imitations of the original "sequence of motion and fact," the presentation of which still evades Hemingway's best efforts. If he fails, however, it would seem less a function of the author's skill than a property of the act of writing itself. After all, a "simple statement of the method does not convey the feeling," and the difficult "facts" are to be read, oddly enough, only by those who need not rely on reading because they have been personally present at the corrida.

In the latter case no writing could ever suffice to make the bullfight truly present, while in the former case it would appear that the bullfight can only be truly represented by "flowerishness." The writer is forced against his own principles, which were to have begun with the "simplest things" and the "real thing," into an unconscionable exercise of rhetoric. In either case Hemingway faces a predicament. Language is either always inadequate to convey real things or constantly standing in the way of the real thing, transmuting all that is into representations that liberate a linguistic freeplay: capes become jibs, bullfighters become planted trees, description becomes flowerishness. Yet Hemingway's statement of the problem is also clearly rhetorical. Reading this passage, we cannot be sure whether Cagancho's suertes are the real thing or a brilliant pose or whether we are meant to know the bullfight as it truly is instead of just words on a page. But in another sense the problem is immaterial. As Hemingway, waving a cape of words before our eyes, draws us on and then thoroughly confuses us with meanings that slide from our grasp, we find that we have already *experienced* the play of the argument. As Hemingway addresses it, the problem of language is not to be solved but to be enjoyed for the way it affords opportunities to the master rhetorician to play upon (and for) his audience.

"[S]tart your writer to talking of words and he will go on until you are wearied" (71), Hemingway states during a discussion with the Old Lady, and that aphorism keys a persistent sense in the book that its focus is an inquiry into the various strategies of representation writers have at their disposal. During "A Natural History of the Dead," for instance, Hemingway refers us to the drowning mules at Smyrna and notes that the "numbers of broken-legged mules and horses drowning in the shallow water called for a Goya to depict them," and then adds, strangely: "Although, speaking literally, one can hardly say that they called for a Goya, since there has only been one Goya, long dead, and it is extremely doubtful if these animals, were they able to call, would call for pictorial representation of their plight but, more likely, would if they were articulate, call for someone to alleviate their condition" (135). Like so many of the discussions with the Old Lady, the tone of this passage oscillates between the grave and the facetious. And it seems to come apropos of nothing. Few readers, one would think, would pause to consider whether the broken-legged mules were literally calling for a Goya; the metaphor would remain buried and unremarked. Few would think, as it were, to call Hemingway on his choice of phrase. But in choosing to make the throwaway phrase "called for a Goya" remarkable, Hemingway draws attention to the nature and fact of representation itself. The mules themselves are in many senses beyond representation; they cannot represent themselves, being inarticulate; they are in need of mercy, not painting or writing; their plight is so extreme that representation merely glosses the true horror of the event. And the passage occurs in the midst of a self-referential dialogue about the alleged difficulties and failures of Hemingway's own writing: "It's very hard to write like this," "You wrote about those mules before," "I won't write about them again" (135). Metaphorical representation thus plays a complex role in this debate with the Old Lady. It obscures the truth, so that Hemingway is forced to explore the supplemental qualities of his prose and attempt to find a mode of "speaking literally." It points to the possibility that events may be beyond representation, in which case no amount of speaking, whether literally or metaphorically, could suffice. But it also points to Hemingway's determination to put on display all the rich and abundant resources of language. If an innocuous phrase like "called for a Goya" can be called into question and exploited for nuances that seem entirely at odds with the dramatic situation, one might ask whether the play of meaning could not "go on until you are wearied" and one seeks, along with the Old Lady, to interrupt the flow of words and return Hemingway to the "simplest things."

Such seems to be the case, at least, with Hemingway's mazy and enigmatic consideration of the term "suerte," which he initially states refers to "Everything that is done by the man in the ring" and is "the easiest term to use, as it is short. It means act" (16). But Hemingway immediately begins a quarrel with his own translation of "act," for the "word act has, in English, a connotation of the theatre that makes its use confusing." The "easiest term" quickly reveals an interpretive dilemma: whatever *suerte* means, it does not simply mean "act." In one of the more remarkable passages of the book, Hemingway later returns to the meaning of *suerte* with a greatly different effect. The first "act" of the bullfight, the "suerte de varas," Hemingway terms the "trial of the lances," and continues: "Suerte is an important word in Spanish. It means, according to the dictionary: Suerte, f., chance, hazard, lots, fortune, luck, good luck, haphazard; state, condition, fate, doom, destiny, kind, sort; species, manner, mode, way, skilful manoeuvre; trick, feat, juggle, and piece of ground separated by landmark. So the translation of trial or manoeuvre is quite arbitrary, as any translation must be from the Spanish" (96). This "important" word—really, the most important word, since it purports to represent everything a man performs in the ring—turns out to the most complex, for it is shown to possess all the connotative quality Hemingway earlier scorned in the term "act." And the dictionary does not even mention "act" or "trial," the author's own translations! Worse still for a determinate understanding of *suerte*, Hemingway's glossary defines the term *suertes* differently as "all predetermined manoeuvres in a bullfight; any move in a bullfight which has rules for the manner of its execution" (451).

The usage of *suerte* is crucial in several ways to an understanding of *Afternoon*, not least because, if the term defines everything that is done by the torero, a "quite arbitrary" translation can only defer indefinitely our full possession of the "real thing" that happens in the ring. Hemingway's discussion places appropriate emphasis on the role of language and textuality, though, as so often, he juggles the question of that role. On the one hand, language seems to have a clear and unequivocal ability to name things apprehended in a nontextual world, just as suertes performed in the ring must adhere to "fundamental rules" (16) that are "predetermined" (451). In this sense, signifiers seem to have a secure and fundamental relationship to the signified. Hemingway's glossary in some ways assures us of this linguistic function. "*Mona:* silkcovered button worn at the base of the bullfighter's pigtail" (421) reads one entry. By contrast with the lengthier English translation, the signifier *mona* seems to have a density of being or absoluteness that persuades us of the authenticity of the original Spanish. By unfolding the implications of the word into English, the glossary seems to affirm that the original is self-identical with itself and thus in need of no translation to a Spanish speaker. The problems of translating from one language to another merely confirm the competence of native speakers to stand in the presence of stable meanings.

On the other hand, Hemingway's various attempts to define *suerte* bespeak a contradictory sense that all language is fundamentally metaphorical and thus perpetually in need of supplemental translation. So *suerte* is revealed to have hitherto unsuspected depths of meaning that Hemingway's early reference to the "easiest term" that "means act" completely obscures. How then can we be sure that a "skilful manoeuvre" performed in the ring does not include, say, overtones of doom, destiny, or luck? (Surely Hemingway implies it does.) If so, which, and in what proportion? We might argue that such overtones would be perfectly apparent to an expert speaker of Spanish. When, for instance, Hemingway glosses *agujas* variously as "needles," the "bull's horns," and the "top forward ribs beside the shoulder blades" (380), a Spanish speaker might have no trouble in distinguishing agujas (needles) from agujas (horns) and agujas (top forward ribs). Nonetheless, such a feat would seem possible not because of the innate significance of the term but because of whatever context the speaker uses to negotiate the term into significance. But it would not seem possible to prevent other trace significances from accruing in any context we care to adduce.

These two possibilities—that signifiers possess determinate meaning only in specific contexts, or that signifiers simply offer an unstable freeplay of meanings—are both entertained in *Afternoon*. Though Hemingway doubts the translation of *suerte* as "act," for instance, he later seems to employ the theatrical connotations of the word deliberately ("Act one is the act of the capes" in which the "bull has the greatest opportunity to display his bravery or cowardice" ("Act two is that of the banderillas" [96]). Similarly, though "trial" is a "quite arbitrary" translation, its appearance in the text signals a lengthy play of associations between the bullfight and the Spanish Inquisition (the muleta cloth is fastened with a "thumb screw," while the "first act is the trial, the second act is the sentencing and the third the execution" [97, 98]). The trajectory of each signifier is thus marked by a kind of digressive play that keeps opening up further referential positions. "Act" means suerte, but its ability to mean a scripted performance first puts it out of bounds and then brings it back as it merges with meanings clustered around "trial"; "trial" means suerte, but it is first labeled "quite arbitrary" and then employed to translate, as it were, one Spanish institution into another. In both cases the signifiers seem to have no innate or determinate meaning, though context usually creates the illusion that there is.

But contexts are themselves unstable, as the very last words of *Afternoon* (in the Bibliographical Note) both argue and demonstrate: "When a volume of controversy may be written on the execution of a single suerte one man's arbitrary explanation is certain to be unacceptable to many" (487). Framing the meaning of *suerte* anew, and warning of the profound intertextuality of the term, this addendum implies an infinite proliferation of possible contexts and meanings. As if multiple dictionary definitions were not enough, we now face a situation in which each suerte potentially contains volumes, and in which each volume, registering only controversy and arbitrary explanation, leads us further from absolute knowledge. *Suerte* and its accompanying English translations is thus an important word to *Afternoon*. It suggests fundamental rules for the performance of predetermined actions in the ring while participating in a metaphorical play that puts in question the availability of fundamental and predetermined meanings.

The linguistic play surrounding the term *suerte* is still more evident in what some critics have taken to be the book's main thesis, and even an important insight into the history of bullfighting: Hemingway's investigation into the decadence of bullfighting. "It is a decadent art in every way," he proclaims at one point, adding that "like most decadent things it reaches its fullest flower at its rottenest point, which is the present" (68). The problem, as Hemingway sees it, is that the "modern technique of bullfighting . . . has been made too perfect. It is done so close to the bull, so slowly and so completely without defense or movement on the part of the matador, that it can only be accomplished with an almost made-to-order bull" (161). Along with smaller and meeker bulls, the growing reliance on graceful cape-work makes the "original moment of truth . . . the killing" into a "tricky business" (174) that features imitation (rather than the original) and lies (rather than the truth), and that fosters incompletion in the "decay of a complete art through a magnification of certain of its aspects" (70). In this sense, as several critics have pointed out, the book contains a quest for origins—a golden age of bullfighting—now ruined in the decadent world of modernity by commercialism and an unhealthy obsession with one aspect of the corrida.

Yet the issue of contemporary decadence is less clear-cut than Hemingway sometimes makes it sound. Belmonte, the man whose "decadent . . . impossible . . . almost depraved style" is most responsible for bringing about this narrow emphasis on cape-work, is after all a "genius and a great artist" and a revolutionary who could "break the rules of bullfighting and could torear . . . as it was known to be impossible to torear" (69). But it is not only that the "beautiful unhealthy mystery" of Belmonte turns out to be more complex than Hemingway's argument about the art's "rottenest point." Immediately after the comparison between Belmonte and Joselito, for instance, Hemingway adds: "indeed decadence is a difficult word to use since it has become

138

little more than a term of abuse applied by critics to anything they do not yet understand" (70–71). There is a clear implication that Hemingway (unlike other critics) does understand something of the subtle usages of the term. But this "difficult word" does imply the problematic status of Hemingway's own argument; his caveat in the first chapter that "every year I know there is more to learn" specifically asserts that he does not yet understand bullfighting in any complete way. Moreover, the anecdote about Jean Cocteau and Raymond Radiguet that closes the chapter imputes a very different kind of decadence. Noting Cocteau's riposte to his lover ("Bébé est vicieuse—il aime les femmes" [71]), Hemingway states: "So you see, madame, we must be careful chucking the term decadence about since it cannot mean the same to all who read it" (71). It is possible that Hemingway's irony is doubled-edged here and that we are meant to recognize Cocteau's asseveration of his lover's decadence as merely proving his own. Nevertheless, even the fact of a permanent standard of decadence would not erase the plenitude of meanings it possesses to a speaker like Cocteau and to a multitude of readers.

The possibility that a term like decadence has no meaning except that which hinges on the context of a specific discussion directs us to an even more important twist Hemingway imparts to the debate. For Hemingway himself puts his account of decadence in question with his brief chronicle of previous appraisals of bullfighters. Since 1873 (the accounts Hemingway has been reading date from this year), "bullfighting has always been considered by contemporary chroniclers to be in a period of decadence" (240). Thence follows a very funny history of critical judgments, where Don Luis Mazzantini is "no good" until after his retirement, whereupon he becomes "that colossus of the sword" (240, 241), and Belmonte's big bulls, once he begins to work closer to the bull than Guerrita, become "of course, parodies of the giant animals he, Guerrita, had killed" (242). Bullfighting chronicles turn out to be a parody of respectable histories. Swerving between savage criticism and hagiography, they present a chaos of inflationary accounts, hyperbole, partiality, and sycophancy. Bulls are swollen to great size in these accounts (Hemingway has "looked up the weights and the photographs" to prove it) and reputations seem to depend mostly on how long the bullfighters have been dead. Documents themselves have no documentary value: hence Hemingway doubts whether contemporary accounts of Pedro Romero, who fought before 1873, will enable a "true judgment to be formed" (243) of his skill.

In this case, the problem is not that bullfight historians disagree over the meaning of the word *decadence*, or that they judge bullfighters in different ways, but that they consistently and arbitrarily employ the term in complete disregard of the actual skills of the matadors. We could attribute this lugubrious consensus to a mere idiosyncrasy of the discourse of bullfighting, which leaves open the possibility of truly discovering and naming its golden ages and periods of decadence. Hemingway's claim to have completed his scholarly research (after 1873) into bullfighting history, photos, and statistics grants him nominal authority to write this detached and clear-minded history. He even purportedly settles the issue of the true golden age of bullfighting (he plumps for Lagartijo and Frascuelo). Disingenuously, however, he settles the issue by drawing on the "different sources I have read and all contemporary accounts" (243). The strategy merely returns Hemingway to the accounts whose rhetoricity he has taken such delight in exposing in his own deliciously rhetorical chronicle of the chroniclers. Should we then consider Hemingway's arguments for a contemporary period of decadence in bullfighting as a victory for neutral judgment and careful scholarship or as a return to the tone and historiography of those who always consider bullfighting to be in a period of decadence? However much we attempt to extricate Hemingway from a history of arbitrary judgments, his work reproduces that history too exactly, and draws attention to that reproduction too firmly (and amusingly), to be easily distinguished.

Hemingway's account of a history of dubious chroniclers thus raises doubts about his allegations of decadence. But we might also question whether he is carrying forward *an* argument about decadence in the sport. That assumption is not self-evident, particularly in light of the fact that some readers have read *Afternoon* as a problematically fragmented work. Its "miscellaneous materials" might be collated, as Peter Hays interestingly points out, under the rubric of a "modern omnium-gatherum, like the great Renaissance essay collections using a single topic as a focus by Robert Burton or Sir Thomas Browne"; but, as Hays himself admits, *Afternoon* is "several books masquerading as one."[6] The masquerade is easily broken. The abrupt dramatic interludes with the Old Lady, who is even more abruptly thrown out (190), the sometimes scurrilous literary essays, the anecdotal narratives, and the multiple appendices all suggest an almost Melvillean embracing of polyvocal structure. Everywhere we lack the logical transitions that would bridge

6. Benson, 75; Peter L. Hays, *Ernest Hemingway* (New York: Continuum, 1990), 63.

disparate modes of writing and provide a countervailing sense that its fragments metonymically adduce a whole. Omissions, which Hemingway in his
iceberg theory of writing implied could guide the reader to an ideal plenitude,
emerge here as the corollary of a pervasive disregard of narrative cohesion.

The possibility arises, then, of reading Hemingway's thoughts about decadence as a series of relatively independent arguments, by turns serious and
whimsical, within a narrative structure that draws attention to its bricolage.
On a smaller scale, too, the idea of bricolage seems appropriate to a logic of
obsessive transformation in the book whereby ostensibly direct statements are
modified, supplemented, metaphorically displaced, and contradicted. The
long disquisition on the death of horses in the ring in Chapter 1 provides a
fine example, even though, on the surface, it promises exemplary corroboration of the seemingly straightforward principle of synecdoche whereby parts
truly made would represent the whole: of the "three acts in the tragedy of the
bullfight," Hemingway remarks, it is the "first one, the horse part, which indicates what the others will be, and in fact, makes the rest possible" (98). The
horse part that makes everything possible, however, is problematic not just
for its ethical but for its rhetorical dilemmas: "The question of why the death
of the horse in the bull ring is not moving, not moving to some people that
is, is complicated; but the fundamental reason may be that the death of the
horse tends to be comic while that of the bull is tragic. In the tragedy of the
bullfight the horse is the comic character. This may be shocking, but it is true"
(6). This short passage begins with a statement that turns out to be a more
complicated question than it appears, for the assertion that the death of the
horse is not moving demands a quick supplement in favor of greater precision
("not moving to some people that is"). But the supplement itself hides the
need for a further question: who are "some people"? Hemingway himself has
just undercut any assumptions we might have about who responds to bullfights: "there was no difference, or line of difference, so that these people
[those he introduced to the bullfight] could be divided by any standard of
civilization or experience into those that were affected and those that were not
affected" (4–5). The passage next attempts to establish a "fundamental reason," which is suddenly dis-established in the hesitant "may be" and further
undermined by the vague statement that the death of the horse "tends to be"
comic. The following sentence returns to secure positions (the bullfight is a
tragedy; the horse is comic), preparing the way for the declaration in the next
sentence that "it is true." But what is true quickly unravels with the revelations

that, first, the nature of the comedy varies ("the worse the horses are . . . the more they are a comic element"), second, when horses are gored "they are not comic; but I swear they are not tragic," third, the comic is actually the "burlesque visceral accidents which occur," fourth, that there is "nothing comic by our standards in seeing an animal emptied of its visceral content," fifth, the horse is "as comic when what it is trailing is real as when the Fratellinis give a burlesque of it in which the viscera are represented by rolls of bandages, sausages and other things," and sixth, disembowelings are sometimes "due to their timing . . . very funny" (6–7).

What, then, are we to make of a comedy in which the comic principle is embodied at times in the horses themselves and at other times in certain accidents of "timing"? The convolutions of Hemingway's argument are more than simply appropriate to a complicated question that has perhaps no final answer; they signify the author's own perfectly timed comic play with the rhetorical possibilities of language. In one sense the entire passage is a burlesque—a kind of disemboweling—of Hemingway's own aesthetic principles. The "simplest things" are here conveyed in outrageously long-winded and contradictory fashion. Moreover, the "actual things" themselves seem to vanish before our eyes. The horses' viscera, trailed around the ring, are described nonviscerally as "the opposite of clouds of glory." The Fratellinis are said to burlesque the horses' disembowelings by representing the viscera with "rolls of bandages" (of all things!), but Hemingway's horses are already only representations of horses: they are "parodies of horses," which are even held to look "like birds, any of the awkward birds such as the adjutants or the wide-billed storks" or "a little as a dead pelican does." The last thing that can be done with these parodic bird-horses, it seems, is to see them as they really are; alternatively, if this is how they really are, Hemingway seems unable to present them without the most skillfully managed contrivances of the rhetorician. One of the "simplest things of all and the most fundamental," violent death, turns out to be puzzlingly indeterminate. The example of the horses, which follows hard upon this statement, suggests that this book about bullfighting demands an aesthetic of complexity rather than criteria like "simplest things."

The carnival of perspectives and tone-changes occurring in Chapter 1 puts in question the extent to which we can develop a holistic attitude toward the horses' deaths and thus the extent to which we can know the whole tragedy (or tragi-comedy?) the first part makes possible. The first part itself is composed of many disintegrating parts, as the narrative mimics horses trailing pieces of themselves around the ring. We might then view this passage on the horses, which Hemingway himself views as crucial to what follows, as the work of a bricoleur from whose scattering of possibilities we can pick and choose—or as the work of someone immersed in the polysemous potential of a text that first exposes its vitals and then disingenuously invites us to mistake burlesque for the pure and uncompromised "real thing." Do we read multiple independent arguments or one argument that unravels itself? My point is again not that we should choose or that the book asks us to choose, but that both lines of argument highlight Hemingway's rhetorical games. Both, equally, put in doubt the possibility that this book reaches for a "real thing"— some elemental force, some absolute truth—embodied in, yet beyond the reach of, writing itself.

The kind of debate Hemingway opens with his account of the horses, later intensified by the only superficial victory of "straight talk" over "flowerish-ness" in his description of Cagancho's art, and everywhere implicit in the met-aphoric gorings, woundings, failures, self-dramatizations, and self-doubts that this narrative embodies, still invests the famous dying fall that concludes the main body of the text. Chapter 20 centers on an elegiac lament for lost experi-ences but is also an equivocal meditation on the aesthetics of (in)completion. "If I could have made this enough of a book it would have had everything in it" (270) the chapter begins, and Hemingway continues with a well-known paean to the experience of Spain: "If you could make the yellow flames of candles in the sun . . . make clouds come fast in shadows moving over wheat and the small, careful-stepping horses; the smell of olive oil; the feel of leather; rope soled shoes; the loops of twisted garlics . . . then you would have a little of Navarra. But it's not in this book" (275).

One is tempted to remark along with Hays, "But, of course, it is in the book; you have just read it." There is a sense in which the careful selection of detail in this last chapter does imply some of the range of experiences— people, places, sensations, history—Hemingway associates with the bullfight. But there is also a sense in which the chapter completely discredits its con-cluding notion that "any part you make will represent the whole if it's made truly." An aesthetic allowing metonymic purchase on the whole truth should not need "everything in it," for existing parts would already represent the whole; a feeling for whatever has been omitted should have been given "as strongly as though the writer had stated them" (192). This litany of Spanish experiences only makes us aware of the multitude of things that could have been put in; it suggests, as Messent says, an "impossible wholeness."[7] More profoundly, the chapter turns on the "problem . . . of depiction" for a writer who wishes to stand in the presence of the "actual things" that language can only *represent*. The poignant tone of "If you could make . . . But it's not in this book" arises from an absence that writing can hardly assuage. The "actual things" are actually not in the book, and the writer is left to gesture at a vanished presence whose loss is felt the more intensely as representations accumulate.

I have argued so far that Hemingway's claims for an aesthetic of truth-telling, wholeness, action, and the "real thing" simply fail to describe the complicated rhetorical games of *Death in the Afternoon*. The book is fragmented and riven with contradictory statements masquerading as confident truths, so that elements of doubt and undecidability intrude into what appear to be the most fundamental rules governing aesthetic, moral, psychological, and bull-fighting experience. Abstract-seeming aesthetic issues take on a different and deeper resonance, however, once we begin to activate the correlations between style and masculinity that Hemingway intimates and that his scholarly readers have tended to interpret with such ease. But Hemingway's text places in doubt the very act of making that correlation. It would, for instance, certainly seem possible to find Hemingway, as Mary Jacobus writes, "on the side of everything in language that is multiple, duplicitous, unreliable, and resistant to . . . binary oppositions" (40) and thus speak of Hemingway's style in terms of "*écriture féminine*."[8] The claim itself comes as no surprise. Many feminist critics have noted (as does Jacobus) that the concept of *écriture féminine* advanced by theoreticians like Luce Irigiray and Hélène Cixous can be used to describe the productions of twentieth-century avant-garde writing in general and not a specifically female textual economy.

The possibility of a Hemingwayesque *écriture féminine*, on the other hand, seems febrile in the context of what seems to be the book's unmitigated promotion and celebration of masculine roles at the bullfight. Whatever Hemingway's narrative strategies, the book's concern with courage, nobility, cojones, violent death, and honor, all bound up in the conflict between bull and bull-

---

7. Hays, 66; Messent, 138.

8. Mary Jacobus, "The Question of Language: Men of Maxims and *The Mill on the Floss*," in *Writing and Sexual Difference*, ed. Elizabeth Abel (Chicago: University of Chicago Press, 1982), 40.

fighter, both male, suggests that it is devoted to, and indeed obsessed by, the art of being a man. Though Hemingway specifically mentions women who enjoy the spectacle of the bullfight, so that it would not do to generalize too quickly about how female readers individually or collectively are identified in the book, Hemingway seems more obviously concerned with the conduct not of people but of males, and not just of males but of "full-sized" men. His writing seems to partake of the same self-conscious claims on virility. During his first-chapter apologia for writing a book about bullfighting, for instance, Hemingway argues that violent death is "one of the subjects that a man may write of" (2). His phrasing provocatively allows "man" multiple significances (something that is typical of *Afternoon*). Does this statement suggest that violent death is a topic any male, or possibly any person, may write about? Or does the subject demand, as Max Eastman puts it in his critique of *Afternoon*, a "full-sized man"?[9] The distinction is vital because in the latter case the culturally loaded and culturally specific meaning of *man* leads us back to a rhetoric of truth and authenticity. To be a man as opposed to any adult male signifies in Western culture a set of (somewhat ill-defined) characteristics underpinned by a code of authentic behavior. One cannot fake manhood; fake men are only male; males putting their manhood on display are faking; a man is somehow complete for manhood cannot be eroded or increased in the face of changing circumstances. This essence of authentic manhood appears in the bullfighter's quest for "true, not tricked, emotion" (12) and in the writer's desire to avoid being a "fake" (54). In facing death directly and honestly, it would seem, the writer partakes of the same transcendent manliness imbuing the torero.

The history of scholarship on *Death in the Afternoon*, however, demonstrates that this uncomplicated redaction of the relationship between writer and fighter is scarcely complete or conclusive, for critics have tended to read Hemingway's attempt to turn writer into torero as an exaggeration or overintensification of masculine characteristics. While critics have concurred in reading the bullfight as a powerful source of masculine meaning and value for Hemingway, they have taken his claims for masculine authenticity as a stylized pose. By and large, that is, critics have refused to see his performance as "manly" at all. It is on this basis that *Afternoon* sometimes functions as a watershed in what we might call "regression" theories of Hemingway's work,

9. Max Eastman, "Bull in the Afternoon," *New Republic*, June 7, 1933, 94.

145

which, by integrating individual works into an overarching thesis, seek to comprehend the faltering trajectory of his career. J. Bakker, for instance, argues that *Afternoon* marks a transition point in Hemingway's career whereby the earlier hero, characterized by a "great susceptibility to feeling and emotion," gives way to the later hero, who is portrayed, to the detriment of the fiction, as a man of action. For Broer, too, Hemingway's fascination with the torero in *Afternoon* encourages in subsequent work an "unnerving impulse toward confessionism and exhibitionism—toward the melodramatic display of costume and ritual and toward sensationalistic shows of bravado." His idea may be indebted to Edmund Wilson's attack in *The Wound and the Bow* (1947): the book is "partly infected by a queer kind of maudlin emotion, which sounds at once neurotic and drunken. He overdoes his glorification of the bravery and martyrdom of the bullfighter"; when the author drops the "disciplined and objective art with which he has learned to concentrate in a story the light of the emotions that flood in on him, he straightway becomes befuddled, slops over"; in short, the "whole thing becomes a little hysterical." Philip Young joins the chorus: though the "bullfighter is the man with the code, whom the hero studies, admires and emulates," the book's problem is the "rather hysterical or blood-drunken manner" in which the subject is presented.[10]

This sense that the potentially authentic expression of manly characteristics has here transformed into fake "exhibitionism" is the substance of Max Eastman's infamous review of *Afternoon,* entitled "Bull in the Afternoon." Though Hemingway, according to Eastman, despises the "sentimental poppycock most regularly dished out by those Art nannies and pale-eyed professors of poetry," the author himself falls into the same trap. The book on bullfighting Eastman considers "juvenile romantic gushing and sentimentalizing of

10. Bakker, 6; Broer, 114; Edmund Wilson, *The Wound and the Bow* (Oxford: Oxford University Press, 1947), 93; Young, 68, 69. Herbert J. Muller had already argued in 1937 that *Afternoon* was a "boyish glorification of blood and death, at bottom an adolescent and sentimental performance." Other similar critiques of the book include Maxwell Geismar, who admits that the book includes the "braggadocio, the rather sophomoric, sophisticated smartness which marked his earlier work"; and Richard B. Hovey, who argues that in this book Hemingway has "gone in for a phony mysticism" that "replaces an affirmation of life with a mystique of death." Herbert Muller, *Modern Fiction: A Study of Values* (New York: Funk and Wagnall, 1937), 401; Maxwell Geismar, "Ernest Hemingway: You Could Always Come Back," in ed. McCaffery, 158; Hovey, 103, 105.

simple facts," which ironically arises out of Hemingway's obsession with killing and bloodshed. The "commonplace that Hemingway lacks the serene confidence that he *is* a full-sized man" leads the writer to romanticize the bullfight in what Eastman terms, brilliantly, a "literary style . . . of wearing false hair on the chest." That inflated bravado masks a "child's fairy-story writing." Romanticism obscures the kind of manly "straight talk" that is so crucial, for "a man cannot grow to his height without self-knowledge."[11] Eastman, then, joins Broer, Bakker, Wilson, and many others, in reading *Afternoon* in terms of an obsession with manhood gone awry, which so far distinguishes Hemingway from the experience of authentic manhood that, for Eastman, the author simply produces the kind of sentimental (and by association feminine) gush that the "full-sized man" had eschewed.

Accounts like these do problematize the relationship of writer to fighter, but they leave intact, and indeed depend on, the preservation of an authentic experience of manhood. Terms like "macho," "sentimental," "feminine," and "romantic" are bound into a complicated value system depending for its stability and endurance on a signifier—the masculine—that not only centers the system but actually signifies being centered in the strong, autonomous (male) self. So Eastman recuperates an ideal form of masculinity when he argues that "a man cannot grow to his height without self-knowledge"; and Broer too accepts that at other times Hemingway does achieve an authentic expression of manliness. Something analogous to Hemingway's "real thing" thus underpins their work: if the "actual things . . . which produced the emotion" displace writing and speak, as it were, directly to the observer, so does Hemingway's writing in *Afternoon* displace the essence of true manhood—existing in some ideal form outside the book—and render it into "exhibitionism" and sentimentality. According to these critics, Hemingway's work should not be a stylized representation of masculinity but embody a masculine style; his business is not to represent modes of masculinity but to present the "real thing"; his role is not to exhibit masculine roles in self-alienating gests but to be the "full-sized man."

In a series of odd inversions marking the discourse on *Death in the Afternoon*, then, critics have turned the bullfight—which they concur in reading as a powerful source of masculine meaning and value for Hemingway—against the author. His "disciplined and objective art," confronted by the discipline

11. Eastman, 94–97.

of the matador, "slops over"; the matador's performance transforms into exhibitionism; his display of heightened emotion tips over into hysteria; the matador's killing becomes a "blood-drunken" manner. To judge by the preponderance of critical interpretation, a concept of manliness and aspects of the matador-hero (his grace, courage, power) must be rescued from an exaggeratedly tough masculine pose. Yet that pose turns out to be a hysterical and thus infamously "feminine" manner of presentation. "[G]ushing and sentimentalizing" are the marks of one who lacks confidence in being a "full-sized man," as Eastman says; blood-lust coexists with feminine style. Such arguments can be seen as a partial answer to the uneasy liaison between the book's depiction of male courage and its *écriture féminine*. What appears to be Hemingway's unsavory fascination with male violence can be written off not as an extreme form of maleness—which might impugn the authenticity of the masculine values critics wish to privilege—but as a perverse excrescence of femaleness. As Eastman writes, "gushing and sentimentalizing" are the marks of one who lacks confidence in being a "full-sized man." The answer is to return to the (masculine) discipline embodied in the bullfight but never consistently performed in Hemingway's own prose.

These critics nonetheless convey a deep suspicion of something *outré* about Hemingway's style in *Afternoon* that confuses the straightforward assimilation of the principles and ideals of manhood for which Hemingway has always seemed to stand. And they are right. But these accounts have transformed insight into critique because they have assumed that a book about male bullfighters by Hemingway must celebrate the essence of manhood in terms of honor, courage, endurance, and cojones. They have assumed, furthermore, that the conjunction of writer and fighter requires Hemingway to write those same principles into his style. In accordance with Young's dictate "the style *is* the man," most critics have felt justified in arguing that Hemingway's unrestrained "slop" must therefore represent his wounded or anxious or adolescent sense of manhood. I want to argue instead that Hemingway's representations of masculinity arising from the bullfight are scandalous, not because he tries and fails to create a style commensurate with a "full-sized man," but because he views manhood (on display in the arena) and style (on display for readers) as *theatrical*. The bullfight, then, need not be rescued from Hemingway's hysterical or gushy depiction of it; nor should it represent the ideal of disciplined manliness by which his sentimentality can be known and censured. Its articulation of manhood-as-performance instead leads to a critique of the very codes of masculinity it has always been held to exemplify.

In one of the odd dialogues with the Old Lady, for example, Hemingway's narrator agrees with the Old Lady's characterization of three bullfighters as "most valorous and manly chaps" (70). A few pages later, this association between courage and manliness is tested by the bullfighter Maera, who, despite six attempts to kill the bull with the pain of a dislocated wrist, refuses to kill the bull easily because "his honor demanded that he kill [the bull] high up between the shoulders, going in as a man should, over the horn" (81). Hemingway concludes his description with the remark: "Era muy hombre" (82). The scene seems to describe a classic example of the masculine code. Maera displays grace under the pressure of a dislocated wrist and possesses the fortitude to administer death in terms of a code of conduct that prescribes what "a man" should do. In the next paragraph Maera's honest courage is even parlayed into the beginnings of a lesson in morality: Maera is much of a man, as Hemingway explains in Spanish, but in "Spain a man feels that the less he pays his subordinates the more man he is, and in the same way the nearer he can bring his subordinates to slaves the more man he feels he is" (82). Maera (who does not treat his subordinates this way) presumably upholds a true standard of manhood that informs every moment of his performance with the bull. In contrast, men in general subscribe to a code of fake mastery. Economic mastery of other men therefore displaces domination of the bull; an illusory feeling of power displaces the man of integrity; standards bound into transient historical circumstances displace transcendent masculinity.

Nonetheless, the circumstance of "a man" feeling that "the less he pays his subordinates the more man he is" is worrying in the sense that it begins to erode the foundation of an effective typology of manliness. Though we might like to believe in the hierarchy of the true man (Maera) over the fake (economic man), Hemingway makes clear that in the cultural environment of Spain to pay a subordinate less actually is seen as conduct befitting a man. By this competing model of manliness, Maera is not even a "man," and Belmonte, who pays Maera little as a member of his cuadrilla, could more justly claim the epithet "muy hombre." Like Hemingway's point about decadence, the term manhood "cannot mean the same to all who read it" (71) Whether or not Hemingway might distinguish between true and fake (economic) manhood, we have to admit that (according to Hemingway) to a Spaniard both ways are equally authentic. This discussion seems to do scant justice to the tone of this passage, but it does have the advantage of posing the question of what actually constitutes the measure of manhood. Performing actions "as a man should," which seems a self-evident justification of Maera's superiority, turns out to be inadequate, for going in over the horn and paying a subordinate less both appear to be appropriate measures of manliness in Spain. Still more problematically, other bullfighters who go in over the horn seem not to be men, or are characterized as less of men. Barrera, for instance, goes in once "to try his luck at getting the sword in without exposing himself in any way," a method that, "while it keeps within the letter of the rules, is the negation of the whole spirit and tradition of the bullfight" (248, 249). The "really brave" Fortuna is also "brave and stupid" (260). And Cayetano Ordonez, when he nerved himself to fight well, gave performances that were the "brave actions of a coward" (90).

If going in over the horn is what a man should do, but does not guarantee manliness of Maera's type, we must look for manhood in some essential and integral characteristic of the individual, such as the valor that is "so absolute and such a solid part" (78) of Maera. What, then, are we to make of the matador Luis Freg who, with his seventy-two severe horn wounds in twenty-one years, seems still more valorous than Maera himself, but whose valor seems intensely problematic? Freg's terrible gorings, Hemingway writes,

> had no effect on his valor at all. But it was a strange valor. It never fired you; it was not contagious. You saw it, appreciated it, and knew the man was brave, but somehow it was as though courage was a syrup rather than a wine or the taste of salt and ashes in your mouth. If qualities have odors, the odor of courage to me is the smell of the sea when the wind rips the top from a wave, but the valor of Luis Freg did not have that odor. It was clotted and heavy, and there was a thin part underneath that was unpleasant and oozy. (263)

The passage is remarkable for its metaphoric power but also for the fact of metaphoric transcription itself. Underscored by doubled modifiers (it is not only "as though courage was a syrup" but "somehow . . . as though"), a slippage occurs between what the observer "saw" and what the writer is able to say. This essence of valor, when captured in language, is knowable only in terms other than itself; it constantly evades the moment when we might recognize authentic valor for what it is. If we look elsewhere in the book for definitive accounts of what valor is, moreover, we find only an elaboration of modes of valor: Martínez's valor is "almost humorous" (262), Fortuna's "dumb" (262), Zurito's "mystic" (262), Litri's "nervous" (254), Villalta's "conceited" (262) and "semi-hysterical" (253). Beyond that, valor lacks an integral and lasting relationship to its possessor: "Courage comes from such a short distance; from the heart to the head; but when it goes no one knows how far away it goes" (222). Freg's valor is not only weirdly "clotted and heavy," but subject to disappear entirely at any time.

In trying to establish the connection between valor and manhood, then, we have at least two unsatisfying options. We can try to infer courage from acts that can nevertheless be performed uncourageously, or mystically, or nervously; or we can know courage from an essence that is actually unnameable or named only in a series of metaphoric displacements. The related concept of honor, which demanded that Maera kill the bull "high up . . . as a man should," only makes the attempt at definition more fraught with problems. Attempts to describe Hemingway's ethics have naturally gravitated to his definition of the Spanish *pundonor,* which means "honor, probity, courage, self-respect, and pride in one word," and which Hemingway insists is an accurate description of the Spanish character: this "honor thing is not some fantasy that I am trying to inflict on you. . . . I swear it is true" (91, 92). Hemingway's conclusion, however, puts in question the extent to which honor can be truly known: "Honor to a Spaniard, no matter how dishonest, is as real a thing as water, wine, or olive oil. There is honor among pickpockets and honor among whores. It is simply that the standards differ." Honor, it turns out, is as negotiable as terms like valor or decadence. How shall we ever distinguish true honor from fake if, as Hemingway implies, its meaning is malleable and confined to specific contexts—and if honor can even mean dishonesty? If standards simply differ, our criteria of judgment must also be confined to specific contexts, and we could not know the difference between an honest individual's and a dishonest individual's honor. Nor could we completely know the difference between honor and dishonor, for the only way to do so would be to affirm an absolute standard of honor that did not differ from situation to situation. As a corollary, if we were to distinguish between honor and dishonor in the specific context of bullfighting, the distinction might have no relevance to any other context: we could not generalize our findings into a definition of manhood itself.

All of this bears directly on Hemingway's representation of authentic manhood. In an early essay on Hemingway, Lincoln Kirstein, iterating the familiar criticism that the author's thinking about men is "infantile, naive and limited," argues succinctly that he "divides most males . . . into two classes, those with balls and those without. . . . He allocates his maleness according to his prejudices and has always in mind his two categories."[12] In fact, the subtle play of meaning in terms like honor and valor suggest a much richer, polyvocal discourse on manhood. Passages like the one on Maera begin to lose their ostensible stability and clarity when placed alongside a multitude of other instances that fray or overburden definitions. At best, it seems, the text can only point outside itself to the actual things that words cannot put down and say "At this point it is necessary that you see a bullfight" (63), "if you should ever see the real thing you would know it" (207). Kirstein's transcription of Hemingway's most famous metonym, however, suggests a way out of the dilemma: manliness can be summed up by a man's cojones. In this way, the male part will represent a masculine whole whose intricate and possibly unnameable aspects cannot be articulated directly. Early in *Afternoon*, for instance, we are informed that Anglo-Americans are "fascinated by victory, and we replace the avoidance of death by the avoidance of defeat," which is, Hemingway remarks, a "very nice symbolism, but it takes more cojones to be a sportsman when death is a closer party to the game" (22). The pursuit of victory is held to be a metaphoric displacement of the authentic game of life and death, which demands instead a quality (cojones) that cannot be fake or merely symbolic. Hemingway's glossary implies a similar point: here, cojones is glossed as "testicles; a valorous bullfighter is said to be plentifully equipped with these. In a cowardly bullfighter they are said to be absent" (396). The glossary seems to emphasize the central function played by the term *cojones* in the book's signifying systems: it carries the ability to mark the difference between man and not-man; between valorous fighter and coward.

It should be noted, however, that the very quality that makes cojones useful as a sign of manhood is precisely its status as metaphor. One could not otherwise distinguish between a heroic and cowardly bullfighter on the basis of equipment that both actually possess. Kirstein implies as much when he remarks that Hemingway allocates males to his two classes—"those with balls and those without"—on the basis of "prejudices" alone. Hemingway's own work implies as much: Jake Barnes seems to have cojones even though he may lack testicles. It is because there is no natural and necessary relationship be-

12. Lincoln Kirstein, "The Canon of Death," in ed. McCaffery, 60.

tween the signifier *cojones* and its signified (testicles) that the term can be liberated to mean the valor, gutsiness, and pride befitting a man. Put simply: a man does not draw valor from his testicles, but his testicles draw meaning when associated with his valor. At the moment of valorous action, they become symbolic (and thus cojones). The point is crucial in several ways. Importantly, it would suggest that *cojones* has reference to gender—the systems of signification that construct terms like man and woman—rather than sex, which leaves open the possibility not only that a Jake Barnes might possess cojones but that a woman, such as Pilar in *For Whom the Bell Tolls*, might "have cojones" and thus be, metaphorically, a "man." It would not be nonsense to emend Hemingway's line to read "it takes more cojones to be a sportsman or sportswoman when death is a closer party to the game." Hemingway is far from writing the male body. Meaning lies not in male genitalia but in the rich possibilities of signification, so that a valorous bullfighter can *be said to be* plentifully equipped with cojones. The essence of manhood is that man is metaphor.

There are several corollaries to this statement. Most importantly, to turn Hemingway's glossary on its head, it is not that cojones signify the presence or absence of valor; the amount of valor signifies the presence or absence of cojones. A man, that is, cannot be said to have cojones until he has demonstrated valorous action. Cojones are always in the process of *being signified*. Unfortunately, as I have shown, the very meaning of valorous action is in doubt because we hesitate between seeing it as translatable only in an intricate series of other metaphors, and thus constantly being modified, or seeing it as tied to the immediacy of a specific situation. In either case, one can define cojones only in supplemental ways: we would need to know whether the man had, say, Zurito's mystic valor or Villalta's semi-hysterical valor, or, alternatively, the circumstances under which mystic or semi-hysterical valor was demonstrated. What we cannot know is the nature of cojones in a pure or direct state, standing outside the play of language, outside the exigencies of particular situations, and outside the observer's evaluation. A crucial implication of a metaphorics of manhood is that meaning arises out of verbal transactions between members of a linguistic community—in this case those versed in the language of bullfighting. Meaning is relational. A brave bullfighter can only be "said to be plentifully equipped" with cojones; the bullfighter's valor is rhetorical and contingent on the one who speaks his valor into being. The matador's performance is always, in part, being performed by others.

While critics have always derived values like bravery, honor, ritual, and discipline from the corrida, in fact, only cursory attention has been paid to the way in which the fact of performance in the arena shapes Hemingway's conception of masculinity. In part this may be because critics have read Hemingway's complex sense of the bullfight as a denial of theatricality. Early on Hemingway rejects the theatrical connotations of the word "act." A similar concern lies behind his criticism of the matador Sanchez Mejias, of whom Hemingway is so contemptuous that he chooses to "devote little space to him in this book." Sanchez Mejias was "very brave, but he laid his bravery on as with a trowel. It was as though he were constantly showing you the quantity of hair on his chest or the way in which he was built in his more private parts. That is not the function of bravery in bullfighting. It should be a quality whose presence permits the fighter to perform all acts he chooses to attempt, unhampered by apprehension. It is not something to club the public with" (94). Hemingway's contempt for Sanchez Mejias is somewhat amusing in light of Max Eastman's later attack on the author's "literary style . . . of wearing false hair on the chest," which led to the infamous shirt-ripping episode in Maxwell Perkins's office I have already described. The passage, however, seems to be a serious attempt to distinguish a sincere display of cojones (for Sanchez Mejias is "very brave") from a fake. Bravery in a bullfighter, then, seems to be an internal quality that should allow performance (in the sense of carrying something out); it need not be, and indeed should not be, dramatized. The private (parts) should not become public. Sanchez Mejias is, as it were, too much the rhetorician, allowing hollow figures to replace the "quality whose presence" signifies the real thing. In an appropriate counterpoint, Hemingway's text elaborates the deficiencies of Sanchez Mejias's style with garish figuration. Fakery is signaled textually by one showy metaphor (it "was as though he were constantly showing you the quantity of hair on his chest") and then another, the phallic joke in "club the public," to which the Old Lady predictably makes the ingenuous rejoinder "I have never been clubbed with it yet." In a sense Hemingway out-performs Sanchez Mejias in dramaturgy. The bullfighter, after all, does not literally club his public with his private parts, but Hemingway's conceits have the capacity to generate a potentially endless linguistic gamesmanship: private parts leads us by association to club, which then leads to the Old Lady's digression and the author's off-color retort: "Madame, you will be clubbed silly with it if you ever see Sanchez Mejias" (94).

As this example suggests, one of the book's great concerns is with theatrical modes of fakery, and it is worth exploring the issue of theatricality in order to provide a context for a fuller discussion of the way in which Hemingway poses the problem of authentic masculinity. A "serious public" at the bullfight, for instance, should know the "faked from the sincere" (42), a distinction that reminds us of feeling "defrauded" (50) at paying good money to see a poor show. Everywhere, in fact, Hemingway registers a landscape of fake display. During the "girl inspection" before the bullfight begins, for instance, using glasses will "destroy for you some of the greatest and most startling beauties who will come in with cloudy white lace mantillas, high combs and complexions and wonderful shawls" (41). The one who inspects inappropriately, however, is known as a pseudo-looker: a "voyeur" (41). Madrid, a little later, is said to lack "phonies" and "disgusting fakes like the gypsy caves at Granada" (51). In keeping with that spirit of Madrid being the true "essence" of Spain, the Prado makes no attempt to "theatricalize or set off masterpieces" so that the "tourist looking in the red or blue guide book to see which are the famous ones feels vaguely disappointed. . . . the pictures are so simply hung and easy to see that the tourist feels cheated" (52). The Prado's method, no doubt, can be related to Hemingway's own desire for a sincere and "pure" writing, which at other times is distinguished from "flowery" (14) writing, "fake" (54) writing, and "erectile" (53) writing, and all four from something like journalism, which offers a particular version of events tempered by the element of "timeliness" (2).

These modes of theatricality correspond to a wide array of fake performances inscribed within the bullfight itself. Most bulls, Hemingway asserts, are now put to death in a "parody of the true way to kill" (232); the matador Alfredo, in attempting to remedy his "vulgar" way of performing the dangerous veronica, is "substituting various picturesque tricks with the cape for that one irreplaceable test of a fighter's serenity and artistic ability" (230); the work of the young Bienvenida seems to Hemingway to "smell of the theatre," though if so it is a "more subtle trick than any we have seen yet" (167). These faked ways of giving emotion are to be differentiated from the slight value possessed by "picturesque" bullfighting, which also characterizes a kind of inadequate observing (the "picturesqueness that you want when you are still in the spectacle stage of appreciation" [42]). Adorno, the glossary tells us, refers to "any useless or flowery theatricality performed by the bullfighter to show his domination over the bull," though this may be "in good or bad taste" (380). The kind of "flowery work" demonstrated by Gallo has some value, but performed alone will "deprive the spectators of the real part of bullfighting, the man deliberately passing the bull's horns as close and as slowly as he can past his own body and to substitute a series of graceful tricks, valuable as ornaments to a faena, for the sincere danger of the faena itself" (215). Sanchez Mejias presumably represents another type of performer, as one who does bravely invite danger but "laid his bravery on as with a trowel."

Once again, Hemingway draws up a series of seemingly stable oppositions: the "real part" of bullfighting confronts "flowery" adornment; the pure veronica counters picturesque tricks; the sincere or intended act (suerte) undermines theatrical display. These oppositions have their counterparts in the rhetorical schemas that mark Hemingway's account of writing. Flowery work with the cape, for instance, corresponds to the "worst of flowery writing" Hemingway employs to describe a veronica. More profoundly, the discourse of the faked bullfight refers us to the fear of metaphoric displacement that underpins Hemingway's most important aesthetic statements in this book. Just as Hemingway seems to wish to obviate the substitutive play of language itself in his quest for the "real thing," so does fake fighting substitute "various picturesque tricks" and "a series of graceful tricks" for real bullfighting. Fake fighting is thus a metaphor tricked out as synecdoche: though adorno actually may be part of a complete faena, it bears only a metonymic relationship to the authentic pass, which involves the man "deliberately passing the bull's horns as close and as slowly as he can past his own body." The trick pass bears none of the transcendent emotion invested in the real thing, which, by definition, allows for no substitution; the trick merely mimics the real in a parody of plenitude. It is essentially empty—a flowery metaphor representing and thus lacking the rich presence of the real thing.

As Hemingway's images everywhere make clear, this process of metaphoric substitution emerges in various forms of theatrical display. Only when the matador works dangerously close to the bull, as Hemingway comments at one point, can one see whether his grace is an "altogether inherent quality and not a pose" (211–12). This distinction between inherent, non-substitutable qualities and actions that are extrinsic, posed, and metaphoric is a compelling way of thinking about Hemingway's aesthetics of performance. Gallo's work with the bull, which Hemingway uses to exemplify flowery grace without substance, is defined as "pure spectacle" (213)—perhaps an appropriate counterpart to those spectators who are still at a "spectacle stage of appreciation." Pure spectacle does not so much oppose the real thing as become a kind of perfect simulacrum, and in so doing marks a hollowed-out form of rhetoric-ity; Gallo's passes were "beautiful to see" but the "negation of true bullfight-ing" (214). This form of aesthetic perfection that contains a peculiar absence or lack has one more twist, for we find that Gallo himself can be imitated: "it was only good if he did it. His imitators only showed how unsound it all was" (213). Oddly, the value of Gallo's theatrical performance is rescued only to be once again removed. His performance cannot be altogether empty if it can be considered "good" and compelling enough to attract imitators. On the other hand, if his imitators merely demonstrate the original's unsoundness, we must harbor the suspicion that there was nothing authentic to imitate.

Hemingway's animus against forms of fake theatricality, however, should not obscure the fact that true bullfighting—which Gallo's "pure spectacle" is held to negate—itself depends on display. True beauties at the corrida also expose themselves to the gaze, and the simply hung pictures in the Prado are after all meant for inspection; for Hemingway, their simple frames actually dramatize their lack of pretension. And the bullfight is always a performance staged before an audience, whose presence is crucial for more reasons than the fact that, as Hemingway comments in the text to one of the photographs, the bullfight is a "commercial spectacle." Attempts to understand the meta-phorical significance of the bullfight in *Death in the Afternoon*, however com-pelling their outcomes in formulating ideas about ritual, courage, masculinity, and code heroes, have always seriously undervalued the role that performance plays in unsettling and compromising firm epistemological positions. Indeed, the whole value of the bullfight resides in its performance, where "perform-ance" is understood to signify in several interlocking senses: the bullfight must be watched; it is a series of acts taking place in unfolding time; it demands quality action (as in the phrase "high performance"). It is for this reason that Hemingway invites his readers to see a bullfight, for if "I were to describe one it would not be the one that you would see, since the bullfighters and the bulls are all different" (63); it is for this reason that the complete faena is so rare, particularly in this decadent age; and it is for this reason that Hemingway emphasizes the temporality of the art of bullfighting, which is an "imperma-nent art" that "finishes with whoever makes it" (99). The only connotation of "act" that seems out of bounds for Hemingway is "theatricality," which, as we have seen, implies something like "show for its own sake" as part of the book's discourse on modes of fakery. But the bullfighter must (ideally) adhere to a scripted series of acts and possess a charismatic ability to transmit emotion to the audience.

The climactic moments of a great faena, however, place the issue of performance in a quite different light. When the "arrogant slowness" of the veronicas "becomes, for the seeming minutes that they endure, permanent" (14), and when a complete faena "takes a man out of himself and makes him feel immortal while it is proceeding" (206), we seem to approach a mythic and transcendent moment—an "original moment of truth, or of reality" (174), as Hemingway puts it—that has occasioned some important scholarship focused on myth and ritual. In some ways, that scholarship has respected the performative dimensions of the ritualized bullfight. As we have seen, Christian Messenger's account of the mythic role played by the Ritual Sports Hero does emphasize the "witnessing of his deeds," because "ritual demands that celebrants share in the power and beauty of the performance."[13] For Messenger and Allen Josephs, however, performance is merely a vehicle to transcendence of the secular, the profane, and the historical. The climax of the performance destroys, as it were, the fact of performance. According to this logic, the perfectly executed killing needs no interpretation or even description; it is ecstatic, untranslatable. Hemingway's account of his first bullfight allows that "I could not see in my mind exactly what happened" (234–35). But Hemingway "remembered in the midst of this confused excitement having a great moment of emotion when the man went in with the sword" (234), an assertion underscored by the earlier comment that "if you should ever see the real thing you would know it" (207). All that remains, it seems, is to elaborate some of the prosaic facts that surround but should never be confused with this intuitive flash.

But Hemingway never frees the transcendent moment of killing from the fact of performance. As the bullfighter is "playing with death, bringing it closer, closer, closer, to himself," Hemingway writes at one point, he "gives the feeling of his immortality, and, as you watch it, it becomes yours. Then when it belongs to both of you, he proves it with the sword" (213). Again, the "complete faena" is described as "moving all the people in the ring together and increasing in emotional intensity as it proceeds, carrying the bullfighter with it, he playing on the crowd through the bull and being moved as it responds in a growing ecstasy of ordered, formal, passionate, increasing disre-

13. Messenger, 251.

gard for death" (206, 207). The complete faena is portrayed as relational and communal, and the moments of ritual transcendence Hemingway describes all record a negotiation between artist and audience. While the matador does face the bull alone, that solitary encounter must itself be placed within the context of the gazes that supply the rationale for the fight and determine the emotional outcome. The solitariness of the matador is a function of the crowd's desire for solitary conflict inscribed within the traditional rules of the corrida. The "moment of truth" (68) signifies a conjoining of action and gaze rather than a point where performance yields to a transcendent "real thing." No act (or suerte) taking place in the bullring can be whole or self-identical with itself; each is hollowed out and alienated from itself by the presence of the watching other; each is profoundly gestic. Each act demands negotiation by others, even if we trust Hemingway when he claims that we need only experience the complete faena (we already "know" it) rather than have it explained by an intermediary. A complete faena could not be complete without an audience; a faena performed in utter isolation could give no emotion. In this respect, it is notable that the amateur capeas (or "town-square bullfights with used bulls") lack both the productive role of the audience and the emotion Hemingway desires. Where the fight is "more enjoyable to player than to spectator," watching gives way to participation, and the capeas are characterized by many men trying to perform simultaneously, which leads occasionally to a "very barbarous, messy" (24) group killing of the bull.

The fact that performance (doing) in the arena cannot be separated from dramatic performance (showing) is crucial to an interpretation of the aesthetic, ethical, and intellectual implications of Hemingway's bullfight metaphor, particularly with respect to the issue of masculinity. Though Hemingway disparages theatricality, the "spectacle stage of appreciation," and Sanchez Mejias's "showing you . . . the way in which he was built in his more private parts," the effect is not to place the fact of performance out of bounds but to determine its role more exactly. The bullfighter still needs to give a charismatic display; the audience needs to observe carefully and expertly; the man in the ring still needs to show cojones, though this display should imply internal qualities. To the extent that bullfighting is a metaphor for masculinity, we cannot ignore the role of performance in the fashioning of manhood, nor the fact that manhood is fashioned, or constructed, rather than a permanent and unchanging essence. Manhood stands somewhere between metonymy and metaphor. To kill a bull correctly and bravely one must *be* a man (so that the killing is a natural part of one's essential being). Confusingly, however, that manliness can only be *represented* (so that "essential" being becomes contingent on the quality of the display). The very nature of the bullfight is to be intensely metaphorical and to transform every act taking place in the arena into a representation of something else and for someone else. It makes impossible the act of distinguishing essence from the representation of it.

Because the interrelationship between matador and audience is such that "if a really good bullfighter is to come and to remain honest, sincere, without tricks . . . there must be a nucleus of spectators that he can play for" (163), it is not surprising that *Death in the Afternoon* is as much a compendium of forms of spectating as it is of forms of bullfighting. If "the spectator did not impose the rules, keep up the standards, prevent abuses and pay for the fights there would be no professional bullfighting in a short time and no matadors" (164), Hemingway comments, and his apothegm seems most necessary because the alleged decadence of bullfighting owes much to its audiences. Bullfighters tend to parody the true way of killing in part because the audience allows and even encourages abuses, as it does when applauding Vicente Barrera for "cheating in the killing because he performs a trick with skill, assurance, and security" (249). If "they prefer tricks to sincerity they soon get the tricks" (163), Hemingway asserts. For that reason, the initiate at the bullfight will want a "good public" (42) as well as good bulls and good matadors. A good public, it appears, is hard to find. It is not the "public of a one bullfight fiesta where everyone drinks and has a fine time, and the women come in costume, nor is it the drunken, dancing, bull-running public of Pamplona, nor the local, patriotic, bullfighter worshippers of Valencia" (42); nor, presumably, would it be the Bilbao crowd that demonstrates "how tough a crowd can be and how thoroughly bullfighters can be terrorized" (39). Madrid, Hemingway claims, provides a good public, though, in a typical strategy of confident assertion followed by subtle questioning, even this claim demands important caveats: "not the days of the benefit fights with elaborate decorations, much spectacle and high prices, but the serious public of the abonos [those holding subscriptions] who know bullfighting, bulls, and bullfighters" (42).

Like Hemingway's inquiry into decadence, where ostensibly authoritative statements turned out to need qualification and sometimes radical revision, the significance of these different crowds emerges not in isolation but contextually. His critique of bullfight audiences in Chapter 4 should be read as part of an exhaustive typology of modes of seeing. The chapter begins by detailing the best kind of fight to see (a novillada), where to see a fight (Madrid), where to sit (the barreras in the shade), and when various ferias take place. Visiting Aranjuez, moreover, the author juxtaposes book knowledge (one can "find the sights in Baedeker" [40]) with the actual sights of the "professional cripples and horror and pity inspirers" lining the road, so that one walks a "dusty gauntlet between two rows of horrors to the ring" (40). These horrors demand a different form of visual representation: "The town is Velasquez to the edge and then straight Goya to the bull ring" (40). (These two painters later find their modern-day counterparts in the two watercolorists who paint "attractive souvenirs" [43].) Straight Goya transforms instantly to the "girl inspection" that is a "big part of bullfighting for the spectator," only to return as the glasses destroy some of the "greatest and most startling beauties," who are revealed in with all their "gold teeth and flour-covered swartness" (41). With another abrupt wrench, we move from beauty that masks horror to a scene of violent death that sometimes conveys a supreme aesthetic experience: "if you never look at girls the glasses are good to watch the killing of the last bull" (42). The passage then modulates into a discussion comparing picturesque bullfighting to picturesque places (Aranjuez and Ronda), though by the end of the chapter the picturesque has yielded to a display of dishonor: the "great style" (45) of matador Chaves's fighting, as Hemingway mordantly calls it.

Hemingway infuses this account of modes of representation with a sarcastic critique of iconology: beauties that the glasses inspect and destroy; Granero, who spends a half-million pesetas on "publicity, propaganda" for himself (which contrasts with the colorful advertising posters that also publicize the corridas); the narrow-minded Valencians who "worship bullfighters, Valencian bullfighters, rather than enjoy the bullfights" (45), and who take on new "idols" every year; and someone from Grau, Chaves's home town, who inscribes a "public monument" (a urinal) with Chaves's shame (46). At the same time, the chapter contains a critique of icon-breakers—the tough Bilbao enthusiasts who argue that bullfighters are "all alike—all cowards, all fakes" (38), and perhaps even the spectator who, destroying fake beauties, nonetheless finds a beautiful girl in "some box you might not have noticed without the glasses" (41). Finally, we might note the concluding clash of gazes that penetrates the hollowness of Chaves's performances: "the one time I saw him a year ago he was not so well fed looking as formerly and standing in the

161

shade he began sweating the minute he saw the bull come out" (46). Ending on a note of realistic assessment and mordant irony, the chapter completes its tour of constantly varying perspectival modes. Advertising posters modulate to Baedekers, professional displays of horrors to Velasquez and Goya, girl inspections to assessments of crowds, icons to monumental urinals. In the same way, pragmatic information on how to watch gives way to the icon-fashioning of a commercialized spectacle, while picturesque descriptions of what can be seen yield to the incisive gaze that exposes Chaves's cowardice.

Chapter 4, with its compendium of ways of gazing and ways of representing, suggests something of the profound epistemological and narrative implications that modes of seeing have for Hemingway. That acme of the Madrid audience, the "serious public of the abonos who know bullfighting," attests to the collusion between watching and knowing: to watch in a perceptive way is to "know"; and to "know" implies refined vision. We might even argue that the goal of the chapter is to transform readers into the "serious public of the abonos" by offering instruction about modes of knowledgeable gazing—an interpretation that sits well with the typical view of Hemingway as a writer promoting expertise as the foundation of ethical behavior. Under this rubric, we could read Chapter 4 as an inversion of the earlier meditation on the deaths of the horses: whereas the significance of the horses' deaths becomes progressively more indeterminate under the piling-up of digressive and even contradictory statements, Chapter 4 cleanses and clarifies our sight, leading us from the perils of icon-making and -breaking to objective knowledge. The chapter leads us, as it were, to the "real thing." What the "serious public of the abonos" experience at the successfully performed "moment of truth," we experience in a flash of knowledge—as, for instance, the truth of Chaves's bullfighting comes suddenly clear.

The more crucial implication of this argument is that our role as readers reprises that of a good public in the construction of significance: we not only observe a panoply of modes of seeing but participate in evaluating them. We distinguish, for instance, between icon and urinal, just as a serious bullfighting public distinguishes between trick and sincerity and then proceeds to enforce those values in subsequent fights. The reader's role at the arena of writing matches the equivocal role of the bullfighter's audience, which does not perform but whose presence is nonetheless constitutive of the performance. Throughout *Death in the Afternoon*, we are invited to view the construction of meaning as a kind of performance: as a series of interpretive acts (or

suertes, perhaps) that must be carried out in conjunction with the text. Nowhere is this clearer than at the heart of Chapter 4, where the long description
of the town of Ronda keys this chapter's fascination with the gaze. During his
description, Hemingway notes that the "entire town and as far as you can see
in any direction is romantic background" (43), perfect for a "honeymoon or
an elopement," and observes that "you can see it if necessary without leaving
the hotel, beautiful short walks, good wine, sea-food, a fine hotel, practically
nothing else to do, two resident painters who will sell you watercolours that
will frame as attractive souvenirs of the occasion; and really, in spite of all
this, it is a fine place" (43). Ronda appears to be a town, as it were, at the
"spectacle stage of appreciation" (42), where "romantic" evokes both the love
interest Hemingway sees as appropriate to the town and a kind of flimsy picturesqueness associated with the attractive watercolors. To see the town from
the hotel is to be, in terms Hemingway has just employed for bullring gazers,
a "voyeur, a looker in the worst sense; that is a looker rather than a do-er" (41).

But until Hemingway remarks that Ronda is a fine place "in spite of all
this," we miss completely the ironic undertones of his description. "That is
where you should go if you ever go to Spain on a honeymoon," pronounces
Hemingway, and there is no reason to doubt this information offered by a
knowledgeable insider. Nor, since Hemingway usually plays the gourmand
straightforwardly (as he does two paragraphs later when evoking the beer,
shrimps, and paella in Grau), is there any reason to suspect Ronda and its
"beautiful short walks, good wine, sea-food" as being anything other than the
seat of pleasurable hedonism. What appears to be a non-ironic description of
a romantic landscape is turned retrospectively into a romantic (or simplified,
flimsy, exaggerated) narrative. Without knowing it we have been knowing
picturesquely; without recognizing it we have been seeing insincerely. The
ironic twist of "in spite of all this," restructuring narrative and vision together,
reveals that the putative facts about Ronda were all along subject to a clearer
and more accurate way of knowing. In support of that latter point, we might
adduce the end of passage on Ronda, which concludes with a quite unroman-
tic description of buzzards feeding on the dead horses on the rocks below the
town, where they are thrown after being killed in the ring.

That ironic twist, moreover, invites us to act on our new knowledge: we
circle back to revise what we have seen and the way we have seen it, and thus
to perform a new (and more pragmatic) interpretation. In the process, the

twist transforms us from lookers (voyeurs) to doers, from lovers of the picturesque to knowers, from those at the "spectacle stage of appreciation" to a "serious public," from those deceived by rhetoric to those desiring firm
denotative statements, and from romantics to realists. The passage on Ronda
thus demonstrates what we might call an interpretive suerte: an act (or really
enacting) of reading that reminds us of the bullfighter's controlled maneuvers
and that matches Hemingway's own aesthetic of the "real thing," which also
disavows the sentimentality of faked or clichéd emotions. Our knowledge of
Ronda also does not emerge directly and purely from the text; it depends
upon our performance of it. Reading becomes an active process of re-vision.
We are compelled into a pursuit of the real Ronda, which can only be discovered by moments of recognition (seeing the irony), looking again (an act of
rereading), and reenactment (activating different linguistic codes). Thereafter,
as we carry out other interpretive suertes, we may be less easily gulled into the
fraudulently sincere.

Reading the passage on Ronda as a kind of narratalogical schooling in appropriate suertes certainly evokes the book's concern with things that are real,
unfaked, stable, and clearly perceived. But it also does scant justice to the
complexity of Ronda. One problem is that the narrative act that asks us to see
ostensibly forthright statements like "attractive souvenirs" as merely rhetorical is itself rhetorical. In its complicated acts of concealment and whimsical
revelation it draws attention to the process of figuration: to what was not
stated clearly, purely, and simply. Indeed, nothing at Ronda seems to escape
the purview of language. Language, we come to know, always embodies a particular point of view (we see romantically or ironically or truly); but vision is
always and already at the mercy of language (otherwise seeing, as a pure and
pre-linguistic mode of knowing, would never allow us to misinterpret Ronda's
scenery). Knowing and seeing truly is a function of language, not a pre-linguistic function that escapes rhetoricity. The problem of seeing and writing
the "real thing" is exemplified by the buzzard-haunted corpses at the end of
the passage. Befitting the abrupt juxtapositions and transformations of tone
and perspective in this chapter, that Goyaesque conclusion counters the picturesque aspects of Ronda; but it also, in some unquantifiable way, modifies
Hemingway's own humorous critique of the picturesque. If Hemingway can
write "in spite of all this, it is a fine place," should we now add "in spite of
that, it is a place of blood and death"? Should we read this conclusion as the
ultimate iconoclasm—for, as Hemingway tells the Old Lady, all stories end in

death—and thus the "real thing"? Should we see Ronda as a "fine place" in spite of both its picturesqueness and its aspects of Gothic horror? Or as a "fine place" precisely because of unflinching acceptance of death? After all, its very name evokes its siting in a "circle of mountains" and its buzzards who "circled" over the town and "ring": in circular fashion, death merely offers life to Ronda's seafood-loving tourists and hungry buzzards.

My point is not that we should, or should be able to, choose between these (and other) readings, but that the supposition that we are now seeing and reading clearly rather than romantically, ensuring that we finally know the truth about Ronda's scenery, is itself subject to rhetorical transformation. Ronda is a fine place "in spite of all this" that once seemed fine (until we were disillusioned); but the buzzard-picked horses put in doubt how, or whether, Ronda is a fine place. We cannot simply circle back to some purely visible knowledge that existed prior to the act of reading; we can only, as it were, keep circling the ring. The ontological basis of our reading the passage on Ronda, then, lies not in the information we gather about the place, as if "actual things" could be gleaned apart from the act of speaking them, but in the act of performance that invites us to know certain things as a function of the way we are knowing them. What this suggests is that our interpretive suertes demand the same kind of ambiguity that marked the bullfighter's. Drawing on the flexibility Hemingway's own definition of suerte provides (96), we might say that we *hazard* interpretations; we allow for the *haphazard;* we *juggle* modes of interpretation; we fall precisely for the *trick,* the one term that Hemingway labors to efface from his work. Just as the bullfighter never escapes theatricality, so our performance of the text calls into play the confusing "connotation of the theatre" (16) Hemingway early wished to rule out precisely because it evokes the ontological insecurity of the stage—the gest— where the meanings of actions are strangely hollowed out and made subject to the dynamic interplay of actor and audience, and where comprehension of the "real thing" is intensely problematic. In reading about Ronda we also enact interpretations that have no absolute foundation. If we choose to believe that buzzards eating dead horses is the real, underlying truth, we will merely be performing an interpretation that the text nowhere guarantees. In forcing us to undergo certain transformations in point of view, the passage moves us not toward an ontologically stable or real perspective but toward the suspicion that we must keep circling the hermeneutic ring. Like the bullring itself, Ronda implies a multiplicity of further performances.

There is no doubt that a rhetoric of authenticity invests virtually every page of *Death in the Afternoon* and that one can therefore comprehend the rationale behind Messent's point that Spain is "another version of Hemingway's 'real thing'; a restorative good country where 'authenticity' marks the heroic masculine figure [the matador] who stars in that repeated ritual which signifies 'true' cultural value."[14] I have tried to show, however, that in this book real things, authentic behavior, heroic masculinity, and true cultural values are everywhere subject to rhetorical performance. The bullfighter, who supposedly centers the ritual event within a matrix of masculine values (discipline, grace under pressure, courage, and so forth), is not exempt from what Hemingway at one point contemptuously calls "flowerishness" and at other times celebrates in the spectacular rhetorical flourishes and theatrical suertes of his art. If the notion of an *écriture féminine* seems nonsensical in the context of *Death in the Afternoon,* it is not because Hemingway fails to give full linguistic play to *jouissance* in a text that is supposed to concern the simplest things of life (like death, violence, and male aggression). The book does, however, chart a way of recovering a pertinent concept of masculine writing that eschews the familiar emphasis on virility and phallogocentrism (such as hard prose and stubby verbal forms) where (private) parts stand in for the whole. That concept can best be articulated as a mode of performance, though as self-dramatization rather than the "sequence of motion and fact" that famously underpins an aesthetic of action. Masculine writing for Hemingway emerges when men and language are staged rhetorically before a watching eye. And like the men in his fictions who seek legitimating audiences before which to perform, men and language call upon the interpreter not once but insistently. In this sense of manhood as dramatic performance the matador, that rhetorician of the ring, does indeed stand forth as the exemplary figure.

14. Messent, 139.

CHAPTER 5

Trophy Hunting as a Trope of Manhood in *Green Hills of Africa*, "The Undefeated," and *The Garden of Eden*

"INCHES DON'T MEAN ANYTHING," claims Pop, the white hunting guide, toward the end of Hemingway's autobiographical novel *Green Hills of Africa* (1935).[1] But his assurance is belied by the scene just enacted, in which Hemingway, returning to camp with his fifty-two-inch kudu horns, confronts hunting companion Karl's—"the biggest, widest, darkest, longest-curling, heaviest, most unbelievable pair of kudu horns in the world" (291). At fifty-seven inches, Karl's "big one" (293) easily wins this phallic-seeming display of prowess. This climactic scene, despite Hemingway's eventual assertion that by the morning his jealousy was "all gone and I have never had it again," portrays a drama of manhood-making that is replayed several times in the novel. An earlier rhino kill, for instance, is in Hemingway's mind "wiped . . . out" (86) by Karl's near-thirty-inch rhino horn—a rhino whose "smaller horn was longer than our big one, this huge, tear-eyed marvel of a rhino, this dead, head-severed dream rhino" (83–84). Karl constantly overmatches Hemingway's kills by getting "trophies that made mine dwarfs in comparison" (86), and Hemingway as often succumbs to the jealousy of a trophy hunter out-trophied. The castration-anxiety implicit in the description of Karl's "head-severed dream" of a rhino evokes an odd all-or-nothing approach to manhood, in which the other's horns do not merely overshadow but nullify his. In a way, this display of phallic power ironically validates Pop's statement: because in certain circumstances inches do mean everything, it is *Hemingway's* inches that suddenly "don't mean anything."

That Hemingway invests with sexual significance this business of compar-

1. Ernest Hemingway, *Green Hills of Africa* (New York: Scribner's, 1935), 292. This work will hereinafter be cited parenthetically by page number in the text. Parts of the section on *Green Hills of Africa* were first published as "Trophy Hunting as a Trope of Manhood in Hemingway's *Green Hills of Africa*," *Hemingway Review* 13, no. 1 (1993): 36–47.

ing horns and of shooting rifles that "pulled off with a jerk" (101) is not particularly surprising in light of work we have already considered. In his short
story "The Doctor and the Doctor's Wife," the doctor, fresh from his humiliation at the hands of Dick Boulton, turns to his shotgun for consolation,
pumping shells in and out of the magazine in a masturbatory display of the
phallic power he could not muster in the public encounter with Dick. The
shotgun signifies the technological superiority that hastened the appropriation of the Indian lands; it connotes the most spectacular trophy hunt of all
considered in terms of game killed, lands seized, and men overmatched. Humiliated in the territory of his own garden, the doctor can only perform for
his own self-delight the mythic role of the territory-seizing pioneer equipped
with superior weaponry. As we have seen, a similar scene takes place during
the fishing trip to the Irati River in *The Sun Also Rises*, where Bill's desire to
show off the size of his catch has him asking "How are yours?" "How big are
they really?" Jake's reluctance to display his in this masculine show-and-tell
reflects badly on Jake's potency, already imputed in his answer: "They're all
about the size of your smallest."[2]

Acquiring and displaying trophies, Hemingway suggests, creates a relationship with other men that is profoundly sexual in the sense that it informs
the construction of a masculine self accurately measurable against the other's
"manhood." Horns, fish, and firearms stand in for a phallic power that in turn
represents the authority, toughness, and prowess of the inner man. The trophy thus becomes a complex trope for the construction of masculine identity.
What scholarly appraisals of Hemingway's preoccupation with masculinity
have rarely recognized, however, is that trophy-hunting and -display subvert
the codes of masculinity so long attributed to his male characters. In particular, they subvert the heroism of autonomous action, best expressed by Earl
Rovit in his claim that Hemingway "prized the adamant separateness" of the
"isolate self."[3] Trophy-display reveals manhood to be a performance created
out of the relationship between the hunter, his display, and his audience,
rather than a permanent characteristic of special men. Manhood is not an
essence; it must be represented in an economy of actions and appraisals. It
belongs to a theater of signs and their interpreting audiences; it must be interpreted as gest. It thus implies simultaneously a textual and scopic economy,

2. Hemingway, *Sun*, 120.
3. Rovit, 37.

for the sign *manhood* must not only be read as part of a signifying system but actively watched into being. Hemingway is less concerned with the fact that manhood signifies the transformation of males into men than with the theatrical process by which it is signified.

The problem that Hemingway confronts in *Green Hills*, then, is not so much what inches mean but that they mean anything at all, for this emphasis on the trophy necessitates a transference of meaning and authority from the self to the dramatic moment of self-display and to the object that signifies the inner man. For Hemingway studies, as we have begun to see, the implications of this shift in emphasis from autonomy and individualism to performance and representation are immense. Manhood demands to be understood as sign rather than essence; as the temporary function of signifying relationships rather than as an abiding and innate characteristic; as the product of those relationships rather than as an originary and transcendent element that controls and centers the signifying process. It becomes, in and of itself, a trope, constructed out of complex events, codes of behavior, and signifying glances that are themselves subject to dramatic slippage and transformation. As the example of Hemingway's fifty-two-inch kudu horns suggests, trophies within this theater of masculine representation have an unsettling tendency to become mere tropes, emptied of the true substance of masculinity they supposedly embody. The corollary is that the fashioning of manhood becomes subject to a potential superabundance—a freeplay—of meaning. Manhood, metaphorically projected through the trophy, is party to its own self-subversion.

Green Hills of Africa has always received particularly short shrift among Hemingway's critics, in part because they have so often seen the book as a hyperbolic and even embarrassing celebration of Hemingway's aggressively masculine tendencies. Early on, Philip Young criticized the author for exaggerating the code of masculinity that had previously served him so well; Young portrays this Hemingway as a rather anemic man "who had so completely cut himself off from the roots that nourish . . . that he had developed a vitamin deficiency." In contrast, Mark Spilka in *Hemingway's Quarrel with Androgyny* (1990) takes the book to task for rejecting the androgynous impulses that (according to Spilka) inspired Hemingway's best work, but which the author in his middle years abandoned for a new "masculinist hardening." The only full-length study of the book, A. Carl Bredahl and Susan Lynn Drake's *Hemingway's "Green Hills of Africa" as Evolutionary Narrative* (1990), attempts to rescue the book against the grain of previous critiques by underscoring the book's commitment to the heroic individual—Hemingway himself—who "integrates intellectual, physical, and aesthetic activities" and who has (in the spirit of Rovit's "isolate self") "developed the ability to function from within."[4]

Anomalous as their evaluation of *Green Hills* might be, Bredahl and Drake's interpretation of the Hemingway hero clearly seeks to restore the book to the conventional and well-traversed terrain of Hemingway studies. According to feminist and non-feminist critics alike, the concept of the Hemingway "hero" and "code hero" evokes the solitary male testing his spirit and prowess against the pressure of outside forces and other men. An exemplary moment in *Green Hills* is the foray into dangerous tall grass where Hemingway tests his nerves against the African guide, who is finally forced to do the calling off (117). Prowess and insight won in solitude is supposed to characterize the archetypal journey of the white male into the wilderness, like Karl who, according to Pop, will "find himself off by himself" (63) and like Hemingway who, also according to Pop, will "enjoy it, being by yourself" (17). The hunt for trophies forces the lone white male to venture into the wilderness in order to bring back tokens of his power, metonymically incarnated in those huge phallic horns. In the novel where Hemingway makes his famous comment that "All American literature comes from one book by Mark Twain called *Huckleberry Finn*" (22), the Hemingway persona might be seen as merely another white male venturing into the wilderness, replete with black guides and moments of sexually charged male bonding once away from P. O. M. (Poor Old Mama), this latter-day version of the stay-at-home Widow Douglas, who remembers to ask in the middle of a conversation about hunting "What about lunch?" (206) and at another point scolds "Go take your bathi [*sic*]" (60).

Rifles so obviously take on phallic significance and the size of horns so clearly measure manhood in *Green Hills* that it is hard to see how Hemingway subverts archetypal narratives of manhood-fashioning in American literature as well as posing real questions about dominant critical conceptions of his work. But the Hemingway persona, constructed as a potential code hero to a

4. Young, 98; Mark Spilka, *Hemingway's Quarrel with Androgyny* (Lincoln: University of Nebraska Press, 1990), 235; A. Carl Bredahl and Susan Lynn Drake, *Hemingway's "Green Hills of Africa" as Evolutionary Narrative: Helix and Scimitar* (Lampeter, Wales: Edwin Mellen Press, 1990), 61. See also J. Bakker's point that Hemingway abandoned his function as an artist to the "single-minded, unreflective mentality of the man of action." Bakker, 128.

generation of readers, in fact consistently undermines the premises of male autonomy so long attributed to his stories. Though Pop "believes you should hunt kudu alone" (9), guides in fact always surround, direct, and sometimes prevent Hemingway's killing. From the opening scene in the blind built by Wanderobo guides to Hemingway's short-lived triumph after killing the great kudu that was to transform Karl's, M'Cola says, into "a little one, a nothing" (232), Hemingway never hunts without guides, never hunts without the applause of the guides or Pop, and never hunts without an anticipated hero's return to Poor Old Mama back at camp. Oddly, but quite properly, Hemingway describes the accidental killing of a second big kudu as an anonymous group action: "We all knew we had killed the other kudu that I had mistaken for this one" (232).

It is of course possible to argue that Pop, in prescribing hunting "by yourself," simply does not consider the African guides and gunbearers worthy of mention. If so, it is a mistake Hemingway does not make. Hemingway can be criticized in a number of ways for his representation of the African "natives," but their presence at the various masculine dramas he describes is essential for his developing discourse of manhood. After the kudu killings, for instance, Hemingway participates on at least three separate occasions in a significant Masai ritual for celebrating a kill: "they all shook hands in a strange way that I had never known in which they took your thumb in their fist and held it and shook it and pulled it and held it again, while they looked you in the eyes, fiercely" (231–32). The ritual transforms the killing grounds into a stage (soon to become a tableau as Hemingway captures the dead kudu on film). Like the "kid," the bullfighter in Chapter IX of *In Our Time*, whose bravery is recognized as "the crowd hollered and threw things down into the bull ring," Hemingway finds the significance of his actions through the approval bestowed on him by public consensus. His power, derived symbolically in the first place from the phallus and transferred to rifle and then thumb, is constituted equally by that empowering male gaze as the Wanderobo-Masai looked him "in the eyes, fiercely."

Hunting forces a demonstration of prowess—a process of performing, Hemingway claims, "something you feel sure you can perform" (116). Yet for Hemingway performance becomes just that: a drama of manhood-fashioning acted out before an audience that crucially affects his sense of manhood by approving or scorning his efforts. Hemingway presents himself as the antithesis of Karl, who finds it "hell . . . to shoot in front of everybody" (63) and whom Hemingway rattles "trying to get him to speed up." By contrast, Hemingway thrives on the pressure of an audience. For Hemingway, who likes to shoot in front of everyone as a self-confessed "damned show-off" (63), the rifle is both a sign of manhood and a stage prop, assisting him to display his virility, yet shaming him when fired improperly, which in fact happens when he takes ten shots to kill an antelope before an amused and embarrassed crowd of onlookers. After finally killing the antelope, he "turned away without looking toward him [the antelope]" (82), a gesture that indicates his shame before the intense watching of the spectators. Yet he cannot dispense with spectators. His first words on returning with the magnificent kudu horns are "Look at them, Pop" (290). After killing the kudu, Hemingway arranges six cartridges in a row and names each after the animal whose death the cartridge represents, while commanding his tracker and an old man to "look!" and then again, "Look, M'Cola!" (241).

But Hemingway is always aware of manhood-making as a theatrical event played out before an audience, and makes it particularly evident in *Green Hills of Africa.* The scene of arranging the six cartridges is prefaced by his comment "I've got the braggies" and followed by "That's a hell of a big piece of bragging. That'll hold me for tonight" (241, 242). Similarly, Hemingway self-consciously diagnoses his flamboyant speeches on American literature as "verbal dysentery" (29) and allows Poor Old Mama to state sarcastically, "You were getting awfully profound." From the first scene of the novel, in fact, manhood-making is associated with the theater. When the truck passing the blind spoils their chances of finding game on the salt-lick, the "theatrical one of the two trackers stood up" to announce "It is finished" (2). Later, M'Cola is said to see Hemingway shooting birds as "the clown of the piece" (37); during another hunt, Hemingway observes Poor Old Mama watching "like someone enjoying a good musical show" (102); Hemingway's belated trip to the new kudu country is said to be a "one-man show" (212); and Pop (in order to deflect the seriousness of his remarks) walks away from Hemingway "with comic stiffness" (198).

The decision to hunt a different section of the country, moreover, allows the introduction of a new tracker whom Hemingway immediately despises as "that theatrical bastard" (163), probably because Garrick, as Hemingway labels him, functions as his double, reflecting back to Hemingway his own performances. On first meeting the tracker, Hemingway refers to him as "Loud Mouth, the . . . theatrical genius who was giving a gesture-by-gesture reproduction of How B'wana Simba Killed His Last Kudu" (163). Prior to that display, Hemingway, posturing, wants the interpreter to translate his own boast: "Tell him I am B'wana Fisi, the hyena slaughterer . . . B'wana Fisi chokes them with his naked hands." Later, Hemingway describes this little piece of theater: a "Masai walked down the center of the valley while we were glassing it and when I pretended I was going to shoot him Garrick became very dramatic insisting it was a man, a man, a man!" (172). "Don't shoot men?" asks Hemingway, assuming his tracker's own pidgin-English and very dramatic about his supposed ignorance. Self-consciously, he owns up to "clowning for M'Cola." Later, tracking a wounded sable, Hemingway admits "I had always sworn to Pop that I could out-track M'Cola but I realized now that in the past I had been giving a sort of Garrick performance" (269). Like Hemingway's boastful pledge of killing six animals with six cartridges, Garrick at one point "simulated the killing of half a dozen kudu" (164). And like Garrick, who after the successful hunt for the kudu "was playing the victorious leader home from the chase" (278), Hemingway soon plays the role of the returning hero bearing the spoils of victory: "I shouted and we all commenced to shout and blew the klaxon and I let the gun off, the flame cutting up into the dark and it making a great noise" (290).

This seriocomic business of dramatizing (or failing to dramatize) one's prowess in *Green Hills* carries profound implications for the way we read Hemingway's conception of manhood-fashioning. However completely hunting allows one to perform "something you feel sure you can perform" (116), performance in *Green Hills* always involves an unsettling negotiation between the primary meanings of the word: performance as an unfolding in action of one's will, and performance as conforming one's actions to an audience's expectations. The two cannot be separated, for Hemingway's actions nowhere stand apart from his spectators' evaluation of them. Though Hemingway in a sense controls this theater of manhood through his sagacity and skill as a hunter, performance always compromises the integrity and autonomy of the "one-man show" by ceding decisions about the actor's prowess to an audience. Being coterminous with the staging of masculine authority, manhood is thus necessarily transient; it is constantly being emptied of significance in order to be re-created during the next display of prowess. Celebrated one moment in the Masai ritual of thumb-pulling, Hemingway is the next humiliated on finding his kudu horns fail to measure up to Karl's. It is not that the horns change shape, but that the meaning of their shape depends on the interpretation temporarily bestowed within constantly changing dramatic contexts.

As a startling corollary, performance threatens the ontological stability of actions undertaken by an agent whose very purchase on what really happened hinges in part on the interpretation of others. The killing of the first lion, for instance, remains "confused and unsatisfactory" (40), even though later evidence (the one bullet found in the carcass being from Hemingway's Springfield) proves that Hemingway rather than P. O. M. killed the lion. M'Cola and the other Africans back at camp celebrate P. O. M. as the lion's slayer, and there is a sense in which the celebration alone allows P. O. M. to lay claim to actions she never performed. P. O. M. does not believe Hemingway's statement that "You killed him" (43); on the other hand, she seems genuinely to want to "enjoy my triumph." Hemingway, who really "rolled [the lion] over" (42), finds this potential sign of his masculine prowess transformed into a confusion that, going on his own account of a fairly straightforward sequence of events, should never occur. The ensuing celebration of P. O. M. interprets Hemingway's performance (killing the lion) as a non-performance (he was not *seen* to kill the lion)—a misreading that gains sudden legitimacy when it is found to govern Hemingway's feelings of confusion and dissatisfaction.

Two interesting implications emerge from this scene. First, the celebration of P. O. M. seems to outweigh not only the physical evidence of the bullet and Pop's and Charo's testimony that Hemingway rolled over the lion but Hemingway's own interior confidence in the meaning of his action. What should be undisputed evidence becomes suddenly subject to an interpretation that retains its effect even when we know what really did transpire. Hemingway's action and his knowledge of his action, which we might expect to be brashly and in this case justifiably untouched by any apprehension of doubt, seem instead subject to an unwarranted but quite powerful play of meaning. Second, as this statement already implies, the celebration of P. O. M. is not hollow or farcical. If Hemingway feels "let down" at the absence of "heroics" and "drama" (41) during the shooting of the lion, the same cannot be said of the dance that ensues: "*Hey la Mama! huh! huh! huh! Hay la Mama! huh! huh! huh!*' they sang the lion dance with that deep, lion asthmatic cough in it" (42). The scene suggests the dilemma at the heart of Hemingway's feelings of confusion. Celebrating P. O. M.'s miss as though it were a kill actually does lend it an aura of authenticity; failing to celebrate his kill, by the same token, hollows out the significance of his action. Hemingway's actions are his own, yet their meaning is problematic in a situation where meaning must be staged and communally celebrated. Interpretation in this scene is therefore not completely at the mercy of arbitrary decisions made by M'Cola; what is telling is the extent to which those decisions take on weight and legitimacy when performed in a successful dramatization.

Once we see how prominently acts of display function in the fashioning of manhood—and simultaneously unsettle assumptions about what manhood is—the deeper meanings of trophy-measurement become clearer. Trophies bear an unexpectedly important role in comprehending and evaluating the performances that produce them. Manhood does not exist securely and completely prior to the acquisition of trophies; trophies acquired in the pursuit of manhood come to embody it. Thus the experience of hunting that does not produce trophies frustrates both Hemingway and Karl: the latter is "pale, and gaunt looking" (151) and "not himself, nor anything like himself" (152) when unable to locate the longed-for kudu, while Hemingway feels "rotten sick" (272) over the sable bull he wounds then loses. "I wanted him," Hemingway adds, "I wanted him damned badly." Likewise, as the lion-slaying demonstrates, the acquisition of trophies without appropriate public recognition degrades the original display of prowess. Though at times Hemingway finds contentment in the simple experience of pursuit (he claims to be "altogether happy" [6] after a fruitless day spent in the blind), such moments are contained within Hemingway's larger quest for the trophies that alone seem to signify completion and satisfaction.

As visible and permanent signs of what a man has accomplished, trophies promise to stabilize a process of manhood-fashioning that is always subject to the unsettling scrutiny of others and thus never completely controlled by any individual. Yet by the same token trophies turn male authority and autonomy into parodies of themselves. If manhood must be associated with a competitive display of the "tangible things" (86) that represent and signify the original displays of prowess, then it must remain subject to circumstances outside the control of any individual, such as the availability of appropriate animals, the constant possibility of being out-trophied, or even having the trophy assigned to someone else. The fate of Hemingway's magnificent kudu horns is an obvious example. Like Belmonte in *The Sun Also Rises*, whose return to the bull ring from retirement is ruined by the greater skills of Romero despite the fact that Belmonte's skill is in itself more than adequate, Hemingway is humiliated by the competitive display that follows the hunt even though the original hunt had seemed to prove his manhood.

As long as "all the tangible things we had to show" (86) remain the measure of manhood, manhood itself is constantly in danger of being voided when not displayed or when trophies are out-displayed. M'Cola, the guide, will not move from the first big kudu until Hemingway has measured its horns and pronounced "Big! Big! . . . Twice as big as B'wana Kabor [Karl's]" (233). But after seeing Karl's "big one," Hemingway does not want to "see mine again; never, never" (291), spurning now the competitive display he would otherwise gladly have made. Hemingway's two kudu, when over-matched by Karl's before Pop, P. O. M., and Karl himself, do not diminish but nullify his hard-won sense of masculinity, just as Karl's enormous rhino horn "wipes out" Hemingway's. Masculine authority, in other words, cannot be fashioned cumulatively or incrementally from trophies gained, nor can it be fashioned retrospectively out of an accumulation of trophies. So despite the fact that Karl has out-performed him in every other category of hunted animal and should thus stand on the mere size of his trophy collection as the virile hunter personified, Hemingway's massive kudu horns still promise his accession to the leading role in this drama of masculine display. Those fifty-two-inch kudu horns counterbalance the fact that Karl has shot the "best buff, the best waterbuck, and the best lion" (63) and transform his kudu horns into "nothing." Even so, they are themselves then negated by Karl's more impressive fifty-seven-inch specimen.

In Hemingway's theater of manhood-making, manhood is thus paradoxically represented by trophies. They must be impressively displayed to recall the original moment of killing, yet are just as easily out-displayed on a stage that conflates manly self-possession with the male's possessions. The authority pertaining to trophies is claimed by an individual yet is bestowed dialogically by the audience (for a trophy does not signify manhood in itself nor to a single man). That authority, moreover, when overshadowed by a superior performance, is found suddenly to reside nowhere. Manhood and trophy become "nothing," while the audience registers its embarrassment or disapproval. The trophy, as sign, can signify nothing until the individual situates it conspicuously within a complex communal drama pieced together out of appropriate gestures, glances, comparative measurements, and ritualistic approvals. Carried off successfully, trophy-display may for a moment—*the* moment of display and approval—signify its possessor's manhood. Yet the individual is impotent, despite hunting skills demonstrated or imagined, to make the sign signify anything at all. The trophy is nothing without the man; but the man, allegedly autonomous, cannot make the trophy mean "manhood" in a theater where roles are assigned communally. Such problems contribute to the precariousness of manhood for Hemingway: precarious because it cannot function without trophies and precarious because it cannot function with trophies in any reliable way.

Manhood in *Green Hills of Africa* arises out of a display of prowess that must be reconfirmed in the ritual of trophy-display. For that reason, trophies represent *lack*. They represent what must be supplemented in the original experience in order to consolidate the individual's sense of manhood. They dispute the possibility that manhood might be essential, non-representable, and thus permanently outside the play of shifting contexts and meanings. Yet trophies themselves are not identical with the manhood they supposedly represent. Though Hemingway would have nothing to show for his hunting prowess without the trophies, the characters in *Green Hills* do not (to use Derrida's terminology) stand in the presence of Hemingway's manhood when they observe his rhino or kudu horns. The trophies are an attribute and consequence of their signifying context; they too must be negotiated into significance. As the display of the rhino and kudu horns demonstrates, that negotiation drastically transforms the meaning of trophies. The sign (the horns) fluctuates between presence and absence. It signifies the plenitude of Hemingway's masculine powers when his horns were to make "nothing" of Karl's trophies, then suddenly signifies his humiliation as the horns vanish during the display of Karl's "big one."

This unsettling trajectory of the sign seems resolved by Hemingway's subsequent revelation that in the morning his bitterness over Karl's kudu horns "was all gone and I have never had it again" (293)—at least, presumably, until the moment of re-creating the scene during the writing of the book. The morning, it appears, renews the meaning of the horns and restores the efficacy of the sign by way of a final absence, in this case the loss of the envy for which the horns were primarily responsible. But Hemingway's resolution is oddly constructed given the nature of the problem it is meant to address. Hemingway comes to terms with Karl's kudu by seeing that when "you put them side by side they looked all right" (293) because the horns were "all . . . big." But this solution places him squarely within the obsessive competition that, Pop says, "Spoils everything." Hemingway, that is, attempts to move beyond competitive display by revisiting the original relationship between trophy-size and manhood that he has already surreptitiously questioned. We could only believe that the horns really did look all right in the morning if the previous night's fiasco had been an aberration or if some event had changed the rules of manly display. The book, however, suggests the opposite: that manly display constantly problematizes the security and continuity of manhood. The final transformation is consistent with what we have identified as the transient and compromised nature of manhood-making—and thus not final at all.

All of this relates in fascinating ways to Hemingway's rewriting of his Papa Hemingway persona in *Green Hills*, where the opportunity to inflate the legend couples with his claim in the foreword that he will "write an absolutely true book," as though promising an autobiographical exposure of the man behind the legend. The foreword, however, goes on to deflect attention from Hemingway to "the shape of a country" and "the pattern of a month's action," thus initiating a pattern of revelation and deferral that *Green Hills* repeats over and over. Self-exposure in print is clearly to be both desired and feared. The displacement of emotion and meditation into action that seems so characteristic of Hemingway's fictions runs the risk of being reversed here as Papa Hemingway holds forth pretentiously about literature and portentously about the white man's exploitation of Africa ("A continent ages quickly once we come," "The earth gets tired of being exploited" [284]). But Hemingway just as often refuses to endorse his pronouncements by deliberately assuming the Garrick-mask and thereby owning up to the "braggies" (241)—a self-conscious revelation of his need to stage himself self-consciously before an audience, which, far from revealing the true Hemingway, has the effect of implicating him in just one more staging.

Interestingly, it is precisely this stagy aspect of *Green Hills* that critics have always noted and usually derided. Edmund Wilson set the tone early by criticizing the homage (he claims) Hemingway pays to his own literary personality, which, Wilson writes dryly, "appears here in a slightly absurd light." Hemingway, Wilson adds, is "beginning to be imposed on by the American publicity legend which has been created about him." John Chamberlain concurred in his review of Hemingway's book, referring to it as "all attitude, all Byronic posturing." For critics like John Raeburn and Scott Donaldson, *Green Hills* is one more sign of how Hemingway increasingly invested his charismatic personality into his books after the late 1920s, to the detriment of his work.[5] Bearing witness to his own aggrandizement, Hemingway, so this common line of argument goes, lost the detachment that his code heroes most famously represent and replaced it with an inflated sense of self.

Yet the common image of Hemingway as a rather adolescent writer who needs to occupy the literary stage while being afraid of emotional exposure misrepresents his complex role in *Green Hills.* Perhaps the best example is the long scene with Kandinsky, where Hemingway, blossoming into garrulous life under the German's persistent questions, expounds on subjects ranging from America's great writers to the value of his own work: he knows the "brilliant people," he has experienced the pitfalls inherent in the business of writing, he senses and strives to reach the "fourth and fifth dimension that can be gotten" (27) in writing. Though Hemingway modestly allows P. O. M. to claim the title of America's greatest living writer for him (19), the scene does provide him with an opportunity to put forward his credentials as a literary scholar whose sources of authority lie in the experiences accruing to a famous, practicing writer. It is his artist's need for an "absolute conscience . . . to prevent faking" (27) that permits him to distinguish good American writers like Henry James and Mark Twain from the gentlemen "men of letters" (20)—and indeed from the "brilliant people" he knew in Paris.

As one would expect from his discourse on fake writing in *Death in the Afternoon,* Hemingway's treatise on literary matters is much concerned with distinguishing good writing from various modes of rhetoricity. His account of Herman Melville, for instance, produces this telling exchange with Kandinsky:

"We have had writers of rhetoric who had the good fortune to find . . . how things, actual things, can be, whales for instance, and this knowledge

---

5. Wilson, "Letter to the Russians about Hemingway," in ed. Meyers, *Critical Heritage,* 216, 218; John Chamberlain, "Books of the Times," in ed. Stephens, 150; Raeburn, *Fame,* 72–79; Scott Donaldson, *By Force of Will: The Life and Art of Ernest Hemingway* (New York: Viking, 1977), 6–9. Others have complained of Hemingway's "grinding need for self-justification," of his "belligerent self-righteousness." Fewer critics have enjoyed Hemingway's inflated presentation of himself; but for Bernard De Voto it was Hemingway's excellent "clowning," and for Ronald Weber the "forceful, mercurial presence of Hemingway himself," that distinguished the book. Young, 97; Bakker, 124; Bernard De Voto, "Hemingway in the Valley," in ed. Meyers, *Critical Heritage,* 211; Ronald Weber, *Hemingway's Art of Non-Fiction* (New York: St. Martin's Press, 1990), 91.

is wrapped in the rhetoric like plums in a pudding. Occasionally it is there, alone, unwrapped in pudding, and it is good. This is Melville. But the people who praise it, praise it for the rhetoric which is not important. They put a mystery in which is not there."

"Yes," he said. "I see. But it is the mind working, its ability to work, which makes the rhetoric. Rhetoric is the blue sparks from the dynamo."

"Sometimes. And sometimes it is only the blue sparks and what is the dynamo driving?" (20)

Here, the term *rhetoric* conveys the familiar sense of superfluous language alienated from any useful and generative function; and it suggests by implication a contrasting situation—presumably Hemingway's own—in which true words and "actual things" go hand in hand. This usage echoes through the conversation with Kandinsky: New England writers divorce language from "the words that people always have used in speech" (21); Hemingway can read naturalists only when they are not being "literary" (21); the conclusion of *Huckleberry Finn* is "cheating" (22); ambitious authors in quest of money write "slop" (23); and critics' claims about various "masterpieces" (24) are untrue. Hemingway can only imagine a nonrhetorical language—again, by implication, his own—that might exist "without tricks and without cheating" (27).

But another connotation of rhetoric—that of persuasive eloquence— gradually makes itself felt in this passage. Indeed, Hemingway's peroration begins with a subdued recognition of the function of the orator. Speaking of the joy of having a daughter, Kandinsky concludes after some labored casting for the appropriate term ("how shall I say? Yes, it is like—what do you call") that it is the "Heinz Tomato Ketchup on the daily food" (18). Hemingway applauds "That's very good." His comment does more than politely note Kandinsky's striking metaphor and his command of English; it draws attention to the rhetorical effect (and effectiveness) of the German's conversation. Hemingway, in other words, interprets Kandinsky's struggles to find and carefully formulate an eloquent conceit as a fundamentally rhetorical performance designed to impress his public. Later, Hemingway acknowledges choosing a rhetorical strategy when, in response to Kandinsky's question about what harms a writer, he thinks "I was tired of the conversation which was becoming an interview. So I would make it an interview and finish it" (28). In this context, his reply ("Politics, women, drink, money, ambition") is deliberately rhetorical. We cannot tell whether this statement reveals Hemingway's true feelings about what harms a writer, for his intent here is not so much to reveal truths as to bring about a desired effect (closing the conversation). As such, this re-sponse seems distinguishable from earlier remarks that Hemingway himself confesses form a "damned serious subject" (26).

The seriousness of Hemingway's remarks in this passage, however, are constantly entangled with the very forms of rhetoricity that he seems so con-cerned to bracket off as "slop" or as useful only in certain narrow contexts. For "slop," in the form of repeated allusions to the ailment from which he is recovering as this book opens (amoebic dysentery), is also made to invest his serious remarks. Hemingway prefaces his comments with an acknowledgment that his tongue is "loose. . . . too bloody loose" (19); in the aftermath of the conversation, he refers to his profound comments as "verbal dysentery" (29). This emetic discourse—which takes place just before a lunch specified as "Grant's gazelle chops, mashed potatoes, green corn, and then mixed fruit for dessert" (29)—also regales its readers with a bizarre menu of food metaphors, beginning with Kandinsky's Heinz ketchup, moving to "plums in a pudding," then "angleworms in a bottle, trying to derive . . . nourishment from their own contact and from the bottle." During the conversation Hemingway is also offered nourishment from a bottle: beer to loosen his tongue (19, 22) and a gimlet to quell it (28). We might read the entire passage as a complicated game with processes of ingestion and digestion. That game, incidentally, con-tinues through the book in such scenes as a hyena eating its own entrails (38), Hemingway carrying a tripe bag (a reedbuck's stomach turned inside out), Hemingway carrying his intestine outside his body (283), and the trailing of a wounded buffalo by its bloody dung (113).

The point, however, is that while writing off the superfluous rhetoric of a Melville and the slop written by commercially motivated authors Hemingway caps Kandinsky's Heinz ketchup metaphor with tropes of his own, some of them (like New York writers compared to angleworms in a bottle) even more brilliantly contrived than his guest's. We might put this down to a demonstra-tion on the part of a superior writer of how to produce sparks from a dynamo that truly generates energy. Or, to switch to the trope that informs the rest of the book, we might put it down to a demonstration of how to out-trophy another man's tropes, in the sense that Hemingway's metaphors are verbal trophies displayed to a receptive audience in the cut-and-thrust of masculine competition. Yet we have Hemingway's retrospective word for it—another trope—that his entire conversation can be read as "verbal dysentery." At this point, the discussion, like the reedbuck's stomach and like Hemingway's own prolapsed intestine, can be turned inside out. Should we interpret Hemingway's use of metaphors as an indication of his superior authorial powers or as more loose slop, introduced in contempt of his own aesthetic? Are we to understand the put-downs of the brilliant people in Paris and the New York angleworms as the true gen, conferred on us by this brilliantly satiric insider, or as loose slop vented in the manner of ambitious writers, who wish only to sell books on the strength of their literary fame? Should we read the passage as a wry, self-conscious reflection on the very process of slopping over into metaphor or as a self-congratulatory literary puff?

The problem with such questions is that, perhaps misleadingly, they probe the question of what Hemingway means rather than the effect he means to generate. The more important possibility we must consider is that his discourse has all along been a rhetorical performance designed to sway an audience rather than to reveal truths about writing and writers. His striking use of tropes to buttress an attack on rhetoric suggests, after all, a deliberately ludic element to his discourse, hinting that we should pay attention not so much to the wisdom of his remarks as to their function and purpose. His statement that his lecture has been nothing more than "verbal dysentery" asks us to do more than reassess his ideas; it invites us to see ideas as eloquent moves in a rhetorical game. It is in this spirit that Hemingway draws attention to Kandinsky's trope as a deliberate rhetorical display, that Hemingway pretends to forget his train of thought and invites Kandinsky to coax him on (20), and that Kandinsky refuses to be persuaded (28). Though Hemingway professes to be dealing with a "damned serious subject," we cannot really be sure whether his remarks are serious or part of an elaborate oration inspired by and designed to run rhetorical circles around Kandinsky's conceit of the Heinz ketchup. His very claim for a "damned serious subject" seems subverted by an understated but persistent sense in the discussion with Kandinsky that Hemingway, ingesting beer and emitting dysenteric words, is indulging himself too freely. Scatology stands in for a playful overindulgence in metaphor. That "damned serious subject," dysenterically turned inside out, can be read as scoring a brilliant rhetorical point in a game where ideas are staged and upstaged. It is therefore not surprising, given the scene's concern with bodily and verbal discharges, that Hemingway concludes his peroration by advocating the upsetting properties of drink, asking Kandinsky—rhetorically—"Don't you ever want to change your ideas?" (28).

It might be argued that in the long run there is little difference between reading this scene as a straightforward presentation of Hemingway's fondest literary beliefs or as a devious questioning of his own rhetorical performances. Whether we read this as extravagant bombast or a subtle inquiry into the dynamics of self-presentation, the Hemingway persona again manages to take center stage. Actually, the implications of interpreting Hemingway's harangue as a rhetorical performance are profound. What is most interesting about *Green Hills* in this case is not so much Hemingway's scandalous representation of his literary self as the way that representation iterates the scandal of manhood-making. Hemingway reproduces the performances males undergo in order to demonstrate their acquisition of manhood by staging himself in such a way as to question whether his persona, by turns self-justifying, self-satisfied, self-promoting, and self-deprecatory, ever coheres. Hemingway's self-staging, in fact, makes his identity indeterminate. Because the long Kandinsky episode that opens the book establishes Hemingway's credentials as a public figure so thoroughly, we can never tell the difference thereafter between the true Hemingway self (which presumably exists prior to any public representation) and further avatars of his own public image. Like the making of men, the fashioning of Hemingway's persona always depends on its relationship to an audience. In both cases, performance becomes a prerequisite of authoritative identity and self-reliance; it initiates the process of self-aggrandizement, without which, it seems, identity and authority must collapse altogether. Hemingway performing his role as he-man writer and Hemingway writing about masculine performances both point toward the existence of a mutable self, capable primarily of dramatizing and promoting a series of fantasies about male autonomy and power, but lacking a fully developed, consistent, authoritative self prior to the moment of performance.

In *Green Hills*, these fantasies of masculine authority are shaped during the communal negotiations whereby hunter-writer, audience, and trophy become wedded in moments of intense watching. Like the writer and the famous literary personage, the hunter requires his audience. Like the hunter, the writer must stage himself while denying—or at least re-staging—the implications of that staging, lest he elevate stagecraft itself into a position of primacy over its agent. Self-display thus occupies an ambiguous position in *Green Hills*. On the one hand, the self can be constituted only through display, and various aspects of Hemingway's persona are therefore obsessively paraded before us. On the other, self-exposure is to be feared because the process of self-revelation, by revealing the male's dependence on it, must always compromise autonomy. Self-exposure runs the risk of unmasking the *lack* of self prior to its rhetorical aggrandizement—a performance that allows it to begin to take on depth, weight, and shading.

To negotiate the problems of self-display calls on all of Hemingway's powers of invention. The image of a masculine self liberated from the interference of a supporting cast of other hunters, women, guides, and gunbearers must be floated even while he acknowledges his debt to the legitimating nature of the spectacle. His success at the first task is evident in the fact that almost all critics have accepted his fictional presentations of autonomy in hunters (and elsewhere bullfighters, warriors, and even impotent journalists) at face value. It is evident, too, in the fact that critics have simply embraced Hemingway's tendentious remarks on literature—or written them off as tendentious— rather than attending to the process of rhetorical hollowing-out they imply. But Hemingway focuses not so much on male fantasies of being off by oneself as the insecurities those fantasies are designed to mask, and acknowledges that, whenever men accede to manhood in his fictions, the mask has already disappeared. What makes *Green Hills of Africa* such a fascinating work is that Hemingway asserts so strenuously the ideal of the autonomous male yet, driven by the imperatives of the "damned show-off" within himself to hunt trophies, is willing to explore the subversive premise that trophy-hunting, as a rhetorical measure of man, constrains the very idea of manhood.

STUFFED BULLS AND PIGTAILS IN "THE UNDEFEATED"

"The Undefeated" bears every sign of being the bellwether story of a collection whose title, infamously, promises a world of men without women. Striking what Cyril Connolly called the volume's "note of ferocious virility," the story indulges its concern with men competing and fighting heroically.[6] Women— unless we count the bullfight critic's "date at Maxim's at twelve" (22)—are not even mentioned in the story.[7] Not surprisingly, critical interpretations have

6. Connolly, *Without*, 111.
7. Ernest Hemingway, *Men Without Women* (New York: Scribner's, 1927), 22. This work will hereinafter be cited parenthetically by page number in the text.

emphasized a thematics of lonely endurance and courage in the face of defeat, exercised by a protagonist who approaches the status of what Earl Rovit calls "archetype Man." Carlos Baker's reading in this respect is exemplary: Manuel Garcia and Jack Brennan, the hero of "Fifty Grand," "show, in crucial situations, the courage which has sustained them through their earlier careers. . . . Manolo earns the right to keep his *coleta*, the badge of the professional matador, by a courage that is much greater than his aging skill, or, for that matter, his luck."[8] Though Baker does not specifically say so, his reading implies that the bullfighter is loath to surrender the badge of his manhood. Gored and anaesthetized, Manuel still has the strength in the story's final scene to insist that Zurito not cut off his coleta, that phallic-seeming pigtail whose function is to embody his will to strive and endure (and perhaps to display his prowess in the ring once again). In this reading, to agree with Baker that the "bullfighter's pigtail is the sign at the center" of "The Undefeated" is also to argue for the centrality of a code of manly conduct, embedded in Manuel's personality, displayed through his heroic actions in the ring, and represented by the phallus-coleta.

This interpretation, however, does not account for the problematic aspects of the representation of manhood in this story. Though Baker invites us to think carefully about the coleta as a sign of manhood, he makes the understandable assumption that the sign bears a transparent and self-evident relationship to Manuel's professional honor and thus to his manly courage. Baker's invitation actually demands, and deserves, much more attention. First, his presupposition that the coleta represents an immanent principle of courage that has sustained Manuel in the past and still informs his actions in "crucial situations" ignores the pigtail's complex and shifting narrative role as it is alternately concealed, displayed, threatened, and preserved. The coleta, which is supposed to supply prima facie evidence of the courageous deeds Manuel Garcia can "show" in the ring, is scandalously subject to its own codes of (non)display. Second, Baker fails to describe the process whereby fictive audiences in the story watch and interpret signs, trophies, and actions, transforming the arena and the narrative itself into spaces where various and variable perspectives are performed, negotiated, and emptied of absolute significance. Whereas Baker desires to read beyond the temporary situation of Manuel's performance to the principles and values that shape it, the fictive

8. Rovit, 68; Baker, *Writer as Artist*, 122.

audiences see only temporality and situatedness. They exist to pay testimony to the fluidity of acts of performance, when whatever values emerge are just as surely transformed or displaced by ensuing situations. Third, Baker omits all mention of the crucial work that must be undertaken by readers in order to negotiate a sign (the coleta) that is placed under such intense interpretive pressure by the story's fictive audiences. We are forced to confront the process whereby critics (in the main) reach a conclusion about Manuel's coleta that is diametrically opposed to the opinion of everyone in the story except Manuel himself.

This last point reprises the by-now familiar attack by reader response critics on formalist analyses, which, as Stanley Fish writes, tend to "assume that meanings can be specified independently of the activity of reading [when] it is in and by that activity [of reading] that meanings—experiential, not positivist—are created."[9] My point, however, is not to criticize Baker's (excellent) work for its formalist tendencies but to argue that omissions in readings of Hemingway's narrative can be as revealing of critical presuppositions about masculinity as readings of Hemingway's narrative omissions. For Baker, in accord with most other readers of the story, the coleta is central but not an interpretive crux because the meaning of the sign has already been disposed, and thus precedes its acquisition by a male character. The coleta is the sign at the center and the sign that centers the meanings of Manuel's actions; his actions are unproblematic to the extent that he fights to hold on to the meaning of the sign. What Baker does not consider forms the substance of my argument: the possibility that the meaning of the story's central sign is articulated by means of its display and by the nature of the interpreting audience, and the further possibility that the story urges a reading experience on its actual audience that accords with that promulgated by the various watchers and "readers" within the text. Like Hemingway's trophy horns in *Green Hills of Africa*, the coleta takes on meaning during moments of performance; but we shall also have to ask how and why our interpretive performances match or diverge from those of the fictive audiences. The pigtail, that sign of "archetype Man," is not so much central to "The Undefeated" as the point at which interpretive performances can be seen at work upsetting the center of stable and determinate meanings—and, for that matter, the center of stable and determinate men.

9. Stanley Fish, *Is There a Text in This Class? The Authority of Interpretive Communities* (Cambridge: Harvard University Press, 1980), 120.

The story's concern with signs and trophies of manhood is registered early and enigmatically in the first scene, when Manuel, walking into Retana's office, immediately positions the promoter amidst bullfighting memorabilia and under one trophy in particular: "A little man sat behind a desk at the far side of the room. Over his head was a bull's head, stuffed by a Madrid taxidermist; on the walls were framed photographs and bull-fight posters" (1). The stuffed bull, which hangs directly above Retana as if to evoke some subtle identification between bull and man, plays an unexpectedly important role. In one way it helps to shape the specular economy of the scene, for, after the narrator thrice records Retana looking at Manuel, the bullfighter looks not at Retana but at his trophy: "Manuel looked up at the stuffed bull. He had seen it often before. He felt a certain family interest in it. It had killed his brother, the promising one, about nine years ago. Manuel remembered the day. There was a brass plate on the oak shield the bull's head was mounted on. Manuel could not read it, but he imagined it was in memory of his brother" (2). The bull's head awakens two kinds of memory in Manuel: the particular day of his brother's death and a history of past dealings with Retana (for Manuel has presumably frequented the office to have "seen it often"). Consequences follow as Manuel's gaze is in turn reframed by Retana's. The promoter "saw him looking at the stuffed bull's head," and his interpretation of that gaze has some effect on persuading him to hire Manuel: in addition to mercenary considerations, Retana notes the "appeal that Manuel had made to him for a moment when he thought of the old days" (3).

If the trophy leads the two into concord over the "old days," however, it also gives rise to a significant misreading on Manuel's part. His supposition that the trophy head is a memorial to his brother proves to be faulty, for we are given the information he cannot read: "The plate said: 'The bull "Mariposa" of the Duke of Veragua, which accepted 9 varas for 7 caballos, and caused the death of Antonio Garcia, Novillero, April 27, 1909.'" The plaque, in fact, refers to the death of Manuel's brother only in the context of the bravery of the bull, who has the courage and power to kill seven horses while being pic-ed nine times. (By way of contrast, the bull Campagnero, which gores Manuel, accepts only four varas [pics] for the death of two horses.) The "family interest" Manuel feels for the bull's head is thus susceptible to a wide range of interpretations. The trophy head that stands reminiscently for the death of one brother presages, like a memento mori, the goring of another. The head also allows us to pass value judgments on the Garcias. The plaque makes a wry commentary on the forthcoming tribulations of the less promising of the Garcia brothers, who struggles to kill a bull that is much less distinguished than the one his brother fought. If Antonio garners for his family name the reflected glory of the brave Mariposa, Manuel humiliates himself fighting a bull that the "veterinaries won't pass in the daytime" (3).

Possibly, too, the trophy head invites us to reflect on the invidious distinction between the heroic contests of old and the parlous state of contemporary bullfighting. Watching Manuel watch the bull's head, Retana sounds the theme of decadence Hemingway will elaborate at greater length in *Death in the Afternoon*: Retana notes that, in contrast with the head of Mariposa, the "lot [of bulls] the Duke sent me for Sunday will make a scandal." Later, he argues that "There aren't any bull-fighters any more." The head recalls the lost glory of days when men like Antonio Garcia fought fearless bulls. By the same token, it comments ironically on the bulls the "veterinaries won't pass," but which are offered to Manuel because Retana "could get him cheaply." Representing a proud tradition, the trophy head now yields to "Retana's boys" (7), a group of bullfighters characterized by a waiter in a café as a "bunch of camels." We might even see the trophy as representing the head of Manuel himself, sacrificed to deadening commercial imperatives. (Retana claims to have heard a rumor that Manuel has suffered an amputation: "I heard they'd cut your leg off.") The juxtaposition of heads that forges an identity between Retana's living and the mounted bull's dead gaze bolsters that interpretation. It is as if Manuel—or at least his pigtail, which Retana directly threatens in the last scene by handling the scissors—is destined to take his place among the trophies adorning Retana's wall.

This sense that the dead gaze of Mariposa exposes the contemporary bullfighting scene as a living charade finds much evidence in the story. Everywhere the narrative records a landscape of inauthenticity and substitution. Retana's bulls in the nocturnal are those the "veterinaries won't pass"; the floodlit nocturnal is itself a poor cousin of the sunlit corrida (we are told that Zurito "pic-ed in the hot afternoon sun for big money. He didn't like this arc-light business" [14]). Manuel asks Zurito to substitute for Retana's picadors; Retana intends Manuel to "substitute for Larita" (3). And worse: if Retana seriously believes that there "aren't any bull-fighters any more," Manuel could only be a substitute for one who is already a substitute for the great figures of old. As if testifying to the lowly status of Manuel and the nocturnal, the reviewer at the bullfight is the "substitute bull-fight critic of *El Heraldo*" (14), later denominated the "second-string critic" (15). Even the crowd might be seen as a poor second to the daytime aficionados who might have appreciated Manuel's bravery. As for the corrida itself, Manuel's performance is often described by outside witnesses not for itself but in terms of the style of another: he and Hernandez are said to participate in the paseo "like Joselito and Belmonte" (14), while to *El Heraldo*'s second-string critic Manuel's series of veronicas end in a "very Belmontistic recorte" (15). Entering the ring following the burlesque of the Charlie Chaplins, moreover, Manuel leaves it to a hail of cushions and empty bottles (which substitute for the hats and canes being picked up as the paseo begins): to the crowd, his performance smacks of the burlesque.

In this environment of second-string bulls, fighters, and critics, Manuel's claim that "I don't like to substitute" (3) hints at the theme that most critical readings have seized upon: Manuel, despite his flaws and despite the crowd, epitomizes a spirit of true manhood. To Lawrence Broer, for instance, Manuel's "simple and unmitigated pride—pride in his professional skill and in his manly courage—provided at least one positive standard by which an individual might gain honor and dignity in a world where those essentials seemed lacking." His "courage and integrity are incorruptible." Earl Rovit holds that "The Undefeated" exemplifies Hemingway's tutor stories and describes Manuel in terms that dovetail nicely with Broer's: in "The Undefeated," the "tutor figure has already achieved a self-containment or self-definition before he appears in fiction; he already *is,* and the finality of his self-acceptance removes him from the disintegrating experience of *becoming*" (83).[10] For Rovit, Manuel arrives at Retana's door with his manliness, like his suitcase, in hand. He is uncorruptible because already completed as a man, unmitigatedly proud because he need not undergo the disintegrative experience of transforming his personality from immature youth to able man. He follows his chosen path of courage despite the hostility and misapprehensions of the crowd because he is already self-contained and thus committed to a "positive standard" of conduct prior to changing circumstances and to the evaluation of an audience.

In harmony with this standard line of inquiry, Manuel's answer to Reta-

---

10. Broer, 47; Rovit, 83. Kenneth S. Lynn, more recently, has written in a similar vein that Manolo is "an exemplar of Man, that peculiar creature in the world of being who can achieve 'authenticity' only by confronting the burden of his freedom to make choices and by embracing the awareness, without allowing it to demoralize him, that someday he will die." Kenneth S. Lynn, *Hemingway* (New York: Simon and Schuster, 1987), 269.

na's skeptical "There aren't any bull-fighters any more" has to be taken seriously and at face value: "I'm a bull-fighter." In the same way, the "family interest" Manuel feels for the stuffed bull must be interpreted to his credit: though Manuel does not have the skill of a first-rank matador, he has the courage and therefore the right to face up to this trophy of past glories and remark on his affinities to it. Indeed, it might be argued that Manuel represents manly values all the more intensely because he is not a good bullfighter. Struggling to perform the suertes another better bullfighter might perform with ease, he directs our attention away from the aesthetic (and theatrical) aspects of bullfighting and toward the spirit and moral integrity that informs the entire enterprise. Though a substitute, Manuel can be, and usually is, held to exemplify the best tradition of authentic bullfighting. His substitution is an ironic righting of a business in which (at least according to Retana) there are no longer true bullfighters and in which fakes like the bullfight critic are called on to interpret the action. The story thus reframes but ultimately preserves a functional contrast between authenticity and substitution. The critic is a true substitute (truly second-string and second-rate); Manuel is a false substitute (falsely held in low esteem) and thus the figure who redeems the bullfight business's descent into fake meanings and crassly commercial values. Amid scandalously equipped bulls and bullfighters who are a "bunch of camels," Manuel's manly valor teaches an object lesson to a decadent profession.

For those critics who read the story in terms of a Hemingway code of valorous manhood, Manuel's status as tutor is also inscribed in the conflict between his actions in the ring and the fickle observation accorded him by crowd and critic. Until the crowd actively makes its displeasure known, Manuel performs self-containedly without appearing to take note of his audience: at one point he had "not consciously noticed" (19) the trumpet blowing to "change the act to the planting of the banderillos"; at another he gestures "toward a box he could not see high up in the dark plaza" (23). By contrast, the preponderance of the watchers at the bullfight seems insultingly ill-qualified to interpret his performances. The second-string critic is unconscionable in his dereliction of duty. He switches his description of the "veteran Manolo" (15) to the derogatory "aged Manolo" after he "rated no applause" (19) and finally gives up writing altogether, thinking "What the hell was it anyway? Only a nocturnal" (22). The crowd, whose fickleness governs the critic's fluctuating responses, begins by applauding Manuel's efforts and ends by throwing cushions and other detritus into the ring—something that signally affects the outcome of Manuel's faena, for he is gored after tripping over one of the cushions. The crowd, most critics agree, can hardly be said to interpret and define Manuel's complex courage with any accuracy. Though Manuel is not obviously affected by the crowd's animosity, the crowd, one feels, could obviously learn from Manuel's professional dedication, honor, and bravery. Above all, they could learn from the integrity accruing to the isolate man determined to ignore or face down the dishonorable crowd.

For critics like Philip Young and Earl Rovit, who have been instrumental in elaborating the precepts of the Hemingway code, watching is a vital but not essential part of the educative relationship between (in Rovit's terms) tutor and tyro. According to Philip Young, for instance, the code hero (Rovit's tutor) in Hemingway's short stories "introduces and exemplifies . . . the Hemingway 'code,'" the basic principles of which can be articulated by "illustrating it in action."[11] On the part of the tyro, the process of observation signifies lack: that which must be seen in the person of another in order to lead one toward a definition of true manliness. The tyro is he whose incompleteness is signified by the act of watching—and of needing to watch—others. On the part of the tutor, being watched signifies the fullness of his self-containment. The tutor's actions and conduct should be studied and if possible emulated, but his actions, importantly, precede the specific interpretation placed on them and the consequences they cause. No gaze can alter the essential completeness of the man in possession of the code, for, as Rovit says, the tutor arrives on the scene self-defined. The tutor, in terms of Rovit's subtle distinction, cannot always teach, but the tyro can always learn: the meanings and values represented by the tutor are immanent and always potentially recuperable, though this does not mean that the tyro will always see the point of the lesson. We might define the tutor as he who illustrates in action precepts that the reader cannot see as other than what they truly are, though his actions are sometimes subject—as in "The Undefeated"—to the vagaries of interpretive gazes. By this logic, the crowd can only be seen as the negation of both tutor and tyro. It is that entity which invests its being into a continuing process of performance-making. It possesses neither the tutor's self-contained solitariness nor the tyro's wish to learn by watching and thus to achieve independence from the purview of the evaluating gaze.

This hypothesis that Manuel, like Romero in *The Sun Also Rises*, does it

11. Young, 35, 36.

"all for himself inside" while the crowd blindly spurns the opportunity Manuel affords them to watch, learn, and thus satisfy the requirements of the tyro role, is certainly encouraged by various aspects of "The Undefeated." But this straightforward reading of the story misses its complex exploration into conditions of watching, interpretation, and performance. One problem with the stuffed bull's head that figures so crucially in the story's opening scene, for instance, is that it too can be identified with the story's critique of inauthenticity and substitution: the head metaphorically substitutes for the bravery the living Mariposa actually displayed in the ring. It is because the trophy head also functions as a trope that it gives rise to multiple possibilities of interpretation. Mounted on the wall behind and above Retana's head, the trophy can be made to redound to the credit of the promoter: he owns the trophy and thus by extension the heroic feats it implies. But though Retana can mount the trophy he cannot control the trope, which can as easily, and probably with more justice, be made to signify the ironic discrepancy between the promoter and the heroic events he sometimes sets in motion. From the point of view of Retana's desire for glory, the trope/trophy problematically evades his attempt to make it signify, for the dissociation of the trophy from actual heroic events invests it with a capacity to be negotiated into meaning by a variety of interpretive gazes. The brass plate sets upon the head a satisfying interpretation—satisfying to Retana—but cannot prevent Manuel from interpreting the head as a memorial to his brother and cannot prevent us from reading it in ironic juxtaposition to the head of the "little man" who looks at Manuel. The meaning of the trope/trophy, it seems, is not embodied in the head or the explanatory brass plate but in the nature of the gaze that establishes it within a certain context of significance—and this is as true for readers of the text as for the illiterate (or too distant) Manuel and for Retana, who sits with his back to the trophy.

This interpretation of the trophy head bears an intriguing inverse relationship to the way in which most critics read Manuel's character and the nature of substitution in the story, for it appears that Hemingway, scandalously, might value the fact of substitution itself. My reading of the trophy head above is in these terms a scandal. It implies that the trophy's value resides not in the immediate significations bestowed on it by the attached brass plate but in its properties of metaphoric substitution, by means of which the head is able to signify more than the bravery of a bull or the prestige of the trophy's owner. And it implies that one interpretive gaze can substitute for another, so that Manuel's decision that the trophy represents a memorial to his brother is displaced, but not erased, by Retana's vaguely nostalgic feeling that it represents the old, authentic spirit of bullfighting. Nor are those interpretations erased if we substitute the suggestion that the trophy is meant to display Retana's pride in his own accomplishment, or the suggestion that it represents the dead commercial end of those accomplishments. The different gazes to which the trophy is subject in the opening scene of the story do not invalidate possible correspondences between the trophy and the meaning of a character's actions—whether it be Manuel's bravery or Retana's deadening commercialism—but they do put in doubt the availability of final and determinate meanings. An act of interpretation takes on value within the context of a whole range of possible gazes and possible meanings, in which we are always aware of the metaphoric density and richness of a sign like the trophy head.

That challenge to our sense of the legitimacy of the absolute interpretive gaze in the first pages of the story is extended and elaborated in the rest of the narrative. Few of Hemingway's stories build character, scene, and meaning so obsessively in terms of various modes of watching as "The Undefeated." The multiple gazes in the first scene, where Retana looks (thrice) at Manuel, Manuel looks at the bull, and Retana looks at Manuel looking at the bull, sets a pattern that is iterated in numerous later scenes of (self-)appreciation, competition, and humiliation. Retana is one character among many who pay close attention to the visual dynamics of a scene; the second-string critic and the crowd are only some of the many audiences who constantly watch and evaluate other men. Elsewhere, for instance, the coffee boy looks "curiously" (6) at Manuel, while Manuel, looking at the waiters, notes that they do not notice him (7). Zurito, after performing brilliantly with the bull, asks Manuel, "You see that one?" (17), and then continues to vaunt his prowess: "Look at him [the bull] now," and then yet again "Look at him now." When Fuentes comes out to place the banderilleros, Retana's man advises Manuel and Zurito "Watch him now" (20) and then again "Watch him," while the gypsy, after his own sparkling performance, makes a tour of the ring. Zurito later directs Retana's man to "Watch the faena" (25), an encounter that is itself replete with looks exchanged between Manuel and the bull. It is hardly surprising that the story ends with a gaze. With the doctor preparing to operate, Zurito, the last sentence informs us, "stood awkwardly, watching."

A mere enumeration of scenes like this, however, does not register the complex way in which watching in this story both underwrites the construction of the narrative and upsets any simple consideration of the role of the interpretive gaze. One important example is the first conversation between Manuel and Zurito, which turns on several moments of counterpointed and countermanding glances:

"The papers said they never saw a better faena," Manuel said.
Zurito looked at him. (9)

As if to rebuff Zurito's presumably skeptical look, Manuel quickly reverts to the subject of his last performance:

"You ought to have seen me, Manos," Manuel said, reproachfully.
"I don't want to see you," Zurito said. "It makes me nervous."
"You haven't seen me lately."
"I've seen you plenty."
Zurito looked at Manuel, avoiding his eyes. (10)

More is at stake here than the question of whether Manuel's last performance, despite his goring, was a fine one. Manuel's insistence on being seen is in part a power play. It gently invites Zurito to trust the evidence of his own eyes, implying that the picador's refusal to pic for Manuel has no pragmatic basis. Zurito's answer ("I've seen you plenty") perhaps carries a touch of sarcasm: any attention to Manuel's bullfighting would be too much, no attention is "plenty." More importantly, he returns to Manuel's concern with the relationship between knowledge and seeing. Though Manuel pretends to value the presence of the spectator over rumor and conjecture as a basis for knowledge, Zurito instead asks the bullfighter to recognize the depths of his self-deception. In calling upon others to watch him, Zurito implies, Manuel simply cannot see himself. The look that Zurito gives Manuel at the end of this passage is thus in the nature of another telling substitution. Though Zurito has not seen Manuel in the ring, his look across the table stands in for what he must have seen had he been there. It cautions Manuel to substitute clear-sightedness for the dangerous illusion that he can still perform in the ring. Tellingly, Zurito emphasizes his own perceptiveness. He reveals his ability to read the visible traces of the matador's recent history: "Zurito looked at his face. 'You've been in the hospital'" (9). And he concludes his part of the conversation with another bow to rational knowledge. "I'll pic for you and if you don't go big tomorrow night, you'll quit. See?" offers Zurito, where "See?" means something like "Do you understand" or "Do you see what I mean?" In contrast, Manuel makes an emotive appeal on the basis of his dramatic presence in the ring: "You watch me. I've got the stuff."

This brilliantly drawn interchange between the two men deepens still further when we realize the hidden relationship between watching and manhood. For one more thing at stake in this exchange of glances is that which signifies, or signs into being, Manuel's professional (and masculine) attributes: his coleta. The coleta might be said to structure this entire visual contest, for its presence informs the charged play of metaphor that articulates what Manuel does not or should not display. "Why don't you cut off your coleta, Manolo?" (9) asks Zurito, reinforcing his question after the long passage quoted above with flat directives: "You got to cut the coleta," "I'll cut your coleta myself." Zurito's unwelcome advice underpins the struggle between the two men to decide the mode of interpretive watching. The picador's gaze emphasizes signs of weakness and professes skepticism about Manuel's ability to perform. The metaphor of cutting the coleta acknowledges the fact and the nature of Manuel's lack. The coleta is a visible sign of what there is to be seen of manhood in the bullfighter's conduct. It centers the play of metaphor informing the process of manhood-fashioning, in part because it is *the* part that metonymically incarnates the bullfighter's phallic power to wield his sword in the arenas where males stake their claims to manhood. The coleta demands interpretation; it marks the matador as he who exists within an interpretive field; and it defines the interpretive field as that which exists to evaluate performances of manhood. For Zurito the coleta is supernumerary because Manuel no longer controls the play of metaphor, a loss most evident in the fact that he bears a sign that can only be read as signlessness. The presence of the sign on Manuel signifies only absent manhood; its invitation to be read and interpreted signifies what can no longer be seen or what is no longer worth seeing.

Zurito's metaphor (cutting the coleta) thus renders more precisely his statement "I don't want to see you." Zurito does not want to see his friend killed in the ring; but he also does not want to be forced to place Manuel within an interpretive field that can only read the matador's claim on meaning as a humiliating charade. Manuel should see, Zurito seems to be saying, that he should not be seen; he should understand, moreover, that being watched activates metaphoric associations that link abstract concepts of masculinity to the visual dynamics of a particular scene. The coleta invites the gaze, which in turn invites reflection on the wearer's manhood. Though Manuel at first seems to miss the point of Zurito's metaphor—he parlays it first into "I won't have to quit," which represents only one of the picador's meanings—his next words declare his allegiance to Zurito's logic: "You watch me. I've got the stuff." His declaration is designed not merely to demonstrate confidence but to preserve the signifying properties of the coleta and his continuing ability to make them signify. "You watch me" stands in, as it were, for the fact of the uncut coleta, which in turn stands in for whatever complex associations of manhood Manuel and Zurito attach to the act of bullfighting. Manuel ultimately makes his claim for status on Zurito's premises: the matador is determined to place his actions on display and, by showing them worthy of interpretation, to prove himself in a theater of manhood-making.

In this light, Manuel's refusal to look squarely at the value of Zurito's advice is interestingly iterated by an omission of the picador's, who follows his statement "I've seen you plenty" by looking at Manuel yet "avoiding his eyes." The nature of Zurito's (half) glance reveals what is at stake in this play of glances. The men are speaking of a hypothetical performance in the bullring, but the conversation between them in the café itself conforms to a theatrical paradigm, though perhaps more in the spirit of manhood-unmasking than -making. The scene between the two evolves out of a series of evaluatory and defensive glances in which both men are aware of the significance of their role. In pointing out Manuel's likely humiliation in the ring—and in the face of his determination to refuse the obvious—Zurito seems empathetically ashamed for his friend. More particularly, Zurito may be ashamed at having to suggest that Manuel undergo the humiliating ritual of cutting off the iconic coleta. Manuel not only faces shame in the ring, Zurito fears, but experiences shame now as the picador's probing gaze exposes his brave words ("I've got the stuff") as hollow rhetoric. Put simply, Zurito fears the consequence of exposing Manuel's confident assertions as so much theatrical posturing. The scene is reminiscent of an earlier encounter in the café when the waiter and coffee-boy notice Manuel's "pigtail pinned forward on his head" (6). The boy's response is quite different from that of the waiter, who (perhaps slyly) wonders whether Manuel will fight in the burlesque that precedes the bullfight proper: "You in the Charlie Chaplins?" The coffee-boy, however, "looked away, embarrassed." The boy looks away from the scene of Manuel's discomfiture for some of the same reasons that Zurito refuses to meet the matador's eyes. Both are embarrassed by the lack of recognition accorded Manuel's coleta, a feeling intensified by the distinct possibility that Manuel no longer warrants recognition. Both attempt to refrain from theatricalizing Manuel's plight, in part because of a fear that Manuel represents only a theatricalization (and thus hollowing out) of the significance of the coleta. And both, ironically enough, testify to the communal nature of that significance. The humiliation of a coleta that does not signify correctly accrues also to those who desire to negotiate its meanings in a satisfying way. Insofar as they express a sense of shame by looking away, they demonstrate the importance of the community of gazing that should legitimate the matador's—and by extension their— honor and courage. Their goal is to preserve a rich theatricality in which the coleta centers and displays an iconic representation of manhood.

Some of the implications of this argument can be seen more fully if we turn to a reading of Zurito's evasive glance that is more in keeping with traditional interpretations of the story. Despite his assessment of Manuel's weakened condition and despite his confident call for Manuel to "see" the truth, it might be argued that Zurito sells short his own percipience. By not meeting Manuel's eyes, Zurito looks without truly seeing. It is Zurito who will not, or cannot, face up to the truth that allowing Manuel to put his courage to the test is more important than his friend's personal safety. In light of the ensuing scenes during the nocturnal, Zurito's sense of shame could just as easily be accounted his for so badly mistaking Manuel's fortitude and resolve. Manuel's performance, despite the crowd's later impatience, turns out to be worth watching after all; he has indeed "got the stuff." Such an interpretation is intriguing because it accords with the conventional sense that Manuel's watchers constantly misjudge his actions: the crowd, the critic, Retana's man, Zurito, and Hernandez all offer slightly different perspectives on Manuel's performance in the ring, and all, according to conventional wisdom, miss the courage and professional dedication that bespeak his manliness. Zurito's final action in the story—watching Manuel—might then be accounted a kind of poetic justice for one who earlier refused to look his friend in the eye as well as a counterbalance for all those who watched Manuel improperly.

This rereading of Zurito's evasive glance reveals much about prevailing interpretations of Hemingway's concept of manhood, which, as we have seen, is usually held to resist theatrical display. One should not be surprised that Zurito fails to recognize Manuel's true worth, this argument might continue, if Manuel's masculine virtue resides precisely in his resistance to self-dramatization. Though Manuel occasionally acknowledges the crowd's applause in the ring, and though he does salute the president with a formula that is "a little long for nocturnal use" (23), his intent seems less theatrical than a demonstration of the kind of pride in traditional bullfighting values he shows again in his faena. Manuel, too, deliberately eschews the kind of extravagant self-dramatization practiced by Fuentes: "The gypsy came running along the barrera toward Manuel, taking the applause of the crowd. His vest was ripped where he had not quite cleared the point of the horn. He was happy about it, showing it to the spectators. He made the tour of the ring" (22). In contrast, the narrative merely registers a similar moment during Manuel's faena when the bull's "horn drove through one of his sleeves and the bull ripped it off" (28). Fuentes just misses serious injury while Manuel just misses dispatching the bull. The difference between the two actions, we may feel, exists mainly in the capacity of each man to celebrate them publicly. Indeed, there is perhaps a sense in which Fuentes's self-dramatization forces an unnecessary interpretation of his undoubted prowess. His actions could stand alone as an exemplary conjoining of courage and skill; the theater that follows adds nothing except the suspicion that a supplemental display might after all be necessary. As though in recognition of Fuentes's own brilliant skills of self-display, the narrative refuses to record his thoughts during his performance. We therefore have no way of distinguishing his performance from the spirit that motivates it. We cannot be sure that the theatrical impulse that makes him tour the ring does not also inform the moment when he moves ever closer to the bull, causing Retana's man to say "Watch him now" and "Watch him" (21). By contrast, the narrative records enough of Manuel's thoughts during the faena to absolve him of purely theatrical motivations. He is simply determined to fight on even after suffering the wound that makes him feel "broken and gone" (30) and even after the crowd begins to show its unmistakable disdain for his struggles. The manly spirit Manuel epitomizes seems to emerge only when the kind of drama the crowd desires begins to turn sour; it is precisely that which does not translate into brilliant theater. Tellingly, the moment when Manuel seems to bring most dramatic intensity to his bullfighting occurs only by error. As the "hot, black bull body touched [Manuel's] chest as it passed" (24), Retana's man exclaims, "If it was Belmonte doing that stuff, they'd go crazy" (25) and "Why, that one's a great bull-fighter." The bullfighter, however, puts this moment of high drama down to a misjudgment: "Too damn close, Manuel thought." Zurito concurs, immediately sending out Fuentes in support of the shaky fighter.

One way of reading "The Undefeated," then, is to see the story as ironically reversing the demands of the crowd and critic, who demand a bravura display and get raw courage, and who demand self-dramatization and get a selfless devotion to the best traditions of bullfighting. We might in fact see Manuel's courage as all the greater because bad luck or a lack of talent conspires against him. Hitting bone during his first few attempts to kill the bull and thus drawing the wrath of the crowd, Manuel quickly forfeits the kind of skillful display the crowd desires and he wishes to make. In consequence, there is no dramatic need to prolong a display the crowd has already disparaged. Manuel, however, insists on performing correctly—and dangerously. "There was nothing to do but go in" (28) he says after yet another failure to kill, though Hemingway in *Death in the Afternoon* details many safer ways to kill without "going in." One might suppose that it is precisely Manuel's inner and thus invisible determination to perform by the rules that Zurito misses in his assumption that a code of honor must be visible to the observer—indeed, as the very mark of ratiocination. Kenneth G. Johnston does just that, arguing that "Manuel, although bloodied and bowed, is truly undefeated. He has fought and killed according to the rules." Those rules are not merely those of engagement in the bullring but of the Hemingway code, which "permits a character to retrieve victory, usually moral, as he goes down to what the uninitiated would call defeat."[12] The morality of playing by the rules is thus sufficient for Johnston to disregard the aesthetic shortcomings of Manuel's performance.

To the truly perceptive spectator, then, Manuel's drama of manhood must be worthy of applause even when the drama of graceful bullfighting disappoints. The meaning of the final scene, where Manuel fights for the right to keep his coleta, naturally follows the logic of this ironic reversal of the crowd's expectations. The coleta, which is initially "pinned forward on his head, so that it would not show under the cap" (2), which provokes amusement in the waiter (6), and which causes Zurito to insist on its removal, ultimately becomes the dramatic focus of the operating room, where first Retana and then Zurito threaten it with removal before Manuel and Zurito collude to preserve it. Unlike Retana's dead trophy in memory of old times, Manuel's living coleta seems to testify to the enduring power of the bullfighter to make the sign signify manhood. The play of meaning in the story around authenticity and substitution finally resolves in favor of a transcendent moment in which the sign-wielder and his audience (Zurito) stand in the presence of an icon (the

12. Kenneth G. Johnston, *The Tip of the Iceberg: Hemingway and the Short Story* (Greenwood, Fla.: Penkevill, 1987), 88, 87.

coleta) that now possesses a determinate and immutable meaning. Zurito, whose original condition for participating in the nocturnal was that Manuel would cut his coleta if he did not "go big tomorrow night" (10), is now forced to acknowledge that Manuel has indeed gone big. If the display itself causes Zurito to want to wield the scissors, the spirit behind the display allows him to see that the sign has been imbued with a rich plenitude of significance.

As compelling and coherent as this fairly typical reading is, it does not begin to do full justice to more problematic aspects of audience, display, and interpretation in the story. The coleta is indeed "big" with meaning, but it need not, and should not, signify only that Manuel's status as a big man nullifies the weakness of his display. One problem is that the fictive audiences presented in the story are by no means as contemptible and by no means as univocal or unjust in their disparagement of Manuel as Hemingway scholars have tended to suppose. The audience at the nocturnal, for instance, seems quite capable of recognizing expert work in the bullring despite its partiality for the Charlie Chaplins (which Zurito, incidentally, also admires). The critic's slender praise of Zurito's skill ("Zurito resurrected some of his old stuff with the pike-pole" [17]) is drowned by the crowd's response to the extraordinary display that ensues: "'Olé! Olé!' the man sitting beside him shouted. The shout was lost in the roar of the crowd." The crowd's opinion is quickly corroborated by Zurito's vainglory ("You see that one?") and by Manuel's praise: "It was a wonder." Similarly, Fuentes's superb work with the banderilleros, which has even Zurito warning "He's too damn close" (21), draws appropriate and deserved acclaim from the crowd. If we fault the crowd for its shabby treatment of Manuel, then, we must also approve its somewhat paradoxical ability to identify and evaluate the truly impressive work performed by Zurito and Fuentes.

Interpretations of Manuel's work with the bull vary, but they are not illogical. He garners applause for his first passes (15) and for his work with the muleta (25); he gets none for what the critic calls a "vulgar series of lances with the cape" (19), presumably because Manuel sidesteps the charging bull (18–19) rather than holding his position firmly. (By contrast, Manuel's good work with the muleta is grounded in fighting with "his feet firm" [24] and "Firmly planted.") The point is not a minor one if, as the crowd at least seems to believe, poor bullfighting impugns the bullfighter's courage while courageous bullfighting imparts aesthetic and emotional value to the performance. It is on that basis that sidestepping the bull can be seen as not merely a flaw

in the graceful perfection of the bullfighter's stance but as evidence of his trepidation. Poor technique implies a poor nerve. It is on that basis, too, that we
might read the difference between Fuentes's ripped shirt and Manuel's as
being more than a matter of luck, for, in crowding the bull so closely, Fuentes
demonstrates a skill commensurate with the courage displayed and the danger
faced. His audience recognizes his courage by way of his skill and invests his
skill with the courage such close work professes. Conversely, Manuel's uncon-
vincingly messy faena breaks the relationship between skill and courage so
that, though his failures could be imputed to bad luck or to the fact that the
bull is "all bone" (29), the crowd is unable to interpret the one quality by way
of the other. Manuel gives the crowd no reason to read his faena in terms of
the Belmontesque passes for which they applaud him rather than in terms of
the trepidation that causes him to sidestep the bull.

This more complex understanding of the crowd gains some confirmation
from the part played by Zurito, who lays claim, if anyone does in this story,
to the role of tutor that figures so largely in Hemingway criticism. The veteran
picador, whose expertise with the "pike-pole" is so unforgettably demonstrated to the watching audience, plays a quiet but significant counterpoint to
Manuel's efforts. Zurito, for instance, constantly appreciates the importance
of self-dramatization. If Fuentes's theatrical tour of the ring flaunts his prowess too freely, the same can hardly be said of the picador's invitation to "Look"
and "see" the outcome of his own immense efforts on Manuel's behalf. The
attention Zurito wishes to draw to his performance is commensurate with its
quality. Moreover, his years of experience in the ring enable him to appraise
the work of others accurately. He remarks of Fuentes "He's good" (21), and
when Fuentes passes by during his tour of the ring "smiling, pointing at his
vest" (22) Zurito "smiled" as though in mutual recognition of their talent. His
opinion of Manuel thus carries weight. When Retana's man comments "Why,
that one's a great bullfighter" (25) during the faena, Zurito responds "No, he's
not." Zurito perhaps recognizes that some of the drama of Manuel's faena
arises out of poor judgment. His opinion is, at least, a considered one: during
the faena he "looked out across the arena at Manuel" after noting the matador's error, refuses to speak to Retana's man because he was "watching Manuel out in the center of the arena," and then instructs the man to "Watch the
faena."

Zurito's response to Manuel in the final scene thus emerges out of studied
and informed watching. The fact that Zurito does not cut Manuel's coleta

could suggest, as I argued, an ultimate recognition that the bullfighter has really "gone big," in terms of courage if not of a brilliant performance. But the final play with the scissors as they are passed from medical practitioner to promoter to picador implies otherwise: "Zurito was speaking to Retana. One of the men in white smiled and handed Retana a pair of scissors. Retana gave them to Zurito. Zurito said something to Manuel" (31). It is Zurito who apparently instigates this second operation on the operating table and he who is given, or takes, responsibility for carrying it out. He defers the operation not because he suddenly grasps the meaning of Manuel's actions and thus the enormity of cutting the coleta but because of Manuel's remarkable struggle to preserve the symbol of his profession. Zurito's excuse for changing his mind—"I was joking"—is clearly false, and comes too quickly to represent a careful reconsideration of Manuel's performance. And his final comment to Manuel ("You were going great") seems an obvious attempt at reassurance rather than a genuine revaluation of his more critical appraisal during the faena. Indeed, the moment echoes the scene in the café when Zurito looks at Manuel while "avoiding his eyes": in both cases Zurito resists the humiliation occasioned by intensifying Manuel's humiliation. Zurito's eventual refusal to cut the coleta thus does not distinguish him from the crowd's evaluation of Manuel; it merely emphasizes the perceptive but passive watching that still characterizes him in the story's final sentence as he "stood awkwardly, watching" the drugged bullfighter.

This reinterpretation of the role played by the crowd and Zurito might be said to miss the point of critical judgments of Manuel, which argue that the responses of the various fictive audiences within the story, however acute we might now allow them to be, should not prevent us from making a more accurate assessment of Manuel's performance based on an aggregation of eyewitness accounts. In particular, the third-person narrator to which the fictive audiences obviously have no access forces us to judge Zurito correct in refraining to cut the coleta even against the evidence of his expert appraisal. Similarly, our omniscience cannot permit us to make the crowd's (understandable) mistake of equating messy killing with a lack of courage. Being privy to the conjunction of Manuel's thoughts and his actions during his faena surely erases any lingering doubts we might have—despite the doubt of other watchers in the story—that he performs out of fear rather than ill luck. Instead, the third-person narrator might help us understand the constraints operating on the actual crowd, which has no independent means of judging the quality of Manuel's determination and verifying that he has comported himself within the professional and manly codes to which he subscribes.

Yet the information granted us by the third-person narrator is by no means sufficient to establish unequivocally characteristics like toughness, endurance, and honorable victory-in-defeat promoted by "tutor" readings of the story. Like "The Short Happy Life of Francis Macomber," "The Undefeated" presents the dilemma of deeds performed standing in for an integral quality that must exist prior to performance if we are not to mistake acts for the ineffable quality that inspires them. That Manuel keeps placing himself in dangerous situations to confront the bull is undeniable. That such circumstantial evidence signifies Manuel's courage and heroism is debatable. His cyclic return to bullfighting, for instance, allows a quite different perspective on his multiple attempts to kill the bull during his faena. When Zurito remarks "You ought to quit it, Manolo" (10), Manuel replies "I can't." This implication that his return to the scene of bullfighting manifests an uncontrolled compulsion seriously questions the extent to which his deeds in the ring could be considered heroic. His desire to continue confronting the bull even after serious injury might be seen as a symptom of the same neurosis that drives him to return to bullfighting in the first place. The entire faena, not surprisingly, is composed of iterated actions: Manuel running toward the bull, the bull standing fixed, the sword spinning away, the bull bearing Manuel backward or bumping him on the ground. Far from being a man whose perseverance drives forward and invests his actions, we might argue, Manuel is the sum of actions he cannnot avoid or bring under his control and is therefore doomed to repeat. Heroic endurance becomes in this reading decidedly unheroic because of his involuntary subjection to forces that shape him.

Moreover, the final scenes gradually put in doubt the opposition between matador and hostile crowd that underpins so many readings of the story. At the beginning of his faena Manuel ignores the crowd. Facing the bull, he is "conscious of many things at the same time" (26), and all of them concern only the exact sequence of actions he must perform in order to dispatch the bull. Several attempts later, frustrated by the fact that the bull seems to be "all bone" (29), Manuel thinks, "He'd show them." As if on cue, his sword shoots "end-over-ending into the crowd," which responds by suddenly re-emerging as a potent influence on his actions:

> The first cushions thrown down out of the dark missed him. Then one hit him in the face, his bloody face looking toward the crowd. . . . He

stood there watching the dark, where the things were coming from. Then something whished through the air and struck by him. Manuel leaned over and picked it up. It was his sword. He straightened it over his knee and gestured with it to the crowd.

"Thank you," he said. "Thank you." (29)

This scene marks one crux of the story, not least in terms of plot development, for he is gored when tripping over one of the thrown cushions. But Manuel's slip in a sense takes place earlier when, reversing his show of politeness for the return of the sword, he transfers his venom at the crowd to the bull: "Oh, the lousy, dirty bastards," thinks Manuel of the crowd, and then of the bull "All right, you dirty, lousy bastard!" We have already been informed that Manuel's "instincts and his knowledge worked automatically, and his brain worked slowly and in words" (26). By that standard, his descent into obscenity implies that his slow-working brain has begun to erode his bullfighting instincts. Not surprisingly, Manuel's next encounter with the bull, where he is not fast enough to evade the horn, is made in flagrant disregard of the carefully considered maneuvers he had earlier attempted: "He stepped close and jammed the sharp peak of the muleta into the bull's damp muzzle."

Manuel's bravura "He'd show them," which puts his earlier professionalism at the service of defiantly proving something to "them," thus begins to transform his concentration on the task in hand into self-conscious theatricality. Inner confidence yields to the self-defeating impulse to display it to others. The moment signals the end of his self-control and the beginning of his subjection to the dictates of the crowd. After losing his sword, for instance, Manuel can only stand there "watching the dark" as if he is the negative image of the crowd, who sit there watching the lighted arena. In another step away from the straightforwardness of his earlier performance, his "Thank you" hides his true disdain for those "dirty bastards," while it is his anger that provokes his hurried encounter with the bull. In this context, even the action that seems most to evoke his heroism—completing the faena while seriously wounded—reveals the wholly different motivation of responding to the crowd. He thinks "All right, you bastard!" before the final thrust, conflating bull and hostile audience as though to lay both to rest simultaneously. Manuel is motivated still by the impulse to "show them." Oddly, if his anger at the crowd causes him to lose self-control, it also gives him the strength and resolve to complete his task. Though he kills the bull and metaphorically vanquishes his audience, his triumph only underscores his acquiescence to a theatrical paradigm of self-fashioning that both destroys him and provokes his success.

At the very least, then, we should read "The Undefeated" as an anti-tutor story in which Manuel progressively sacrifices the positive values that he at times demonstrated in the ring. Courage transforms into anger, intelligent professionalism into mad haste, self-control into a desire to "show them," and the potentially emotional moment of killing into an aesthetic catastrophe, which ends when Manuel "flung himself onto the bull." One implication of this reading is that it overturns conventional interpretations of the story while preserving all of the features of the Hemingway code, whose values we now know not by what Manuel shows but by what he fails to show. He becomes a poor counterpart of Pedro Romero in *The Sun Also Rises*, performing well when ignoring the crowd, performing badly when aware of the theatrical dimensions of his deeds, and ultimately testifying by his lapses to the aesthetic purity, the perfect disregard of the audience, and the self-contained manliness Romero seemed to demonstrate in *Sun*. If Manuel had like Romero done "it all for himself inside" throughout his performance, so this argument goes, he could not have lapsed into self-destructive fury at his audience nor emphasized the "show" at the expense of his aesthetic, emotional, and manly qualities. The final irony might then come on the operating table, when Manuel's insistence on keeping his coleta can only be read as a desperate attempt to revivify values already forfeited during his conflict with and ultimate submission to the audience. If the primary value lost is that of self-containment, the logical consequence is that Manuel would seek to retain the sign, that obvious—but now surely hollow—show of his manhood.

My point here is not to choose between interpretations of Manuel as heroic matador, incompetent performer, or anti-tutor but to emphasize something of the range of possible readings available to readers who dispense with code and tutor hypotheses as the primary means of approaching Hemingway's representation of manhood. The conflict between matador and hostile crowd, which for most interpretations structures the circumstances within which Manuel shows his heroism, should instead be seen as the story's key problematic. The crowd's potentially reasonable insistence on the matador marrying grace and courage upsets readings that occlude Manuel's aesthetic disasters behind his manly virtues of courage and endurance. And those virtues themselves begin to seem suspect when viewed as a manifestation of an almost neurotic compulsion to return to bullfighting or in light of his abandonment of principled bullfighting in order to "show them." The status of Manuel's manhood is undecidable—or decidable only by choosing one among many possible competing interpretations. The problem I wish to emphasize, however, is not that "The Undefeated" is undecidable but that all interpretations (including that of undecidability) depend on gauging the nature of Manuel's performance in the ring. We cannot abstract a quality of manliness from Manuel's actions because manhood cannot be known until tested, and cannot be tested until proved in a pertinent display. The thesis that Manuel abandons his principles in desiring to "show them" is thus deeply problematic, for we can only know the principles in the first place by the manner in which Manuel displays them, thus matching his claim "I am a bullfighter" to the evidence of his deeds in the ring. Manuel can only always place his qualities on show. Those who see Manuel as courageous because his courage is untainted by any hint of theatricality—which is after all a legitimate interpretation—still miss the point. "The Undefeated" does not suggest that Manuel defies being watched; it suggests only that no one in the story was watching his performance carefully enough.

That last statement forces us to confront a problematic aspect of reading Hemingway that must now occupy our attention in the remainder of this chapter and in the next, for there is in fact an audience who watches Manuel's performance carefully: the story's readers. The lacuna of this and other interpretations of "The Undefeated"—though my discussion has everywhere hinted at its existence—is the special interpretive role granted readers who must possess a privileged knowledge distinct from the misreadings promulgated by the fictive audiences if the values most critics find in the story are to be realized and activated. Responsibility for activating the meaning of the coleta, for instance, must be transferred from audiences within the text to its readers: we register the full meaning of the phallus-coleta, seeing its metonymic relationship to Manuel's manhood, despite the fact that even Zurito wishes to cut it off. That transference is necessary (and problematic), for it allows us to pass over in silence the question of why several different audiences in the story fail to perceive that Manuel is a "man" despite the fact that, according to Rovit, Manuel is not merely a type but the "archetype Man." One would expect that Manuel's courage—like Pedro Romero's work with the bull in *The Sun Also*

Rises, when "even the American ambassador saw" its essential value—could not ultimately be misconstrued.[13]

Most critical readings of "The Undefeated" simply render the watchers' surprising misinterpretation into an unsurprising opposition between a blindly hostile fictive audience and a sympathetically clearsighted reader. Kenneth Johnston's remark that the code permits a character to retrieve victory though going down to "what the uninitiated would call defeat" exemplifies this reader's privilege to construe the meanings of the Hemingway text correctly. Though the crowd, the critic, and probably even Zurito see Manuel as defeated, we (the initiated) can only see them as incorrect, unjust, or simply confused about the priority of the rules of the code over the aesthetic rules.of the fight. Seeing truly counters a regime of false, imperceptive audiences; looking beyond Manuel's aesthetic shortcomings to his moral integrity resists the vulgar crowd's call for a dramatic show. At the same time, our recognition of Manuel's inner manliness makes nonsense of the symbolic near-castration (cutting the coleta) that signals the fictive audiences' derogation of his code. We become initiates in the code in part by watching the efforts of the uninitiated to make sense of puzzling actions only we can decipher. We realize our ability to read Manuel's struggles to fulfill the terms of the code by seeing the various audiences described in the story as fictive exemplars of how not to read. Though few critics recognize the fact, the concept of the Hemingway code encodes not merely a set of values but a set of strategies for reading.

This reinscription of the initiated reader into accounts of the story's hostile fictive audiences is particularly intriguing—because disguised—for those who insist that Manuel focuses a strict opposition between the false audience and the loner invested with the authentic Hemingway code, and who thus deny any theatrical impulse at work in Manuel's bullfighting. Lawrence Broer, like Johnston, notes Manuel's "contempt for the crowd" and then proceeds to link Hemingway's formulation of the code hero to his developing readership: "even as early as 1925 it must have been clear to some readers that Hemingway had introduced, in the character of Manuel Garcia, a strikingly new note into his fiction. Here was a far different sort of hero than Hemingway thus far had been depicting. The earlier hero was a passive or defensive individual. . . .

13. Rovit, 68; Hemingway, *Sun,* 215.

Manuel, on the other hand, is conspicuously in control of his environment."[14] Broer argues, without ever addressing the premises that organize his thinking, for the superior perspicacity of some readers in divining a role that is nowhere specified within the text. Though none of the fictive audiences seem to recognize the values Manuel represents, subtle readers will see that Manuel is "conspicuously" in charge of his environment. Actual readers are the only possible initiates in a story where the uninitiated see only defeat. For Broer and Johnston, the corrective to the fictive audience's ill judgment can only be to put back in play the dependence on watching that the story seems to work so hard to evade. Watching is ruled out as an infallible mode of apprehending manhood—which is anyway a moral and spiritual quality imperceptible to the senses—but then reintroduced in the form of an interpretive gaze to which the tutor must after all make some appeal if the manly values he represents are not to be lost in the pervasive misinterpretations of the fictive audiences.

The work of Earl Rovit suggests a similar equivocation about the roles of fictional and actual audiences. He distinguishes between Hemingway's "ideal portrait" in which his "audience is composed entirely of aficionados like Hemingway" and his "actual practice" in which "both in bull rings and among reading audiences—the spectators are not worthy to share the Host. . . . they can easily become antagonistic to the artist." Rovit reads the relationship between artist and audience in contradictory ways. He notes that Hemingway's hostility to crowds in stories like "The Undefeated" and "The Snows of Kilimanjaro" implies disdain for his own audience: the hyena in "Snows," for example, represents a "distended identification of the audience that the artist must serve."[15] Yet his own interpretations of Hemingway, as we have seen, set up confident distinctions between tutors and tyros that must find their genesis in the ability of at least some readers to match Hemingway's "ideal portrait." The ideal audience of aficionados is written off within the stories yet somehow implied as the antithesis of the carnivorous crowds Hemingway actually depicts so that subtle readers apprehend and carry out the correct role. Not all readers necessarily respond in this way, as Rovit admits. But to the extent that Hemingway's work partakes of archetypal and mythic significance the initiated reader has the advantage of tapping into meanings that must be universally recognizable even if not always recognized.

14. Broer, 48.
15. Rovit, 18–19, 22.

In a story like "The Undefeated," the reader ideally stands in for the fictive audiences, exchanging authentic responses for their paucity of insight. It is important to recognize, however, how thoroughly most interpretations of the story attempt to cover over the traces of this substitution of reader for the story's faulty spectators. The reader's role is conflated with Manuel's lonely heroism insofar as readers assume that his claim "I am a bullfighter" is straightforwardly and unambiguously enacted in the ring. In principle there is nothing to interpret if our knowledge about Manuel's heroism is "conspicuously" obvious. It would seem a truism of formalist modes of interpretation that the reader's work is erased or subsumed within what seems obviously true about a text; and the claim for archetypal truth is a particularly adept way of closing down the potentially unruly intervention of individual readers into the interpretive field. That strategy, however, comes under intense pressure in a story so obsessively concerned with modes of watching and interpretation. It leads Johnston to preserve a role for the initiated viewer in a story concerned only with the uninitiated and Rovit to write off a hypothetical audience that must actually exist if his own insights are to be confirmed.

The implications of this uneasy countenancing of the reader's role are worth exploring, particularly in what it reveals of the potentially destabilizing effect of the fictive audiences on common assumptions about Hemingway's concept of manhood. Traditional interpretations contend that Manuel's essential manliness constructs readers' interpretations in such a way that our task is—can only be—to apprehend the "archetype Man." Though Manuel's actions take place over a period of time, he presumably cannot be said to fashion manhood as if it were a role that must be filled out by manly deeds. Manuel's manhood must have always and already been there, self-contained but ready to take the shape of whatever press of circumstances emerged in the ring. It is thus the reader who must gradually fashion a role appropriate to the enduring qualities displayed in the ring, perhaps entertaining and then dismissing the possibility that Manuel is a failure before arriving at an understanding of his archetypal significance. Manhood is precisely that which is not subject to interpretation, but which structures the reading strategies deployed by the initiated reader. In contrast, the fictive audiences compose a theater of manhood in which there appears to be no archetypal essence of Man. Manhood is instead an arbitrary sign subject to ever-shifting interpretations and, most problematically, to the quality of its staging: hence Retana's man exclaims that Manuel is a great bullfighter while Zurito disagrees, and the crowd applauds one series of passes, remains silent for another, and contemptuously maligns the faena. The sight of the coleta, moreover, causes Retana to say "You don't look well" (2), the waiter in the café to wink and joke, the coffee boy to look "curiously," and Zurito, after witnessing Manuel's miserable faena, to wield those threatening scissors. The mode of watching, as far as the fictive audiences are concerned, constructs (or more often deconstructs) the sign "man." Manhood, for them, exists only in the moment of performance; moreover, since the watchers at the fight do not even see the clear possibility of reading Manuel's courage as a manly quality, it must be that each performance is potentially subject to multiple interpretations.

The multiple scenes of watching described in "The Undefeated" thus afford a wholly different paradigm of reading. They foreground scenes of watching as decisive acts in the construction of knowledge even at the moment when Manuel's heroic endeavors appear to deny most forcefully the perceptiveness of his spectators. They supplant the finality of an all-knowing gaze by creating a shifting play of interpretation in which one audience and one interpretation is constantly being substituted for by others. They adumbrate a narrative in which even Zurito's expert opinion must take its place as one of many, and in which the act of substitution is not so much demonized within a rhetoric of authentic conduct as responsible for the rich polyvocality of the text. And, perhaps most importantly, they realize the actions performed by Manuel in the ring as a piece of theater, not merely in the sense that they are determined to value and evaluate the dramatic merit of Manuel's performance, but in the sense that his very identity as a man is formed, or de-formed, in the act of display. They represent a situation, moreover, in which the interpretive demands and capacities of watchers are as much in play as the identities of men. Even the substitute reviewer is capable of praising Manuel's "Belmontistic recorte" before damning his "vulgar series of lances with the cape." Actions and interpretations are timebound and ontologically insecure. Characteristics that guide viewers to a recognition of manhood must be seen and interpreted. They do not suggest a situation whereby manly characteristics exist prior to the act of display, in which case seeing and interpreting would have been mere adjuncts to the apprehension of immanent manly principles.

This argument sheds light on a remarkable yet completely unremarked problem in Manuel's desperate defense of his coleta on the operating table. Carlos Baker, as we have seen, argues that the scene signifies Manuel earning the "right to keep his *coleta,* the badge of the professional matador"—a prerogative that, once again, must be seen as ratifying the right way to read this scene if all other watchers (including probably Zurito) read it wrongly. But why should it be necessary for Manuel to preserve the badge of his profession (and manhood) at all? If the whole point of the story is to place Manuel's deeds beyond the purview of the interpretive gaze—under whose scrutiny, as the fictive audiences so convincingly demonstrate, it is possible to misinterpret the meaning of actions—the presence of a coleta to manifest Manuel's status should in no way be required. If Zurito had cut off the coleta, in other words, his action (for the percipient reader) should not destabilize the meaning of Manuel's actions in the ring or diminish his status as a man on the operating table. The attention that Manuel pays to his pigtail should by the logic of tutor theories of reading merely draw him back into a mode of display/being watched that such theories categorically discard as the *reason* for the tutor's behavior (though, to be sure, being watched carefully as a prelude to imitation is a salutary *consequence* of that behavior).

In fact, the sign of the coleta bears a crucial relationship to what I have argued are Hemingway's predominant narrative strategies, which substitute actions performed for abstract values like a character's manhood and which are therefore intensely metaphoric. We are constantly made aware of the signs of Hemingway's values, pursuing their traces amidst events, deeds, and material objects like the coleta or the kudu horns that are all resolutely shorn of authorial comment. Though critics by and large seem to have little trouble in perceiving the abstract values to which those actions and objects refer, signs like the stuffed bull's head or the bullfighter's pigtail should give us pause. The coleta is deeply important to tutor interpretations of the story because it seems to lend such obvious interpretive support to actions that simply do not speak for themselves when performed in the bullring. The coleta must be rescued by critics interested in preserving a stable and determinate concept of manhood in Hemingway's work because its metonymic properties, drawing together professional expertise and the fighter's phallic credentials, work too well for critics to see that the sign is, and must be, empty if one is ever to reach an authentic and absolute condition of manhood beyond its metaphoric displacements. But I have suggested that the sign (coleta) is not empty at all: it is the (indeterminately large) sum of all the interpretations to which it gives rise; it marks the point where one mode of interpretive gazing substitutes for another in a nonhierarchical and decentered play of meaning. And it suggests a concept of manhood where metaphors like the coleta are indeed necessary to consolidate temporarily a phantasmagoric theatricalization of identity.

Interpretations that see the reader's role simply as responding to the "archetype Man" embedded in Manuel's struggles, then, are incommensurate with a polysemous narrative and a sign (the coleta) whose value resides only in the course of a particular reading. Lacking verification of Manuel's manly status independent of the deeds he performs and the eyewitness accounts he inspires, interpretations of "The Undefeated" can only end up by reinscribing the question of audience into their strategies and discourse despite the fact—or perhaps because of the fact—that most interpretations ignore the complex role of the fictive audiences. What is at stake in "The Undefeated" is not the Hemingway code but the work of encoding practiced by critics, for the story invites us to negotiate and thus pay attention to our own performance of various interpretive possibilities. In so doing, the story exploits the reader's role as watcher to suggest a problematic construction of manhood by way of trophies and signs. The coleta is fundamentally problematic in that it means anything at all (for manhood should be internal, not signed into being); in the way that it means (for readers of the story, like the fictive audiences, must negotiate, adjudicate, and legitimate certain meanings); and in what it means (for a range of possible interpretations, as we have seen, exist beyond the simple equation of the coleta with manhood). This argument nevertheless begs important questions about the roles potentially and actually played by readers in adjudicating matters of manhood in Hemingway's work, and I elaborate those questions in the following chapter by turning to some of the most remarkable works in Hemingway's oeuvre: those, like "Big Two-Hearted River" and *The Old Man and the Sea,* in which the actions undertaken by the protagonist appear to be witnessed by no one at all.

"TAKE A GOOD LOOK . . . BECAUSE THIS IS HOW I AM":
GENDER ROLES IN *THE GARDEN OF EDEN*

Twice in the published version of *The Garden of Eden* male characters participate in familiar social rituals of manhood-fashioning. The most complex scenes of heroic male action occur late in the novel when David returns in imagination to his father's and Juma's tracking and killing of the great elephant. These scenes are reminiscent of *Green Hills of Africa* in defining an arcane language of signs and signifying glances, the possession of which, as the young David implies, "made the difference between a boy and men."[16] It was "not just that they were men," ponders David about his father and Juma, but that as professional hunters "They knew everything the elephant had done, pointed out the signs of it to each other without speaking." Picking up the trail of the "old bull," at another point, "Juma had looked at David's father and grinned showing his filed teeth and his father had nodded his head." They share, according to David, a "dirty secret" (197) from which he is excluded. These dumbshows of sign-reading and -interpretation constitute a discourse of masculinity; they mark the points at which their expert command over the art of tracking becomes visible and functional as a means of tracking perform- ances of manhood. Scarcely able to read the signs himself, young David is reduced to reading the men reading the signs. He is assigned a subordinate position in these dramas of signifying glances. The first day of the hunt, for instance, becomes a pageant of humiliation as David "watched the two men" while they "looked back at him at regular intervals to check if he was with them" (181). Only after expertly knocking over two birds with his slingshot does David receive a favoring glance: Juma "looked back and smiled this time."

Yet the aftermath of the elephant hunt is strongly reminiscent of the ba- thetic trophy-displays of *Green Hills of Africa*. Sitting beneath the giant tusks on the honored "old men's stools" at the shamba, the hunters receive a heroic welcome. Yet the return merely signals a renewal of the decidedly unheroic drunken binges that preceded the hunt (when "Juma was so drunk we could not wake him" [198]), while, on David's part, his place on the old men's stools is an ironic reminder of his failure—or refusal—to enter the signifying proc- ess by which men are called into being. Though David "look[s] at Juma with his stitched up face and his broken ribs" (219) after the elephant is killed, David refuses to give Juma (or his father) the recognition his father demands from him. Instead, David responds to the secret glance of the elephant whose "eye was alive and looked at David" (217) at the moment of death. The tale is, as the older David says on completing it, a "very young boy's story" (219), both in the sense that it concerns the learned strategies that distinguish men from boys and in the sense that David, by opting out of those strategies, can only remain a very young boy.

16. Ernest Hemingway, *The Garden of Eden*, ed. Tom Jenks (New York: Scribner's, 1986), 188. This work will hereinafter be cited parenthetically by page number in the text.

The other archetypal scene of potent watching in the published version of the novel occurs in the narrative of David's relationship with Catherine, when, in Chapter 1, he lands a fifteen-pound bass in the middle of Grau du Roi. Mastering the strain of his "long pole . . . bent to the breaking point" (14), almost overcome by the "tragic violence" (15) of the fish, David battles in front of his wife, the waiter, and a "procession of people" (15), who watch and then celebrate his sterling display. Appropriately, David tells the watching waiter that "*we've* beaten him" (my italics), for our understanding of his performance owes as much to his audience's celebration of him as to his own heroic actions. Catherine, for one, intuitively construes the meaning of the scene out of a complex sequence of gazes: "I couldn't believe him when I saw him out of the window and you with your mob following you" (17). However disparaging Catherine sounds, the "mob" is crucial. Catherine reads the value of her husband's exploits by how thoroughly they weld a potential multiplicity of perspectives into one; the more his watchers become an undifferentiated mob, the more the heroic meaning of his actions seem beyond the dispute of any individual. Like Romero, who can afford to ignore the crowd because the crowd is so omnipresently *there,* Catherine (and David) can dispense with the mob whose role actually guarantees the meanings of the scene.

The stage is set here for David to transcend the "very young boy's story" of the elephant hunt, where he was relegated to interpreting the signs of real men in action. After the epic struggle with the fish, all seem able to read his starring role in a familiar drama of appraising glances—appropriately punctuated with two kisses for the hero, one from Catherine and one from "a woman from the fish market" (16)! That both manuscript and published text abruptly reverse this expectation, placing the powerful Catherine Bourne quickly in the ascendancy, is a transformation that most critics find easy to ascribe to Catherine's destructive tendencies. As Marilyn Elkins states neatly, Catherine introduces the "dangers of transsexuality and the way in which it can destroy a man's Garden of Eden." Comley and Scholes agree, since for Catherine to "experience what boys feel is to transgress, to break a taboo that is not merely social but religious." Catherine's fate, for these scholars, is proof enough of her fatal power: women like Catherine "must be relegated to the world of the insane or designated as lesbian and, therefore, marginalized as 'other'"; Catherine's "transgression . . . is coded in the Hemingway Text as madness."[17]

17. Marilyn Elkins, "The Fashion of Machismo," in *A Historical Guide to Ernest Hemingway,* ed. Linda Wagner-Martin (Oxford: Oxford University Press, 2000), 108; Comley and Scholes, 59; Elkins, 111; Comley and Scholes, 59.

Such interpretations, as I argued in my analysis of "The Short Happy Life of Francis Macomber," are predicated on a buried logic of consistent manhood: only a man can catch a fifteen-pound bass; therefore David must indeed *be* a man. And the corollary is that if he falls from that lofty eminence, someone else (like the bitch/lesbian/transsexual/mad/woman Catherine) must be responsible.

I shall argue here that David is never more typical of Hemingway's sense of manhood-fashioning than in becoming a man when playing appropriately to the crowd—and then abruptly losing his manhood when Catherine takes center stage. And oddly, but perfectly logically, the character who best draws out the implications of Hemingway's construction of manhood in this novel is *Catherine.* We have seen that for Hemingway not all males are "men" and that, moreover, males do not remain "men" beyond the moment of manly performance; and one consequence, as I have hinted in the case of Pilar, Marjorie, and the woman in "Cat in the Rain," is that all "men" may not be male. In *The Garden of Eden* Hemingway fully embraces that startling premise. The novel suggests that if masculine identity can be traced not to sex but to a gender role, and not even to a constant and deeply conditioned role but to one that is born anew at each moment of performance, then anyone, including a woman, might aspire to and even acquire "manhood." At this point, the idea of manhood is triply decentered: first as something one can acquire in perpetuity; second as a fundamental and causative principle of male identity; and third as a principle necessarily belonging to males. Though Catherine never performs the heroic role associated with Villalta or Romero or even Papa Hemingway in *Green Hills,* her symbolic performance of and intervention in the rites of manhood makes more obvious what Hemingway has always implied: that manhood is primarily a function of staging rather than maleness, and that crossing gender boundaries is a natural consequence of the fragility and temporality of masculine identities. As Catherine constructs herself as a man, manhood itself is deconstructed as performance.

In its manuscript form, writes Mark Spilka, *The Garden of Eden* is "chiefly a novel about haircuts," and it has been relatively easy to read the novel as a "fantasy-laden" work revealing, as Carl Eby explains at length in a recent book, Hemingway's fetish for hair-cutting and hair-styling.[18] The example of

18. Mark Spilka, "Hemingway's Barbershop Quintet: *The Garden of Eden* Manuscript," in *Hemingway: Seven Decades of Criticism,* ed. Linda Wagner-Martin (East Lansing: Michigan State University Press, 1998), 353; Carl Eby, "'Come Back to the Beach Ag'in, David Honey!': Hemingway's Fetishization of Race in *The Garden of Eden* Manuscripts," *Heming-*

Manuel's coleta in "The Undefeated," however, suggests that Hemingway has always been alert to the cultural meanings of hairstyles: the coleta, like the kudu horns in *Green Hills,* functions as a trope of manhood, signifying in an unstable negotiation with an interpreting audience ever-changing definitions of manhood. Catherine's masculine hairstyle and cross-dressing complete the logic of this interpretation. Changing her body-signs does not mean that she becomes male (no one in the novel *mistakes* her for a male); but her actions transfer increasing attention to the sign-systems that constitute definitions of manhood and to the way audiences interpret them. Like the coleta in "The Undefeated," Catherine's mercurial hair-changing reveals much about gests of manhood-fashioning.

The narrative voice, for instance, registers the switching of gender roles during the "sea-change" sex scenes straightforwardly, as if the changes are real: David becomes "my girl Catherine" (25), he feels the "weight and the strangeness inside," he agrees that "Now you can't tell who is who." Perhaps we as readers can; since the narrative always assigns "she" and "he" to Catherine and David, respectively, one might argue that the narrative never fails to distinguish between their "true" sex and the game of gender-role switching they invent. (It would be quite in keeping with the long history of Hemingway scholarship as I have defined it in this study to read the radical implications of gender barriers going down as a way of recuperating what it *really* takes to make a man.) Yet the game is not so much invented between them as a consequence of Catherine's demand and David's acquiescence. The fact that the sign of the hair subverts itself—she looks like a boy but is not—must therefore be recontextualized within the cultural codes that associate passivity with femininity and aggressive action with masculinity. Catherine looks like a boy; but is not; but performs a manly role more persuasively than David; and the narrative labels David "he" but does not overtly refuse Catherine's characterization of him as "girl." Obviously, Catherine-as-man is a trope. But then which part of manliness is not a trope?

What is most remarkable about Catherine's attempts to transform herself into a man, however, is not the overt body-sculpting or even the way in which her tendencies toward aggressive sexuality and autonomous behavior become more pronounced, but the way in which she attempts to appropriate the strategies and signifying systems that have hitherto identified Hemingway's pri-

way Review 14, no. 2 (spring 1995): 99; Carl Eby, *Hemingway's Fetishism: Psychoanalysis and the Mirror of Manhood* (Albany: State University of New York Press, 1999).

mary male characters. After having her hair cropped a second time, Catherine displays herself to David and says "Take a good look. . . . Because this is how I am" (54), suggesting not only her reconfiguration of selfhood based on her looks, but still more intriguingly a new sense of self based on how she is looked *at*. Her new haircuts mark the points at which she begins to participate in a theater of self-fashioning within which Hemingway's male characters have typically been shaped. Hence Catherine is pleased when she and David become the talk of the village; dressed in slacks, she chaperones Marita around Nice while disregarding (but noticing) the rude comments; she constantly invites David to look at her: "Take a good look" (54); "Do I look all right?" (57); "Just look at me" (195), "Look at me," "see how dark we are" (193), "Look at us"; and, like another "damned show-off" (Papa Hemingway in *Green Hills*), she persuades David to sit in a café with her at Cannes to "show off" (98) their matching haircuts. In so doing, she takes her place in the lineage of Hemingway's prominent male characters: the Doctor performing for his son in the operating theater of the Indian Camp; Villalta killing with his "hand up at the crowd"; Romero performing for Brett; Hemingway turning Africa into an arena for his self-aggrandizement in *Green Hills*.

At key points Catherine commands the theater of self-representation, as when she persuades David to follow her lead in dyeing her hair (the narrator tells us) a "silvery northern shining fairness" (91):

> David looked at Catherine and then at his own face in the mirror. His was as brown as hers and it was her haircut.
> "You really want it that much?"
> "Yes I do, David. Truly. Just to try it a little bit. Please."
> He looked once more in the mirror and walked over then and sat down. The coiffeur looked at Catherine.
> "Go ahead and do it," she said. (92)

Though this scene begins with the coiffeur explicitly stating that dyeing Catherine's hair "must be Monsieur's decision," the decisive glance among the complex of gazes that ends the scene is the one Monsieur Jean directs at Catherine looking for her order to begin—the glance that tacitly but unambiguously designates her the director of and star performer in a drama of her own making. By contrast, David looks from Catherine into the mirror to find himself confronting her brownness and her haircut. In observing himself, it is as though he is still gazing at Catherine, to whom the coiffeur then looks by way of confirming her as the cynosure of all eyes. These gazes, importantly, specifically refuse the traditional staging of the woman as prized object of the male gaze and male desire. Catherine appears instead as the figure of authority to whom the coiffeur's interrogative glance is addressed and upon whose looks and look David's very identity seems to depend. Being looked at supplants her "looks"; and being looked at is less important than her command over the kind of gazes directed at her.

It is David whose role becomes increasingly reactive and solitary as Catherine aggressively transforms him to match her own boyish style, overrides his objections to her actions, dominates him sexually, and finally burns his manuscripts. Yet David's passivity should not be misread as irrelevant to the dynamics of their relationship. As he says late in the novel, Catherine "turns my flank so skillfully then finds it is her own and the last fighting is always in a swirl and the dust that rises is our own dust" (211). Like the bullfight David's statement recalls, David and Catherine's conflict demands mutual participation and takes shape, most importantly for our purposes, before an evaluating audience. As audience to her self-fashioning, David plays a crucial yet ambiguous role. Catherine's role-playing depends on his agreement, which underwrites the significance of her actions but forces us to see her actions as a gest. This does not mean that the "real" man wins out over the fake or that Catherine must be punished for her temerity in taking on a masculine role. In taking on a "manly" role, Catherine's actions are contextualized by, and in turn illuminate, the typical failure of Hemingway's men to sustain their manhood within the purview of a theatrical construction of masculinity.

David's role as audience to Catherine's gender-switching underscores, in fact, the lack of autonomy I have claimed lies at the core of Hemingway's vision of masculine identity. Like Papa Hemingway in *Green Hills,* her attainment of identity depends on the contract between performer and audience; her haircuts function like trophies in *Green Hills* to signal her participation in a communal system of gender representation. Tellingly, the major break in David and Catherine's relationship, occurring after Catherine sleeps with Marita, is signaled by a withdrawal of David's legitimating gaze. Returning to the bedroom to find David gone, Catherine communes only with an unproductive mirror gaze: she "looked at the bed and then went to the bathroom door and opened it and stood and looked in the long mirror. Her face had no expressions and she looked at herself from her head down to her feet with no expression on her face at all" (127). David returns later to find himself "shocked at the dead way she looked" and the performer/audience contract irredeemably broken. As Catherine puts it: "There isn't any us. . . . Not anymore."

This contract allows for the invention of gender roles even as it suggests their arbitrary nature, and one other crucial aspect of Catherine's theater of man-making is the strikingly fluid and temporary nature of the various stages of hair-cropping, hair-dyeing, and cross-dressing she undergoes. Relating her experience at the coiffeur in Biarritz, Catherine says "I said I wanted it cut like a boy when he would first go to public school," but that "after he was finished and I looked like the most attractive girl who ever went to Eton I just had him keep on shortening it until Eton was all gone and then I had him keep on shortening it" (55). Her fluid hairstyles signify first boy and then girl and then (perhaps) boy again; the first style signifies Eton until suddenly "Eton was all gone." Signs change unpredictably into ciphers; and in the same way, Catherine's very identity appears in and disappears from the novel. Early on, after Catherine transforms David into Catherine and herself into Peter, we are told that lovemaking leaves them both "dead and empty" (25), and the chapter ends with David thinking "goodbye Catherine goodbye my lovely girl" (26). At other times, Catherine refers to the return of her "Catherine" personality as a kind of resurrection: "Yesterday it was all gone and everything was over and now here I am" (186). These transformations strongly convey Catherine's dissolution into madness. But they convey even more strikingly some of the more troublesome implications of the theatrical nature of man-hood-fashioning. We saw in *Green Hills* that trophies were fragile indicators of manhood to the extent that they were in constant danger of being out-trophied and thus "wiped out"; yet the implications of this voiding of masculinity were often obscured in the novel by Hemingway's braggadocio. The significance of his posturing was masked by the potency *of* his posturing. By contrast, the fluctuating nature of Catherine's performance suggests a recurrent voiding of identity while restoring a sense of existential terror. Catherine's fate, put bluntly, is the potential fate of all Hemingway's male characters.

The implications of this argument run counter to the most persuasive interpretations of *The Garden of Eden* put forth in Mark Spilka's *Hemingway's Quarrel with Androgyny* and J. Gerald Kennedy's "Hemingway's Gender Trouble," in which the novel, as Spilka suggests, is held to "accommodate the late emergence of the feminine in his makeup."[19] Although the androgyny

19. Spilka, *Hemingway's Quarrel*, 306; J. Gerald Kennedy, "Hemingway's Gender Trouble," *American Literature* 63, no. 2 (June 1991): 187–207.

hypothesis highlights the uneasiness I claim Hemingway always entertained toward masculine identities, I find this reading problematic in at least two ways. First, the hypothesis has evoked (though it does not necessarily presuppose) a stable constitution of self; one can become an androgyne by possessing a coherent and stable set of characteristics assembled out of masculine and feminine elements that are, prior to the inception of an androgynous state, themselves cogent enough to enable and maintain an autonomous sense of selfhood. In these readings, androgyny has been stabilized as an attribute or identity possessed by a character prior to interaction with others; it constitutes a sense of self that governs public actions. I emphasize instead the flexibility of roles produced socially and theatrically; Catherine, far from being a single, autonomous, androgynous subject, plays masculine and feminine roles alternately and sequentially, and is *variously* constituted as a subject during her performances.

Second, the androgyny hypothesis misconstrues the narrative doublings and repetitions that pervade *The Garden of Eden:* the physical likeness of Catherine and David; the sequential coupling of Catherine and David, then Catherine and Marita, then Marita and David; the doubling of Catherine and David's story with David's elephant-hunting narrative; and above all the omnipresent mirror gaze. The androgyny hypothesis relies on reading doubling as convergence—the growing physical likeness between Catherine and David, for instance, portending a feminized David and masculinized Catherine. I read doubling as iteration. Catherine becomes a "man" in the same way that males become men; and she fails to preserve that masculinity in the same way that males cease being "men" beyond the crucial moment of performance. Catherine's role-changing thus confirms the origins and discloses the problematic of manhood, and her travails are in turn doubled and reconfirmed by David's elephant-hunting narrative. As Catherine's self is progressively hollowed out in its pursuit of masculine identity, so does David's narrative inscribe a double loss: the loss of a masculine performance neither he nor his father can fully translate into a centered and lasting identity, and a sense of loss *at* a masculine performance in which the display of prowess has such destructive consequences. Like Catherine's mirror gaze that simultaneously surveys herself from head to foot and discloses to herself her own absence, both Catherine and David's persistent quests for masculine identity reveal only the profound loss of center they are forced to keep negotiating.

CHAPTER 6

The Self Offstage: "Big Two-Hearted River" and *The Old Man and the Sea*

"BE A MAN, MY SON," exhorts Sam Cardinella's surrogate Father (the priest) before he skips back from the gallows in Chapter XV of *In Our Time*.[1] The irony—that Cardinella will soon not "be" at all—is not merely a joke at the priest's expense. Hemingway's heroes are typically supposed to comport themselves as men at the moment when being itself is most under threat, and in this sense Cardinella reveals himself desperately in need of the priest's admonition. Lacking dignity and grace, Cardinella shows no sign of "holding tight on to himself" (65) in the time-honored way of Hemingway heroes: he is carried and "held . . . up" by the guards, "[loses] control of his sphincter muscle," is dropped on to the floor, regarded with disgust, and blindfolded. Holding tight is replaced by the straps that hold him immovably to the chair on the gallows. None of the humiliations he suffers need impair his dignity, as numerous examples from Hemingway's work attest. The seriocomic hero of "A Very Short Story" succeeds in holding tight on to himself despite enemas and anaesthetics. The pain-ridden Belmonte of *The Sun Also Rises* prefigures Manuel Garcia in "The Undefeated," who (if we are to trust most interpretations of the story) rises in manly stature the more he resists surrendering to the humiliations inflicted on him by the crowd. Robert Jordan in *For Whom the Bell Tolls*, knowing his death approaches, bravely prepares to buy his comrades some time to escape. But Cardinella, the narrator explains in an enigmatic moment, has been "like that": the guards "were carrying Sam Cardinella. He had been like that since about four o'clock in the morning." The narrator presumably refers not to the fact of Cardinella's being carried but to the state of mind of which being carried is the sign. Cardinella's humili-

---

1. Hemingway, *In Our Time*, 65. This work will hereinafter be cited parenthetically by page number in the text.

ation arises from having to be carried; he lacks the self-control and self-possession a man must exercise despite the disciplinary procedures enveloping him if he is to retain manhood. There is a sense, then, in which Cardinella has had no being as a man for two hours. He inhabits a state of man-lessness, represented in the narrative by the actions performed on his passive body and represented textually by the absence of a specific reference for "that."

As so often in *In Our Time,* Cardinella's humiliation is intensified by his inability to control the theatricalization of his last moments. Unlike Robert Jordan's end, which we anticipate as he looks from behind a tree at his unsuspecting pursuers, Cardinella's is stage-managed by others. The scaffolding on which he is to die is constructed as a stage, for it is built in the corridor of the county jail surrounded by occupied cells. The occupants, we are specifically told, "had been brought in for the hanging." Of the seven unimprisoned men who accompany Cardinella, three seem supernumerary to the proceedings and two have no function beyond that of silent witness. Several other details contribute to this thoroughly unpleasant piece of theater. It is the sight of the "cap to go over his head" that causes Cardinella to lose control of his body, as if testifying to the importance of the moment when his helpless exposure to watching eyes supplants his agency over his vision. At least two of those who are to share Cardinella's fate act in a premonitory refusal to see or be seen: "One of the white men sat on his cot with his head in his hands. The other lay flat on his cot with a blanket wrapped around his head." One implication of Cardinella and the two white prisoners being "like that" is that they surrender themselves completely to the spectatorial eye. Cardinella, refusing to look back at his captors, refusing to look death in the face, can only submit to being seen in whatever posture his captors choose to pose him. (The chair to which he is strapped after disgusting the guards is not his captors' preferred mode of execution.) By metonymic extension, any claim he once had to manhood can now be "seen through." It is exposed not so much by his inability to prevent himself from being watched as by his inability to be seen holding himself bravely, in which case he would still be representing himself as a man. Cardinella is in some senses the polar opposite of Villalta, who does possess the means to dramatize himself sucessfully before an audience. What links the two characters is the fact that in each case being a man should need to be articulated in a theater of self-dramatization.

Cardinella's absolute inability to dramatize himself before his audience of prisoners, guards, priests, and silent witnesses takes on great importance in the context of the remarkable "Big Two-Hearted River," whose two parts surround and counterpoint the story of Cardinella's demise. It is not only that Nick Adams on his trip to the river lacks Cardinella's panoply of spectators; Nick draws no audience at all. The story breaks the narrative logic of individuals performing for an evaluating audience that characterizes so many of Hemingway's works and that operates with such disastrous effect for Cardinella. Profound consequences for understanding Hemingway's construction of manhood ensue. Though the stories of Cardinella and Villalta mask a deeper indebtedness to an ethos of performance, Nick's solitude in "Big Two-Hearted River" argues for a wholly new approach on Hemingway's part to the question of how men resolve their identities. Actions would now seem to be undertaken for their own sake rather than for the sake of demonstrating manly behavior. And the structure of theatrical representation that could have granted Cardinella a dignified exit had he displayed himself differently disappears in "Big Two-Hearted River," leaving Nick without the need to transform space into an arena. The character of Nick Adams postulates the existence of a self-possessed and nontheatrical masculinity, fashioned without an empowering audience. In this respect, Cardinella's heroic opposite must be said to be the Nick Adams of "Big Two-Hearted River" rather than a Manuel Garcia or Belmonte, for these latter characters share with Cardinella a narrative premise that self-dramatization of some kind is a given. They can only represent themselves well or poorly. What they cannot do is take themselves completely out of the purview of an evaluating audience. That is Nick's prerogative alone.

This chapter explores some of the implications of Hemingway's attempt in "Big Two-Hearted River" to imagine an authentic experience of manhood independent of performance, partly by considering the problematic consequences for the construction of identity in Nick Adams, and partly by comparing the effects of Hemingway's other great tale of solitary heroism, *The Old Man and the Sea*. Traditional interpretations of these works frequently view *Old Man* not simply as like "Big Two-Hearted River" but as a kind of apotheosis of the principles of manhood-fashioning found in the earlier work. These narratives of men off alone force us to reexamine the premises of a thesis that portrays Hemingway's men as never truly off alone in their dependence on self-dramatization. Yet important differences between these two stories compel us just as obdurately into examining the ways in which readers have responded, and still might respond otherwise, to narrative dramatizations of undramatized manhood. Though superficially alike, these early and late examples of Hemingway's work are quite dissimilar in the way that they build character, explore questions of masculine identity, and shape the experience of readers. In particular, the presence of fictive audiences at the end of *Old Man* who respond to Santiago's trophy invites us to probe the role that readers are expected to play in judging and approving Santiago's conduct. And it allows us to begin the perhaps more difficult task of considering the effect of critical performances in unfolding traditional interpretations of Hemingway and closing down others that, oddly enough, these traditional critical perspectives sometimes already imply.

If Chapter XV places Sam Cardinella within a panoply of spectators, the opening paragraphs of "Big Two-Hearted River" flaunt the lack of a watching crowd as Nick arrives in Seney to find, unexpectedly, that "There was no town" (133). Now burnt to the ground, Seney also stands in marked contrast to the burned-out town on the Italian front in Chapter VI where Nick tries to make sense of his wounding before the "disappointing audience" of Rinaldi. And unlike the character of earlier stories, Nick does not attempt to play audience to his own posturing. Though this story opens like "The Battler," with Nick watching a train disappear, the taint of male competition and display that has him trying (unsuccessfully) to see his "shiner" in the water is now absent. At the beginning of "Big Two-Hearted River," Nick looks *through* the surface of the water to the trout beneath "keeping themselves steady in the current." Later, Nick closes off his only attempt to speak aloud to himself after his voice "sounded strange in the darkening woods" (139). "Big Two-Hearted River," moreover, transforms the camp inhabited by Bugs and Ad Francis into the "good place" of Nick's camp, devoid of human companionship or conflict. From its beginning, "Big Two-Hearted River" suggests the startling possibility that Nick's earlier travails were more the result of contact with other humans than of specific encounters with demanding females like Marjorie or gay males like Bugs. The presence of an audience in earlier stories compelled men (including Nick) to stand within a field of vision that could not be defined solely by and in terms of the subject, transforming a code of self-determination into a play of theatrical self-fashioning. Isolation in and of itself now appears to be a virtue. "[C]rowded streams" to Nick denote botched rituals: dead, furred trout in the rivers, product of inexpert fishermen, whom Nick, off alone, refuses to emulate. And his bitter coffee at the end of Part I evokes memories of the fishing trip to the Black River, where Hopkins's sudden wealth promotes invidious distinctions between the companions. What "broke up the trip" is not Hopkins's leaving but the conspicuous display of gift-giving that accompanies it.

"Big Two-Hearted River" is a dramatic analogue for what critics have often considered to be the essence of masculinity in Hemingway's work, for Nick's experience of being alone at the river at last bears out, it seems, the many scholarly accounts—both celebratory and accusatory—that equate isolation and heroic masculinity. His solitary endeavors remind us of Benson's "self-reliant hero," Rovit's "isolate man," and Baker's Hemingway hero who must "learn his own way to a great extent independently of every other man."[2] In keeping with this potentially crucial alliance between narrative strategy (depicting a man off alone) and theme (defining an ethos of autonomous manhood), "Big Two-Hearted River" constructs symbolic spaces in ways that recall the arenas of earlier stories but recasts them in a different mode. The "good place" of Nick's camp, for instance, is the culmination of a series of references to arenas in *In Our Time:* the cabin of "Indian Camp," the fenced-in garden and cottage in "The Doctor and the Doctor's Wife," as well as the "big hot bedroom" (88) of "Mr. and Mrs. Elliot" and the claustrophobic room of "Cat in the Rain." Yet this camp differs importantly from all of them in that its space resists the characteristics that defined earlier arenas—not because it lacks human structure but because it lacks the kind of drama that transforms the cabin into an operating theater and the doctor's garden into a potent combination of courtroom and boxing ring. Nick's cleaning of the two trout at the end of "Big Two-Hearted River" recalls the caesarean of "Indian Camp," yet the results of his incisions, "clean and compact," are far removed from the terror and the struggle to dominate the operating theater of the Indian's cabin. The trout suggest a second neat inversion of details from that earlier story. The Indian father is dead when thought to be alive; the trout, dead, when held in the water "looked like live fish." Nick's distinction in "Big Two-Hearted River" is not simply to create his own space but to create one that, hosting no overt exhibition of manhood, brackets off masculine competitiveness as that which broke up a fishing trip to another river and in another time.

Indeed, it is possible to argue that Nick's camp creates a paradisal "good place" demonstrating by contrast the lack or hollowness of prior arenas, and that actions performed there are elevated to a level of archetypal or mythic

2. Benson, 30; Rovit, 37; Baker, *Writer as Artist,* 156.

significance before which earlier experiences seem empty and inauthentic. As Joseph M. Flora has remarked, the story is in one sense Nick's account of Genesis.[3] Nothing suggests that more than his Adamic ability to move into a space devoid of the audience that has, in the stories of *In Our Time*, customarily watched and celebrated tough male roles or derided men's failures, and to enter a realm of experience where actions undertaken in isolation seem restored to a kind of plenitude—where, for instance, the narrative registers the ceremonial opening and eating of a can of pork and beans as if it enacted some primordial rite of bean-eating. Nick in the New World garden can be construed as Original Man, the quintessential man off by himself, representing a state and creating a space to which other damaged or humiliated males in quest of manhood should aspire, and manifesting the kind of self-possession the priest has in mind when he tells Sam Cardinella to "Be a man." Compared to the scene at the Black River or to his father's garden, which enclosed a usurping spouse and a history of land stolen, indebtedness, and labor troubles, Nick's camp signifies an economy of financial and psychic self-sufficiency.

The story's opening paragraphs corroborate this growing sense of a new representation of manhood with a visual economy that only seems similar to earlier stories in the collection. The narrative immediately makes Nick commensurable with the function of sight. His looking and watching in the opening paragraphs unfolds the panorama of burned town, river, hills, and pine plain. And he performs no action apart from watching. The prolonged, steady gaze with which Nick regards the trout "holding themselves with their noses into the current" expresses something of a resurgence of self-control, fortitude, and quiet command over objects apprehended within the field of vision. His acts of looking, unlike similar ones in stories like "Indian Camp" and "The Doctor and the Doctor's Wife," neither situate him in a matrix of competitive glances nor call forth a response from the objects of his gaze (trout, kingfisher, river). Those objects offer no resistance to his gaze; nor yet do they seem dominated by his gaze. The trout pursue their lives with apparent indifference to the fact of their being watched; and the watcher, in turn, avoids the kind of technologically enhanced disciplinary gaze with which Robert Jordan surveys the surrounding country. His acts of looking might even seem equiva-

3. Joseph M. Flora, *Hemingway's Nick Adams* (Baton Rouge: Louisiana State University Press, 1982), 157.

lent to and invisible in the objects apprehended within his visual field were it not for the narrator's persistent reminders of Nick's agency: "Nick looked at. . . . Nick looked down. . . . Nick watched [the trout] a long time. . . . Then he saw them. . . . Nick looked down. . . . It was a long time since Nick had looked into a stream and seen trout." These opening paragraphs thus balance Nick's nearly complete passivity against a subtly iterated suggestion that watching, however inert and receptive its mode, appears capable of thoroughly mediating and potentially governing the field of vision. And they balance passive looking against a particularly keen sense that these moments of watching mark a regenerative return to—or even an advance beyond—the last time that Nick had "looked into a stream and seen trout."

Nick's acts of looking are important to the common supposition that he undertakes this sojourn at the river in order to heal his war-torn psyche. On the one hand, Nick appears to step successfully beyond the example of his father, whose looking and whose demands to be looked at constantly bring him to scenes of sexual and racial conflict. Indeed, because gazing in the company of other men (and sometimes women) leads to having one's visual field mediated by the competitive gaze of the other, the concept of theatrical self-fashioning might be thought to presuppose the kind of warlike struggle to see and be seen that is implied by the doctor's contest with Dick Boulton or by Jake and Bill's show-and-tell at the Irati River. We need not adduce the trauma of war to account for a damaged masculine self, which is always damagingly incomplete if it can never be fully self-possessed, but instead possessed by the evaluating gaze of another. I have demonstrated in earlier chapters that the concept might have more benign consequences in terms of allowing men to fashion changing roles for themselves. But "Big Two-Hearted River" suggests the revolutionary possibility of stepping offstage and thus situating—indeed, rescuing—the self beyond either the warlike or the transformative effects of theatrical self-fashioning. Nick, we might argue, offers up control over the visual field in order to gain a greater measure of self-control. The function of gazing by a man in solitude might allow the recuperation of a damaged self precisely because it rules out the act of gazing as in any way contingent upon a structure of power.

On the other hand, we might argue that Nick's returning self-control is indebted precisely to his rediscovered ability to mediate the entire visual field. His eye, as it were, brings his "I" subtly but powerfully into being. Grammatically, the iteration of "Nick looked at. . . . Nick looked down" continues to place Nick as the predicate of every unfolding sentence. And as the sole spectator, he becomes the subject of every act of looking and perception; he is free to subject any object within the visual field to his gaze. The exception, somewhat paradoxically, is himself. Yet it is completely in line with an ethos of self-possessed manhood that Nick should secure his identity by assuming a prerogative to master all gazes by means of an authoritatively detached stance—one that is, by definition, outside the visual field it seeks to control. A master gaze must not be recognized by another lest the troubling presence of another gaze to which it is subject, and which is outside its own purview, reveal its status as *a* gaze among many. And that master gaze must not even be made aware of itself, lest it appear problematically exterior to itself and thus, being double or split, not detached at all from the acts of watching it purportedly stands indifferently beyond. Nick's perspective must therefore seem not to be perspectival, and his gaze erase all consciousness of itself as a gaze, if the act of gazing is to be interpreted as signifying a self that has been realized, or is now realizing itself, beyond the purview of another's gaze. The narrative's seamless conjoining of acts of watching with objects that seem to exist independently of human interference—so that Nick is passively receptive yet also always in charge of bringing elements of the scene to our attention—supports the contention that he establishes his identity both powerfully and nontheatrically. Nick, as it were, exists for the first time offstage, and in so doing refuses to compromise his command of the subject position. He neither stages himself for others nor becomes the subject of a gaze exterior to his own. And he must be offstage in the sense of being detached from the whole visual field in order to master it completely. So compelling is Nick's offstage experience at the river that performance, far from being the preferred mode of self-fashioning for men, might instead be seen as the problem with manhood-fashioning in a culture that fails to provide satisfactory outlets for (solitary) masculine experience and that urges men toward competitive displays.

It might therefore be argued that the dynamics of a self offstage in a story like "Big Two-Hearted River," where the character of Nick Adams escapes the self-dramatizations found in earlier stories, betrays the shortcomings of any theory of performance in Hemingway's work and validates the numerous exegeses that privilege an account of autonomous manhood. The story seems to suggest that performances of manhood are errors from which true manhood must be rescued and then revived in isolation. For that very reason it is worth pausing at this juncture to explore the irony that few scholarly appraisals of the story actually cast Nick in a heroic mold, preferring to envisage him as a man in search of a manhood that stretches, like his desire to fish the swamp, alluringly ahead of him. The story, Philip Young argues, presents a "picture of a sick man, and of a man who is in escape from whatever it is that made him sick." Carlos Baker, following the lead of Malcolm Cowley, writes that Nick resorts to the river for "therapeutic purposes." Lawrence R. Broer suggests conventionally that the story is an "attempt to find defensive structures by which the brave and simple man might survive in such a [hostile] world" and, much more intriguingly, that the tale represents a bridge between the "sterile and impotent image of the Anglo-Saxon world of *In Our Time*" and the "pattern of ritualized, primitive-defensive behavior that [later] attracts him so strongly to Spain." Nick Adams thus achieves the "same sense of emotional satisfaction in performing these simple, primitive rites as Jake Barnes soon experiences through the ritualized and ceremonial patterns of the bull-fight."[4]

Traditional approaches to "Big Two-Hearted River" thus emphasize the therapeutic boon that isolation brings to a wounded masculine self, though in a surprisingly negative way: isolation is an "escape" and a "defensive structure." By the same logic, Nick has not yet fulfilled the priest's injunction to "Be a man." At best we discover Nick in the process of becoming a man, slowly moving in his beleaguered fashion toward an apotheosis that numerous obstacles—his weariness, the mosquito in his tent, the panic-inspiring trout, the fear of the swamp—conspire to defer. In none of these interpretations, moreover, is the dramatic situation of a man off alone considered to be an exemplary demonstration of pure and essential manhood. Instead, Nick's experience of solitude is bracketed off as a symptomatic response to conditions of wounding that emerged before the story even opens: Nick lying against a wall with a bullet in his spine, (perhaps) watching his father's humiliation at the hands of Dick Boulton, or more generally being brought up in the sterile environment of the Anglo-Saxon world. To critics, the narrative representation of solitude does not therefore necessarily bring about a state of self-possessed manhood, though solitude can be thought of as necessary for a "defensive" structuring of a damaged male self in which the conditions for a secure sense of masculinity can be forged. Those interpretations depending on some variant of a masculine code must at this point read Nick's defensive

4. Young, 19; Baker, *Writer as Artist,* 127; Broer, 39, 46, 44.

reconstruction in the context of those who have already made it to manhood: the kid of Chapter IX, Villalta, and later on in Hemingway's career Pedro Romero or Santiago.

Such at least is the case with Broer's illuminating analysis. Broer, who cites his debt to Young's work on the wound and the code, argues that in *In Our Time* the "highly sympathetic portraits of matadors" in the vignettes, which contrast with stories of Anglo-Saxon sterility, foretell the flowering of Hemingway's interest in a powerful "moral code" for men drawn from the bullfight specifically and from Spain in general. This moral code is designed to counter the deficiencies of the early Hemingway hero, who is a "man without a country, without religion, without relation to any cultural or national past, and without ideological relation to the future."[5] But though bullfighting might be thought an admirable vehicle for emphasizing a psychological imperative toward relationality, possibly constructed around a code of theatrical self-fashioning, Broer actually preserves the autonomy of the masculine hero. Broer's notion of a moral code signifies the professional rules of an enterprise (in this case bullfighting) rather than compliance with the code of a group of people. Hence Manuel Garcia in "The Undefeated," according to Broer, can be heroically committed to his craft despite the ignorance of his actual audience. And though Nick Adams mediates the entire visual terrain of "Big Two-Hearted River," it is Garcia, constantly under the scrutiny of numerous spectators, who is "conspicuously in control of his environment," who is "self-possessed" and a "dominator in every sense." A similar contrast emerges in *The Sun Also Rises* between the "herding instinct of Jake's companions" and the quality of Romero, a "man who lives and works alone."[6] Broer, in other words, finesses the problem of the crowd by defining the important relationship as the one between the individual (bullfighter) and his code. And though code heroes like Romero and Garcia (and presumably Villalta) can only function by demonstrating their prowess to others, Broer subordinates the fact of demonstration to the ritual patterns such behavior is designed to convey. In so doing, Broer broaches unintentionally the problem of why an ethos of masculine autonomy should be epitomized by a matador before a crowd while Nick's "defensive" procedures at the river camp, when he would seem conspicuously in charge of his environment, should appear so puzzlingly incomplete.

5. Broer, 46, 43.
6. Ibid., 48, 49, 51.

Broer's account epitomizes, in fact, the kind of problematic reversals that characterize the discourse on "Big Two-Hearted River," whereby a dramatic analogue for a theory of masculine self-possession is read as a case of damaged identity and a narrative strategy that seemingly grants Nick visual possession of the surrounding territory is read as depicting a precariously temporary quest for manhood. Above all, Broer's subtextual emphasis on the performer (the matador) as Hemingway's quintessential hero strangely—strangely in terms of his own intentions—conceives of masculinity as more pertinent to the bullring than to the isolated river camp. But Broer thereby underscores the extent to which an ethos of performance has shaped what seem to be the most potent moments of masculine action undertaken in *In Our Time* before "Big Two-Hearted River." Villalta, in particular, who becomes "one with the bull" and leaves the "red hilt of the sword sticking out" (105) of the bull's shoulders, is a representation of formidable power expressed through an intense sexual potency. As I suggested at the beginning of Chapter 2 in rebutting most accounts of Hemingway's concept of masculinity, Villalta's potency is inseparable from its staging. The vignette begins by placing Villalta "in front of you" and in front of the roaring crowd, and thereafter every act performed [carried out] leads a double life as a performed [dramatized] act. Villalta dominates the multiple gazes intersecting the arena and in so doing controls both the bull and the play of symbolic meanings informing his acts. The corollary, as I have argued at length, is that Villalta's being as a man depends on variable and temporary conditions of self-fashioning to which he owes his allegiance in the very act of mastering them. Though the sources of Villalta's prowess lie in performance, his performance, crucially, does not seem to be presented ironically. Swinging back from the bull "like an oak when the wind hits it"—a force of nature incarnate—Villalta in Chapter XII underscores the ways in which a potent masculinity might be exercised by and through self-dramatization. Unless we write off the performative aspects of Villalta's bullfighting as somehow out of bounds, Nick's solitary endeavors in the wilderness cannot be thought of as uniquely responsible for bringing about a state of manhood.

Yet there is a sense in which performance can be thought of as the dilemma of manhood-fashioning that Nick must negotiate in the wilderness. For the second problem with reading Nick in "Big Two-Hearted River" as the archetype of autonomous and therefore unsullied masculinity is what so many conventional interpretations imply yet have never considered appropriate to the story, namely that solitude, deemed to help remedy a damaged masculine self, might aggravate or even bring about that damage by denying the protagonist his opportunity to perform for an evaluating audience. Critics, in other words, have insisted that the story represents a parlous state of manhood while excluding as a problematic the process of manhood-fashioning itself, which, conventionally, represents Nick's efforts to discover by means of his solitary activities the pure or primal man within. The difficulties Nick finds in reconstructing a damaged psyche—the metronomic attention he pays to every step of a process, his shakiness on hooking the big, uncontrollable trout, his fear of fishing the swamp—are written off as problems to which manhood will ultimately come as a solution. But many aspects of the story argue that it is precisely the nature of Nick's strategies of manhood-fashioning, pursued in an environment lacking Hemingway's characteristic structure of male performance and evaluating audience, that make the value of his restorative rituals debatable. The point of the story lies not in fishing the swamp—the action that, hovering beyond the bounds of narrative representation, marks a hypothetical cohesion of masculine elements of fortitude and self-reliance—but in the fact that the very nature of the manly gestures available to Nick forever defer the moment when fishing the swamp alone would become a possibility.

The problematic of manhood-fashioning is brought home most clearly in those moments when narrative gaps interrupt the ostensibly seamless recording of Nick's sensations and perceptions. The most obvious—for all that it is rarely recognized in such terms—occurs where Chapter XV, the vignette of Cardinella's hanging, separates the two parts of "Big Two-Hearted River." Here the impersonal and detached narrative voice brilliantly mimics the disciplinary gaze to which Cardinella is subjected. Depicted within a sequence of exterior actions, statements, and glances, he is the focus of this penal theater. He appears exclusively under conditions of performance, witnessed by assorted characters within the story as a body dragged to the scaffold. Responding to the theatricalization of Cardinella's demise, the narrator's detached stance creates a kind of simulacrum whereby we know Cardinella solely through a display of external actions. We may choose to read those actions as pertaining to certain states of mind: being carried "like that," for instance, might signify Cardinella's cowardice; losing control of his bowels might represent a loss of grace under pressure. Or we might choose to read those actions as signifying a complete voiding of identity: Cardinella is nothing beyond the actions that, displaying and representing him, occupy the entirety of his being. The narrative mode of Chapter XV thus contributes to a sense of the progressive annihilation of the masculine I (and eye) under conditions of total theatricality. Those conditions should also obtain, moreover, had Sam Cardinella held tight to himself and demonstrated his contempt for the proceedings while arraigned before the disgusted or terrified eyes of the onlookers. In that case he would still fail to secure the perfect self-possession we have stipulated as Nick's (possible) prerogative at the river camp, where he is alone and, in the senses I have discussed, offstage. Because we can only know his state of mind from his actions, Cardinella can only stage himself or be humiliatingly staged. To the extent that we insist on autonomy as an archetypal condition of manhood, we rule out those male characters who depend on displaying tough, heroic actions in order to make known a sense of their interior worth as men.

But in "Big Two-Hearted River" itself conditions of non-performance—under which we should (at last) be able to stand in the presence of the absolute masculine self, entirely unaffected by any demand for or threat of self-dramatization—lead to a puzzling sense of psychological displacement in Nick's character. This is particularly evident at the point when the profound shock of Nick's battling the dangerously large trout brings about a sequence of thought that culminates in "I" irrupting into the text: "By God, he was the biggest one I ever heard of" (151). The remark draws our attention squarely to Hemingway's curious transformations of narrative voice in "Big Two-Hearted River," for it breaches the narrative logic of third-person omniscient and free indirect discourse that has so far governed Nick's experiences and that leads us to expect phrasing like "he was the biggest one *he* had ever heard of." Shortly before this moment, in fact, the narrator informs us "He had never seen so big a trout" (150). We are attuned early in the narrative to a strategy that replicates the kind of careful control Nick wishes to exert on his environment. He is screened from our gaze, as it were, by the position of a narrator who stands authoritatively separate from Nick or who covertly mediates his thoughts in such a fashion that they appear to be the provenance of a third person (thus "*He* had never seen so big a trout"). Under what conditions, then, is Nick suddenly capable of speaking directly for himself? As brief as it is, this intrusion into interior monologue forces us to the disconcerting possibility that the entire narrative turns upon an erasure of the self-possessed I/eye (for which interior monologue seems the appropriate narrative mode) and the substitution of third-person narration. The irruption of "I" suddenly makes us aware of the kind of self-reflexive consciousness that might have been present from the beginning had not Nick carefully choked off the thoughts and memories (and his actual voice) that would force him to become aware of himself. It suggests the extent to which Nick is at every other point little more than a recording consciousness. By the logic of this reading, the lonely, meditative gazing at nature that early on seemed to portray a character in charge of the terrain visible from the standpoint of the eye/I can now be seen to signify a general and profound sense of displacement that governs the substitution of one narrative mode for another and that reduces Nick to the function of sight alone. Nick is the subject of multiple acts of seeing; but the discourse of I/eye of which he is at least once capable has been appropriated and his subject-position filled with the gaze of a third-person narrator: Nick, not "I," looks at the trout in the river. In these senses Nick stands enigmatically center stage and offstage; speaking once in his own person, thinking once in his own person, and mediating the visual terrain, yet never on other occasions dramatically visible at all.

The story's bravura insistence on solitary experience—Nick alighting to find that "There was no town" of Seney—leads back, by a new route, to the same dilemma that haunted "The Battler." Ad Francis's desperate attempts to dramatize himself disguised a malleable and amnesiac self characterized by incessant transformation rather than stability. In a sense, Nick wishes to iterate Ad Francis's capacity for amnesia; Bugs's certainty that Francis "won't remember nothing of it" is picked up by Nick's knowledge that he could "choke" the bad memories of the Black River. Critics have tended to view this displacement as a psychologically necessary strategy for healing Nick's war-fragmented self and have argued about whether his final promise to "fish the swamp" signifies the completion of that process. Such analyses, however, invert the meanings of Nick's actions. Significant as those actions are on a symbolic level, they cannot fashion a self because Nick constantly defers the self-awareness that would make them psychologically potent. Nick, as Peter Schwenger puts it, has "no way to deal with the emotion . . . except by the very strategies of detachment which threaten him" (46).[7] If Nick comports himself as a man at the sacred river, no one (scarcely even Nick himself) is

---

7. Peter Schwenger, *Phallic Critiques* (London: Routledge and Kegan Paul, 1984), 46. The direct context of Schwenger's comment here is Hemingway's "A Way You'll Never Be."

there to acknowledge and validate it. While the absence of audience removes the need for the puerile self-display of "The Battler" and "The Three-Day Blow," that same absence erases all opportunity for the self-dramatization that empowered characters like the "kid" and Villalta, and that might indeed have accorded Sam Cardinella their heroic status had he possessed their ability to perform in front of a crowd.

"Big Two-Hearted River" delicately probes the question of how and under what circumstances it is even possible to represent a man off alone, if by "man" we mean a male who is self-possessed and self-determined. Taking a cue from critical reactions to the story, I argued that the fact of Nick's isolation does not guarantee an ethos of masculine autonomy. Despite the early promise of Nick's seemingly poised spectatorial role, the story's narrative mode gradually betrays an amnesiac self whose gestures toward self-control involve a profound displacement of the "I" into a depersonalized third-person narrator. For all the humiliation visited upon Sam Cardinella in Chapter XV, the vignette's narrative of a male conducting himself (in this case badly) before an evaluating audience conforms more closely than "Big Two-Hearted River" to the theatrical acts that identify the most authoritative male characters in story after story of *In Our Time.* Whatever therapeutic actions Nick generates from his experience on the river can only be partial gestures toward a manhood whose completion depends on the legitimating function of an audience. It is not the case, then, that a man offstage is unrepresentable in Hemingway's work; but the implications of its representation turn out to be very different from the conventional depiction of the autonomous and self-determined man. Hemingway's exploration of the world of the solitary male suggests a curious dead-end and an intriguing dilemma for a writer so fascinated by masculine experience: how could one successfully write of the nontheatrical situation of being off alone if the masculine self can be constructed only through self-dramatization? The late novella *The Old Man and the Sea* provides Hemingway's only other fully developed answer.

READING THE BONES: SANTIAGO'S AUDIENCES IN
THE OLD MAN AND THE SEA

If the publication of *The Old Man and the Sea* inspired critics and prize committees to reevaluate an author many considered artistically exhausted, the novella itself has generally had the effect of confirming major lines of inquiry into Hemingway's work. Early reviewers and scholars emphasized continuities of philosophy—particularly his philosophy of masculinity—and aesthetic strategy. To Philip Young, for instance, Santiago is the "first of the code heroes to have grown old"; to Arvin R. Wells, borrowing Young's concept, he is the "apotheosis of the code hero"; to Delmore Schwartz, the "old fisherman is the quintessential hero of Hemingway's fiction," for he represents the "solitude which requires absolute courage and complete self-reliance." Joseph Wald-meir puts a similar sentiment in terms that make clear the link between au-tonomous action, self-assertion, and manhood: "A man must depend upon himself alone in order to assert his manhood, and the assertion of his man-hood, in the face of insuperable obstacles, is the complete end and justifica-tion of his existence for a Hemingway hero." Even critics' caveats—and there were many—have the effect of confirming commonplace ideas about Hem-ingway. Robert P. Weeks sees the story as so much fakery; Nemi D'Agostino remarks that the story's "symbolism remains a fictitious disguise," while Claire Rosenfield condemns passages of the tale for its sentimentality and its "patent attempt at manipulating our responses."[8]

Philip Toynbee, in an attack on what he calls a "meretricious" story, sup-plies an intriguing reason for this constellating of critical opinion: the book is "stuffed with the burden of all the theses which had been written about Hemingway's message and philosophy. . . . What must follow, of course, are

8. Young, 96; Arvin R. Wells, "A Ritual of Transfiguration: *The Old Man and the Sea*," in *Twentieth Century Interpretations of "The Old Man and the Sea*," ed. Katharine T. Jobes (Englewood Cliffs, N.J.: Prentice-Hall, 1968), 56; Delmore Schwartz, "*The Old Man and the Sea* and the American Dream," in ed. Jobes, 98; Joseph Waldmeir, "*Confiteor Hominem:* Ernest Hemingway's Religion of Man," in *Papers of the Michigan Academy of Science, Arts, and Letters*, vol. 42 (Ann Arbor: University of Michigan Press, 1957), 146; Robert P. Weeks, "Fakery in *The Old Man and the Sea*," in ed. Jobes, 34; Nemi D'Agostino, "The Later Hem-ingway," in ed. Jobes, 109; Claire Rosenfield, "New World, Old Myths," in ed. Jobes, 51. The list could be extended. According to J. Bakker, "Santiago is the Hemingway hero" whose "ultimate satisfaction lies in the fact that he has asserted his manhood in the face of insuper-able obstacles," despite the "falseness" in the story. Richard Hovey remarks that "we have something of the story as before: a hunt after big game, a test of manly courage, a proof of grace under pressure, and a theme like that of 'The Undefeated.'" Hovey, too, regrets that the stripped-down narrative results in unfortunate oversimplifications, for "the hero this time is for the most part uninvolved with any person other than himself." And Jackson J. Benson argues that the "primitive simplicity of Santiago must be felt as a kind of hypocrisy expressed by an author who seems to be trying to manipulate his audience." Bakker, 229, 232, 231; Hovey, 191; Benson, 185.

the hundred exegeses. The book is doctor-bait, professor-bait."[9] According to Toynbee, the book is the outcome of an authorial and scholarly feeding frenzy. Hemingway feeds off critical opinion and in turn trails in his wake bait to attract further schools of thought, those "hundred exegeses." Toynbee's attack thus makes absolutely unremarkable the number of critics who perceive Santiago as code hero. How could they not when Hemingway had the example of John McCaffery's convenient anthology (1950), and when the opinions of Edmund Wilson, Malcolm Cowley, and Robert Penn Warren were finding more general and systematic form? And Toynbee allows us to read the oddly similar attacks on *The Old Man and the Sea* as a function of Hemingway's same meretricious tactics. These critics perceive that the author is at best parlaying an oversimplified interpretation of his work into narrative form or at worst conforming to critical dictates—impressions that form a particularly delicious riposte to Hemingway's long-standing and very public abhorrence of critics and reviewers.

One consequence of Toynbee's censure, surprisingly, is that by referring to the story only in terms of a complicity between author and audience he obliterates the solitariness of the old man. The novella becomes a kind of group exercise in intertextuality whereby what seem to be Santiago's specific and individualized attributes can only be read as textual echoes of readers' generalized comments about Hemingway's characters. It is not so much that Santiago endures in magnificent isolation as that the enduring legacy of Hemingway heroes who were once truly autonomous and individualized speaks through him. Santiago is never self-defined, Toynbee implies, but a palimpsest: he is not *Santiago* but the Hemingway hero; and not even the Hemingway hero so much as Hemingway's reductive rewriting of the critics' rewriting of narratives that may originally have tendered fluid and powerful conceptions of heroic conduct. The writings of Hemingway's audience—the critics he pretended to despise—have become the subject of the novella. The alleged fraudulence of Hemingway's style and criticisms that Hemingway is trying to steer his material and audience into conformity with preconceived and narrowly conceived notions of heroic manhood all bear out Toynbee's point, as does any interpretation that marks out a quintessential (rather than unique) role for Santiago.

Picking up Toynbee's criticism, Philip Rahv elaborates the notion that hid-

9. Philip Toynbee, "Hemingway," in ed. Jobes, 87, 88.

den audiences play an unexpectedly large role in the novella when he argues that Hemingway's aesthetic self-control has slipped into an unsavory self-dramatization. For Rahv, the story "exhibits" the "credentials of the authentic."[10] The term is neatly chosen, for it bespeaks the story's status as a perfect likeness—a simulacrum—of earlier works. It can only put on exhibition narrative strategies and philosophies that were once an integral function of Hemingway's texts. The narrative crafting that must have been once an act of aesthetic discovery, fresh, original, and ever different, has shifted into a deliberate attempt to recall and display the results of that discovery. The author's role that once must have been detached from, or ancillary to, or at least indistinguishable from the stories themselves has become the governing impulse behind this novella. The novella could not even be considered a self-parody, which would at least imply some conscious reflection about the roles pertaining to an author like Hemingway. It is instead an odd parody of self-consciousness whereby celebrated (and by now routine) ideas are paraded in an attempt to draw responses from a preselected audience of professors and doctors. That Rahv and Toynbee do not fall for Hemingway's trick as good as proves their case, for in not responding like some colleagues they show that this text does not have the power of authentic literature to put its value beyond debate. Such value is demonstrable but, crucially, in no need of exhibition. Toynbee in fact concludes by inviting "any sane critic" to compare this latest work to "The Killers" or "The Undefeated," whose value, in the absence of any discussion about their merits, must simply be self-evident. Such criticisms no doubt tell us much about the proclivities of Rahv and Toynbee, who favor an ethos of originality over (self-)imitation, authorial detachment over the manipulative hand of the writer, and ironic distance over the author's celebration of his own famous ideas. One more hidden irony of Hemingway's supposed volte-face over his old dislike of literary critics is that it is now critics like Rahv and Toynbee who speak for concepts that Hemingway helped shape in the early modernist period, and who even use those concepts as tools to expose the author's contemporary work as counterfeit. Both critics thus interestingly uncover some of the assumptions that go to the reading of Hemingway's work in general.

The primary value of Toynbee's and Rahv's work for our purposes lies in what it reveals about the possible functions of an audience in a fiction that

---

10. Philip Rahv, "Hemingway in the 1950's," in ed. Jobes, 111.

seems to put such considerations out of bounds. A work like *The Old Man and the Sea*, which focuses so intensely on Santiago's solitary heroic struggle against the elements, appears capable only of ratifying principles of masculine conduct that affirm (in Santiago's classic statement) "what a man can do" rather than what a man displays.[11] As the comments of Schwartz and Waldmeir suggest, readers tend to see Santiago as quintessential precisely because he is alone and thus the paradigm of what is usually only intimated in Hemingway's fictions. Because stories like "Big Two-Hearted River" that explicitly fictionalize a man alone are rare in Hemingway's canon—and even then, as we have seen, hardly unambiguous about the psychic health of the solitary man—Santiago's exemplary actions must represent what other male characters covertly desire or unconsciously need in order to attain essential manhood. By this logic, Hemingway must have been searching all along for a narrative vehicle that could dramatize a nontheatrical presentation of manhood and make visible what can be seen only in the absence of spectators.

Toynbee and Rahv turn this logic on its head. Far from noting a thematics of solitude, they read the work as completely dependent on one audience of critics to which Hemingway's ideas are indebted and another to which it is addressed. For them, Santiago's solitude is meaningful only in terms of the various audiences who have construed and who are to construe its meaning; the absence of fictive spectators merely "exhibits" itself to the critic's eye. Santiago is irredeemably a function of the interpretive gaze. It should be noted, however, that for Rahv and Toynbee this return of the repressed audience is exactly the problem with the story. What is suspect is not an aesthetics of authorial detachment and a philosophy of masculine autonomy but Hemingway's failure to implement them—a failure that is all the more profound because the novella speaks so blatantly for the very values it destroys. In distancing himself from the "hundred exegeses" the book will inspire, Toynbee covertly puts into play through the figure of the responsible critic the detached, self-reliant, and self-possessed role Hemingway's heroic male characters used to exemplify but which this novella insists on perverting amid various acts of narrative theater. The responsible critic might even appear all the more self-possessed because Hemingway's abandonment of the principles governing authentic literary art leaves the critic to speak for them alone. The

---

11. Ernest Hemingway, *The Old Man and the Sea* (New York: Scribner's, 1950), 66. This work will hereinafter be cited parenthetically by page number in the text.

disgust that Toynbee clearly evinces for *Old Man,* however, suggests a measure of ambivalence. If Toynbee arrogates Hemingway's now-abandoned role, the critic's act of having to speak of and for an authentic work like "The Undefeated"—that which depends on no other text and makes a claim on no other text, if Toynbee is right—nonetheless marks a potentially perilous moment when what should be self-evident suddenly needs to be made evident after all. Toynbee faces the distinct possibility of having to exhibit the credentials by which authentic texts like "The Undefeated" may be known and thus reproducing the dilemma he sees as a function of Hemingway's text when theatrical representation stands in for self-presence. The act of directing readers to works that are by his definition independent of other texts inscribes Toynbee in a logic of display barely masked by his insistence that their essential worth need not even be spoken. Toynbee's maneuver restores faith in the unique and autonomous text while drawing attention to his own acts of critical performance.

Toynbee's and Rahv's narratives of Hemingway's decline into theatrical narrative can be read very differently. My interpretation of *The Old Man and the Sea* corroborates their sense that the question of audience keeps obtruding in a work where "what a man can do and what a man can endure" seems to position Santiago outside the purview of a watching and evaluating audience. What Toynbee and Rahv see as a problem with the story, however, might be read more profitably as the story's problematics of audience. Though their point about the novella's address to an audience of critics is provocative and worthy of careful consideration, *The Old Man and the Sea,* like "The Undefeated," implies not one but various kinds of audience. The several different groups of spectators whose inspection of the marlin's skeleton closes the story play a particularly crucial role. They restore the act of interpretation as an element of plot. And, retrospectively, they invite readers to compare their experience of the text with those offered within the fictive world of the novella. The fictive spectators do not act as paradigmatic readers so much as bring pressure to bear on the work's actual readers to examine their own interpretive performances, and indeed to see the act of interpretation as a performance rather than a set of responses predetermined by a monologic text. For, in the same way that Rahv and Toynbee read a tale about solitude in terms of its special demands on an audience, this story whose plot so carefully removes spectators from Santiago's scenes of conflict constantly returns its readers to the scene of conflicting interpretations. That these interpretations once again focus on issues of Santiago's manhood is only appropriate to a character whose performance is always under scrutiny and in question.

In the quiet moments before hooking the giant marlin, Santiago observes that "nothing showed on the surface of the water but some patches of yellow, sun-bleached Sargasso weed and the purple, formalized, iridescent, gelatinous bladder of a Portuguese man-of-war floating close beside the boat" (35), which was floating "cheerfully as a bubble with its long deadly purple filaments trailing a yard behind it in the water." The old man reserves much scorn for the Portuguese man-of-war—he loves to see the sea-turtles eating them—for though the "iridescent bubbles were beautiful," they were "the falsest thing in the sea." The reason for Santiago's animus is not on closer inspection obvious, for other creatures of the sea, including the hooked marlin with his purple stripes and "great length and width and all his power and his beauty" (94), hold similar attractions. Presumably Santiago has in mind the notion that beauty itself should not be invested in the business of killing, or that, conversely, correct methods of killing parlay attractiveness into the truly beautiful; the powerful marlin and mako shark (100), whom Santiago depicts as great fighters and great beauties, have no need of tricking their prey. Or perhaps Santiago disdains the fact that the Portuguese man-of-war's beauty is so purposefully on display. We do not even need to note the hollowness of this "bubble" and "gelatinous bladder" to see the connection to other scenes in Hemingway's work where theatrical display appears to be written off as the one truly inauthentic term in a discourse of heroic manhood. In the *Old Man*, this "falsest thing in the sea" perhaps points us toward the truest: the old man himself who, outfacing even the admired turtles who "shut their eyes" (36) when approaching the man-of-war, studies and sees through its deadly deception.

Out at sea, Santiago resolutely sets about reading sea-signs, employing all manner of glances in seeking to interpret the seascape surrounding him: "If there is a hurricane you always see the signs of it in the sky for days ahead, if you are at sea. They do not see it ashore because they do not know what to look for, he thought. The land must make a difference too, in the shape of the clouds. But we have no hurricane coming now" (61). Subtly distinguishing between himself and "they" who inhabit the land, Santiago quietly speaks for his greater abilities of perception. He even implies that his skill only manifests itself on the sea: he ponders that the "land must make a difference" in the shape of clouds as if on land he has never bothered to look for signs of hurricane. From the sea, in contrast, cloud-shapes over land have precise significance: the "strange light the sun made in the water . . . meant good weather and so did the shape of the clouds over the land" (35). The difference the sea makes is that looking must be exercised for practical advantage (and indeed survival). Santiago is "happy to see so much plankton because it meant fish" (35), and, seeing that a bird is "circling again" (37), he comments "He's found fish." The same bird is said to have "got something. . . . He's not just looking" (33). Like Santiago, the bird places vision at the service of purposeful and pragmatic action; "just looking" as an enterprise without design or goal is ruled out as a worthwhile activity. This does not mean that Santiago can render all sign-reading into purposive action. His observation that "Everything that shows on the surface today travels very fast and to the north-east" (40), for instance, makes him wonder "it is some sign of weather that I do not know?" But Santiago accepts the riddle as his limitation. The sign is knowable; and it is partly because all signs in this seascape appear meaningful and decidable that "just looking" seems a particularly pointless endeavor.

Importantly, the act of looking reveals meanings that seem independent of the observer. Skilled observers drawing on a fund of knowledge gained through experience are certainly necessary to realize and act on signs like plankton (meaning fish) and strange light in the water (meaning good weather). But a different perspective on or misinterpretation of natural signs could not disturb their true meaning. Santiago actually ponders "what the sea looks like from [the] height" (71) of an airplane and remembers that from the cross-trees of a turtle boat the "dolphin look greener . . . and you can see their stripes." It could not be said, however, that different perspectives transform the dolphin; Santiago is merely recognizing the logic by means of which the same animal looks different from various angles, heights, and qualities of light. Similarly, sea-readers who mistook the meaning of plankton could not change its significance; they would simply be poor readers. This fact that meanings at sea operate independently of the observer potentially bestows great authority on the independent observer. Plankton continues to signify fish and strange light to signify good weather to the truly perceptive observer even if all other observers who are "just looking" fail to see the connection. Sea-knowledge that operates independently of any communal interpretation or evaluation thus offers crucial philosophical support for a narrative of actions undertaken outside the purview of any watching audience. In particular, it seems to guarantee the meaning of Santiago's manly actions in lieu of the evaluating audience that typically records and negotiates the meaning of deeds performed by Hemingway's male characters. Potentially, we comprehend Santiago's manly credentials with the serene confidence with which he grasps the meaning of plankton. If we did not, the narrative seems to suggest, those meanings would nonetheless be there.

The act of looking positions Santiago within a swiftly changing but eminently readable seascape where confident action depends on straightforward acts of perception that may be undertaken by any experienced individual. But Santiago also shows a preterite ability to see through and beyond what is immediately apprehended by the physical eye. He is a sea-borne seer, his visionary gaze accentuated by his habit of looking into the sun (32–33) and his once-preternatural ability to see "almost as a cat sees" (67) in the dark. At dusk Santiago guides the skiff by the star Rigel (75) even though Rigel, so Robert P. Weeks complains in "Fakery in *The Old Man and the Sea*," is apparently invisible at that hour.[12] Merely seeing "one of the projecting green sticks dip sharply" (41), Santiago knows "exactly what it was": "One hundred fathoms down a marlin was eating the sardines that covered the point and the shank of the hook." Similarly, after the marlin jumps for the first time Santiago finds he can "picture the fish swimming in the water with his purple pectoral fins set wide as wings" (67). As many commentators have suggested, such moments culminate in the scene of the marlin's death when Santiago, nearly fainting with exhaustion, "looked carefully in the glimpse of vision that he had" (94). It is the moment when Santiago realizes the mythic knowledge obtained from this "angling vision into the heart of mysteries."[13] In these senses, Santiago is closer to Pilar than to Robert Jordan, who chooses to trust what is within the field of sight and its technologically enhanced extensions but who rejects, or finds too threatening, the uncanny mode of foresight offered by Pilar when she reads his hand.[14] Santiago, it might be argued, possesses the deeply pragmatic ability to interpret sea-signs through the evidence of his senses as well as the visionary ability pertaining to the mythic quest hero. This

---

12. Robert P. Weeks, "Fakery in *The Old Man and the Sea*," in ed. Jobes, 40. Weeks derides fakeries such as the fact that Santiago sees stars that cannot be seen, endures the struggle with the marlin for three impossibly fatiguing days, and knows from the first touches on the bait that the marlin is a male.

13. Rovit, 90.

14. Hemingway, *Bell*, 33.

mastery of the natural and supernatural spectrum of vision counters the kind of criticism Robert Weeks levels at the novella in complaining that only a description of fish and stars present to the physical eye legitimately conveys Hemingway's own aesthetic of precise, factual detail. For those reading Santiago as quest hero, no extraordinary or transcendent glimpse of nature could be too miraculous.

Santiago understands the true nature of the Portuguese man-of-war, whose deliberate display of beauty foists a merely theatrical (that is, fake) meaning on its observers, as well as the nontheatrical display of sea-signs that do not demand any response from their observers. And he comprehends the numinous, archetypal images that cannot even be apprehended by the physical eye. Santiago thus plays the almost unique role in Hemingway's fiction of a potent observer who is not in turn under surveillance. Indeed, Hemingway quietly emphasizes the old man's ability to evade surveillance. He is soon out of sight of the other fishermen, and in sight only of creatures who do not seem to comprehend him: the tuna with its "big, unintelligent eyes staring" (38), and the marlin whose "eye is huge" (67) but "as detached as the mirrors in a periscope" (96). Moreover, Santiago goes unnoticed by "coast guard and . . . planes" (124) sent out to search for him for the "ocean is very big and a skiff is small and hard to see." Santiago's mastery of vision should then properly be seen as the inverse and the consequence of his removal from the watching and evaluating crowd. Unlike Jake Barnes, Santiago need not place his capacity for expert observation at the service of anyone else or partake in competitive masculine displays. And unlike Barnes or Robert Jordan, he need not stage himself before an evaluating audience. Beyond the confines of the closed arena and watching crowd, it seems, Santiago can indulge the full range of perceptions available to the man off alone. We are close here to agreeing with Joseph Waldmeir's apothegm that a "man must depend upon himself alone in order to assert his manhood" and simultaneously standing Hemingway criticism on its head, for, in terms of my argument, such agreement would make Santiago a unique figure among Hemingway's fictional characters rather than his quintessential hero. A narrative that demonstrates "what a man can do and what he endures" (66) rather than what he performs in front of an audience justifies the preponderance of Hemingway criticism—in this one work.

But doubts about the potent yet monocular role I have sketched for Santiago remain, and not only because of reviewers like Rahv and Toynbee who are skeptical about the originality of Hemingway's novella. Gerry Brenner, in particular, has asked the kind of awkward questions that compel us to revise our understanding of Santiago's role. Brenner asks why Santiago needs to kill the fish if symbolic mastery of the fish is all that counts and, even more important, why Santiago must then expose his mastery to the evaluation of others: if the beautiful marlin is destined to become a "spectacle to stupid tourists," Brenner inquires, "Must Santiago return with the mutilated carcass?"[15] It is worth noting that Brenner's questions anticipate the kind of arguments I made about *Green Hills of Africa* and "The Undefeated." If what counts in the articulation of a masculine self is the experience of comporting oneself as a man, the expression of masculinity in the form of trophies and other signs—whether kudu horns, trout, marlin, bull's ears, or pigtails—should be absolutely immaterial. Santiago has already proven himself, triumphing over his pain and fatigue and over the marlin's strength. One could hardly have thought less of Santiago as a man if the marlin had escaped at the last or even if he had released it. The thrust of the harpoon, which occurs with the marlin already passive and defeated, seems curiously anticlimactic (particularly because a canny sea-reader like Santiago must be aware, and has already half-admitted [68], that there is little likelihood of returning the marlin intact). And returning the trophy to land seems even more superfluous to the business of being a man once Santiago has given his "all" (93) and defined his masculinity most perfectly at the moment of the marlin's death.

A rationale can be found for Santiago's trophy among conventional interpretations of the novella, particularly those that uncover the mythic significances of the text. Earl Rovit's reading is worth quoting at length:

> The kind of experience which Santiago undergoes is an incommunicable one, but it is not without value to the community of men. He has been a champion of mankind for men and not for himself. He has brought back from his isolation a fragmented gift offering to his fellows, an imperfect symbol to suggest where he has been and what he has found there. There are those within the community with the experience and the imagination and the necessary love to project on that skeletal symbol a feeling of the experience which it represents. For them the world has been redeemed; a shaft of knowing has pierced like a thunderbolt into their awareness of

15. Brenner, 177.

what it is to be a man and the image of mankind has been immeasurably enhanced.[16]

For Rovit the presence of the "skeletal symbol" is crucial to persuade the "community of men" to flesh out hidden, archetypal meanings, a task that is actually facilitated by its skeletal nature: because its lack of flesh strips away any commercial value it might have had, spectators cannot confuse "what it is to be a man" with a male's earning power. Moreover, its "fragmented" and "imperfect" nature suggests the extent to which mythic experience is essentially "incommunicable." The "community of men" must intuit from the adventure's bare bones—the quest hero's boon to his people—the archetypal wholeness and plenitude that can only be experienced, not transmitted. Rovit's answer to Brenner's question "Must Santiago return with the mutilated carcass?" is thus to rewrite the context in which the question becomes meaningful. The trophy is useless to *Santiago;* it is the community of men who require a metaphoric glimpse of the "glimpse of vision" Santiago experienced at the marlin's death. For the same reasons, dumping the skeleton at sea could not affect the old man's heroism, though it would of course prove a loss to his community. The fact that the carcass inadequately reveals Santiago's manly "all" should then be seen as a consequence of the shortcomings of representation, which cannot possibly be commensurate with the transcendent and thus unrepresentable experience itself. It would be churlish to accuse Santiago of needing to signify "what it is to be a man" when he is the one who has stepped beyond the bounds of representation.

To Brenner, Santiago's self-representation is the key that unlocks the story's true significance: Santiago, desiring Manolo to hero-worship him and win Manolin back from the "fathers who have demanded Manolin's obedience," indulges a selfish but common-enough desire to dramatize his skill. Santiago must bring home the mutilated carcass "because without proof of his exploit he can not show his superiority to such lesser men."[17] The important distinction between those readings is that for Brenner the activities of fictive audiences within the text and the interpretations of the story's readers make a sudden and profound difference. In Rovit's mythopoeic reading, interpretations of the sign of the skeleton have no effect on the heroic actions that pre-

16. Rovit, 90.
17. Brenner, 180, 178.

cede them, for no amount of (mis)interpretation could add to, detract from, or transform the archetypal plenitude from which this fragmentary gift offering appears. The bones are not strictly in need of readers at all, for a receptive audience is exterior to the universal significances liberated by the story (though the very universality of the story of course makes such an audience a likelihood). The boon the quest hero brings to his community in Rovit's reading becomes in Brenner's the sign of Santiago's theatricality: he is theatrical because he desires to signify his heroism to a watching audience of fishermen, boy, and boy's father rather than acting in complete, sign-less indifference to the opinions of others. Even more surprising, it begins to appear that Santiago must all along have been pursuing his lonely battle with the marlin with one eye on a prospective audience. Though he does not dramatize his deeds for an audience, every action he undertakes is a kind of proto-performance, setting the stage for a triumphal and wholly theatrical return.

The traces of a barely disguised desire for an audience in the novella are in fact present throughout. Away from the pitying or derisive glances directed at Santiago on the Terrace, the old man insists over and over again on his solitude, referring for instance to his habit of speaking to himself and his penchant for going out beyond all other people. "I wish I could show him what sort of man I am" (64) says Santiago of the fish at another point, guilelessly commanding our attention for the show that the old man never appears to make even when he and the fish confront each other face to face. And other potential but absent audiences are frequently on Santiago's mind. Brenner notes the old man's refrain "I wish the boy were here" (56), interpreting it as a prolegomena for his later more blatant bid for an audience. The insight is an acute one. At one point, for instance, Santiago says out loud "I wish I had the boy. To help me and to see this" (48). The moment represents a complicated transaction for the reader. The fact that the boy is not there to see something worth seeing appears to remove all taint of theatricality. If Santiago ever performs for an audience (as he perhaps does when handwrestling or in bringing back the marlin's carcass), he clearly cannot be performing now for the boy. His remark laments and thus underscores the absence of spectators. Yet it demonstrates to the *reader* that there is indeed something worth seeing. Santiago's complaint is something of a red herring. Specifying an onlooker who is absent has the effect of dramatizing Santiago's solitariness; but the spectator-function the absent boy would have provided is transferred to the silently present reader. Indeed, because we cannot help as the boy would have done our only possible role is to "see" and evaluate Santiago's exploits. The very stridency with which the novella rejects audiences for Santiago's exploits at sea, then, keeps putting back into play its rhetorical manipulation of the reader.

But the key to the function of audiences in *The Old Man and the Sea* is Santiago's return with the marlin skeleton, when proliferating fictive audiences mark a more obvious return to theaters of masculinity and pose in suddenly striking ways the question of how readers judge and evaluate Santiago's actions—and why they must. I argue that the conclusion of the narrative forces us to reconstruct the nature of our reading experience by asking us to see it first and foremost as a reading *experience* that has unfolded temporally and is now susceptible to transformation (though, by the same token, the possibility of a saintly Santiago must at first be entertained rather than dismissed as hypothetical). By introducing fictive audiences at such a late stage, *The Old Man and the Sea* invites us to discover retrospectively the reading processes we have undertaken from the beginning, but which have been disguised as the seemingly natural business of recording determinate and possibly universal meanings about (in Rovit's words) "what it is to be a man." In alienating what seemed natural and unproblematic, the novella asks us to act as audience to our own activity and thus belatedly to uncover that activity as a performance that has only temporarily purveyed certain meanings as inalienable and non-theatrical. That logic of interpretive performance enacted by the work has another consequence. As the reader's role grows in importance, a burgeoning awareness of multiple interpretations begins to erode the distinction between the masculine performance the work seems above all to value (an action done truly and well) and the notion of performance as self-dramatization, which *Old Man* seems to write off as unimportant or (in the guise of the Portuguese man-of-war) lethal.

One answer to the question of why Santiago must return with the mutilated carcass is that a series of perspectives on the carcass compel the reader into realizing the power of the interpretive actions of audiences. No fewer than five distinct sets of spectators attend to the marlin's carcass as it drifts in the harbor. Perhaps unexpectedly, given that he confesses "he did not want to look at the fish" (110) after the second shark attack, the old man is himself the first spectator as he "looked back and saw in the reflection from the street light the great tail of the fish standing up well behind the skiff's stern. He saw the white naked line of his backbone and the dark mass of the head with the projecting bill and all the nakedness between" (121). Santiago's backward (and here narcissistic) glance sets in train a series of interpretive glances that corroborate the undoing of his heroism. Looking back at the proof of his endurance and courage suggests to what extent the trophy matters to him; the look confirms that the trophy is worthy of being looked at and that others after Santiago will want to look at it. Manolin iterates this deceptively disinterested glance. In response to the fisherman who informs him that the marlin "was eighteen feet from nose to tail" (122), Manolin replies only "I believe it." But we have been told that the boy has already "been there before" (122) the other fishermen. One implication is that the boy, worried about Santiago, has arisen early; having had time to digest its size, his current lack of interest in it could be put down to his preoccupation with the suffering it must have caused his mentor. Another possibility, however, is that having seen the marlin earlier the boy can safely leave others to exclaim over its size (just as Santiago must know others will exclaim over it). What allows his ostensible disinterest is the enormity of the fish and of the struggle it must have cost the old man, for Manolin (like Santiago) need not dramatize what no one could help looking at.

Santiago's spectacular success is that he stage-manages his return in such a way that his presence is no longer required on stage. Unlike the character of Ernest Hemingway in *Green Hills of Africa,* whose trophy horns are consistently out-trophied and voided of meaning by Karl's triumphs in a theater of masculine display, Santiago sets out a hitherto undreamt-of and surely unsurpassable exhibition of his prowess. If Hemingway never succeeds in playing the part of the father with the biggest (phallic) horns in the earlier book, Santiago masterfully plays "Pop" to Manolin, even making him a gift of the marlin's huge spear ("as long as a baseball bat" [62]) in metonymic tribute to his manly powers and to his powers of mentorship. But though Santiago merely lies in his shack, bestowing gifts on Manolin and Pedrico, while others gaze in awe at the giant skeleton, it could not be said that he has obliterated all traces of the theatricality by means of which he represents his manhood to the community. His theatrical gesture is precisely to remove himself from the stage; he refuses to appear before his peers secure in the knowledge that the trophy, and the damage done to it and the skiff, adequately dramatize his endurance, strength, and skill. Oddly, this interpretation both substantiates and inverts common readings that emphasize Santiago's brotherhood with and likeness to the marlin. Doubling for Santiago, the marlin-trophy bespeaks his mastering and shaping hand. It accounts for Santiago's incapacity or refusal to make his deeds signify by completely and very successfully taking over the signifying function. Santiago's peers cannot help but read these signs: the marlin's enormous size (hence the superhuman powers its capture must have taken), its stripped carcass (hence prolonged shark attacks), the missing gaff and wrecked rudder (hence the old man's efforts to beat off the marauders). Indeed, it might be argued that the carcass's principal function is to represent the act of representation: stripped of all commercial value, it can function only as sign, standing for Santiago and for the acts of theatrical representation he appears not to be making.

The ways in which Hemingway shapes readers' responses in the closing scenes support the sense of a character enmeshed in a complex scheme of stage-management. As I have argued, Santiago's return with the marlin-trophy potentially subverts assumptions about his heroism that have been gradually accruing over the course of his solitary voyage and identifies the real problem of the text as the question of why there is a conclusion at all. The reader cannot know more about Santiago's heroism than at the moment of his supreme victory over the great fish; we see that up until that moment his victory seems to be untarnished by theatrical motivations; reading on ensures the old man's fall into the commonplace of displaying his heroic worth. Why, then, does the reader need to read the sign (the marlin's carcass) that simply refers us back to the story we have just read? One answer is that most readers who enjoy reading the novella experience its conclusion as much more than an iteration of Santiago's story. However intellectually inappropriate the con-clusion may be to a concept of autonomous manhood, its primary function is really a profoundly emotional appeal to the reader to participate in the communal (re-)negotiation of the meaning of Santiago's manly actions. What that process of retrospection suggests, however, is that the sequence of events leading to the death of the marlin, far from being the final word on the old man's masculine prowess, has all along been puzzlingly incomplete, and that the backward glance or retrospect instigated by Santiago is of hitherto unsus-pected importance.

After Santiago falls asleep in his shack, Hemingway carefully defers his awakening until four separate groups of spectators have begun to unfold some of the emotional complexities of the old man's return. To be sure, the specta-tors—the boy who hardly seems to look at all, the fisherman in the water measuring the skeleton, the other fishermen who stand watching, and the

proprietor at the Terrace—seem to play insignificant roles. But the very reticence of their response is crucial. We realize first that perceptive members of
Santiago's community have no need to question or interpret Santiago's adventure. They know what must have happened with the immediacy embodied
in the proprietor's terse "What a fish it was. . . . There has never been such
a fish" (123), Manolin's "*He* didn't beat you. Not the fish," and the waiter's
wonderfully abridged retelling of the story: "Tiburon. . . . Eshark" (127). These
mini-narratives point toward the expert appraisals that need not be elaborated
because no expert could possibly interpret the evidence differently. The fish is
beyond misinterpretation by those who know the sea (though not by the tourists, as we shall discover). Perhaps more to the point, the size of the fish and
the grandeur of Santiago's exploits exceed the boundaries even of expert appraisal. When the proprietor remarks to Manolin, "Those were two fine fish
you took yesterday too" (123), the boy replies, "Damn my fish," as if conventional appraisals were suddenly meaningless. Similarly, his "I believe it" might
suggest to us the pointlessness and even impropriety of measuring a marlin
the like of which has never been measured before. As Carlos Baker writes,
"Santiago knows, has known all along, that there are other standards of measurement than feet or inches on steel tape," and Manolin's reactions bear out
his debt to his mentor.[18]

But the measurer and the silent group of "Many fishermen" (122) do play
important roles. They counter any suspicion that the boy's response is exaggerated or sentimental; indeed, they intensify by their silence and their numbers the grandeur of the marlin precisely because it is their everyday job to
catch marlin. It is therefore not the actual size of the marlin that counts but
the fact that even these experienced fishermen feel the need to watch and put
a number on the incomprehensibly large marlin (and by implication on Santiago's exploits). Moreover, the fact that the measurer calls to Manolin rather
than the other fishermen that the carcass is "eighteen feet from nose to tail"
suggests a new respect for the old man's pupil, who can now order with an
authority borrowed from his mentor "Let no one disturb him." The group of
watchers by the carcass convey a profound collective respect for Santiago and
his deeds that is all the more moving because among the watchers are presumably those who earlier laughed at or pitied Santiago: "many of the fishermen
made fun of the old man. . . . Others, of the older fishermen, looked at him

18. Baker, *Writer as Artist*, 297.

and were sad. But they did not show it" (11). The later description of reticent watching thus inverts the earlier scene on the Terrace. The men watch with awe rather than pity or scorn, and it is again testimony to the overwhelming impact of Santiago's deeds that the spectators have gone beyond shame at their behavior into awe at his. A theater of humiliation has become one of respect.

The fact that it is the older fishermen on the Terrace who do not laugh out of greater respect or experience (knowing that the younger men might also have to suffer bad luck) adds one more twist to this scene, which amply repays their earlier esteem. Their lack of show translates now into the stunned restraint that characterizes all the fishermen; their pitying looks at Santiago are transformed into the display that signifies to the gathered crowd of young and old the plenitude of the old man's manhood. The scene ratifies their wisdom; and the fact that their response is shown to be wise confirms that much old wisdom might be learnt from looking at the marlin's carcass. Part of the emotional complexity of this simple scene lies in the fact that those who earlier scorned Santiago are now forced to look differently through the eyes of their wiser elders. They repeat, in fact, the look-without-show that the older fishermen practiced on the terrace and that Santiago models for us as he "looked back" at the marlin and then leaves it for others to discover and celebrate. Even more subtly, Hemingway introduces us to the skeleton-watchers—Manolin, the proprietor, the fishermen—after their vigil has begun. Since the narrative does not record the beginning of their watching nor whatever variety of responses might have been theirs initially, it gives the impression that the period of watching has been going on for an indeterminately long time. It forecloses any question about why the trophy-skeleton should be gazed at; it merely registers the fact that the trophy has been and is being gazed at by those who have already read the signs and who have had their early differences of opinion about Santiago transformed into unanimity. Awed watching, the narrative maneuvers us into believing, is the only appropriate response because it is the only response the narrative describes.

One emotion the narrative makes available to us at this moment is thus satisfaction that the doubters have been so effectively silenced—a satisfaction doubled because the solemnity of all the watchers at the scene precludes even the need to ridicule those who earlier scorned the old man. We only know to feel that satisfaction, however, because of a more compelling identification with those experts who stand stunned into silence. We interpret their silence as awe because we are familiar with the details of the old man's exploits and can therefore confirm the legitimacy of their response. We have experienced the struggle whose marks the men of Santiago's community endeavor to read, and know beforehand that this is the "biggest fish that [Santiago] had ever seen and bigger than he had ever heard of" (63). Yet there is a sense in which the communal response nonetheless confirms the legitimacy of ours. Though we come to the final scenes as expert witnesses of Santiago's adventure (if not of the sea), we lack precisely what the crowd of spectators possess in abundance: the shared sense of expert knowledge and the consequent ability to forge a communal appraisal of the marlin's significance. While on first reading the text we have no particular reason to disbelieve Santiago's impression that it is the "biggest fish that he had ever seen," we also have no reason to believe that despite his age and experience a bigger one could not have been seen or heard of elsewhere. The proprietor's statement, the measurement of the skeleton, and the crowd's silence do not disclose additional information, but they do inspire us with the confidence of an expert consensus that we, knowing the whole story, can share. In this respect, my argument completely reverses Rovit's claim that a select few among Santiago's fellows can interpret the meaning of his quest to future generations. It would seem more likely that readers might not trust the mythopoeic significance of the quest until expert witnesses have retrospectively guaranteed its extraordinary nature. We see the true extent of the old man's strangeness only when his peers fall dramatically silent; and only their evaluations persuade us that his experience is worthy of evaluation.

One consequence of this short but crucial interval before Santiago awakes is that we awaken to a collective sense of the old man's achievements. What makes Hemingway's tactic so subtle is that he effects a considerable increase in emotional intensity by repeating what we already know; and the fact that Santiago's community repeats what we know disguises our new orientation from a single to a communal perspective. Signs of that change can be found, however, in the tourists' glances and interpretations that complete the novella. Though the (presumably American) tourists see exactly what Santiago and his peers see—the "great long white spine with a huge tail at the end"—the man and woman insist on promulgating a complete misinterpretation of the marlin. Failing to understand the waiter's explanation, the woman comments, "I didn't know sharks had such handsome, beautifully formed tails," which receives only a dull-witted "I didn't either" from her companion. We are suddenly situated within a tangle of (mis)interpretive gestures. The tourists cannot understand the waiter's language or the iconography of great fish, though they do agree (mistakenly) with each other. Like the prey of the Portuguese man-of-war, they are taken in by an aesthetic experience removed from pragmatic reality. Unlike the fishermen who once laughed at Santiago, moreover, they have no way of correcting their misjudgment. They represent a boundary condition in the spectrum of fictive audiences that takes us from the wise, older fishermen to the impetuously scornful (but educable) younger ones and thence to the tourists who are satisfied with the wrong explanation. The tourists' downfall, curiously, is their having to ask for an explanation. The logic of the language of fish and fishing is that it need not be articulated. The question ("What's that?") reveals their lack of the kind of practical experience that frees the members of Santiago's community from having to ask or explain at length the significance of the fish.

A reader might legitimately feel a sense of loss as the numinous quality of Santiago's exploits fades so quickly into dull-wittedness and error. To do so, however, merely confirms and celebrates the difference between tourist and reader. We know that difference in the rapidity with which we understand the waiter's little tale and in the vapidity we remark in the tourists' easy acquiescence to a faulty solution. (In case we speak no Spanish, the narrator even explains that the waiter was "meaning to explain what had happened.") But it is not that the tourists stand as a warning to identify a role we must refuse or a role poor readers might unwittingly enact, for the tourists are not just poor readers. They are simply wrong. The marlin is not a shark. Though we might fail in more abstruse matters like understanding the motivations of a group of silent fishermen or reaching agreement about the moral significance of Santiago's quest, we cannot possibly miss the tourists' simple error, see it as anything but an error, or fail to make the simplest possible substitution of marlin for shark. That righting of error is surprisingly crucial to the reader's role in the final scene of the novella. Like Hemingway's earlier almost invisible iteration of what we already know, this scene works so brilliantly because we are placed in a position of already having made the correct substitution. The reader is helpless to make the wrong decision because the scene so successfully masks the fact that a decision is being made. The scene seems to confirm an ethos of interpretive certitude not by asserting the possibility of correct reading but by withdrawing any question of or even any need to articulate the problem of incorrect reading. As readers of faulty readers, we are barely aware of what we have learnt in order to read the bones accurately.

One effect of this nearly impalpable act of reading is that we find ourselves seeming to enact the role of the fishermen, who also as the very premise of their knowing need not articulate or even consciously bring to mind their comprehension of Santiago's struggle. Like the fishermen, we are sufficiently expert to disparage the inexpert tourists without even considering the sources or manner of our expertise. We share the waiter's ability to make "Tiburon. . . . Eshark" signify as an adequate account of Santiago's struggles. We share the fishermen's ability to look pragmatically at the whole skeleton and the whole story to which it refers rather than confining its handsome tail to a purely aesthetic domain. In the process, we step without really knowing it into a situation where secure knowledge is the condition of the kind of communal experience Hemingway describes. Nonetheless, enough points of difference remain between reader and fisherman to make that security suspect. The fishermen, for instance, read our narrative in reverse: we experience the gradual stripping of the carcass and see the bones as its outcome; they see the bones and read back to what must have happened. And part of what makes the fishermen's stunned tribute to Santiago's exploits so emotionally satisfying to the reader is the abruptness of their response. They act as an emotional exclamation point by immediately confirming the responses that have accumulated for us over the course of the narrative. And they do so by reading, as it were, the bare bones of the fish. Few readers without benefit of the narrative could hope to emulate their skill. Having read the narrative and being in a privileged position to confirm their insight, however, we assume that we can read the bones as well as or better than they. Our relationship to the fishermen's expertise is thus managed by a kind of narrative sleight of hand. The structure of the narrative demands that the fishermen reach their conclusions quite differently from the reader. Our knowing that the fishermen are right, however, disguises the difference in their interpretive experience and in their textual intervention as bone-readers. Difference is experienced as a double affirmation of what really counts: Santiago's heroism.

Like the audience of fishermen whose startlingly different response we read, oddly, as if it were our own, the trophy-sign is put into play as an enigmatic but important component of our negotiation of the tourists' error. As we have seen, the very presence of the trophy poses a dilemma because it runs contrary to the logic that men discover themselves in isolation. Yet by subtly maneuvering us to identify the egregious mistake of the tourists, the narrative asks us to respond to the sign as though it carried the real meaning of the quest. We do not pause to think as we silently correct the tourists that the sign is suspect because it displaces into metaphor the original purity of Santiago's actions, or that it is in fact the tourists who do most to raise to consciousness the metaphoricity of the trophy by showing how easily it can be (mis)interpreted. This is the case partly because we do not pause to think through the implications of or to think that we even are correcting the tourists. Our roles as observers and interpreters barely register as significant; the tourists' error seems self-evident; and for that reason our confident ability to know the true meaning of the bones (by virtue of which we know the tourists' error) passes unchallenged. We are invited against our better intellectual selves into an invisible alliance with the sign that threatens to undo a man's essential autonomy, but in such a way that we read the sign as being identical with whatever makes a man. The "great long white spine" is of course a marlin and not a shark; it is naturally the consequence of a man's great courage; it is Santiago's backbone against the tourists' spinelessness: these or other similar assumptions are what must structure our reading experience in the act of writing off the tourists. We simply expunge—because we know so well—the process of reading that brings us to this act of representation and thus erase from our experience of the text the metaphoricity of the trophy-sign. It is only when we articulate these final acts of reading that we begin to be aware of the potential metaphorical freeplay that opens in the space between the signifier (the bones) and the signified (the sequence of heroic exploits that cause it to signify), and thus begin to ponder the puzzle of why Santiago needs to haul back a trophy to his manhood at all.

My argument suggests that after Santiago's return the narrative compels the reader toward a profoundly satisfying emotional resolution by closing gaps between readers and fishermen and between the reader and the sign, and persuading us that the trophy-sign is identical with and exchangeable for the man. Problematic as it is to a theoretical understanding of Hemingway's concept of manhood, the sign is necessary to a resolution of the reader's experience of the text. The narrative invites us to watch, admire, and judge the trophy and the fishermen's responses to the trophy while Santiago lies sleeping in his shack, thus appearing to solve at a single stroke the dilemma of how the nontheatrical actions of a man off alone can be understood as self-dramatization, and how crucial acts of self-dramatization can be masked by the signs that represent them. The trophy-sign allows Santiago's actions to be retrospectively deemed and now judged as a performance without his ever appearing on stage. It allows us to preserve the illusion of Santiago's heroic independence. And, as we join the other fishermen in a collective appreciation of a man's exploits, the narrative "pays off" with a rare emotional satisfaction all the more striking for being constructed out of one's solitary experience of a solitary man's adventure.

Yet the very strategy that seems designed to preserve the old man's lonely courage—substituting the trophy-skeleton as a trope for Santiago's offstage self—is the one that reveals the narrative's profound emotional and thematic debt to the presence of audiences. Nudging us to inquire "Must Santiago return with the mutilated carcass?" these closing scenes hover on the edge of making us retrospectively aware that our firsthand and ostensibly unshaped experience of Santiago's exploits has been something of a ploy to repress our activities as readers. It appears, in fact, that our firsthand experience of Santiago's deeds can be further enriched and made more meaningful by reprising and reviewing the same information through the eyes of others and that we and the trophy-sign and the late fictive audiences are vital to the shaping and finalizing of Santiago's manhood. By this logic, the concept of a quintessential male performing unstaged actions uncompromised by metaphoric trophies substituting for manhood disappears. The final scenes represent a crucial supplement to what seemed initially a whole and perfect narrative of heroic conduct, revealing the story of Santiago's solitary heroism to have been after all incomplete and his manhood not final or self-evident at all.

As we saw early in this chapter, suspicious readers (like Benson, Rosenfield, Rahv, and many others) have often fuzzily registered their experience as "manipulation," as if they were aware that they have been invited to play a role without quite being able to articulate it. Readers like this experience the text as an exhibit: a rhetorical and artful (rather than artistic) attempt to persuade them of a significance that Hemingway can no longer produce as a simply natural, immanent, and undramatized consequence of his fiction. The problem with the novella is that it is deeply rhetorical; and its rhetoricity is a problem because the primitive simplicity characterizing a real man is not supposed to be rhetorical. Simplicity of style and simplicity of (male) character should both preclude rhetoricity. These interpretations are correct insofar as Hemingway's text theatrically exploits its own processes of construction, leading the reader to experience Santiago's heroism relatively unchallenged before in its closing scenes revealing what seemed to be a direct simplicity of style as a subterfuge and the reader's first-time experience as problematic. But the problematic of the first-time reading, I have argued, need not be a problem; the final scenes can, in other words, *restore* to our imaginations a powerfully emotional sense of a theatrical and rhetorical construction of manhood. In this reading, "manipulation" loses its negative connotations and becomes the strategy through which one begins to recognize Hemingway's delicate grasp of manhood-fashioning.

Santiago may then be "perfectly male" and the "quintessential hero of Hemingway's fiction" but my account of how the narrative seeks to shape spectatorial roles for the reader ironically reverses those claims.[19] Santiago, I contend, is quintessential Hemingway insofar as his exploits take place in anticipation of and before the actual or implied presence of an audience. Santiago's and the narrator's insistence that the old man is alone serves to make us aware of how we fulfill the role Santiago seems to feel lacking; and the multiple audiences in the novella's finale guarantee, and urge us to guarantee, the significance of actions that neither seem perfectly complete nor attest to the perfect completeness of Santiago's manliness. It is that which Santiago's deeds ostensibly lack—an audience—that the novella succeeds so well in manufacturing. As Philip Toynbee notes in his criticism of the book being "doctor-bait, professor-bait," there is a powerful sense in which the novella throughout invites and guides our responses, though Toynbee sees the return of the reader as alarmingly decentering the authentic presentation of a manly hero. But the logic of a theatrical representation of manhood, which I have argued characterizes Hemingway's questioning approach to the construction of masculinity from the beginning of his work, reverses this criticism. *The Old Man and the Sea* composes a studied reinscription of the function of audiences. And its corollary, the undermining of a concept of masculinity beyond the purview of an evaluating audience, implies a work that is—against all the odds—deeply imbued with a theatrical fashioning of manhood.

19. Benson, 176; Schwartz, 98.

Epilogue

WORKING WITH Ernest Hemingway's fiction over the past several years afforded me a vastly entertaining perspective on the dynamics of literary reception. Everyone, I discovered, had an opinion about Hemingway and was more than willing to share it with me, usually immediately, before I had a chance to sketch out my own project. When I did, I typically received some version of the following remark: "Surely Hemingway didn't intend that!" The skeptical force of that remark, repeated so often by scholars and non-scholars alike, is worth contemplating, not least because of its claim on intentionality, which is a subject scholars learnt to finesse long ago. (Who besides students believes in intentionality anymore?) Even when my colleagues were intellectually inclined to understand texts as products of social formations and discourses—and I think most scholars today are—it was as if an exception would have to be made for the charismatic Hemingway. *Pace* Michel Foucault, this author seemed very much a "who," not a "what," and uniquely so as well. In all likelihood my interlocutors were responding to the cultural sign "Hemingway," which has become an icon for tough, individualistic masculinity, fused with whatever pieces of biography they knew. Still, all rationalizations aside, my colleagues, as much as my one-story-in-high-school friends, were disposed to read the character of Hemingway's fiction in tandem with the character of the author—and did so with a passion that both surprised and pleased me.

As the preceding chapters imply, I prefer to approach the biographical Hemingway by way of his writing. Hemingway's work as a whole, I have argued, represents masculinity in terms of its staginess, tropes, symbolic performances, and rhetoricity, and in terms of its complicated relationships to audiences who witness and evaluate. The range and depth of Hemingway's concern with theatrical representations of manhood, the sheer number of avenues explored, the consistency of his interest in such matters throughout his career, persuade me that it is time, finally, to discard the "dumb ox" approach to this writer—along with the thesis that he was always trying to flee the implications of his own refined (or "feminized") sensibility.[1] This approach at least offers a way beyond the interminable double bind in Hemingway studies whereby his real-life posturings have been taken as an interpretive framework for his writings, and what appear to be the worst of his writings have merely underscored what seems commonsensical and obvious about his life.

One advantage of my interpretation here is that it allows a different perspective on what has always appeared to be the worst of Hemingway: his pose of machismo in life, and the way that pose seemed to infect his later work amid a welter of "kid-stuff bravado . . . tight-lipped posturing . . . [and] endless narcissism," so that it began to read "like cheap Hemingway parody," like "Hemingway . . . playing Hemingway."[2] This study implies that what so many readers regard as Hemingway's unfortunate fall into stylistic self-parody perhaps as early as the 1930s might be *prized* instead as an exploration of rhetorical representations of masculinity—culminating in a narrative, *The Old Man and the Sea,* that masquerades, wittily, as the quintessential Hemingwayesque exposition of a man off by himself. Such an approach opens up the possibility that Hemingway was self-consciously engaged in questioning and perhaps even unraveling his own stylistic and thematic concerns. This kind of stylistic challenge could be construed in various ways. Hemingway might have chosen in a work such as *Old Man* to parody the lineaments of his style (or the way critics came to perceive it); or perhaps he was on the verge of self-parody in some enigmatic narrative borderlands where we as readers may never quite know how to position ourselves. Or we might argue—and this is the interpretation I emphasize in this book—that Hemingway was always interested in a range of rhetorical strategies as a mode of masculine display. Hemingway playing Hemingway at least becomes an option to play off against Hemingway trying to "be" Hemingway and failing, and it implies that Hemingway was at least more self-consciously reflective about masculine self-dramatization than allowed by most of his readers. Perhaps most importantly, this emphasis puts us in mind of the Brechtian *Verfremdungseffekt* and of Butler's estranging pa-

1. Wyndham Lewis, "The Dumb Ox: A Study of Ernest Hemingway," in ed. Meyers.

2. Irving Howe, review of *Islands in the Stream,* in ed. Meyers, 568; John Aldridge, *After the Lost Generation: A Critical Study of the Writers of Two Wars* (New York: McGraw Hill, 1951), 200; Isaac Rosenfeld, "A Farewell to Hemingway," in ed. Stephens, 329.

EPILOGUE

rodic repetition as a way of noticing the acts of gendering that textualize Hemingway's characters.

The key to my interpretation of Hemingway, however, is not an event or pattern in his life or a passage or pattern in his work that would once and for all reveal the truth about how he understands masculinity as performance, but a new estimation of the very concept of theatricality. My claim that theatricality lies everywhere in Hemingway's life and work, it should now be clear, is fairly unexceptionable. The real difference lies in my refusal to interpret any sign of rhetorical play as a failure of manly self-possession or to write off bombastic or aggressive maleness in terms of a lugubrious theatricality. It lies in my refusal, in other words, simply to follow the party line of dismissing Hemingway's theatricality as self-parody, adolescent posturing, exaggerated masculinity, or rhetorical display—and then to extend the logic of performance into the rest of his work. I have argued instead that theatricality is that which overthrows the possibility of establishing a self-possessed masculinity beyond the reach of rhetoricity or the contingency of audience, and that it is, moreover, principally responsible for the richness of Hemingway's work on masculinity. In this sense, it does not matter whether we believe that Hemingway thought of Harry Morgan or Robert Wilson as exemplary men. As Brecht's man on the slippery slope need not be aware of the social formations underpinning the act of falling over in order for the audience to grasp the point of the gest (that it signifies losing face), so Hemingway's gests do not require an intending author. It only matters that they make it *possible* to view masculinity (in Butler's words) as incredible. The emphasis, really, is on the work of the audience. It is quite conceivable that Brecht's audience—like Hemingway's audience of scholars—will see only a man falling over and thus utterly fail to grasp the gest. But this is a failure that can be unlearned. Once one is aware of how disruptively audiences can participate in the fashioning and unsettling of meaning, there is no going back.

The other skepticism concealed in "Surely Hemingway didn't intend that!" is, I think, over the extent to which Hemingway could have been responsible for a *critique* of masculinity. I have argued in this study that Hemingway's theaters of manhood do represent a thoroughgoing critique of any concept of "full" or transcendent manhood, and that there is no "real thing" in his fiction to which men should aspire, however much his characters and critics might like to believe so. I have also argued that Hemingway's work invites an analysis of power relationships (as with Jake Barnes and Romero, Robert Jordan

HEMINGWAY'S THEATERS OF MASCULINITY

and Pablo, Frederic Henry, the young Nick Adams, and "Papa" Hemingway himself), such that the act of being or becoming a man is decentered, or subtly problematized, or on occasion downright demolished. This does not mean that the trope of theatricality always has to function as a critique of Hemingway's male characters. In *For Whom the Bell Tolls,* for instance, I showed that theatricality could be viewed as a counter to the totalitarian male gaze. And we need not read characters such as Santiago in *Old Man* or Manuel in "The Undefeated" as being diminished by their debts to self-display—though self-display is surely at odds with the way they understand themselves. I have preferred, in fact, to emphasize in this study the ever-changing ways in which Hemingway employed the trope of performance in order to construct, over the course of his career, a multi-angled inquiry into masculinity, while keeping in mind the predominantly critical edge I find characteristic of Hemingway's fiction.

I want to conclude by noting that this study raises important questions and thereby opens up new vistas of study. Simply to remark, as I did in the previous paragraph, that Hemingway's work implies a critique of some constructions of masculinity but not of others suggests a need for some hard theoretical analysis. How many modes of masculinity are there? How far might this kind of critique be consistent with a feminist critique—or does it require an entirely new analysis? How might this new critique interpret the main thrust of Hemingway scholarship to date, given that it has presented him as though he were principally interested in delineating idealized states of manhood, and as though his theatrical poses were the elements most threatening to a charitable interpretation of his life and work? Where did those poses come from? What relationship to his cultural horizon led Hemingway to a theatrical representation of manhood? And, crucially, how might that horizon, understood in terms of the revisionary textual analyses I have conducted here, have shaped the work of other modernists? I am tempted to say, in the spirit of Hemingway's famous mea culpa at the end of *Death in the Afternoon,* "If I could have made this enough of a book it would have had everything in it" (270). This book does not; and my attempt to address the questions I outline above will mean another one.[3] But perhaps that is merely guaranteed by the complexity of Hemingway's probing, multifaceted, ever-shifting representation of men and by the challenge it levels at contemporary discourses on masculinity.

3. To be published by the University Press of Florida in the next few years.

Ashley, Schuyler. Review of *In Our Time*. In *Ernest Hemingway: The Critical Reception*, edited by Robert O. Stephens, 10–11. New York: Burt Franklin, 1977. First published in *Kansas City Star*, December 12, 1925.

Backman, Melvin. "Hemingway: The Matador and the Crucified." In *Hemingway and His Critics: An International Anthology*, edited by Carlos Baker, 245–58. New York: Hill and Wang, 1961.

Baker, Carlos. *Hemingway: The Writer as Artist*. Princeton, N.J.: Princeton University Press, 1952.

———, ed. *Hemingway and His Critics: An International Anthology*. New York: Hill and Wang, 1961.

———, ed. *Ernest Hemingway: Critiques of Four Major Novels*. New York: Scribner's, 1962.

Bakker, J. *Ernest Hemingway: The Artist as Man of Action*. Assen, Netherlands: Van Gorcum, 1972.

Bal, Mieke. "His Master's Eye." In *Modernity and the Hegemony of Vision*, edited by David Michael Levin, 379–404. Berkeley: University of California Press, 1993.

Baym, Nina. "Actually, I Felt Sorry for the Lion." In *New Critical Approaches to the Short Stories of Ernest Hemingway*, edited by Jackson J. Benson, 112–20. Durham: Duke University Press, 1990.

Beach, Joseph Warren. *American Fiction, 1920–1940*. New York: Macmillan, 1941.

Beck, Warren. "The Shorter Happy Life of Mrs. Macomber." *Modern Fiction Studies* 1, no. 4 (November 1955): 28–37.

Beegel, Susan. *Hemingway's Craft of Omission: Four Manuscript Examples*. Ann Arbor: UMI Research Press, 1988.

Benson, Jackson J. *Hemingway: The Writer's Art of Self-Defense*. Minneapolis: University of Minnesota Press, 1969.

Berger, Maurice, Brian Wallis, and Simon Watson. *Constructing Masculinity.* New York: Routledge, 1995.

Beversluis, John. "Dispelling the Romantic Myth: A Study of *A Farewell to Arms.*" *The Hemingway Review* 9, no 1 (fall 1989): 18–25.

Birringer, Johannes. *Theatre, Theory, Postmodernism.* Bloomington: Indiana University Press, 1991.

Brecht, Bertolt. *Brecht on Theatre: The Development of an Aesthetic.* Trans. John Willett. New York: Hill and Wang, 1964.

Bredahl, A. Carl, Jr., and Susan Lynn Drake. *Hemingway's "Green Hills of Africa" as Evolutionary Narrative: Helix and Scimitar.* Lampeter, Wales: Edwin Mellen Press, 1990.

Brenner, Gerry. *Concealments in Hemingway's Works.* Columbus: Ohio State University Press, 1983.

Brod, Harry, ed. *The Making of Masculinities: The New Men's Studies.* Boston: Unwin Hyman, 1987.

Brod, Harry, and Michael Kaufman. *Theorizing Masculinities.* Thousand Oaks, Calif.: Sage Publications, 1994.

Broer, Lawrence R. *Hemingway's Spanish Tragedy.* University, Ala.: University of Alabama Press, 1973.

Brook, Peter. *The Empty Space.* New York: Atheneum, 1980.

Brooks, Cleanth. *The Hidden God.* New Haven: Yale University Press, 1963.

Burgum, Edwin Berry. "Ernest Hemingway and the Psychology of the Lost Generation." In *Ernest Hemingway: The Man and His Work,* edited by John K. M. McCaffery, 308–27. Cleveland: World Publishing, 1950. First published in *The Novel and the World's Dilemma* (Oxford: Oxford University Press, 1947).

Butler, Judith. *Gender Trouble: Feminism and the Subversion of Identity.* New York: Routledge, 1990.

Chase, Cleveland B. "Out of Little, Much." In *Ernest Hemingway: The Critical Reception,* edited by Robert O. Stephens, 41–42. New York: Burt Franklin, 1977. First published in *Saturday Review of Literature,* December 11, 1926.

Cheatham, George. "The Unhappy Life of Robert Wilson." *Studies in Short Fiction* 26, no. 3 (summer 1989): 341–45.

Civello, Paul. "Hemingway's 'Primitivism': Archetypal Patterns in 'Big Two-Hearted River.'" *Hemingway Review* 13, no. 1 (fall 1993): 1–16.

Cixous, Hélène. "The Laugh of the Medusa." Translated by Keith Cohen and Paul Cohen. *Signs* 1 (summer 1976): 865–80.

————. "Castration or Decapitation?" Translated by Annette Kuhn. *Signs* 7, no. 1 (autumn 1981): 41–55.

Comley, Nancy R., and Robert Scholes. *Hemingway's Genders: Rereading the Hemingway Text.* New Haven: Yale University Press, 1994.

Connolly, Cyril. Review of *Men Without Women.* In *Hemingway: The Critical Heritage,* edited by Jeffrey Meyers, 110–12. Boston and London: Routledge and Kegan Paul, 1982. First published in *New Statesman,* November 26, 1927, 208.

Cooperman, Stanley. *World War I and the American Novel.* Baltimore: Johns Hopkins University Press, 1967.

Cowley, Malcolm. "Hemingway Portrait of an Old Soldier Preparing to Die." In *Ernest Hemingway: The Critical Reception,* edited by Robert O. Stephens, 298–300. New York: Burt Franklin, 1977. First published in *New York Herald Tribune Book Review,* September 10, 1950.

————. *A Second Flowering: Works and Days of the Lost Generation.* New York: Penguin, 1980.

Cunliffe, Marcus. *The Literature of the United States.* London: Penguin, 1954.

D'Agostino, Nemi. "The Later Hemingway." In *Twentieth Century Interpretations of The Old Man and the Sea,* edited by Katharine T. Jobes, 108–109. Englewood Cliffs, N.J.: Prentice-Hall, 1968. First published in *Sewanee Review,* summer 1960, 491–92.

Davidson, Arnold E. "The Ambivalent End of Francis Macomber's Short, Happy Life." *Hemingway Notes* 2, no. 1 (spring 1972): 14–16.

Davidson, Arnold E., and Cathy N. Davidson. "Decoding the Hemingway Hero in *The Sun Also Rises.*" In *New Essays on "The Sun Also Rises,"* edited by Linda Wagner-Martin, 83–107. New York: Cambridge University Press, 1987.

Derrida, Jacques. "Structure, Sign, and Play in the Discourse of the Human Sciences." In *Writing and Difference,* translated by Alan Bass. Chicago: University of Chicago Press, 1978.

De Voto, Bernard. Review of *Green Hills of Africa.* In *Hemingway: The Critical Heritage,* edited by Jeffrey Meyers, 210–13. London: Routledge and Kegan Paul, 1982. First published in *Saturday Review of Literature,* October 26, 1935, 5.

Donaldson, Scott. *By Force of Will. The Life and Art of Ernest Hemingway.* New York: Viking, 1977.

Eagleton, Terry. *Against the Grain.* London: Verso, 1986.

Eastman, Max. "Bull in the Afternoon." *New Republic,* June 7, 1933, 94–97.

Eby, Carl. " 'Come Back to the Beach Ag'in, David Honey!': Hemingway's Fe- tishization of Race in *The Garden of Eden* Manuscripts." *Hemingway Review* 14, no. 2 (spring 1995): 98–117.

———. *Hemingway's Fetishism: Psychoanalysis and the Mirror of Manhood.* Albany: State University of New York Press, 1999.

Elkins, Marilyn. "The Fashion of Machismo." In *A Historical Guide to Ernest Hemingway,* edited by Linda Wagner-Martin, 93–115. Oxford: Oxford Uni- versity Press, 2000.

Farrell, James T. "The Sun Also Rises." In *Ernest Hemingway: Critiques of Four Major Novels,* edited by Carlos Baker, 4–6. New York: Scribner's, 1962.

Fetterley, Judith. *The Resisting Reader: A Feminist Approach to American Fic- tion.* Bloomington: Indiana University Press, 1978.

Fiedler, Leslie. *Love and Death in the American Novel.* New York: Stein, 1966.

Fish, Stanley. *Is There a Text in This Class? The Authority of Interpretive Com- munities.* Cambridge: Harvard University Press, 1980.

Flora, Joseph M. *Hemingway's Nick Adams.* Baton Rouge: Louisiana State University Press, 1982.

Foucault, Michel. *Discipline and Punish: The Birth of the Prison.* Translated by Alan Sheridan. New York: Pantheon, 1977.

———. "The Eye of Power." In *Power/Knowledge: Selected Interviews and Other Writings, 1972–1977,* translated by Colin Gordon et al. New York: Pan- theon Books, 1980.

Frye, Northrop. "Novels on Several Occasions." In *Ernest Hemingway: The Critical Reception,* edited by Robert O. Stephens, 333. New York: Burt Frank- lin, 1977. First published in *Hudson Review,* winter 1951, 611–12.

Gajdusek, Robert E. "*A Farewell to Arms:* The Psychodynamics of Integrity." *Hemingway Review* 9, no. 1 (fall 1989): 26–32.

Gannett, Lewis. "Books and Things." In *Ernest Hemingway: The Critical Re- ception,* edited by Robert O. Stephens, 289. New York: Burt Franklin, 1977. First published in *New York Herald Tribune,* September 7, 1950.

Gebhardt, Richard C. "Hemingway's Complex Values." *Hemingway Review* 1, no. 1 (fall 1981): 2–10.

Geismar, Maxwell. "Ernest Hemingway: You Could Always Come Back." In *Ernest Hemingway: The Man and His Work,* edited by John K. M. McCaffery, 143–89. Cleveland and New York: World Publishing, 1950.

Gilbert, Sandra, and Susan Gubar. *The War of the Words.* Vol. 1 of *No Man's*

Land: The Place of the Woman Writer in the Twentieth Century. New Haven: Yale University Press, 1988.

Griffin, Peter. *Along with Youth: Hemingway, the Early Years.* New York: Oxford University Press, 1985.

Gurko, Leo. *Ernest Hemingway and the Pursuit of Heroism.* New York: Thomas Crowell, 1968.

Hays, Peter L. *Ernest Hemingway.* New York: Continuum, 1990.

Hemingway, Ernest. *In Our Time.* New York: Scribner's, 1925.

————. *The Sun Also Rises.* New York: Scribner's, 1926.

————. *Men Without Women.* New York: Scribner's, 1927.

————. *A Farewell to Arms.* New York: Scribner's, 1929.

————. *Death in the Afternoon.* New York: Scribner's, 1932.

————. *Winner Take Nothing.* New York: Scribner's, 1933.

————. *Green Hills of Africa.* New York: Scribner's, 1935.

————. *For Whom the Bell Tolls.* New York: Scribner's, 1940.

————. *The Old Man and the Sea.* New York: Scribner's, 1952.

————. "The Short Happy Life of Francis Macomber." In *The Snows of Kilimanjaro and Other Stories.* New York: Scribner's/Collier, 1986.

————. *The Garden of Eden.* Edited by Tom Jenks. New York: Scribner's, 1986.

Hemingway, Leicester. *My Brother, Ernest Hemingway.* Cleveland: World Publishing, 1962.

Henricksen, Bruce. "The Bullfight Story and Critical Theory." In *Hemingway's Neglected Short Fiction: New Perspectives,* edited by Susan F. Beegel, 107–21. Ann Arbor: UMI Research Press, 1989.

Hicks, Granville. *The Great Tradition.* New York: Macmillan, 1933.

————. "Small Game Hunting." In *Hemingway: The Critical Heritage,* edited by Jeffrey Meyers, 213–16. London: Routledge and Kegan Paul, 1982. First published in *New Masses,* November 19, 1935, 23.

Hoffman, Frederick J. *The Twenties: American Writing in the Postwar Decade.* New York: Free Press, 1966.

Hovey, Richard B. *Hemingway: The Inward Terrain.* Seattle: University of Washington Press, 1968.

Hutton, Virgil. "The Short Happy Life of Macomber." In *The Short Stories of Ernest Hemingway: Critical Essays,* edited by Jackson J. Benson. Durham: Duke University Press, 1975.

Hyman, Stanley Edgar. Review of *The Portable Hemingway.* In *Hemingway:*

The Critical Heritage, edited by Jeffrey Meyers, 424–25. Boston and London: Routledge and Kegan Paul, 1982. First published in *New York Times Book Review,* September 13, 1953.

Irigaray, Luce. *Speculum of the Other Woman.* Translated by Gillian C. Gill. Ithaca, N.Y.: Cornell University Press, 1985.

Jackson, Paul R. "Point of View, Distancing, and Hemingway's 'Short Happy Life.'" *Hemingway Notes* 5, no. 2 (spring 1980): 2–16.

Jacobus, Mary. "The Question of Language: Men of Maxims and *The Mill on the Floss.*" In *Writing and Sexual Difference,* edited by Elizabeth Abel, 37–52. Chicago: University of Chicago Press, 1982.

Jay, Martin. "In the Empire of the Gaze: Foucault and the Denigration of Vision in Twentieth-Century French Thought." In *Foucault: A Critical Reader,* edited by David Couzens Hoy, 175–204. Oxford: Basil Blackwell, 1986.

Johnson, Edgar. "Farewell the Separate Peace." In *Ernest Hemingway: The Man and His Work,* edited by John K. M. McCaffery, 130–42. Cleveland and New York: World Publishing, 1950. First published in *Sewanee Review,* July–September 1940.

Johnston, Kenneth G. *The Tip of the Iceberg: Hemingway and the Short Story.* Greenwood, Fla.: Penkevill, 1987.

Josephs, Allen. "Toreo: The Moral Axis of *The Sun Also Rises.*" *Hemingway Review* 6, no. 1 (fall 1986): 88–99.

J. R. "Hemingway's Gamy Dishes." In *Ernest Hemingway: The Critical Reception,* edited by Robert O. Stephens, 141–42. New York: Burt Franklin, 1977. First published in *Cincinatti Enquirer,* November 4, 1933.

Kennedy, J. Gerald "Hemingway's Gender Trouble." *American Literature* 63, no. 2 (June 1991): 187–207.

Killinger, John. *Hemingway and the Dead Gods.* Lexington: University of Kentucky Press, 1960.

Kirstein, Lincoln. "The Canon of Death." In *Ernest Hemingway: The Man and His Work,* edited by John K. M. McCaffery, 59–65. Cleveland and New York: World Publishing, 1950. First published in *The Hound and Horn,* January–March 1933, 336–41.

K. S. Review of *Men without Women.* In *Ernest Hemingway: The Critical Reception,* edited by Robert O. Stephens, 62–63. New York: Burt Franklin, 1977. First published in *Boston Evening Transcript,* January 7, 1928.

Lawrence, D. H. Review of *In Our Time.* In *Hemingway: The Critical Heritage,* edited by Jeffrey Meyers, 72–74. Boston and London: Routledge and Kegan Paul, 1982. First published in *Calendar of Modern Letters,* April 1927, 72–73.

Lee, A. Robert. Introduction to *Ernest Hemingway: New Critical Essays,* edited by A. Robert Lee, 7–12. London: Vision Press, 1983.

Leverenz, David. "Manhood, Humiliation, and Public Life: Some Stories." *Southwest Review* 7 (fall 1986): 442–62.

Levin, David Michael. "Decline and Fall: Ocularcentrism in Heidegger's Reading of the History of Metaphysics." In *Modernity and the Hegemony of Vision,* edited by David Michael Levin, 186–217. Berkeley: University of California Press, 1993.

Lewis, Robert W. *Hemingway on Love.* Austin: University of Texas Press, 1965.

Light, James F. "The Religion of Death in *A Farewell to Arms.*" *Modern Fiction Studies* 7 (summer 1961): 169–73.

Lockridge, Ernest. "Faithful in Her Fashion: Catherine Barkley, the Invisible Hemingway Heroine." *Journal of Narrative Technique* 18, no. 2 (spring 1988): 170–78.

Lounsberry, Barbara. "The Education of Robert Wilson." *Hemingway Notes* 5, no. 3 (spring 1980): 29–32.

Lynn, Kenneth S. *Hemingway.* New York: Simon and Schuster, 1987.

"Marital Tragedy." In *Ernest Hemingway: The Critical Reception,* edited by Robert O. Stephens, 31–32. New York: Burt Franklin, 1977. First published in *New York Times Book Review,* October 31, 1926.

Martin, Jay. *Harvests of Change: American Literature 1865–1914.* Englewood Cliffs, N.J.: Prentice-Hall, 1967.

Matthews, T. S. "A Hemingway You'll Never Be." *New Republic,* November 27, 1935, 79–80.

McCaffery, John K. M., ed. *Ernest Hemingway: The Man and His Work.* Cleveland and New York: World Publishing, 1950.

Messenger, Christian K. *Sport and the Spirit of Play in American Fiction: Hawthorne to Faulkner.* New York: Columbia University Press, 1981.

Messent, Peter. *Modern Novelists: Ernest Hemingway.* New York: St. Martin's Press, 1992.

Meyers, Jeffrey. *Hemingway: A Biography.* New York: Harper/Perennial, 1985.

———, ed. *Hemingway: The Critical Heritage.* Boston and London: Routledge and Kegan Paul, 1982.

Moddelmog, Debra A. *Reading Desire: In Pursuit of Ernest Hemingway.* Ithaca, N.Y.: Cornell University Press, 1999.

Morris, Lawrence S. "Warfare in Man and among Men." In *Ernest Hemingway: The Critical Reception,* edited by Robert O. Stephens, 44–45. New York: Burt Franklin, 1977. First published in *New Republic,* December 22, 1926, 142–43.

Nagel, James, ed. *Ernest Hemingway: The Writer in Context.* Madison: University of Wisconsin Press, 1984.

"The New Hemingway." In *Ernest Hemingway: The Critical Reception,* edited by Robert O. Stephens, 304–305. New York: Burt Franklin, 1977. First published in *Newsweek,* September 11, 1950, 90–95.

Nye, Andrea. "Assisting at the Birth and Death of Philosophic Vision." In *Modernity and the Hegemony of Vision,* edited by David Michael Levin, 361–78. Berkeley: University of California Press, 1993.

Ong, Walter J., S. J. "The Writer's Audience Is Always a Fiction." *PMLA* 90, no. 1 (January 1975): 9–21.

Palin, Michael. *Hemingway's Chair.* New York: St. Martin's Press, 1998.

Phelan, James. "Distance, Voice, and Temporal Perspective in Frederic Henry's Narration: Powers, Problems and Paradox." In *New Essays on "A Farewell to Arms,"* edited by Scott Donaldson, 53–74. Cambridge: Cambridge University Press, 1990.

―――. "The Concept of Voice, the Voices of Frederic Henry, and the Structure of *A Farewell to Arms.*" In *Hemingway: Essays of Reassessment,* edited by Frank Scafella, 214-32. New York: Oxford University Press, 1991.

Pound, Ezra. "A Retrospect." In *Literary Essays of Ezra Pound,* edited by T. S. Eliot, 3–14. New York: New Directions, 1968.

"Preludes to a Mood." In *Ernest Hemingway: The Critical Reception,* edited by Robert O. Stephens, 7. New York: Burt Franklin, 1977.

Presley, John W. " 'Hawks Never Share': Women and Tragedy in Hemingway." *Hemingway Notes* 3, no. 1 (spring 1973): 3–10.

Priestley, J. B. Review of *A Farewell to Arms.* In *Hemingway: The Critical Heritage,* edited by Jeffrey Meyers, 136–37. Boston and London: Routledge and Kegan Paul, 1982. First published in *Now and Then,* winter 1929, 11–12.

Pullin, Faith. "Hemingway and the Secret Language of Hate." In *Ernest Hemingway: New Critical Essays,* edited by A. Robert Lee, 172–92. London: Vision Press, 1983.

Raeburn, John. *Fame Became of Him: Hemingway as Public Writer.* Bloomington: Indiana University Press, 1984.

———. "Skirting the Hemingway Legend." *American Literary History* 1 (spring 1989): 206–18.

Rahv, Philip. "Hemingway in the 1950's." In *Twentieth Century Interpretations of "The Old Man and the Sea,"* edited by Katharine T. Jobes, 110–12. Englewood Cliffs, N.J.: Prentice-Hall, 1968. First published in *Image and Idea: Twenty Essays on Literary Themes,* ed. Philip Rahv (New York: New Directions, 1957).

———. Review of *Across the River and into the Trees.* In *Ernest Hemingway: The Critical Reception,* edited by Robert O. Stephens, 319–21. New York: Burt Franklin, 1977. First published in *Commentary,* October 1950, 400–402.

Read, Alan. *Theatre and Everyday Life: An Ethics of Performance.* London and New York: Routledge, 1993.

Reynolds, Michael S. *The Young Hemingway.* New York: Basil Blackwell, 1986.

———. *Hemingway: The Paris Years.* New York: Basil Blackwell, 1989.

———. "Hemingway's West: Another Country of the Heart." In *Blowing the Bridge: Essays on Hemingway and "For Whom the Bell Tolls,"* edited by Rena Sanderson, 27–35. New York: Greenwood Press, 1992.

———. "*A Farewell to Arms:* Doctors in the House of Love." In *The Cambridge Companion to Hemingway,* edited by Scott Donaldson, 109–27. Cambridge: Cambridge University Press, 1996.

Rosenfeld, Isaac. "A Farewell to Hemingway." In *Hemingway: The Critical Reception,* edited by Robert O. Stephens, 329–32. New York: Burt Franklin, 1977. First published in *Kenyon Review,* winter 1951, 147–55.

Rosenfeld, Paul. "Tough Earth." In *Ernest Hemingway: The Critical Reception,* edited by Robert O. Stephens, 9–10. New York: Burt Franklin, 1977. First published in *New Republic,* November 25, 1925, 22–23.

———. Review of *In Our Time.* In *Hemingway: The Critical Heritage,* edited by Jeffrey Meyers, 67–69. Boston and London: Routledge and Kegan Paul, 1982. First published in *New Republic,* November 25, 1925, 22–23.

Rosenfield, Claire. "New World, Old Myths." In *Twentieth Century Interpretations of "The Old Man and the Sea,"* edited by Katharine T. Jobes, 41–55. Englewood Cliffs, N.J.: Prentice-Hall, 1968.

Rovit, Earl, and Gerry Brenner. *Ernest Hemingway.* Boston: Twayne, 1986.

Sanderson, Rena, ed. *Essays on Hemingway and "For Whom the Bell Tolls."* New York: Greenwood Press, 1992.

Scafella, Frank, ed. *Hemingway: Essays of Reassessment.* New York and Oxford: Oxford University Press, 1991.

Schenk, Celeste M. "Charlotte Mew." In *The Gender of Modernism: A Critical Anthology,* edited by Bonnie Kime Scott, 316–20. Bloomington: Indiana University Press, 1990.

Schorer, Mark. "The Background of a Style." *Kenyon Review* 3 (winter 1941): 101–105.

Schwartz, Delmore. "Ernest Hemingway's Literary Situation." In *Ernest Hemingway: The Man and His Work,* edited by John K. M. McCaffery, 114–29. Cleveland and New York: World Publishing, 1950.

———. *"The Old Man and the Sea* and the American Dream." In *Twentieth Century Interpretations of "The Old Man and the Sea,"* edited by Katharine T. Jobes, 97–102. Englewood Cliffs, N.J.: Prentice-Hall, 1968.

Schweickart, Patrocinio. "Reading Ourselves: Toward a Feminist Theory of Reading." In *Gender and Reading,* edited by Elizabeth Flynn and Patrocinio Schweickart, 31–62. Baltimore: Johns Hopkins University Press, 1986.

Schwenger, Peter. *Phallic Critiques.* London: Routledge and Kegan Paul, 1984.

Scott, Bonnie Kime. Introduction to *The Gender of Modernism: A Critical Anthology,* edited by Bonnie Kime Scott, 1–18. Bloomington: Indiana University Press, 1990.

Seydow, John J. "Francis Macomber's Spurious Masculinity." *Hemingway Review* 1, no. 1 (1981): 33–41.

Spilka, Mark. "The Death of Love in *The Sun Also Rises."* In *Twelve Original Essays on Great American Novels,* edited by Charles Shapiro, 238–56. Detroit: Wayne State University Press, 1958.

———. "The Necessary Stylist: A New Critical Revision." *Modern Fiction Studies* 6 (1960): 283–97.

———. "Warren Beck Revisited." *Modern Fiction Studies* 22 (1976): 245–55.

———. *Hemingway's Quarrel with Androgyny.* Lincoln: University of Nebraska Press, 1990.

———. "Hemingway's Barbershop Quintet: *The Garden of Eden* Manuscript." In *Hemingway: Seven Decades of Criticism,* edited by Linda Wagner-Martin, 349–72. East Lansing: Michigan State University Press, 1998. First published in *Novel* 21, no. 1 (fall 1987): 31–45.

Stephens, Robert O. ed. *Ernest Hemingway: The Critical Reception.* New York: Burt Franklin, 1977.

"Stiff Upper Lip." In *Ernest Hemingway: The Critical Reception,* edited by

Robert O. Stephens, 144. New York: Burt Franklin, 1977. First published in *Time,* November 6, 1933, 59–60.

Stoneback, H. R. "From the rue Saint-Jacques to the Pass of Roland to the 'Unfinished Church on the Edge of the Cliff.'" *Hemingway Review* 6, no. 1 (fall 1986): 2–29.

Strychacz, Thomas. "Dramatizations of Manhood in Hemingway's *In Our Time* and *The Sun Also Rises.*" *American Literature* 61, no. 2 (1989): 245–60.

———. "Trophy Hunting as a Trope of Manhood in Hemingway's *Green Hills of Africa.*" *Hemingway Review* 13, no. 1 (1993): 36–47.

———. "*In Our Time,* Out of Season." *Companion to Hemingway,* edited by Scott Donaldson, 55–86. Cambridge: Cambridge University Press, 1996.

———. "The Sort of Thing You Should Not Admit: Hemingway's Aesthetic of Emotional Restraint." In *Boy's Don't Cry? Rethinking Narratives of Masculinity and Emotion in the U.S.,* edited by Milette Shamir and Jennifer Travis, 141–66. New York: Columbia University Press, 2002.

Svoboda, Frederic J. "The Great Themes in Hemingway: Love, War, Wilderness, and Loss." In *A Historical Guide to Ernest Hemingway,* edited by Linda Wagner-Martin, 155–72. New York and Oxford: Oxford University Press, 2000.

Tate, Allen. Review of *The Sun Also Rises.* In *Hemingway: The Critical Heritage,* edited by Jeffrey Meyers, 93–95. Boston and London: Routledge and Kegan Paul, 1982. First published in *The Nation,* December 15, 1926, 642, 644.

Tompkins, Jane. "Women and the Language of Men." In *Old West–New West: Centennial Essays,* edited by Barbara Howard Meldrum, 43–59. Moscow: University of Idaho Press, 1993.

Toynbee, Philip. "Hemingway." In *Twentieth Century Interpretations of "The Old Man and the Sea,"* edited by Katharine T. Jobes, 112. Englewood Cliffs, N.J.: Prentice-Hall, 1968. First published in *Encounter,* October 1961, 86–88.

Trilling, Lionel. "An American in Spain." In *Ernest Hemingway: Critiques of Four Major Novels,* edited by Carlos Baker, 78–81. New York: Scribner's, 1962.

Van Gunten, Mark. "The Polemics of Narrative and Difference in *For Whom the Bell Tolls.*" In *Essays on Hemingway and "For Whom the Bell Tolls,"* edited by Rena Sanderson, 143–57. New York: Greenwood Press, 1992.

Waldmeir, Joseph. "*Confiteor Hominem:* Ernest Hemingway's Religion of

Man." In *Papers of the Michigan Academy of Science, Arts, and Letters,* vol. 42, 349–56. Ann Arbor: University of Michigan Press, 1957.

Warren, Robert Penn. "Hemingway." *Kenyon Review* 9, no. 1 (winter 1947): 1–28.

Way, Brian. "Hemingway the Intellectual: A Version of Modernism." In *Ernest Hemingway: New Critical Essays,* edited by A. Robert Lee, 151–71. London: Vision Press, 1983.

Weber, Ronald. *Hemingway's Art of Non-Fiction.* New York: St. Martin's Press, 1990.

Weeks, Robert P. "Fakery in *The Old Man and the Sea.*" In *Twentieth Century Interpretations of "The Old Man and the Sea,"* edited by Katharine T. Jobes, 34–40. Englewood Cliffs, N.J.: Prentice-Hall, 1968.

Wells, Arvin R. "A Ritual of Transfiguration: *The Old Man and the Sea.*" In *Twentieth Century Interpretations of "The Old Man and the Sea,"* edited by Katharine T. Jobes, 56–63. Englewood Cliffs, N.J.: Prentice-Hall, 1968.

West, Ray B. "*A Farewell to Arms.*" *The Art of Modern Fiction,* edited by Ray B. West and Robert W. Stallman, 622–33. New York: Holt, Rinehart, and Winston, 1949.

Whitlow, Roger. *Cassandra's Daughters: The Women in Hemingway.* Westport, Conn., and London, England: Greenwood Press, 1984.

Wilshire, Bruce. *Role Playing and Identity: The Limits of Theatre as Metaphor.* Bloomington: Indiana University Press, 1982.

Wilson, Edmund. *The Wound and the Bow.* Oxford: Oxford University Press, 1947.

———. "Letter to the Russians about Hemingway." In *Hemingway: The Critical Heritage,* edited by Jeffrey Meyers, 216–21. Boston and London: Routledge and Kegan Paul, 1982. First published in *New Republic,* December 11, 1935, 135–36.

Woolf, Virginia. Review of *Men Without Women.* In *Hemingway: The Critical Heritage,* edited by Jeffrey Meyers, 101–107. Boston and London: Routledge and Kegan Paul, 1982. First published in *New York Herald Tribune Books,* October 9, 1927.

"Writer." In *Ernest Hemingway: The Critical Reception,* edited by Robert O. Stephens, 13. New York: Burt Franklin, 1977. First published in *Time,* January 18, 1926, 38.

Wyatt, David. *Prodigal Sons: A Study in Authorship and Authority.* Baltimore: Johns Hopkins University Press, 1980.

Wylder, Delbert E. *Hemingway's Heroes.* New Mexico: University of New Mexico Press, 1969.

Young, Philip. *Ernest Hemingway: A Reconsideration.* New York and Toronto: Rinehart, 1952.

Zabel, Morton Dauwen. In *Ernest Hemingway: The Critical Reception,* edited by Robert O. Stephens, 295–97. New York: Burt Franklin, 1977. First published in *The Nation,* September 9, 1950, 230.